704

GHOULS,
GIMMICKS,
AND GOLD

GHOULS, GIMMICKS, AND GOLD

Horror Films and the

American Movie Business,

1953–1968

KEVIN HEFFERNAN

Duke University Press

Durham and London 2004

© 2004 Duke University Press
All rights reserved
Printed in the United States of
American on acid-free paper ∞
Designed by Amy Ruth Buchanan
Typeset in Scala by Tseng
Information Systems, Inc.
Library of Congress Cataloging-
in-Publication Data appear on
the last printed page of this book.

CONTENTS

ACKNOWLEDGMENTS

I would like to thank Ken Wissoker and Christine Dahlin at Duke University Press, two energetic, thorough, and gracious editors. Also, Duke's Natalie Kozin and Southern Methodist University's David Sedman helped me though the logistical and technological thicket of book illustrations in the digital age. The Hamon Arts Library and the G. William Jones Film and Video Collection at Southern Methodist University, the Wisconsin Center for Film and Theater Research, the Library of Congress Motion Picture Archives, the Reading Room at the British Film Institute, and the Microforms Collection at the University of Delaware Library provided access to key documents. Forbidden Media of Denton, Texas, and Southern Methodist University's Norwick Center for Media and Instructional Technology provided video and DVD copies of many wonderful and obscure films.

Donald Crafton, Rick Worland, Joe Dante, and Kim Bernstein provided generous and detailed comments on several drafts of this project. I am also very grateful for the comments, feedback, and support of Tino Balio, Teresa Becker, Harry Benshoff, David Bordwell, Allan Bryce, Noël Carroll, Margaret Dew, Nicole Fries, Tom Gunning, Scott Higgins, Michele Hilmes, Lea Jacobs, Henry Jenkins, Vance Kepley, Dick Klemensen of *Little Shoppe of Horrors*, Tim Lucas of *Video Watchdog*, Greg Luce of Sinister Cinema, Denis Meikle, Clyde Putman, Paul Ramaeker,

Doug Riblet, Max J. Rosenberg, Harris Ross, Sara Ross, Eric Schaefer, Eric Smoodin, Jonathan Sothcott, Rafael Vela, John Waters, and Justin Wyatt.

The Division of Cinema-Television at Southern Methodist University provided generous support for much of the work that made this project possible. My students in "Great Directors: The Horror Film" and "Screen Artists: Cinema of Sex and Violence" were of great help in clarifying some of the ideas that follow. The Division also provided a summer of teaching and research in London, which was invaluable in giving me the opportunity to conduct research for chapters 2 and 5, and a fall sabbatical in 2002 helped me finish the project.

I am also very grateful for the love, support, and generosity of my four favorite women: My friend, Kim Bernstein; my mother, Nell Heffernan; my wife, Sylett Strickland; and our daughter, Spencer Ciaran. I dedicate this book to them.

INTRODUCTION

When a young person hears the words "horror film" or "movie monster," the images that come to mind are likely to be those of Freddy Krueger and his menacing finger blades from *A Nightmare on Elm Street*; the hockey-masked and homicidal Jason of the *Friday the 13th* films; or *Child's Play*'s malevolent devil doll, Chucky. At the dawn of the twenty-first century, these horrific icons of the New Hollywood have become familiar through the merchandising of a wide variety of franchised products: video games, model figures, soundtrack CDs, and fan magazines circulate through the market and make these monsters as widely known as Disney characters, rock stars, or other media celebrities.

When, on the other hand, a member of the baby boom generation hears those same words, he or she is more apt to picture a lumbering Boris Karloff in the flattened skull and electrode bolts of *Frankenstein* (1931); Bela Lugosi in cape and tails from *Dracula* (1931); and Lon Chaney in yak-hair makeup from *The Wolf Man* (1941) or, in the famous chiaroscuro production still from *The Mummy's Ghost* (1944), bandaged and withered. Both fans and casual viewers almost always use terms like "classic" and "famous" (as in the fan magazine *Famous Monsters of Filmland*) to acknowledge the wide circulation and familiarity attained by these earlier images over their sixty-year existence in theaters, television, and other commodity forms.

Famous monsters of the 1930s: the Monster (Boris Karloff) in *Frankenstein* (Twentieth Century-Fox).

How did one set of iconography come to permanently replace the other as both commercial products and images of shared fear, loathing, and delight?

The movies that introduced the "classic" images given above are, no less than their contemporary counterparts, the products of a very specific period in American film history. This earlier era was characterized by an industry that carefully guarded its long-term financial interests through a system in which a handful of very powerful firms exercised rigid control of the movie business. During the Hollywood studio era, which stretched from the early 1920s to sometime in the early 1960s, five companies — Paramount, Twentieth Century-Fox, Loew's, Inc. (the parent company of Metro-Goldwyn-Mayer), RKO, and Warner Bros.— were vertically integrated, producing films, distributing them worldwide, and showing them in profitable company-owned chains of theaters. The theater chains owned by these companies were often located in different parts of the country: Warner's Stanley and First National chains were in the Middle Atlantic region, Paramount's Publix Theaters were in Chicago and the Midwest, and so on. The studios' most popular star vehicles premiered in their own first-run theaters and played a week at premium (but affordable) ticket prices. The lucrative first-run theaters owned by the "Big Five" comprised only 15 percent of the total theaters in operation but garnered nearly 70 percent of the nation's box-office receipts.[1]

Two smaller companies, Columbia and Universal, produced films and distributed them but owned no theaters. United Artists served only as a distributor for a wide array of independently produced films, most notably the prestige features of Samuel Goldwyn, David O. Selznick, and Walt Disney. Beneath these "Little Three" companies, at the very bottom of the industry, was a group of small studios known collectively as "Poverty Row." These companies, which included Republic, Monogram, Grand National, and Producers Releasing Corporation (PRC), produced B films for the lower half of double bills.

Each of the major studios released an average of a film a week, and these firms favored each other in booking engagements in their profitable first-run theaters. In contrast, independent theaters and circuits not affiliated with the majors were forced to wait until a box-office hit's first run in the big houses had played out and the film was withdrawn for a period of "clearance." These "subsequent-run" engagements, which usually included a supporting B feature, garnered a much lower ticket price, running as they did after a film's novelty had largely worn off. In addition, independent theaters would often have to buy an entire season's worth of releases from the studios, months before the films had been produced or reviewed in the trade press, in order to have access to one or two sure-fire hits with major stars. This practice, known as block booking, often resulted in films sitting on a shelf in the projection booth, unplayed but fully paid for. Such practices created an adversarial relationship between independent exhibitors and the major Hollywood firms, and it appeared to many that collusion between the major studios served as a powerful barrier to entry into the business. In 1938, the antitrust division of the Department of Justice filed suit against the Big Five studios for illegal restraint of trade, and the case would wind its way through the courts for the next ten years.

During the studio era, virtually every company produced some horror films, particularly during the "horror boom" of 1931–1933.[2] In fact, Paramount garnered an Academy Award for Fredric March's lead role in *Dr. Jekyll and Mr. Hyde* in 1932. For most of the studio era, however, the horror genre was most readily (and resourcefully) exploited by the weaker of the studios. Against the odds of the onset of the Depression in the first half of the thirties, Universal achieved success with its Frankenstein and Dracula pictures. These modest but highly influential genre films, Thomas Schatz points out, were characterized by expressionist art direction and the signature stylings of stars Boris Karloff and Bela Lugosi, director James Whale, screenwriter John Balderston, and cinematographer Karl Freund. Universal suffered only modest losses in 1932 to 1933, the depth of the Depression for Hollywood, whereas more ambitious companies such as Fox, RKO, and Paramount posted huge losses and ended up in bankruptcy or receivership.[3]

In the late thirties, Columbia put Boris Karloff on contract for films such as *The Black Room* (1935) and *The Man They Could Not Hang* (1939). In the forties, RKO, always the weakest of the Big Five, produced stylish B supporting features such as *Cat People* (1942) and *I Walked with a Zombie* (1943) through their production unit headed by Val Lewton. Finally, Poverty Row produced many low-budget horror films with featured players in the lead roles, including Majestic's *The Vampire Bat* (1933) with Lionel Atwill, Monogram's *The Ape Man* (1943) with a fading Bela Lugosi, and PRC's *Bluebeard* (1944) with John Carradine. Unlike the major studio releases, which were booked to exhibitors for a percentage of the box office, B pictures from Poverty Row were booked for a flat fee and served as the bottom half of double features on subsequent-run engagements of major releases.[4]

The industry's self-censorship mechanism, the Production Code Administration of the Motion Picture Producers and Distributors of America, depended for enforcement on studio ownership of first-run theaters: films denied a code seal were not shown in the profitable houses controlled by the majors. This formed a powerful barrier to producers or distributors who sought to differentiate their product through subject matter untouchable by the major studios. Some such efforts were successful, however. Eric Schaefer's *Bold! Daring! Shocking! True! A History of Exploitation Films, 1919–1959* meticulously details the production, distribution, and exhibition circuit for low-budget films featuring forbidden images of nudity, drug addiction, childbirth, and venereal disease that operated in a sort of regionally based parallel universe to Hollywood's national theater chains and distribution channels. The theaters that showed these films were often located in downscale urban areas and instituted an adults-only admission policy. These exploitation films were distributed on a states-rights basis in which regional distributors oversaw their bookings into local theaters. The films themselves were independent features with very low production values (including flubbed lines, hasty camera reframings, and even out-of-focus shots); films imported from abroad; and reissues of Poverty Row films under salacious new titles. Even rereleases of major studio films were occasionally exploited in this way: Tod Browning's *Freaks*, released by MGM in 1932, was issued years later by exploiteer Dwain Esper under the title *Forbidden Love*.[5]

Most filmgoers, however, preferred the stars and conventional genres of films from Hollywood. After the fabulously lucrative years of World War II, during which the rationing of consumer goods diverted disposable income to moviegoing, the American film industry was hit with a number of setbacks. Between 1947 and 1948, television ownership skyrocketed, increasing by over ten times to 175,000 sets, on its way to 90 percent penetration by the end of the fifties.[6] Also in 1947, a public-relations disaster loomed as Hollywood, for the first time, became the subject of investigation in the hearings of the House Committee for Un-American Activities. Consumer durable goods like automobiles and home appliances, snapped up by a public hungry after decades of Depression and war rationing, diverted discretionary income from movie tickets, and the huge migration to suburbia moved many upscale consumers away from the downtown first-run movie houses. Then, in May of 1948, the U.S. Supreme Court rendered its decision in the decade-old Big Five antitrust case in a series of consent decrees. *United States v. Paramount, et al.* ruled that vertical integration, block booking, and excessive clearances constituted illegal restraint of trade. The Big Five were ordered to sell off their theater chains and stop block booking.

This began a period of convulsive change for the production, distribution, and exhibition branches of the movie business. Movie attendance plummeted and studios cut back on production. The major companies, now focused on maximizing profits through fewer and costlier releases, began an aggressive move into new technology like widescreen projection, stereo sound, and 3-D, both to compete with television and to profit from the sale of equipment to exhibitors. The Production Code, which had depended for enforcement on studio ownership of the premium theaters, began a decades-long weakening.

In *Sure Seaters: The Emergence of Art-House Cinema*, Barbara Wilinsky notes that it was the independent and neighborhood exhibitors in whose interest the Justice Department had tried to act in the first place. These exhibitors, known in the trade as "nabe operators," were now squeezed between a serious shortage of releases from the studios, expensive equipment upgrades in order to play the studios' successful CinemaScope and 3-D releases, and exorbitant rentals from distributors. The long-term effect of the *Paramount* decision was to place the nabe operator in an even more precarious position in relation to the distribution arm of the film industry. Wilinsky charts the postwar conversion of many subsequent-run houses into art theaters within this context.[7] Some of these struggling neighborhood theaters also formed the major venues for the changing industry of the horror film during the fifties and sixties: smaller distributors like newly formed American International Pictures (AIP), which began business in 1954, were able to reach a new audience of teenage filmgoers by booking their films into neighborhood theaters desperate for product. This period saw the American movie business change from the chaotic poststudio era to the conglomeration of the New Hollywood.

Most studies of the horror genre skip consideration of the role that economic necessity played in the postwar horror film. Some writers privilege aesthetic histories and attempt to chart the evolution or devolution of the genre in terms of iconography, narrative conventions, or representations of violence. Examples of this kind of genre history include Carlos Clarens's *Illustrated History of the Horror Film*, S. S. Prawer's *Caligari's Children: The Film as Tale of Terror*, and Noël Carroll's *The Philosophy of Horror*.[8] Other writers attempt to trace the social evolution of the genre and, despite their denials of a simplistic causal relationship, chart a reflection of a larger social reality in the movies themselves. This reality, according to these studies, can be understood in terms of changing gender relations, the evolution of a consumer-based economy, or even the increased brutalization of the public by a violence-saturated media, and these theories comprise the dominant mode of writing on the horror film of the past twenty years. Its distinguished exemplars include Robin Wood's widely reprinted "An Introduction to the American Horror Film," Carol Clover's *Men, Women, and Chain Saws*, David Skal's *The Monster Show*, Andrew Tudor's *Monsters and Mad Scientists*, Tony Williams's *Hearths of Darkness*, William Paul's *Laughing/Screaming*, and Harry Benshoff's *Monsters in the Closet*.[9]

These writers along with dozens of others have immeasurably increased the depth and richness of our encounters with horror movies, and the more groundbreaking of these works (here I am thinking of Wood and Clover) have radically expanded the range of films deemed worthy for serious analysis by critics and teachers. Much of the moral and intellectual force of their argument was marshaled against dismissive counterclaims that these films were lurid, primitive expressions of the most callous and mercenary impulses of a debased commercial film industry. Still, a cultural or aesthetic account of the horror film unmoored from its economic history seems to me wholly inadequate. Topical and sensationalist genre films often serve very particular economic functions within the industry, and cultural analyses that do not take into consideration these particular functions miss a vital part of film's historical dimension.

For this reason, I have chosen the postwar popular cinema of the fifties and sixties, a period of massive changes in the film industry, and I have attempted to chart the different functions that horror films played in the period that saw those changes. I argue that there was a major cultural and economic shift in the production and reception of the horror film that began at the time of the 3-D horror film cycle of 1953 and ended with the adoption of the Motion Picture Association of America (MPAA) ratings system and the subsequent development of the adult horror film in 1968. This period, 1953 to 1968, coincided with the most precipitous and sustained decline in box-office attendance in the postwar period.[10] Divorced from their theater chains as the result of the Supreme Court's 1948 *Paramount* decision, the major studios cut back on production and adopted a blockbuster policy of fewer productions at higher budgets, hoping to produce hits that would command high rentals from exhibitors. This shift created fallow periods in the release schedule, and even the major theater chains, no longer affiliated with the Hollywood studios, found themselves with little product to play, particularly in the autumn and spring seasons. The *Paramount* decision was designed in part to strengthen the bargaining power of the independent exhibitors vis-à-vis the collusive behavior of the studios' distribution oligopoly. But, in reality, the *Paramount* case had the unintended effect of exacerbating the effects of market forces, including a shortage of product, which in turn placed the former subsequent-run exhibitor in an even more precarious position.

The industry made many changes to adapt to these conditions, including technological innovation, new patterns of distribution, increasingly aggressive advertising campaigns, independent production, co-productions with the film industries of Great Britain and elsewhere in Europe, and the sale of features to television. The low-budget genre cinema of the fifties and sixties plays an important part in all of these adaptations. The "upscaling" of genres through the use of color, wider screen size, major stars, and presold properties like best-selling novels —all of which is evident in the western, domestic melodrama, musical, and science fiction genres in the fifties—was generally slow to come to the horror film. Even Hitchcock's *Psycho*, produced for Paramount in 1959, was shot in black and white with his television crew. Still, technological innovation played a crucial role in the postwar horror film: the 3-D boom of 1952–1954 contained several horror films that were box-office hits, including *House of Wax* (1953) and *Creature from the Black Lagoon* (1954).

The ghouls, gimmicks, and gold of this book's title refer to, respectively, the production, distribution, and exhibition branches of the movie business. I place at center stage the sometimes cooperative, sometimes confrontational relationship between the exhibition and distribution branches of the industry, for it is this relationship that drove the production end of the industry toward the development of the low-budget genre films that characterized much of this phase of the post-studio film industry. For example, technological innovations such as 3-D and CinemaScope coincided with an increasingly confiscatory split between distributor and exhibitor, with the distributor retaining as much as 70 percent of first-run box-office receipts. Furthermore, 3-D was all about the sale of hardware (whether special viewing glasses or stereo sound) to exhibitors. Such practices almost led to open warfare between Hollywood and all but the largest theater chains. Similarly, the cutbacks in production and seasonal droughts in the release schedule of the majors virtually forced some exhibitor circuits to enter production; later, I will examine the Houck theater chain's foray into production in the late fifties.

Product shortage also created the opportunity for cagey independent producers such as William Castle to use idle studio space at Columbia and Allied Artists to make horror and other films earmarked for release during the relatively idle months in the distribution calendar. Castle began his run of gimmick-laden horror films in the late fifties in releases like *Macabre* (1957), *House on Haunted Hill* (1958), *The Tingler* (1959), *Thirteen Ghosts* (1960), and *Homicidal* (1961). Also by the mid-fifties distributors of genre double bills had begun to exploit threadbare neighborhood theaters, formerly part of the subsequent-run pipeline during the studio era and now desperate for first-run product, in huge multitheater openings supported by massive saturation advertising on TV and radio.

Thomas Doherty's *Teenagers and Teenpics* is a very successful attempt to trace the reciprocal relationship between cultural and industrial forces in this period. Doherty recounts the crippling effects that several events had on the motion picture industry, including the *Paramount* decision, the rise of television, the demographic trend toward suburbanization, and the siphoning of disposable income to monthly payments on consumer durables. At the same time, he notes, because of their disposable income American teenagers were becoming one of the most sought-after demographic groups by the culture industry. The motion-picture industry, like the recording industry, successfully exploited this new market through a genre cinema aimed at youth *"to the pointed exclusion of their elders."* [11] However, Doherty's chapter on "horror teenpics" places an almost exclusive emphasis on discourses of juvenile delinquency and stock characters in films such as *I Was a Teenage Were-*

wolf (1957), which were, he points out, derived from their counterparts in social-problem films like *Rebel without a Cause* and *The Blackboard Jungle*. The broad trends Doherty outlines leave little room for a discussion of film style and narration, and the end point of his study, 1960, signals a major shift in the aesthetic, technological, economic, and social function served by the horror film in the movie marketplace. Indeed, the increasing importance of the international market and coproductions, the shift to color, and the more explicit depictions of sex and violence in the genre were all part of this shift.

Despite my interest in providing an economic framework for understanding the nature and functions of horror films in the fifties and sixties, I am not an economic determinist. These films are too interesting to be reduced to being mere by-products of changes in the movie business in the postwar period. The horror movies of the baby boom era retain their ability to frighten, astonish, and delight audiences. The eighties and nineties have seen a dizzying succession of remakes, sequels, and homages to horror films from this period, ranging from *Psycho* and *Night of the Living Dead* to *Ed Wood*, *Godzilla*, *Village of the Damned*, *Diabolique*, *Little Shop of Horrors*, *Not of This Earth*, *Invaders from Mars*, *House on Haunted Hill*, and *Thirteen Ghosts*. Videocassette and DVD reissues of the originals continue to constitute a profitable and increasingly upscale niche of the home video market.

Further, the fifties and sixties saw immense artistic changes in the horror genre. Decades of audience familiarity with characters (mad scientist, entranced heroine, suave vampire), plots (invasion, mysterious voyage, science gone awry), themes (forbidden knowledge, transgressive sexuality), and settings (desert island, old house, laboratory) led filmmakers to increasingly stylish and outlandish variations on established formulas. Thomas Schatz's *Hollywood Genres* asserts that filmmakers respond to increasing audience awareness of genre conventions by following a pattern of increasing self-consciousness in their deployment.[12] Notably, a genre moves from an experimental phase, in which the conventions are introduced (say, the German expressionist *schauerfilme* of the twenties such as *The Cabinet of Dr. Caligari* [1919] and *Nosferatu* [1922]) through a classical phase in which the conventions achieve stability (for example, the thirties films by Universal such as *Dracula* and *Frankenstein* [both 1931]).

In this book I trace the horror genre's evolution through its two phases. The first is the refinement phase, characterized by the increasing psychological complexity of the characters and by technological innovation, such as in the color movies of Hammer Films, the widescreen

Poe adaptations of American International Pictures, and the gimmick films of William Castle (and their major-studio pastiche, *Psycho*). The second phase is the baroque, in which the conventions, now completely familiar to audiences and filmmakers, are exaggerated and stylized almost to the level of parody. This latter phase is signaled by the eccentric art-film stylings of the later AIP Poe adaptations such as *Masque of the Red Death* (1964) and *Tomb of Ligea* (1965), the wild sexuality of Italian horror films such as *The Horrible Dr. Hichcock* (1962) and *The Whip and the Body* (1963), and the graphic violence of George Romero's *Night of the Living Dead* (1968).

A fascinating and nuanced reading of fifties horror films and literature is Mark Jancovich's *Rational Fears: American Horror in the 1950s*.[13] Jancovich persuasively argues that commonplace critical assumptions about fifties horror movies as reactionary cold war parables are largely mistaken. Even the "invasion narratives" such as *Thing from Another World* (1951) and *Them!* (1954), he argues, display a profound unease with the increasingly managed and rationalized social institutions and psychic life of the postwar period. He traces the motif of alienation, abjection, and dissolution of personality through a range of films and novels of the period and ends his study with a consideration of *Psycho* as a continuation of, rather than a break with, popular culture of the fifties.

There is, of course, a direct link between industrial conditions and the increasingly bizarre hype used to sell films like *Psycho* ("No one will be admitted after the film begins!") and, by extension, the growing outlandishness of the films themselves. The horror film is itself often a site of struggle between two kinds of filmmaking: the self-effacing classical norms of a cinema of narrative integration draw the spectator's attention to the most important story details (say, a slowly turning doorknob or a looming shadow) in an unobtrusive way. By contrast, the wilder, more primitive "cinema of attractions" draws attention to the act of display, often revealing forbidden, shocking, or astonishing spectacle such as a tentacled monster, a female vampire in a diaphanous gown, or a close-up of a knife entering vulnerable flesh. The cinema of attractions, according to filmmaker Sergei Eisenstein and others, is capable of directly eliciting physiological responses from the spectator. Linda Williams has written of the lowbrow "body genres" of melodrama, horror, and pornography, which deploy both elements of classical narrative and eruptive moments of stylist excess and spectacle in the service of eliciting this physical response.[14]

Tom Gunning has argued that early cinema was structured around moments of exhibitionistic display of attractions, and short films from

Trade ad for Allied Artists's 1957 double bill of *Attack of the Crab Monsters* and *Not of This Earth* (G. William Jones Film and Video Collection, Southern Methodist University).

the turn of the century often consist of a single shot that displayed the conjurer's sleight of hand, a staged cockfight, or, my favorite, the electrocution of an elephant. For Gunning, one of the strongest markers of the cinema of attractions is the moment when the conjurer looks into the camera. This look is not of a subject caught unawares but rather a gesture "undertaken with brio."[15] He further claims that this earlier regime of attractions pulses under the surface of the later cinema of narrative integration. In fact, he asserts, it is often a catalog of a film's attractions that form the substance of publicity for the classical film.[16] For example, Allied Artists's 1957 double bill of *Attack of the Crab Monsters* and *Not of This Earth* was heralded with the exclamation, "Terrorama!" These films, sold to exhibitors as a preconstituted package, were advertised by a tandem of posters, the artwork for which preceded the scripting and shooting of the films themselves. The huge pincers of the monster crabs that clutch the heroine in one poster are echoed by the position of the woman's fingers over her own eyes in the poster for *Not of This Earth*. Underneath the woman's terrified gaping mouth is a list of the film's privileged moments of spectacle: "SEE The Fiend with the Death-Ray Eyes! SEE Vampire Creatures from Outer Space! SEE Beauty Trapped by King-Size Mollusks!" Both the female victims in the posters and the

"Step Right Up!" The sinister mountebank invites the
Hollstenwall fairgoers into the sideshow tent in *The Cabinet
of Dr. Caligari* (G. William Jones Film and Video Collection,
Southern Methodist University).

anatomically improbable crab monster feature eyes that stare out at the
viewer.

In the poststudio era horror film of the fifties and sixties, the narrative voice of both the films' publicity and the films' deployment of
style and story is the fairground conjurer, familiar to horror audiences
from at least as early as *The Cabinet of Dr. Caligari*. This figure, whose
broad theatrical gestures and direct entreaties to the crowd to step into
his tent and view the curiosities contained there, is repeatedly cited in
fifties movie trade papers in references to the film publicity's "ballyhoo":
trade sources portray purveyors of horror films like Castle and AIP's cofounders Samuel Arkoff and James Nicholson as mountebanks, tricksters, or conjurers. Arkoff, Nicholson, and *I Was Teenage Werewolf*'s producer Herman Cohen were, in *Time* magazine's 1960 phrase, "the three
Merlins" of horror, and a 1958 *Variety* headline asked, "Is [the] carny
come-on necessary?" In fact, the supposed Caligari-like thrall of the
postwar pitchman over the American fairgoers was the subject of much
social criticism of the fifties. Examples of these critiques range from
from Frederick Wertham's 1953 condemnation of the horror comics,
Seduction of the Innocent, to Vance Packard's 1957 exposé of advertising
psychology in *The Hidden Persuaders*.

The fairground midway from which these conjurers played their
sleight of hand was the motion picture and television marketplace. In
order to track the circulation of horror films through theatrical and tele

vision distribution I chose the Philadelphia market as a test case, for the following reasons. First, the city and its surrounding suburbs has a large and diverse population, and the increased suburbanization of the area's middle-class population was fairly typical of large cities during the period of this study. Therefore, changing patterns of distribution and theater construction undertaken to serve this population created problems for the urban neighborhood theaters that the distributors of genre films attempted to exploit.

Second, drive-ins and auditorium "hardtop" theaters from the greater Philadelphia area were often assembled into temporary theater "chains" for area-wide multiple playoffs of genre-film double bills, a practice that became increasingly important to the horror film in this period. Finally, Philadelphia was (and is) a major media market ripe for exploitation by saturation advertising by a very diverse group of television stations, which became crucial to film distributors and program syndicators as a market for genre features over the course of the sixties. I consulted the Wednesday and Friday movie listings in the *Philadelphia Inquirer* for theater shows and times and used that paper's *TV Week* from the Sunday edition for television listings of movies and other television programming in order to follow over a period of several years the programming decisions of theater owners and TV station managers. Through this method I arrived at a series of conclusions about the relationship between patterns of distribution and exhibition of horror films in the fifties and sixties.

For an overview of the changing industrial context in this period I followed several trade sources, particularly *Variety* and *Motion Picture Herald*. The latter was particularly important in clarifying the issues covered in this book because it devoted a large amount of space to exhibitors' comments about specific films, their audiences and box-office performance, changing patterns of distribution, and the cost of technological upgrade. Both the "Letters" section of the journal and the "What the Picture Did for Me" columns provide a forum for small-town, rural, and inner-city nabe operators to voice their concerns about the changing industry during this volatile period. In addition, the conservative cultural orientation of the publication made it particularly sensitive to issues of community relations and local censorship during this period of atrophy in the Production Code, as well as to the issues of increased visibility of the international art cinema and the rise of the youth audience.

Transcripts of the hearings before the Senate Select Committee on Small Business in 1953 and 1956 provided a huge wealth of detail on the changing movie marketplace, the plight of the small and subsequent-run exhibitor, and the technology race of 1953. Also, the committee's final reports in 1953 and 1956, titled *Motion Picture Distribution Trade Practices*, provided additional information about the Senate's ultimate refusal to step in as arbiter of conflicts between distribution and exhibition. Popular magazines including *Time, Newsweek, Business Week*, and the *New York Times Magazine* were very helpful in tracing the wider response to issues central to this study, such as the 3-D craze in 1953 and the commercial boom in horror films in 1958–1959. *Broadcasting* magazine was a very important source for information on the mid-sixties explosion in UHF and color television as well as on the standardization of feature-film programming by local television stations.

I attempt in this volume to analyze the economic, aesthetic, technological, and cultural factors that changed the horror film through several cycles of popularity from the end of the studio system to the dawn of the New Hollywood. Chapter 1, "Horror in Three Dimensions," examines the technological race of 1952–1954 and the brief 3-D cycle. I outline there the broad issues faced by some small exhibitors in the rush to upgrade their theaters, and I discuss how two successful horror films in 3-D, Warner's *House of Wax* and Universal-International's *Creature from the Black Lagoon*, used the stylistic and narrational norms of the horror genre to negotiate the often conflicting demands of showcasing the new process and maintaining a cinema of narrative integration. This conflict was often expressed in the critics' distaste for "gimmick" shots of objects flying at the audience.

Chapter 2, "The Color of Blood," analyzes *Curse of Frankenstein* (1957), the first of Hammer Films's color remakes of 1930s Universal classics. *Curse of Frankenstein* is a watershed film, both for its origins in the growing trend of international coproduction and for its groundbreaking use of color and explicit gore. Chapter 3, "Look into the Hypnotic Eye!" describes the seasonal product shortages faced by many exhibitors in the mid-fifties and the production efforts of theater chains and an ambitious minor studio, Allied Artists, to use wildly hyped exploitation films to increase their market share. Chapter 4, "'A Sissified Bela Lugosi,'" charts the middle career of horror icon Vincent Price. After a major supporting role in Twentieth Century-Fox's *The Fly* (1958), Price's unique star persona was used by William Castle in black-and-white, gimmick-laden programmers like *The Tingler* (1959), and then by American International Pictures and Roger Corman in their slightly upscaled color and widescreen adaptations of Edgar Allan Poe.

Chapter 5, "Grind House or Art House?" traces the rise of the art theater in the postwar product shortage and the efforts of two small distributors, Distributors Corporation of America (DCA) and Astor Pictures, to serve a range of theaters with a combination of art films and low-budget genre films. As Joan Hawkins notes in *Cutting Edge: Art-Horror and the Horrific Avant-Garde*, these two categories can be quite fluid, both commercially and aesthetically,[17] a concept that helps explain Astor's miserable failure in distributing what is now considered one of the supreme masterpieces of the horror genre, Michael Powell's art-horror hybrid *Peeping Tom* (1960).

Chapter 6, "American International Goes International," describes the tremendous importance of international coproduction, particularly with the Italian film industry, for the horror film in the mid-sixties. One of AIP's commercial and artistic successes from this production trend was Mario Bava's *Black Sabbath* in 1964. Chapter 7, "Television Syndication and the Birth of the 'Orphans,'" recounts the insatiable demand for color features brought about by the mid-decade explosion in color television and UHF. Again, imports from Europe played a huge part in this development, and I trace the circulation of a number of feature-film packages through the Philadelphia television market in the late sixties.

Chapter 8, "Demon Children and the Birth of Adult Horror," outlines the growing trend of the acquisition of the major studios by huge multinational conglomerates interested in developing a "leisure core" of related products and services. Paramount's 1968 release of Roman Polanski's *Rosemary's Baby*, produced by reformed schlockmeister William Castle, intersects with many of these trends. Chapter 9, "Family Monsters and Urban Matinees," situates the 1968 release of *Night of the Living Dead* in the efforts of art-film distributor Continental Releasing to straddle several of its markets, including the kiddie matinee, the inner-city nabe house, and the horror market with a single release. I conclude this book with a discussion of the ways in which the industrial and cultural trends of the period of this study were intensified and refined in the New Hollywood of the seventies and eighties.

CHAPTER 1

Horror in

Three Dimensions:

House of Wax and

Creature from the Black

Lagoon

n a historical survey of three-dimensional motion pictures, R. M. Hayes writes, "There have always been two thoughts on *House of Wax*: one, it is a classic film of the horror genre, and two, it is claptrap exploitation of the worst kind. There seems to be no middle ground."[1] Lowbrow associations continue to plague 3-D films, and modern viewers' experience of 3-D movies is probably limited to an eighties or nineties revival screening of *House of Wax* (1953), *Dial M for Murder* (1954), or perhaps a midnight showing of camp sci-fi outings such as *Spacehunter: Adventures in the Forbidden Zone* (1983), the campier westerns such as *Comin' at Ya!* (1981), or the campiest sexploitation films such as *The Stewardesses* (1969). These films are often remembered as a collection of tedious linking scenes inbetween "gimmick shots" of body parts, hurled objects, or, in John Waters's account of the all-male porn film *Heavy Equipment* (1977), "life itself" flying off the screen.[2]

But the brief 3-D boom of 1952 to 1954 was a crucial time in which technological, economic, and artistic changes rocked the production, distribution, and exhibition branches of the movie business. The stereoscopic feature was one of a large number of technological innovations that had profound economic consequences for theater owners, and films such as *House of Wax* and *Creature from the Black Lagoon* (1954) were early indicators of the way genre films would be made, marketed, and exhibited over the next thirty years. Most important, the technological race of the early fifties, in which the production and distribution branch of the industry rapidly innovated 3-D, widescreen, and stereo sound, left many neighborhood theaters and subsequent-run theaters with huge bills for technological upgrades and a severe shortage of product to play. This would have a tremendous effect on the market for the horror film in the next decade.

The technological changes of 1952 and 1953 were part of an escalating struggle between manufacturers of equipment and centralized distribution on one hand, and the more diffuse branch of exhibition on the other. The newly divorced production-distribution branch of the industry sought to profit from the sale of new technology to the exhibitors both in the actual monies paid for the installation of the equipment and in increasingly confiscatory rental terms for the highly publicized films showcasing that new technology. In the case of 3-D, what was being sold to exhibitors was not so much the films themselves as the competing hardware systems needed to exhibit 3-D films (and the stereo sound systems with which the 3-D systems were packaged), which were vying with one another to become the new industry standard.

The first major-studio release in 3-D was *House of Wax* by Warner Bros. in 1953. *House of Wax* was able to negotiate the often conflicting demands of showcasing the new process and maintaining a cinema of narrative integration through the unique narrative and stylistic features of the horror genre. Despite the encumbrances of special viewing glasses and a complex interlocking mechanism that enabled two projectors to run in sync (a process that necessitated an intermission to change reels an hour into the film), *House of Wax* was one of the box-office sensations of 1953. The 3-D era's other horror success was Universal-International's *Creature from the Black Lagoon* in 1954. *Creature* was released in a wide saturation campaign, booked into dozens of theaters in some areas and supported by massive advertising in television, radio, and newspapers. The upscale trimmings of *House of Wax*, such as color and period costumes, were completely absent from *Creature from the Black Lagoon*. The latter film was highly derivative of films like *King Kong* and *The Thing from Another World*, which privilege shock and gimmick shots over the moving camera and depth staging of *House of Wax*. For this type of exploitation of 3-D to occur, exhibitors had to wait for an inexpensive, single-projector system of 3-D to be introduced via the Moropticon process in 1954.

In 1953, almost all of the major studios were aligned with at least one major manufacturer in an attempt to adopt an image or sound technology that they hoped would become the new industry standard. The first major technological sensation of the "new era," though, did not come from a major studio. Cinerama bowed in a program of shorts, *This Is Cinerama*, at the Broadway Theater in New York in early 1953. Developed by inventor Fred Waller, Cinerama consisted of three projectors running in synchronization on a 142-degree curved screen. Cinerama added to the illusion of depth with six-track stereophonic sound. The Cinerama program consisted of travelogue footage featuring the Grand Canyon, the canals of Venice, and a bullfight in Spain. By the year's end,

Variety reported that *This Is Cinerama* had brought in $6.5 million in its engagement in six cities.[3] However, the tremendous outlay of money needed to convert a theater to Cinerama was a major impediment to its implementation as anything like an industry standard. Estimates of conversion cost varied from $70,000 for basic equipment to as high as $150,000 including construction costs, consulting fees, and labor.[4]

The most successful technological innovation from this period is Twentieth Century-Fox's development of CinemaScope, as detailed in John Belton's *Widescreen Cinema*.[5] According to Richard Hincha, the cost for conversion to CinemaScope was $25,000 for a large theater, $15,000 to $17,000 for a medium-size two thousand seat house, and about $10,000 for a small house.[6] As Belton points out, both of the exhibitor trade organizations—Allied States Organization, which represented smaller independent theaters, and Theater Owners of America, the organization of larger first-run theaters and chains—objected to Fox's insistence that exhibitors purchase the entire CinemaScope package, which included special lenses, an expensive metallic curved screen, and magnetic stereo sound.[7] Eventually, Fox withdrew the stereo-only policy and saw the sale of CinemaScope packages increase significantly throughout 1954 and 1955.[8] In fact, the sale of CinemaScope technology to the exhibitors was handled by a Fox subsidiary, CinemaScope Products Inc.,[9] and by September 1954, Fox had spent about $10 million on the development and marketing of CinemaScope, while exhibitors had spent nearly $67 million for the equipment. Thus, according to Hincha, "Fox may have reaped sizable profits in this area."[10]

The most famous, and I think the least understood, technological innovation from this period was 3-D. As early as the twenties, filmmakers had begun to simulate binocular separation of the right and left eyes' views by printing the left and right images in red and green on a single strip of film. During projection, the red and green viewers worn by the spectators filtered out the opposite eye's views.[11] The brain then fused the two images into one and was fooled into thinking that it was perceiving three dimensions through this "window." Several short films were released in this so-called anaglyph process in the 1920s by Pathé, Educational Films, and others. It was the anaglyph process that was used by engineer John Norling to produce a pair of 3-D shorts that were released by Metro in 1936 and 1938 with narration by humorist Pete Smith under the title "Audioskopics."[12]

In 1939, the Chrysler Corporation contracted with Norling, now working for the Polaroid Company, for a 3-D film to accompany its exhibit at the New York World's Fair.[13] Norling and Polaroid developed a system for binocular 3-D cinematography based on the polarization of light through chemically treated filters. As with the earlier color filters, the polarized glasses worn by the spectator register slightly different images for the left and right eyes.[14]

The first system of polarized 3-D cinematography used by Hollywood was developed in the late forties by a firm outside the Hollywood studio system. The Natural Vision Corporation was formed by Milton Gunzburg and his optician brother Julian who, along with camera-operator Friend Baker, developed a physically enormous system of two sync-geared 35mm Mitchell cameras shooting at a forty-five degree angle through two mirrors pointing at the subject. Projection of the Natural Vision system required two interlocked projectors with polarized filters installed in the port holes of the booth. Spectators wore Polaroid viewers, and the double-projector system required an intermission to change reels. Both the glasses and the intermission were seen as drawbacks, and several Hollywood studios rejected the process.

In 1952, independent producer Arch Oboler, who had become famous as a radio writer and director of both the long-running horror series *Lights Out* and the prestige anthology series *Arch Oboler's Plays*, produced, wrote, and directed *Bwana Devil* in the polarized 3-D process. Oboler's film was shot in Anscocolor and featured Robert Stack, Barbara Britton, and Nigel Bruce in a story of railroad workers in Africa plagued by repeated and violent attacks by ravenous lions (the "bwana devil," or king of the beasts). Virtually every sequence was blocked to foreground the new process, with an almost static tableaux of carefully arranged actors in alternating dialogue and action scenes, the latter featuring hurled spears, growling lions, and rifles pointing into the audience for maximum 3-D effect.

None of the major distributors were interested in the film, but former RKO studio chief George J. Schaeffer, Gunzburg's associate, secured bookings for the film in Hollywood and Los Angeles.[15] Despite wretched reviews, the film became a huge novelty success. At Thanksgiving in 1952, when *Bwana Devil* was released in Hollywood and Los Angeles, the company was telling *Motion Picture Herald* that the system "can be installed in any theater in the nation at a cost a good deal under $100."[16] In fact, by the time all needed equipment was purchased, including a special high-reflection screen (the projection and viewing filters drastically reduced image brightness), the cost was more like $3,000. Oboler sold the rights to the film outright to United Artists, which immediately rushed the film into general release in February.[17]

Bwana Devil grossed over $1.3 million in its first month of general release in thirty key theaters, including a record-breaking run at the Warner Aldine in Philadelphia in spite of a huge snowstorm.[18] *Variety* predicted that the film would gross between $4 million and $5 million domestically,[19] but the film's subsequent-run engagements came up against a glut of 3-D releases from the majors, and the film ended 1953 with a gross of $2.7 million.[20]

Exhibitors who made a bid for first-run engagements of *Bwana Devil* found themselves paying a fifty-fifty split with United Artists as well as paying half the cost of the Polaroid viewers. United Artists claimed, as would other distributors of 3-D films, that these terms were the result of the high price of prints (each reel was printed twice, one for each projector) and the need to manufacture and circulate multiple trailers for the 3-D and flat versions of the film.[21] This expense, as well as the confiscatory terms exacted by the distributor from the exhibitor, would later be a larger impetus for the development of a single-projector system.[22]

Of course, exhibitors, not the public, were the consumers of the new technology, and money flowed into the Gunzburg coffers before a single ticket had been sold. In 1953, Natural Vision secured a one-year distribution deal for the special glasses crucial to the process. The Gunzburg company bought one hundred million pairs from Polaroid for 6.7 cents apiece and sold them to exhibitors at 10 cents apiece, realizing a two million dollar profit in 1953 from these transactions alone.[23] Polaroid, who for a time had completely cornered the market on 3-D viewers, saw its stock rise 33 percent in the early months of 1953.[24] The subsidiary role that the movies themselves played in 3-D's financial success was noted by producer George Jessel, who bitingly predicted in early 1953 that "one year from now the studios will be making nothing but glasses."[25]

For *Bwana Devil*'s highly profitable first run, the film was released only to first-run and first neighborhood-run theaters. Virtually all of the major chains installed 3-D for the first cycle of polarized features. Loew's spent $300,000 to convert its New York chain of thirty-one theaters to 3-D for the release of *Bwana Devil*.[26] Chain exhibitor Robert Lippert even installed 3-D in his Hollywood drive-in theater, the Starlight, with plans to install it in twenty-three more.[27] The major chains were in the position to raise their ticket prices to pay distributors for the "new era" pictures. Cinerama had started the "ticket tilt" (*Variety*'s phrase), and special releases in widescreen, 3-D, and later road-show releases in Todd-AO enabled first-run chains to raise their prices across the board, even for standard releases.[28]

At a meeting of small-theater trade group Allied Central of New Jersey in summer 1953, affiliates claimed that 3-D was most profitable first for the manufacturers and deliverers of equipment, second for the producers and distributors of films, and finally for the exhibitor.[29] The expense of upgrading houses to 3-D, the high rentals charged for stereoscopic features, and the excessive prereleases (high-profile, extensive engagements before a film's official "first run") in theater chains would frustrate the small houses throughout the 3-D period. In October, the Society of Motion Picture and Television Engineers conducted a survey of the five thousand theaters that had converted to stereoscopic 3-D and found that 68 percent were circuit houses and only 28 percent were independents.[30]

For a typical theater, the lenses, screen, and interlocking mechanism of the dual-projector system cost about $1,500, with stereo sound running an additional $10,000.[31] A small exhibitor complained in *Variety* that "while the big chains use stockholder money for new installations, we have to dig into our own pockets."[32] This situation was exacerbated by International Association of Theatrical and Stage Employees projectionist union rules that three projectionists be employed to run 3-D films. The owner of a six hundred seat independent house in Minnesota recognized that the films were merely a conduit through which to sell equipment to theaters. A letter to an exhibitors' trade journal complained, "The distributors who sold us rock bottom budget pictures for big film rentals and the glasses manufacturers who charged us a dime for glasses that probably cost about a cent to manufacture, were the ones who made the dough."[33]

The subsequent-run playoff of *Bwana Devil* in 3-D demonstrated both how difficult the terms were for showing 3-D films for the small exhibitor and how important the glasses were to the economics of 3-D. Whereas first-run theaters could raise their ticket prices enough to compensate for the fifty-fifty split with United Artists on the cost of the viewers, subsequent-run houses found that patrons balked at the ten-cent ticket increase that kept the theater from taking a loss on the glasses.[34] This was bitterly noted by a New Jersey exhibitor, who said, "We're doing so much business with 3-D that we're going out of business."[35] After spending $3,000 to convert equipment and paying the 55 percent distributor split, the neighborhood theater often found itself in the red.[36]

This problem was later made even more acute when major studios began to release their own 3-D features in incompatible systems. In fact, the failure of the industry to standardize 3-D systems was an issue discussed in Senate Small Business Committee hearings on distribution trade practices in April 1953 and again in 1956. Allied States Organization's general counsel Abram Myers told the 1953 committee that "unless prompt action is taken to prevent the freeze-out of the independent by means of the pre-releasing of pictures and the production of depth pictures by multiple processes and the withholding of apparatus from independents, [other unfair trade] practices will become academic."[37] The hearings were a forum for small theater owners and their trade organizations, particularly Allied States Organization,[38] to posit an "artificial" product shortage designed to drive the small theater owner out of business and to transform the film industry from a "mass" to a "class" business.[39] Smaller exhibitors complained about exorbitant rentals, long first runs (which brought films to their theaters virtually played out), and other distribution practices.[40]

The majors pressed on in their technological innovation. One of the production and distribution companies hoping for major gains in the technological sweepstakes was Warner Bros.[41] Its stereophonic sound system, Warner Phonic, was the company's most important bid in the technology race. RCA designed the Warner Phonic system, which made its debut in April 1953. The Warner Phonic system combined a conventional optical soundtrack with magnetic tracks on the coated film for the left, right, and surround channels.[42] The earlier work by RCA on a four-track magnetic reproducer for stereo sound formed the basis of the Warner Phonic system.[43]

An RCA trade ad for Warner Phonic in *Variety* announced "3-Dimensional Sound in [Warner's] exciting 3-D motion picture!"[44] In fact, Warner's use of 3-D in 1953–1954 was an effort to capitalize on its novelty in order to sell the Warner Phonic system to exhibitors. This is why the studio called its stereo system "3-D sound." A trade ad in *Motion Picture Herald* announced, "From the studio that first successfully introduced sound to the motion picture screens of the world . . . the screen's first complete electronic merger of dimension-camera and dimension-microphone in their most fully dreamed-of relations."[45] Production head Jack Warner rhapsodized that Warner Phonic "bears a comparison with our early ventures into sound such as *The Jazz Singer* and *The Singing Fool*. Revolutionary as these pioneer pictures were, I hardly need point out the tremendous improvements in sound process over the last quarter-century."[46] On a promotional tour for the studio, actor Frank Lovejoy announced to *Variety* that after talking with audiences, "even more than 3-D, exhibitors and the public alike are excited about stereo sound. Everyone is convinced that it's just a matter of time before all films, including flats, will be using it."[47]

On the other hand, *Variety* noted that many reviewers hated "cacophonous" sound,[48] and letters to trade publications from exhibitors balked not only at the price of directional sound but also at its disorienting effects. Indeed, one Omaha theater owner complained that, at times, stereo sound "is actually confusing to some patrons."[49] It is precisely this dizzying and shocking effect of stereo sound that provides the context of Warner's premiere showcasing of its new sound system. The feature that introduced Warner Phonic was the horror film *House of Wax*, which, fittingly, was also the first 3-D feature released by a major studio.

The horror film, like the western, detective thriller, and novelty short, was a downscale genre that could upscale itself through the conspicuous use of new technology. According to Bosley Crowther, it was precisely the crisis of the "average film" that was the source of so much anxiety in Hollywood. The film industry would always have a small number of blockbusters on which it could rely, but "it is on the sale of the average picture that the whole movie industry is pegged. If it cannot sell the ordinary picture, it cannot live. . . . Thus it is that they are thinking first of all of the possibilities of 3-D in imparting magnetism and novelty, they hope, to the average film."[50]

House of Wax was released in April 1953 after being rushed through production in an effort to beat to the theaters Columbia's *Man in the Dark* as the first major studio release in 3-D. In 1933, the studio had used the same story in *Mystery of the Wax Museum* to highlight its brief excursion into two-strip Technicolor. Warner's decision to make its initial foray into Natural Vision a remake of an earlier success was part of an industry-wide tendency for studios to remake previous hits updated by new technological systems. Other 3-D or widescreen remakes of earlier hits included Columbia's *Miss Sadie Thompson*, Fox's *How to Marry a Millionaire* (both 1953), and Warner's *A Star Is Born* (1954).[51]

The horror film was particularly amenable to the bizarre effects that could be achieved through a foregrounding of 3-D and stereophonic sound. The stylistic and narrational norms of the horror genre proved particularly well suited to negotiating the conflicting demands between the cinema of attractions ("3-D gimmicks," in the trade parlance of 1953) and the cinema of narrative integration. Also, the setting of the film, a wax museum, motivated the film's obsession with realism and verisimilitude in the visual arts, as well as the relationship between beauty and ugliness; classical art and fairground sensationalism; and, most important, violence and sexuality.

Set at the turn of the century, *House of Wax* tells the story of Henri Jarrod (Vincent Price), a sculptor specializing in hyperrealistic wax recreations of historical and mythological figures. After an investor, Sidney Wallace, delays his promised investment in a new museum for Jarrod's work, Jarrod's business partner, the philistine Matthew Burke, attempts to burn down the waxworks for the insurance money. In a furious struggle with Burke amid the melting wax statues, Jarrod appears to perish in the fire. Months later, Burke is murdered by a hideously disfigured black-cloaked ghoul, and Burke's sleeping mistress, Kathy (Caroline Jones), is injected with a fatal drug dosage. When Kathy's innocent young friend Sue Allen (Phyllis Kirk), discovers the body, she is chased through the foggy city streets by the shambling ghoul in the film's most famous sequence. Later, Kathy's body is stolen from the morgue, and Jarrod turns up alive, embittered, and wheelchair-bound. He opens up the House of Wax, a chamber of horrors designed to showcase horrific crimes and scenes of sexual violence. Sue becomes convinced that Kathy's body is on display in the museum, covered with wax, but her suspicions are dismissed by the police department's Lieutenant Brennan (Frank Lovejoy) and her own boyfriend, Scott Andrews. Eventually, the police confront Jarrod's assistant, Carl Hendricks, as Sue conducts her own investigation and discovers Kathy's body beneath the wax in the Joan of Arc display. In Sue's struggle with Jarrod, his waxen mask is destroyed, revealing him as the murderous ghoul. But before Jarrod can scald Sue to death in the molten wax, Scott overcomes Jarrod's henchman Ygor (Charles Bronson, né Buchinsky) in a violent struggle, and the police break down the door. As the naked and bound Sue screams in terror, Jarrod falls to his death in the cauldron of boiling wax, and Lieutenant Brennan, in the nick of time, moves the gurney on which she is tied as the boiling wax cascades out of the cauldron.

In keeping with its genre, *House of Wax* highlights a mode of storytelling that draws on a set of organizing principles that predate the cinema with origins in the carnival, circus, or sideshow. These have been present in the genre at least since *The Cabinet of Dr. Caligari* (1919). The figure of Caligari, the ancestor of Henri Jarrod and countless other movie madmen, is simultaneously a psychiatrist, carnival barker, and hypnotist. He can be seen as an emblem of the forces that mediate between the genre's eruptions of shock and spectacle and the efforts of the narrative to both impel and contain them. Likewise, in *House of Wax* the restlessly roaming camera, the mordant Jarrod leading the public (and the filmgoer) through the gruesome displays of the chamber of horrors, and the famous paddleball-wielding carnival barker outside of Jarrod's display are all examples of these stylistic and narrative figures. This figure leads our surrogates, the characters in the film, from the normal world of the carnival midway into the inverted and horrific space of the inner sanctum.

In many horror films, the narrative's storytelling process is often enacted in a magician or trickster figure who accompanies his acts of sorcery with elaborate gestures to the audience that have their origins in the deliberately distracting sleight-of-hand of the stage magician. In the case of *House of Wax*'s use of 3-D and stereophonic sound, the violation of the proscenium space signaled elsewhere by the magician's gesture to the audience is achieved through spectacular displays of 3-D or surround-sound channel effects. For example, in the mortal struggle between Jarrod and Burke as the museum burns, the crackling flames appear to spread from the screen to the back of the theater. When Burke throws a chair at Jarrod, it appears to fly off the screen and over the audience's heads. Then, a loud crash is heard from the surround channel at the back of the theater. Perhaps the most astonishing 3-D effect in the film occurs during the final fight between Scott Andrews and Ygor, when Ygor suddenly stands up in the extreme foreground and appears to jump from the theater row in front of the spectator onto the screen.

These moments of shock and spectacle can downplay elements of "telling," or narration, in favor of "showing," a process that historian of early film André Gaudreault has called *monstration*.[52] Gaudreault has written of the two "divergent regimes" of the cinema that remain co-present throughout the entire history of film. The first, "exhibitionist confrontation," apposite to any discussion of 3-D, is characterized by a seemingly unmediated rapport between the viewer and the onscreen spectacle. The most distinctive element of this regime is the look of the magician (or *monstrateur*, in Gaudreault's phrase) directly into the camera in the early trick films of Georges Méliès and other filmmakers. This regime is the basis of the cinema of attractions that, according to Eisenstein and others, was capable of eliciting an immediate physiological response from the spectator in the manner of a fairground spectacle.[53] The second regime, "diegetic absorption," is constructed through norms of spatio-temporal continuity and the unobtrusive direction of the spectator's attention familiar to worldwide moviegoing audiences through the later classical Hollywood cinema and its many overseas variants.

In the horror film, many elements of the cinema of attractions—the presence of an onscreen master of illusions, a restlessly roaming camera often unmoored from any character (which Gunning calls the "unseen energy exploring space"), even the direct stare of characters into the camera—continue to exist alongside (and often in conflict with) the more self-effacing mode of the classical system. Here we can see one

House of Wax: Henri Jarrod and the wax sculpture of Marie
Antoinette (Warner Communications).

of the reasons for Warner's use of the *House of Wax* story to showcase
the Natural Vision process. The generic norms of the horror film were
uniquely suited to achieving a balance between integrated narrative and
scenes of shock or spectacle, an obsession of industry discourses on 3-D
during the period of *House of Wax*'s production and reception.

Vincent Price's Henry Jarrod is first seen lovingly caressing a nude
female bust in clay, and his ensuing argument with Matthew Burke, his
business partner, could be emblematic of the film industry's own de-
bates in 1953 about 3-D's use of violence and verisimilitude. "There are
people in the world who love beauty," Jarrod tells Burke; to which Burke
replies, "But more who want sensation, shock." Burke complains of
"sinking money" into Jarrod's "historic peepshow," a prescient phrase,
and Jarrod offers to buy out Burke after showing the wax display to
his friend Bruce and visiting art critic Sidney Wallace. The cultured
Wallace's visit to the museum contrasts with the philistine Burke's dismissal of the displays; then, Jarrod takes him on a tour designed to showcase both the sculptor Jarrod's work and Natural Vision's cinematography.

As the living actors move across the Warner Bros. set among the wax
figures, Wallace exclaims, "These groups are like dimensional paintings
of the old masters. It's not only a great show, it's an art exhibit." Here
Wallace is echoing those who saw 3-D cinematography as serving the
classical values of balance, harmony, and proportion; those like Martin
Quigley who remarked in a *Motion Picture Herald* editorial that "the
great test of 3-D films actually is in 'normal' scenes rather than trick

scenes."[54] Further, the gestures toward highbrow and middlebrow culture evinced by the historical figures presented in wax help to tame the gruesome elements of both Jarrod's display (modeled, the film's dialogue suggests, on Madame Tussaud's in London) and Warner's *House of Wax*. The period setting of the film also foregrounds costumes and production design in an effort to balance the horrific shock effects with a more upscale spectacle. This is precisely the strategy Hammer Films would use later in the decade for their lush and gory gothics.

Further, the central set of binary oppositions within the film, human flesh/sculpted wax and phenomenal reality/represented illusion, is in many ways a condensation of the discourses surrounding three-dimensional cinematography that circulated throughout the trade and popular press. *House of Wax*'s insane sculptor Henri Jarrod's impossible quest for verisimilitude and knowing the body, particularly the female body, is mirrored in the impossibility of total verisimilitude that haunted the inventors and innovators of Cinerama, anamorphosis, stereophonic sound, and binocular 3-D cinematography.

The fetishism that underlies Jarrod's relationship to his wax creations is underscored in two of his wax exhibits from the beginning of the film, Joan of Arc and Marie Antoinette; and the necrophilia implicit in his rapt attention on them will become explicit after he loses the use of his hands in the fire. He complains of never having found a perfect model of Joan, and he says of the figure, "I've done her over a dozen times, haven't I, my dear, and still she doesn't complain." It is in the figure of Marie Antoinette, his masterpiece, that the film's economy of fetishism, verisimilitude, and sexual violence reaches outrageous proportions in Jarrod's paean: "People say they can see my Marie Antoinette breathe, that her breast rises and falls . . . Her eyes follow you wherever you go . . . They're made of glass . . . They're inserted into the sockets from inside by way of the hollow neck before the head is attached to the body. Forgive me, my dear, for discussing your intimate secrets."

The "intimate secrets" of women proved to be an obsession in discussions of three-dimensional cinematography in 1953: the knowing and probing of the female body was a large part of the discourses surrounding three-dimensional cinematography. About six months after the premiere of *House of Wax*, *Newsweek* reported that radiologists at the University of Rochester School of Medicine had demonstrated a technique of 3-D cinefluorography in which a female patient drank a sample of barium, sat on a revolving stool, and was photographed through a fluoroscope screen by a stereoscopic camera. After the film was developed, "doctors in the audience, wearing Polaroid glasses, got a 3-D view

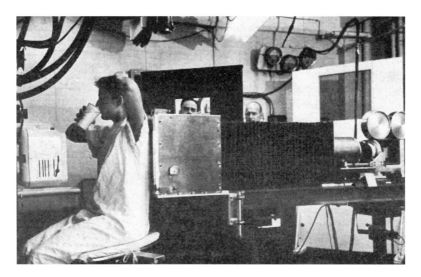

3-D and the radical visibility of the female body: cinefluorography at Rochester University, 1953 (*Newsweek* October 12, 1953).

through the patient's head, neck, and chest. They watched the passage of barium through the chest part of the esophagus, and the living, moving organs as the patient talked and swallowed." A photograph of the session was captioned, "A new look at internal organs in motion."[55]

This increased visibility of the female body was not always welcome. Several exhibitors complained to trade journals about the "horrible rendering of aging actresses" in the stereo process,[56] and Hollis Alpert, in his review of Columbia's *Man in the Dark*, saw fit to point out that "you can now clearly see the mole under the chin of Audrey Totter."[57] Bosley Crowther remarked in the *New York Times* that 3-D "naturally shows up the devices of make-up that have been contrived to conceal blemishes and age. The Max Factoring of the ladies becomes disillusioningly plain, and the 'dome doilies' of balding actors are cruelly revealed."[58]

One of the highlights of the film is Jarrod's pursuit of Sue through the darkened streets in a scene that has no precedent in the 1933 version of the film. The swirling fog (which recalls the smoke from the museum fire), chiaroscuro lighting, moving camera, and directional sound effects mark the sequence as a setpiece of Natural Vision and Warner's stereo sound process. After hearing Sue's screams on finding Kathy's body, a boarder from her rooming house emerges onto the street and blows a whistle to summon the police, while Jarrod chases Sue through the fog. Several shots are staged along a deep-space diagonal, with Sue running in the background and Jarrod advancing on her in the fore-

House of Wax's 3-D setpiece: the chase through the foggy streets (Wisconsin Center for Film and Theater Research).

House of Wax: The paddleball-wielding carney barker (Warner Communications).

ground with the camera tracking in to follow them. When Sue rounds a corner and momentarily escapes his view, she hears a horse-drawn carriage in the distance in a Warner Phonic directional sound effect. Her cry of "Cabbie!" alerts Jarrod to her location, and he sees her just as the carriage fails to halt and rounds the corner (here the sound moves from one side of the auditorium to the other). She flees him again and hides around another street corner, as a medium shot of Jarrod shows him listening intently for a sound to give away her location. She removes her shoes to avoid detection and runs down the cobblestone street in her stocking feet, arriving at Mrs. Andrews's house. Sue's loud bangs on the door and cries for help provide more directional sound, and she is pulled inside to safety.

Nowhere is the interplay between the cinema of attractions and the cinema of narrative integration in *House of Wax* more pronounced, however, than in the sequence that follows the film's intermission and reel change. The camera cranes down in front of the museum marquee, bearing "House of Wax and Chamber of Horrors," a spectacle not unlike what 1953 movie patrons had encountered outside of the theater earlier in the evening. A loud string melody introduces the film's famous carnival barker and his paddleball, a comic inflection of the cinema of attraction's onscreen master of illusions. The nondiegetic music and the bouncing of the ball motivates several directional sound effects, and as the barker looks directly into the camera, he punches the ball seemingly off the screen and into the faces of the film audience.[59] "Careful, sir, or I'll tap you on the chin. Look out, duck!" he addresses the filmgoers, as he takes aim at "somebody with a bag of popcorn." Next, he lists the attractions contained within the museum behind him, including Little Egypt, the mechanically undulating dancer, yet another female "mannequin" on display for male titillation and about whom he appropriately conjectures, "Is she wax, or is she flesh and blood?"

The scene then introduces the young Millie and her two female friends, who enter the museum in search of voyeuristic thrills and who will serve as focal figures for the audience throughout Jarrod's tour of the chamber of horrors. The wheelchair-bound Jarrod, now fully evincing the baroque Vincent Price acting style, introduces the morbid exhibits, which are a darker and more sensational reflection of the high-culture displays seen in the beginning of the film. Virtually all of the exhibits in the new House of Wax depict sexualized violence, and Jarrod leads the audience through them with the punning gallows humor of the contemporaneous E.C. horror comics "masters of ceremonies" or of Alfred Hitchcock's later television introductions. Of the execution of

Anne Boleyn, Jarrod declaims, "Henry . . . invented the shortcut to divorce." Of the dying figure of Marat, stabbed in his bath by Charlotte Corday, Jarrod remarks, "The poor man was dreadfully embarrassed," and Millie, dutiful viewer of both waxworks and 3-D, cranes her neck to get a glimpse of Marat's penis in the bathtub.

Jarrod's tour continues with a prehistoric man dragging a woman into a cave to rape her ("Ladies, this is how our ancestors carried his bride across the threshold"), and an active guillotine chops off a woman's head, which then tumbles toward the camera. Next, we see William Kemmler, the first prisoner to be electrocuted, strapped into the electric chair, then a woman stretched out on a rack. Millie gets nauseous, and her friend asks her, "Is it your corset?" to which she replies, "No, it's my stomach. Turned over." An undeterred Jarrod shows them the modern Bluebeard, at his feet yet another woman supine, nude, and dead. This time, Millie faints, tumbling directly into the camera, and Jarrod, with a supercilious shrug, offers her friends smelling salts like a "nurse" on duty in a 1950s theater lobby. He continues his tour, introducing the wax-covered body of Matthew Burke, Jarrod's own former business partner, as "one they're still talking about" (just like the makers of the quickly made, sensationalist exploitation films that would characterize fifties and sixties low-budget cinema). In a high-culture allusion amid all of these lowbrow horrors, Jarrod quotes *Macbeth*: "Foul deeds will rise, 'though all the world o'erwhelm them to men's eyes."

House of Wax abounds in images of eroticized torture and necrophilia, from the loving caresses Jarrod gives the corpse of Kathy in the morgue to the orgasmic moaning of the nude and bound Sue strapped to Jarrod's wax mold. Men's desire to possess and control the physical beauty of women is woven into the fabric of the film's plot, and many contemporary reviewers objected to the film's violent attractions of voyeurism and misogyny. Unlike the fast playoff of a saturation booking campaign, where a film plays for only a week in a huge number of houses, *House of Wax*'s measured release at inflated ticket prices was unable to protect it from excoriating reviews.

As had been the case with *Bwana Devil*, the vast majority of scorn heaped on the film concerned its emphasis on shock and attraction at the expense of narrative.

John P. Sisk, writing in *Commonweal*, described *House of Wax* as a film in which "violence is exploited with almost lyric intensity," and he says of the film's viewer, "If you had escaped the orgiastic participation you felt dirtied, as if in the atmosphere of perversion." This strain of imagery characterizes Sisk's entire review: "Such intimacies are an in-

House of Wax: Jarrod, Sidney Wallace, and the embalmed Burke (Warner Communications).

The Cabinet of Dr. Caligari: Caligari and the somnambulist Cesare (G. William Jones Film and Video Collection, Southern Methodist University).

vasion of privacy and suggest titillating peep-shows in penny arcades. They violate a compact: the implicit agreement, on the part of the audience to remain in their seats, on the part of the actors to remain on the stage. When audience and actors intermingle the essential tension breaks down; the result may be orgy, nightmare or ecstasy but it is not drama."[60] Parker Tyler's essay in the *New Republic* is even more explicit. "Not only are the frontiers of esthetic experience challenged by stereoscopic vision," he writes, "but also put into question (see the final sequence of *House of Wax*) is the disputed margin between pornography and artistic representation."[61]

In addition to the charges of pandering and pornography, many critics used words to suggest that both the film and its enthusiastic audience were primitive, antedated, or barbarous. *Time* magazine mocked the stereophonic sound, used "mostly for recording eerie musical effects and the screams of ingenues."[62] Robert Kass in *Catholic World* also complained of the "seem[ingly] experimental" directional sound that "assails your ears."[63] The film's absence of stars and lowbrow genre status were also pilloried by the *New Yorker*: "Having invested nervously in a system they don't know much about, [the filmmakers] have hedged their bets by applying the technique to something they know *all* about—stories whose powers of stupefaction are equaled only by their age."[64] In *Motion Picture Herald*, Terry Ramsaye wrote of the first wave of 3-D and widescreen films: "Their predominant aspect is the theme of high violence and colossal mayhem served with gore and destruction. It is pitched at the primitive levels . . . all to the delight of the savage juvenile mind."[65] All of these references to peep shows, arcades, primitive, or antedated stories or techniques, as well as the violation of proscenium space, suggest that what these critics found most offensive was *House of Wax*'s foregrounding of the cinema of attractions at the expense of the classical norms of a cinema of narrative integration.

Outraged reviewers were unable to prevent the film from finding an enthusiastic audience. *House of Wax* made its debut at the Paramount Theater in New York on April 16 and began nationwide prerelease on April 23.[66] The Los Angeles Paramount opened the film with a twenty-four-hour premiere beginning with a "Midnight Spook Matinee" the night before opening day and ending with a "Night Owl's Premiere" at four o'clock the following morning.[67] Warner's *Curse of Frankenstein* would be unveiled exactly the same way at the New York Paramount four years later. In the first week of its prerelease engagement, *House of Wax* had broken house records in Detroit and Chicago,[68] and by the end of May the film had been in first place in box-office returns nationwide for four straight weeks.[69] For the month of May the film grossed almost $2 million and was held over at many of its prerelease engagements.[70]

Nonetheless, the phenomenal box-office success of *House of Wax* would prove to be short-lived because of the limited number of houses equipped to exhibit the film in its two-projector Natural Vision system. As early as mid-June, *Variety* would report that "'The House of Wax' is showing signs of melting." By early summer, only about 2,000 theaters were equipped to show 3-D films, and Warner was forced to wait for more conversions rather than pushing up the date of the film's inevitable wide release in the flat, non–3-D format.[71] The main reason for the exhibitors' reluctance to equip for 3-D was the lack of a standardized system for projection.

Besides *House of Wax*, the only horror film to make *Variety*'s top-fifty grossers of 1953 was Warner's release of *The Beast from 20,000 Fathoms*. This story of an Arctic atomic blast that frees a giant, prehistoric, dragonlike reptile that decimates New York City featured special effects by Ray Harryhausen. If this story sounds familiar, it is because both the film's plot and Warner's saturation distribution campaign were based on the previous year's highly successful reissue of *King Kong*. For its rerelease, RKO featured an aggressive television advertising campaign and extensive giveaways through radio stations and department stores.[72] Warner hyped *Beast* in the same way, opening the film in over 1,400 theaters within a two-week period in late June and early July, backed with an intensive "day after day after day" television ad campaign,[73] for which Warner paid an unprecedented $200,000.[74] The studio would duplicate its success the following summer with *Them!*, a science fiction thriller about marauding giant ants, which was booked in over 2,100 theaters.[75] This saturation booking of lowbrow genre films during fallow periods in the industry release schedule would be refined over the course of the decade by AIP and others and would eventually be used in the blockbuster summer months for New Hollywood genre films including *Jaws* (1975). It was not until early 1954 and the release of Universal-International's *Creature from the Black Lagoon* that these two divergent trends, multiple openings and 3-D, would be exploited by a single film. Before this could happen, distributors and exhibitors had to wait for an industry standard for 3-D technology.

Crucial to standardization was the exhibitors' need for a single-projection system that would eliminate the expensive interlocking of projectors and the intermission reel change. Several companies developed competing single-projection systems, such as the Nord, Vectograph, and Norling systems, but each had technical or financial drawbacks for exhibitors or distributors.[76] The cheapest and most workable single-projection 3-D system would come from a company whose main business was the highly profitable manufacture and sale of 3-D glasses. Because the playoffs of 3-D films were constantly hampered by a lack of stereo viewers, Matthew Fox's Depix Company of Long Island began to make and distribute polarized viewing glass under the brand name Pola-Lite.[77] Depix was immediately sued by Polaroid for patent infringement as well as for copyright violation in Depix's use of the name Pola-Lite, which Polaroid claimed was an illegal appropriation of its trademark.[78] By August, Pola-Lite was manufacturing over seven million pairs of folding-temple 3-D glasses per week in its five plants in the United States and Canada.[79] Finally, Depix formed the Moropticon Corporation to manufacture an inexpensive, easy to install single-projector 3-D system marketed to exhibitors. A standard 35mm projector could be converted to 3-D in minutes by attaching the Moropticon prism lens to the front of the unit.[80]

Another company with yet another 3-D system, Al Zimbalist's Tru-Stereo Corporation, made *Robot Monster* in 1953 to showcase their process. Zimbalist was prepared to offer the system to independent producers at a cost of $5,000 per film.[81] Zimbalist's debut feature was sold at a lower price to small exhibitors: 35 percent of rentals up to a certain figure, then a fifty-fifty split. The film was shown under these terms at three theaters in Hollywood[82] in a doomed attempt to duplicate the success of *Bwana Devil*. *Robot Monster* is an end-of-the-world horror film featuring a gorilla-suited actor wearing an antennaed diving helmet who kidnaps the last surviving earth female. The zero-budget Zimbalist production later became a huge late-night TV cult favorite, and has been rhapsodized as such by critics as varied as novelist Stephen King and right-wing faux film historian Michael Medved.[83] However, in its beauty and the beast story, low-cost 3-D system, and reduced rental terms for exhibitors, *Robot Monster* presages one of the most successful releases of the second 3-D wave, Universal's *Creature from the Black Lagoon*.

Universal had been the first studio to release a film in both 3-D and widescreen with its issue in May 1953 of *It Came from Outer Space* in 1.85 widescreen and polarized 3-D.[84] By the time that Universal announced that it was contemplating an "underwater film in 3-D," *Variety* and other industry insiders were calling 3-D "yesterday's wow." Any depth film in the future would succeed, said the journal, on the ability of a producer to come up with a story particularly well suited to the process as well as the availability of a workable single-strip 3-D system.[85]

Universal decided to use the Depix/Pola-Lite Moropticon system to open *Creature* in a very wide release with an intense publicity campaign. *Motion Picture Herald* had predicted that the Pola-Lite system was an innovation that could be used to "give the average theater what it needs for a change of pace, something radically different now and then, a bit of novelty and special sensation."[86] This accurate forecast shows how the arrangement between Universal and Moropticon/Pola-Lite was a mutually beneficial one: Universal could reap the profits from a successful saturation booking exploitation campaign, which it knew it could place in a variety of theaters because of the ease of installation of the Moropticon system. Pola-Lite, for its part, offered "a free Moropticon system to any exhibitor who buys at least 2,500 pairs of glasses a month for twelve months," according to *Motion Picture Herald*. "The big money is still in the glasses; their sales, running month after month at ten cents a pair, would come to more in the long run than sales of the single projector."[87] Pola-Lite contracted with RCA and Altec Services to install its system in theaters, a process that cost the exhibitors only one hundred dollars and carried no burdensome or expensive stereo sound system piggybacked on the 3-D system.[88] Thus, *Creature* was able to use 3-D as an added attraction to what would become the dominant characteristics of the production and distribution of genre films over the next decade, a modest budget and a wide opening supported by saturation advertising.

Creature from the Black Lagoon was directed by Jack Arnold with the underwater scenes directed by Jack C. Havens. *Creature* makes extensive use of process shots for many of the film's exterior boat scenes, unlike, say, the deep-space natural vistas of Warner's big-budget 3-D western *Hondo* (1953). Whereas "upscale" 3-D films like *Hondo* and *Miss Sadie Thompson* had largely eschewed hurling depth effects for a less intrusive, naturalistic blocking of action, Arnold concentrates all of *Creature*'s 3-D effects into scenes of violence and shock with above-water linking scenes hurriedly executed to move the film forward to the next underwater or mayhem set piece. The film does not efface signs of its modest production budget: virtually two-thirds of the film's above-water scenes take place on the sunlit exterior of the anchored barge, and Havens's underwater scenes dispensed with synchronized dialogue or sound effects.

Creature from the Black Lagoon's status as an exploitation programmer is signaled not only by its relatively low budget and emphasis on violence and 3-D trick shots; its derivative screenplay is a successful retread of elements from other well-known horror and sci-fi hits. Harry Essex's screenplay contains motifs culled from both Howard Hawk's

Pola-Lite courted exhibitors with its inexpensive and easy-to-install 3-D system (Wisconsin Center for Film and Theater Research).

production of *The Thing from Another World* (1951) and the RKO classic *King Kong*, which had been recently (and successfully) rereleased. *The Thing* featured a group of scientists trapped in a polar research station as an enormous humanoid plant creature kills them one by one for the blood it needs to survive. *Creature's* central narrative situation is a group of scientists trapped in an Amazon tributary as the creature, an enraged amphibian gill-man, attacks them for invading his lair. In fact, one of the suspense set pieces of *The Thing*—the sentry's watch over the frozen monster as the electric blanket slowly melts the block of ice in which it is imprisoned—is replayed in *Creature* as the scholarly Dr. Thompson guards the drugged gill-man in its underwater cage while the gill-man is, unbeknownst to him, regaining consciousness.

The human antagonists in *The Thing* are Captain Henry, whose main concern is the safety of the crew and the scientists, and the misguided cold war quisling Dr. Carrington, who insists on keeping the Thing alive in the interest of science even after it has killed several people. Only Carrington's death in the claws of the monster stops his collaboration. Between Henry and Carrington circulates the Hawksian heroine Miss Nicholson, who is Carrington's research assistant and the romantic foil to Captain Henry. In *Creature* a more overtly romantic triangle is formed by research institute director Mark Williams, the swimsuit-clad scientist Kay, and her scientist paramour, hero David Reed. Mark is bitterly jealous of Kay's love for David, and the antagonism between Mark and David propels much of the dialogue of the film. *Creature* diverges from *The Thing*, however, in having the hero want to bring the gill-man in alive and his antagonist wanting its corpse as a trophy.

The reason for this difference can be found in the *Creature's* other source, *King Kong*. The Cooper-Schoedsack production of 1933 has had an almost incalculable influence on every beauty and the beast story since. The Mark-Kay-David triangle in *Creature* is based on the triangle in *King Kong* between impresario Denham, Ann Darrow, and the sailor Driscoll. In *Creature*, Mark Williams, head of the Institute for Maritime Biology, is desperate to exploit for increased funding for the institute the Devonian fossil found by Dr. Carl Maia. "If there's the chance of any publicity, just try and keep him away," David says of Mark before their trip to the lagoon.

Nöel Carroll cites as one of the literary sources of *King Kong* Arthur Conan Doyle's *Lost World*, which Carroll describes as an "apology for colonialism."[89] A similar apology is at work in *Creature's* script, which depends on troubling racial and ethnic stereotypes implied by a sort of hierarchy of humanity and evolution in the film's characters. The white scientists David, Mark, and Kay occupy the highest rung of the evolutionary ladder, followed by the patrician Latin scientist Carl Maia; then by his double, the barge captain Lucas; then by illiterate natives, including Luis and Tomas, who are largely cannon fodder for the monster; and then finally by the gill-man himself. Just as the natives of Skull Island worship Kong, Lucas explains the "native" superstition of the gill-man who lives underwater. Of course, the violation of this order is suggested by the film's more important romantic triangle: David, Kay, and the creature itself. Indeed, David shares some features with the creature. Both remain unchanged by time: the gill-man is a Devonian throwback, and David is praised by Maia and others for looking the same as he did years ago as a student. And we first glimpse both the scuba-geared David and the gill-man as shadowy underwater figures obscured by plants. David's scientific curiosity about the creature is characterized by a compassion Mark finds incomprehensible. "You sound as though I'd put the harpoon through *you*," he snorts after a skirmish with the creature.

Carroll points to the beauty and the beast motif in *Kong* as a latter-day instance of jungle adventure author Edgar Rice Burroughs's "favorite plot device, the abduction of women by non humans." Unlike the Burroughs novels, however, *Kong* emphasizes the "heroic exploits of the abductor"[90] and portrays the beast as childlike, thus gaining a remarkable level of audience sympathy.[91] While the creature is never given this level of psychological complexity, he is, like Henri Jarrod, deeply wronged by the world and clearly smitten with the film's heroine. In fact, the film's famous 3-D set piece, the creature's swimming inches away from the unaware Kay just below the surface of the lagoon, bears a remarkable similarity to the foggy chase scene in *House of Wax*. The slowly swirling mist from the darkened street is reprised in the bubbles and refracted beams of light in the water while the gliding camera dynamizes the space and gives it a shimmering, chiaroscuro otherworldliness. Of course, the graceful synchronized strokes of Ricou Browning's creature are closer to Kong's shy courtship than to Jarrod's twisted, shambling pursuit of Sue Allen. This lyrical passage in *Creature* is an isolated interlude, however: the second half of the film is an almost nonstop barrage of radical frontality and violent 3-D gimmicks with flying bats, underwater spear guns, and air-propelled cloudy nerve poison shot into the audience's faces. The creature's final attack on the barge contains an almost archetypal 3-D shot of the gill-man slowly advancing toward Chico (and the camera) staring with fish-eyed rage into the spectator's eyes as the soundtrack is filled with his labored amphibian breathing.

The low-cost, easily installed Moropticon single projection 3-D sys-

The creature's underwater lair was a showcase for misty chiaroscuro and a range of striking 3-D effects (Wisconsin Center for Film and Theater Research).

tem allowed Universal to release the film in a saturation booking campaign designed for fast playoff to a wide array of audiences, as well as for insulation against the poor reviews the film was guaranteed in the middlebrow press. In March, Universal announced "a series of 17 territorial saturation openings backed by an all-out promotional campaign using radio, TV, and newspapers."[92] The film had eight separate openings in Chicago alone.[93] Further, the distribution deal for exhibitors to play 3-D films had drastically fallen, from the 50 percent under which *Bwana Devil* and *House of Wax* had been sold to the 35 percent, or even less, that was included in the terms for 3-D programmers like MGM's *Arena* and United Artist's *I, the Jury*.[94]

Creature from the Black Lagoon was a huge success, spawning two sequels and continuing the series of the William Alland and/or Jack Arnold unit at Universal begun with *It Came from Outer Space* in 1953. Arnold directed the first sequel to *Creature from the Black Lagoon*, titled *Revenge of the Creature*, in 3-D (Depix had lost a patent infringement suit over the name "Pola-Lite," so Polaroid provided the glasses for the 1955 sequel),[95] as well as *Tarantula* (1955) and *The Incredible Shrinking Man* (1957) both flat in 1.85 widescreen. Films in the trend not directed by Arnold include *This Island Earth* (1955), *The Mole People* (1956), *The Creature Walks among Us* (1956), *Curucu, Beast of the Amazon* (1956), and *The Deadly Mantis* (1957). This series of films, dubbed "weirdies" by *Variety*, netted the studio over $8.5 million through 1957,[96] and it outlasted 3-D by almost five years until Hammer Films's *Curse of Frankenstein* and American International Pictures's *I Was a Teenage Werewolf* spun the horror genre into an entirely new direction in 1957.

At the time of the release of *House of Wax*, *Variety* reported that the curtailment of product from the majors was creating an opening for the independent producer making flat films. The trade journal featured an interview with producer Alan Dowling who had just finished the low-budget *Donovan's Brain* with Lew Ayres for eventual United Artist release. *Variety* asserted that "Dowling feels distribs will look to the indies to round out their release dates."[97] Another growing opportunity for the independent producer was a number of small distributors who had begun business in the middle of the decade and who now were available to provide programmers for product-hungry theaters. Less than a year after *Donovan's Brain*, a new company named American Releasing Corporation would distribute *The Fast and the Furious*, an exploitation film about a club of hot-rod racing teenagers, and the end-of-the-world sci-fi horror film, *The Day the World Ended*. American Releasing would soon change its name to American International Pictures.

In fall 1953, North Central Allied's Bernie Berger, speaking at Senate hearings on behalf of the small theater owner, asserted that nabe operators often found a "shortage of desirable pictures on the breaks" between major releases into subsequent run. This left either the option of closing the theater or playing exhausted features, whether widescreen, 3-D, or flat, months after their initial release.[98] Just three months earlier, critic Bosley Crowther noted that the move toward CinemaScope super productions such as *The Robe* released at a high cost to exhibitors appeared to be part of an attempt to "garner the bulk of the movie revenue from a limited number of annual productions released to a few thousand— or perhaps one-fourth—of the nation's theaters. Where this would leave the other theaters . . . no one knows."[99] The answer to this question is crucial to understanding the nature of the horror film in the rest of the decade.

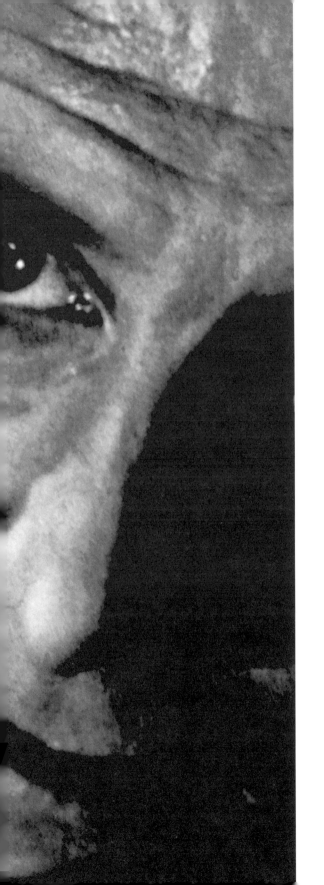

CHAPTER 2

The Color of Blood:

Hammer Films and

Curse of Frankenstein

In a nineteenth-century Swiss charnel house, an impeccably gloved hand pulls a small jar out of a leather case. Offscreen, a coughing, raspy-voiced morgue attendant, who speaks with an inexplicable Cockney accent, demands money from the owner of the case. After a price is negotiated, two disembodied eyeballs, still trailing blood and fleshy matter, plop into the jar of liquid as the tubercular coughs from the morgue attendant continue offscreen. The gloved hands fussily recap the jar and place it back into the leather bag.

Awash in such grisly images, *Curse of Frankenstein* was released in the United States in summer 1957 by Warner Bros. and grossed over $3 million in the world market in less than a year.[1] The film launched the worldwide success of tiny Hammer Films from England as the major reinterpreter of horror myths from studio-era Hollywood, and it marked the high-profile genre debuts of two of the most enduring horror stars of the fifties and sixties, Peter Cushing and Christopher Lee. Much has been written about the film's innovative use of color and explicit gore as well as the production values that belied its $400,000 budget.[2] The filmmakers took advantage of many changes in the international film industry in the late fifties to get the film successfully financed, produced, and distributed. In particular, Hammer exploited a relationship with a silent American partner, Eliot Hyman of Associated Artists Productions (AAP), a distributor of feature films to TV. Hyman would remain partnered with Hammer as AAP grew into Seven Arts in the sixties and eventually bought all of Warner Bros. late in that decade.

Curse of Frankenstein is an important transitional work in the history of the horror genre. The film had to negotiate copyrights held by Universal-International through striking artistic innovation. Hammer, its partners, and distributor Warner Bros. had to respond to changes in the increasingly internationalized film market in order to deliver a product suitable for the outrageous and baroque publicity stunts that came to characterize the horror film in the late fifties and early sixties. The film itself typifies the changes the horror genre was undergoing during the period and extends the narrative and stylistic trends already visible four years earlier in *House of Wax*.

As Denis Meikle notes in his indispensable book on Hammer Films, *A History of Horrors*, the company had been in business, in one form or another, since 1934.[3] Its founder, retail entrepreneur and sometime stage comedian William Hinds (with the stage name Will Hammer), acquired a stake in distributor Exclusive Films during the mid-thirties. Hammer, along with Exclusive's majority partners the Carreras clan (grandfather Enrique, son James, and grandson Michael), distributed short subjects to theaters throughout the war. During this period, however, the lion's share of the company's profits came from ancillary holdings in hotel ownership, music publishing, jewelry shops, and show business promotion.

After the war, British film producers faced an uphill battle. Hollywood's international distribution network was successfully exploiting the decimated film industries of former allies and enemies alike. In the United Kingdom, American distributors often undersold domestically produced British films with more popular Hollywood product, and this practice funneled huge amounts of currency out of Britain's weakened economy. Meikle notes that in 1947 the British government "imposed a punitive 75 percent import tax on American films in an attempt to stem the flow of currency out of the country. This was to lead to a retaliatory export ban, and with domestic production curtailed due to the severe winter, cinemas soon became starved for product."[4] Even after reciprocal agreements between Hollywood's Motion Picture Export Association and the British government ended the import ban, British cinemas faced a severe product shortage. Thus in 1949 Hinds, along with James Carreras, incorporated Hammer Film Productions as a subsidiary of distributor Exclusive and began making supporting features for the British market. These films included the thrillers *Room to Let* (1949) and *Stolen Face* (1951), the comedy *What the Butler Saw* (1950), and the science fiction dramas *Spaceways* and *Four-Sided Triangle* (both 1952).[5] The company's fortunes took a turn in summer 1953 when it successfully negotiated screen rights with the BBC for an adaptation of Nigel Neale's alien-invasion horror serial, *The Quatermass Experiment*. Hammer's 1956 feature versions of the story, the *Quatermass Xperiment* and its sequel, *Quatermass 2*, would begin a decades-long association of Hammer Films with the horror genre.

During this period, Hammer's product was also distributed in the United States: *Four-Sided Triangle* and the Robin Hood–themed *Men of*

Sherwood Forest had been picked up by small U.S. distributor Astor Pictures (see chapter 5), and in 1951 the company struck a deal with American theater-chain owner Robert Lippert, whose Screen Guild Pictures turned out low-budget programmers for his and other product-hungry theaters. This reciprocal arrangement allowed Hammer's English distribution arm, Exclusive, distribution rights to Lippert features like the science-fiction drama *Rocketship X-M* (1950). More important, it gave Hammer's own product access to the U.S. market.[6] After the Lippert deal ended in 1955, United Artists released Hammer's Quatermass horror films, retitled *The Creeping Unknown* and *Enemy from Space* for U.S. distribution. Hammer's programmers were helped in the U.S. market by leading roles from known Hollywood performers in the autumn of their careers: Howard Duff is the lead in *Spaceways*; Paul Henreid plays the main character in *Stolen Face*; and Brian Donlevy is the title scientist in the Quatermass films.

International casts in British movies became even more common after the middle of the decade, when American investment began to pour into British film production at every level. The reason was the British Film Finance Company, or "Eady Levy," a pool of production money fed by a tax on each cinema ticket sold in the United Kingdom and made available to British film producers. The fund was intended to aid in the production of British commercial films for the domestic and international market, but U.S. producers and distributors soon learned to invest money in films produced in England or its territories while making certain that the production company met the minimal legal standard to qualify as a "British" corporation through the hiring of the required number of British personnel. The American production investment would then be augmented, sometimes by as much as 50 percent, with Eady funds. Contributions to the fund were voluntary for the period of 1950 to 1956 but became mandatory in 1957, thereby dramatically expanding the amount of money available for producers.[7] Thus, in 1957, American coproductions from Columbia's blockbuster *Bridge on the River Kwai* to American International Pictures's low-budget horror programmer *Cat Girl* were able to take advantage of funds from the Eady levy.

The influx of American money kept the British film industry active during the postwar economic downturn, while American studios often enjoyed savings in production costs. So it was in 1957 that Eliot Hyman, head of Associate Artists Productions, a successful syndicator of Hollywood films to American TV, invested 50 percent of the budget for a color remake of the Frankenstein story to be produced by Hammer. Most (if not all) of Hammer's investment came from Eady funds. Hammer retained 50 percent of the producer's share and Hyman had the other half.[8]

Hyman initially proposed that the Frankenstein project proceed from a script written by American screenwriter Milton Subotsky, who, with business partner Max J. Rosenberg, would later found Amicus, which produced an innovative series of episodic sixties and seventies horror classics such as *Dr. Terror's House of Horrors* (1965), *Torture Garden* (1968), and *Tales from the Crypt* (1972).[9] Although years later Michael Carreras would remember that Subotsky's script was "abysmally written,"[10] it contained a number of striking elements, including a flashback structure from the insane asylum in which Victor Frankenstein is imprisoned. The novel's characters of M. Krempe, Victor's uncouth and unsympathetic teacher at Ingolstadt, and Henry Clerval, Victor's friend, were condensed into "Paul Krempe," a private tutor who served as confidant and voice of conscience to Victor. Subotsky also included the attempt to steal a wizened scientist's brain for the monster. All of these elements would remain in Hammer's final product.[11]

Meikle recounts the reaction of Universal-International's legal department once the project was announced in the trade papers. The American studio objected to the registration of the title *Frankenstein* and reminded Hammer and Hyman that copyrights on all material original to the 1931 version of the film (and the stage plays on which that screenplay had been partially based) would be zealously enforced by Universal's legal department.[12] In particular, Jack Pierce's makeup design of the monster, made famous by Boris Karloff, could not be used in Hammer's conception or execution of the character. Even after Subotsky extensively rewrote the script, producer Anthony Hinds, son of company founder William, saw elements in the story that reminded him of Universal's *Bride of Frankenstein* (1935).[13] Michael Carreras and Max Rosenberg exchanged several letters about the script's inclusion of a mistaken theft of "the brain of a criminal lunatic" for the monster, which Rosenberg admitted "resembl[ed] in idea, if not incident, the first Universal picture."[14] At one point, Hyman even offered to send 16mm prints of all of Universal's Frankenstein films to Hammer's Wardour Street offices for point-by-point inspection by James Carreras and Anthony Hinds, "providing that [it] remained a purely confidential matter."[15]

In the end, Hammer decided to rework the story into something completely original, and the scriptwriting duties were given to one of Hammer's youngest writers, Jimmy Sangster.[16] *Curse of Frankenstein*, the film that resulted from the efforts of screenwriter Sangster, director

Terence Fisher, and actors Peter Cushing and Christopher Lee, turned
to elements from Mary Shelley's novel and *The Cabinet of Dr. Caligari* to
differentiate its approach to the Frankenstein myth from the old Universal films. The film that resulted from this combination of elements
bears distinctive traces of both the low-end horror film—popularized
by Roger Corman in *It Conquered the World* (1956) and *Not of This Earth*
(1957) and William Castle's later *House on Haunted Hill* (1958)—and
the more overtly "literary" costume melodrama in color. Hammer and
its American partners saw color as a crucial element in avoiding the
supporting-feature fate of Hammer's previous American releases, *The
Creeping Unknown* and *Enemy from Space*. Like the 3-D effects and period
setting of *House of Wax*, the color in *Curse of Frankenstein* served the
efforts of the filmmakers to give the film a high-end gloss in Hollywood's
"color-optional" period of the late fifties and to add an extra emphasis
to the unprecedented levels of onscreen gore that the film offered as its
major attraction.

In *A Heritage of Horror*, one of the first systematic appreciations of
Hammer's films, critic David Pirie tried to rescue *Curse of Frankenstein*
and other Hammer horrors from the pillory of both contemporary reviewers and "purist" horror critics such as Carlos Clarens by situating
Hammer in the tradition of the English gothic.[17] Pirie brings out highly
suggestive readings of many films in the Hammer oeuvre by seeing in
them a continuation of characters from the English gothic novel. The
persecuted woman, the fatal woman, the vampire or fatal man,[18] as well
as motifs of the prioress and the malevolent convent,[19] are all key elements in the Hammer approach to the horror film, and surely Peter
Cushing's performance as Baron Victor Frankenstein is the very em-
bodiment of the "gaunt face and piercing eyes" of the gothic vampire.[20]

In a break with the expressionist Universal Frankenstein films, *Curse
of Frankenstein* contains many elements of a female gothic film like
Rebecca (1940) or *Secret beyond the Door* (1948). Its plot concerns a naive
young virgin, Victor's cousin Elizabeth, who comes to an ancient manor
to marry a mysterious and distant man, Victor himself, whose aloof
manner and frequent absences appear to hide a secret in an unexplored
region of the manor. The female servant, Justine, is openly hostile to the
new arrival, and it is only Paul Krempe, laboratory assistant and close
friend to the husband, who acts as ally and protector to the young bride.
After an exploration of the hidden dangers of the house, in which the
husband is revealed to be the perpetrator of an awful crime—in this
case the creation of the monster—the male protector and the young

bride appear to constitute a normal heterosexual couple at the film's end.

But Sangster, Fisher, and Cushing worked an audacious transformation of these narrative elements by focusing not on the suspicious young bride (as in the gothic novel) or on the pitiful monster (as in the Universal films) but on the ruthless, sadistic, and odiously suave Baron Victor Frankenstein himself. Meikle describes Cushing's Baron Victor Frankenstein as "a veritable serpent in a silk dressing gown,"[21] and it is Victor who narrates the film in flashback from his prison cell. Within the flashbacks, we meet not the neurotic and driven scientist as played by Colin Clive in the Universal films but rather a cold, misogynistic, and sociopathic aristocrat who murders Professor Bernstein, an elderly scientist, to put his brain into the monster. Not only does this Baron Victor Frankenstein sexually exploit Justine, the maid—and, when she is pregnant with his child, lock her in the lab to be murdered by the monster— he even gazes longingly at his bride Elizabeth as a possible source of spare parts for his experiments. Nowhere is Curse of Frankenstein's refinement of the horror genre signaled more strongly than in this radical recentering of the story on the personality of the baron himself. In fact, Hammer's working title for the project had been "Frankenstein and the Monster," as if the studio were acknowledging the widespread confusion of the nameless monster with its creator and placing the scientist back at the center of the story.

Audiences who sat in theaters in 1957 saw the auditorium go dark and, after the Warner Bros. logo appeared, the following intertitle was framed against a swirling red fog: "More than a hundred years ago, in a mountain village in Switzerland, lived a man whose strange experiments with the dead have since become legend. The legend is still told with horror the world over—It is the legend of—THE CURSE OF FRANKENSTEIN."

Surely no one in the theater needed this information in order to construct a coherent story from the images and sounds that would follow. But this brief prologue signals that what we are about to see is a retelling of a familiar story. Sangster told the British trade press about his refinement of the Frankenstein myth as the film was being screened for the first time in 1957: "The whole concept of horror is different. The public is more hard-boiled since the Frankenstein pictures of the thirties. So many horrible things have happened since then that a film has to be really tough to get the desired reaction. But that doesn't mean you have to use a bludgeon. There is, now, the horror of implication."[22] The "horrible things" to which Sangster is referring, include, of course, the Nazi death camps, which made the figure of the remorseless scientist experimenting on human subjects one of the most feared and repulsive monsters of the postwar period. In fact, Hammer's sequel to *Curse, Revenge of Frankenstein* (1958), made many of these parallels explicit, with the Josef Mengele-like Baron Frankenstein presiding over a free clinic, whose impoverished patients unwittingly provide parts for his experiments. This, along with *Revenge*'s onscreen disposal of corpses in a giant furnace, was greeted with outrage and disgust by many British reviewers on the later film's release.

Director Terence Fisher acknowledged the delicate balancing act involved in leavening familiar elements of the horror genre with explicit gore, elegant mise-en-scène, and occasional touches of black humor. He repeatedly stressed the role of restraint, without which the eruptions of Grand Guignol violence would lose their impact, and suggested that "macabre" was a more fitting term for his work than "horror." "Humor, of course, is important in horror, both the intentional and accidental kinds," he told *Kinematograph Weekly*, a British trade journal. "We have found quite ordinary lines can become unintentionally funny in a horror setting . . . By and large, though, a few giggles during a horror film can be taken as a compliment—it shows the picture is really doing its work, that the audience is really gripped."[23] Fisher then cites the moment in *Curse of Frankenstein* that cuts abruptly from the death screams of the maid Justine, trapped in the laboratory with the rampaging monster, to a quiet breakfast table where Victor coos to Elizabeth, "Pass the marmalade, will you, dear?"[24]

Curse of Frankenstein delights in such "images of bourgeois splendor juxtaposed with those of madness, decay, and death."[25] Color is central to this process: Hazel Court's Elizabeth is dressed in cool blues and pastels. Peter Cushing's Baron Frankenstein sits at breakfast in an eggshell morning jacket and blue cravat, and assistant Paul Krempe wears a grey evening jacket in the elegantly appointed drawing room. This palette, along with the earth tones of the prison sequences, are contrasted with the eruptions of highly saturated colors in the lab scenes, in which primary-colored dry cell batteries, glowing-pink generator lights, and (of course) bright-red Eastmancolor blood splash everywhere.

In *An Illustrated History of Horror and Science Fiction Films*, Carlos Clarens criticizes *Curse of Frankenstein* for containing a monster that "is negligible as a dramatic character."[26] It is true that the character has little psychological depth. But, like *The Cabinet of Dr. Caligari*, *Curse of Frankenstein* establishes a fascinating series of inverse parallels between the doctor and his automaton. In fact, Hammer planned to remake *Caligari* a year after the success of the company's first horror hits,[27] and the earlier German film probably influenced Phil Leakey's design for Christopher Lee's *Creature*. The suave and graceful Baron is at home in both the drawing room and the dissecting theater, but Lee's creature moves in a "puppet-like walk, which suggests a deformed animal in pain," in Pirie's description.[28] Cushing's failure as a creator, however, is mirrored by his failure as a narrator, and like Francis, the madman confined to the mental hospital in *Caligari*, no one believes his story that the monster ever existed: Victor is forcibly restrained by the guards in an action that replays Francis's final imprisonment in the German film. Victor's first gesture when the priest enters his cell and threatens to leave is to put his hands around his throat, just as the monster had done to him in the laboratory. In a virtually identical composition, Victor later attempts to strangle Paul when he refuses to corroborate his story.

The theme of the double, or doppelganger, is one of the defining features of gothic horror. Dr. Jekyll and Mr. Hyde and the monster/creator dyad of the Frankenstein myth are two of its most famous examples. Hammer's approach to the Frankenstein story, signaled by the working title "Frankenstein and the Monster," was to place this relationship at the center of their story (two previous Terence Fisher films, *Stolen Face* and *Four-Sided Triangle*, had turned on the doppelganger plot). In *Curse of Frankenstein*, such overt thematic material is contained in the film's series of doublings and displacements that mock the presumptions and pretensions of Baron Frankenstein. The first pair of character doubles are Victor and Paul. The two struggle for possession of Elizabeth, and Paul in parallel and rhyming scenes objects to both Victor's desire to build a man and Elizabeth's desire to honor the arranged marriage with Victor. In fact, when the adult Elizabeth first arrives at the manor, she attempts to kiss Paul, believing him to be Victor. Paul is the only male character in the film who enters Elizabeth's room, and it is he who speaks the last line of the film to Elizabeth, "Come on. I'll take you home."

The film's most complex and sustained set of oppositions involves Victor, Professor Bernstein, and the monster. Victor's Aunt Sophie tells him near the beginning of the film that he is "the sole remaining heir of the Frankenstein family," and Professor Bernstein remarks moments before his death that he is "all alone in the world." As the two scholars relax in the drawing room with Elizabeth, they strike identical poses with brandy snifters and cigars. The professor expresses regret at his life spent in scholarship and childless solitude: "One can spend too much of

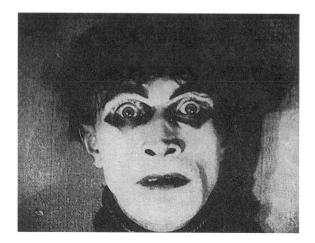

Cabinet of Dr. Caligari: Cesare awakes (G. William Jones
Film and Video Collection, Southern Methodist University).

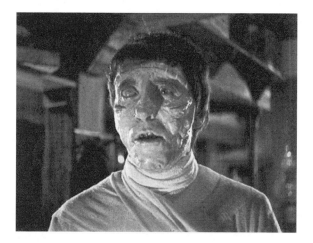

Curse of Frankenstein (Warner Communications).

Curse of Frankenstein: The baron and Professor Bernstein
(Warner Communications).

one's life locked in stuffy rooms searching out obscure truths—searching, researching, until one is too old to enjoy life." This is one option that Victor has before him, although ironically he will not live to be too old to enjoy life, his ensuing brain transplant in *Revenge of Frankenstein* notwithstanding.

A series of parallels between Professor Bernstein and his later incarnation as the monster forms a ghoulish running joke on Victor's aspirations for his creation. While Elizabeth and the baron entertain the professor, Paul enters the drawing room from the rear and is surprised to find the professor visiting. Paul will arrive later in the film and meet the professor in identically blocked shots under entirely different circumstances, first as a disembodied brain in the Frankenstein family crypt and finally as the monster whom he finds trying to strangle the baron in the laboratory and whom he later watches performing pitiful dog tricks for Victor. The monster itself, which does not appear until late in the film—its first stirrings of life signal the beginning of the film's third act—is a twisted reflection of the characters around it. Its first appearance, staggering around the laboratory and ripping the gauze off of its face, is a brutal mockery of Victor's lecture to Paul on physiognomy: "One's facial character is built up of what lies behind it—in the brain. A benevolent mind and the face assumes the patterns of benevolence. An evil mind, then an evil face. [When the brain of a genius is in the monster] then the facial features will display wisdom and understanding."

The Professor's "benevolent" repose in his white funeral shroud finds its inverted double in the bandaged and repulsive monster's first appearance. Similarly, the monster is given the hands of Bardello, "the world's greatest sculptor," but these magnificent hands hang limply at his side and are emphasized only in the murders of Justine and a blind hiker in the woods. The monster's reciprocal relationship to the characters around it are characterized by a series of visual rhymes at almost precise intervals throughout the film, one near the end of each act: the cutting down of the highwayman from the gallows to form the torso of the creature is replayed twice in the fall of the professor to his death from the balcony and the monster's flaming descent into the acid. This motif is reversed in the revelation that Victor has exhumed the monster after Paul has shot and killed it in a tilt-up shot from Victor in the laboratory to the monster hanging from a hook.

Cushing's baron and his doppelganger, the hapless monster, are, like *House of Wax*'s Henri Jarrod and the hulking brute Ygor, postwar incarnations of Dr. Caligari and the somnambulist Cesare. Also like *House of Wax, Curse of Frankenstein* often foregrounds the cinema of attractions in its process of telling and showing: the abject helplessness of the Baron's narration to the priest in his jail cell is contrasted to his status as master of illusion and spectacle within the tale that he tells.

Similarly, Victor's entreaty to Paul to discover the unknown, like Caligari's invitation to the Holstenwall fairgoers to step inside his tent and see the mysteries within, is couched in terms of discovering new boundaries and transgressing old ones. "What we've done up to now is nothing," he tells Paul after they have brought a drowned dog back to life. "It's nothing compared to what we will do. We've only just started, just opened the door. Now it's time to go through that door and see what lies beyond."

Of course, the realm discovered by Frankenstein is a series of ever-closing spaces, beginning with the zone behind the locked laboratory door and ending with the guillotine at the film's end. Along the way, there are other diminishing spaces: the innermost room of the laboratory contains the pit of acid, where Victor disposes of the head severed from the hanging highwayman, and the interlocking spaces of the Frankenstein family crypt is where the baron violates the resting place and the bodily integrity of the murdered Professor Bernstein. In fact, the vat of acid and the vault in the crypt are very likely the identical prop in Bernard Robinson's economical mise-en-scène. Both of these enclosed spaces recall the tank of fluids in which the monster is given life, an enclosed space that simultaneously evokes womb and coffin.

The young and handsome baron remains impeccably dressed and mannered in the story that he tells, controlling both the domestic space of the manor and the charnel-house laboratory where he holds dominion over the various disembodied limbs and organs and the abject monster they eventually constitute. Early in the film, Paul and Victor succeed in bringing back to life a dead dog in an amniotic container that prefigures the huge cauldron that gives birth to the monster. When Frankenstein puts the stethoscope up to the dog's sternum and hears the first stir-rings of its heart, his gaze turns almost into the camera as the camera tracks in and the strings on the soundtrack play James Bernard's five-note leitmotif that characterizes Frankenstein's obsession. Later, as he attempts to convince Paul to construct a human being out of body parts, a long master shot in the drawing room is interrupted by a medium close-up of Victor as he says, "We've done the whole, now we must do parts. Limbs, organs [here he turns to face the camera], now we must build." Like the wheelchair-bound Jarrod leading patrons through the chamber of horrors, Victor is Paul's (and our) tour guide through the for-bidden sights of the laboratory. The baron examines a recently acquired eyeball through a magnifying glass, which enlarges his own eye to mon-strous proportions. Soon after, Paul enters the laboratory and Victor as-sumes his role as monstrateur, announcing to Paul, "I've decided to let you see my progress." Flipping back the sheet that covers the monster's face in its tank, he is shocked to hear Paul's response: "It's horrible!" This parallels an earlier scene immediately following Elizabeth's arrival when Victor brings back from Liepzig the severed hands of the recently deceased sculptor Bardello. In what must have been the outer limits of permissible gruesomeness in 1957, he had unwrapped the bloody limbs from their cloth and butcher's paper shroud and murmured to Paul, "What about these, eh? Have you ever seen anything so beautiful?"

Victor's role as monstrateur and hypnotist in the procurement of parts for the monster reaches its climax in his murder of Professor Bern-stein. Escorting the exhausted old man up to bed, he pauses on the bal-cony and says, "I would like to show you a painting just before you re-tire. It's this one at the top of the staircase here. It was purchased by my father and illustrates one of the early operations." He says, "If you stand back, you can see it better." When the old man steps back to look at the painting, Frankenstein pushes him to his death. The painting is Rembrandt's *The Anatomy Lesson of Dr. Nicolaes Tulp* from 1632. The Rembrandt illustrates not "one of the early operations" at all but an au-topsy on a pallid and grimacing cadaver. The monstrateur figure of Tulp is pulling the cadaver's exposed tendons out of its arm with a pair of forceps (reprising Frankenstein's unveiling of Bardello's hands) and the juxtaposition of the cultured and well-dressed men with the charnel-

Curse of Frankenstein: The vat of life-giving chemicals (Warner Communications).

Curse of Frankenstein: The obsessed Baron Frankenstein (Warner Communications).

Curse of Frankenstein: "If you stand back, you can see it better" (Warner Communications).

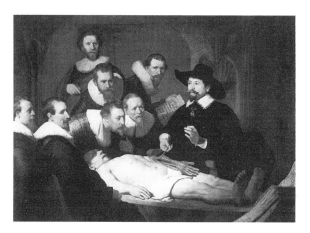

Rembrandt van Rijn, *The Anatomy Lesson of Dr. Nicolaes Tulp*, 1632 (Hamon Arts Library, Southern Methodist University).

house subject matter, along with the deep earth tones and chiaroscuro lighting of the painting, parallel some of the most distinctive elements of the film in which it is contained. The presence of the gruesome but elegant old master painting in this film is yet another of the film's ambivalent gestures to both high art and lowbrow sensationalism.

Victor's last turn as the master of illusion comes when he brings Paul into the laboratory on the wedding night to show him the results of his brain surgery on the reanimated monster. Frankenstein makes the pitiful monster stand up, come toward him, and sit down on the hard floor, the spastic automaton barely able to perform the tricks that Victor could easily have taught the resurrected dog from earlier in the film. The pathetic monster then slumps to the ground on a mat of straw in an identical composition to that of the imprisoned Victor awaiting public execution at the guillotine, which also recalls the highwayman cut down from the gallows and coldly beheaded by the baron earlier in the film.

Curse of Frankenstein was distributed worldwide by Warner Bros. The company that had released *House of Wax* was deeply invested in the British film industry: Warner was a partner in both Associated British Pictures Corporation and that company's profitable subsidiary, the ABC theater chain. Warner also owned its namesake theater, the Warner in London's West End, the marquee of which was permanently emblazoned with "The Home of Warner Bros."[29] This showcase first-run theater and the ABC circuit were a highly profitable conduit through which Warner releases passed in their United Kingdom playoff. *Curse of Frankenstein* broke box-office records throughout the United Kingdom, despite its "X" certificate by the British Board of Film Censors, which restricted its audience to patrons over sixteen.

The upscale norms of realism and literariness accentuated by the film's period setting, restrained performances, and intricate (but economical) mise-en-scène were not characteristic of efforts to promote the film: *Curse of Frankenstein*'s American run was widely reported in trade sources as beginning the more outrageous publicity gags that William Castle and others would refine for the rest of the decade.[30] For the film's New York premiere at the Paramount, the theater hired a man to walk up and down the sidewalk carrying "his own severed head" under his arm and, in a gesture that anticipated Castle's 1958 *Macabre* campaign, handed prospective patrons cards that said, "You will see *Curse of Frankenstein* at your own risk." In a move that recalled Universal's promotions of the thirties,[31] a "nurse" was on hand to administer smelling salts.[32] Warner's trade ad in *Motion Picture Herald* proclaimed, "'The *Curse* of

The pitiful monster in *Curse of Frankenstein* (Warner Communications).

The imprisoned baron, condemned to death, in *Curse of Frankenstein* (Warner Communications).

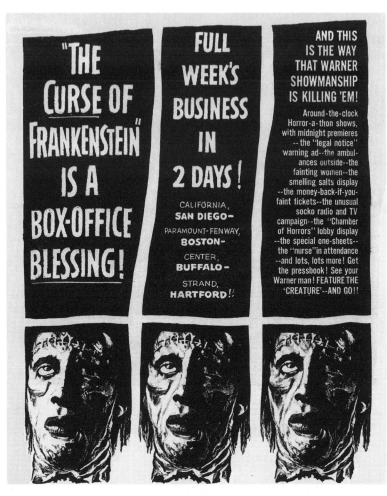

Warners's 1957 trade ad for *Curse of Frankenstein* (Wisconsin Center for Film and Theater Research).

Frankenstein' Is a Box-Office *Blessing!*" and cited the "'nurse' on duty" as one of the many "way[s] that Warner Showmanship is Killing 'Em!" along with lobby displays and massive radio and TV ads and the "money-back-if-you-faint tickets." The three columns of the ad, each forming an exclamation point with what looks like the Christopher Lee monster's severed head forming the bottom point, evokes the "[three] SEEs" entreaty of AIP and Filmgroup ads ("SEE Vampire Creatures from Outer Space! SEE Beauty Trapped by King-Sized Mollusks!" etc.) It also cleverly sidesteps Universal's copyright on the Boris Karloff conception of the monster.

At the California Theater in San Diego, the film received a twenty-four hour "horrorthon" premiere with screenings at midnight, 3 A.M., 9 A.M., noon, and 3, 6, and 9 P.M.[33] In the film's subsequent run in the Bronx, the DeLuxe Theater removed one of the monster's eyes on the two-sheet poster and replaced it with a flashbulb.[34]

The Curse of Frankenstein's overwhelming success at the box office was noted as one of the highlights of the 1957 movie season by *Variety* in January 1958. Its extraordinary artistic influence on the horror genre can be seen in the period settings of Roger Corman's later Edgar Allan Poe adaptations for AIP (see chapter 4) and the Italian horror films of the early sixties (see chapter 6). In fact, the Italian films often featured credits full of Anglicized pseudonyms in an effort to misrepresent the films as Hammeresque British productions. According to *Variety, Curse of Frankenstein*'s more than $2 million in rentals called into serious question whether the picture business in 1958 would be characterized by "blockbusters or some gimmicked entry." Warner's release of the Hammer production was also credited with the revival of older horror films on television and the proliferation of midnight screenings, live spook shows, and other carnival-style promotions.[35]

As a result of the success of *Curse*, Hammer developed very lucrative relationships with several of the major U.S. distributors. For their follow-up to *Curse of Frankenstein, Dracula* (U.S. title: *Horror of Dracula*, 1958), Hammer struck a deal with Universal-International to distribute the film in the United States, and the company was able to use copyrighted elements from that studio's Dracula pictures. They would do the same with other Universal properties, remaking that studio's successes with *The Mummy* in 1959, *Curse of the Werewolf* in 1961, and *Phantom of the Opera* in 1962, and they eventually featured a Karloff-like conception of Mary Shelley's monster in *Evil of Frankenstein* (1964). Like Warner, Universal was heavily invested in Britain: they were part owners of distributor J. Arthur Rank and its exhibition circuit, the Odeon Theater chain. Hammer's Universal coproductions were released by Rank throughout the United Kingdom, although they played in ABC circuit houses rather than in Rank's Odeon chain.[36]

In 1960, Columbia acquired a 49 percent interest in Hammer, allowing the American distributor to exercise significant managerial control over production policies and distribution strategies while still qualifying as a British company eligible for quota consideration and production subsidies.[37] Hammer head James Carreras would continue to rely on U.S. distributors because of their far-reaching film exchanges. "The American companies have the best access to the world market," he told *Variety*, "There's no British distributor who can match it."[38] This internationalization of the horror film, largely begun by Hammer, would continue for over a decade. By March 1964, *Variety* opined that American-financed genre pictures produced abroad "may be the most significant development in the continuing production of exploitable programmers."[39]

Back in the United States, the product shortage was showing no signs of abating. Increasingly, exhibitors scrambled for films to show, regardless of country of origin. The efforts of exhibitors like Robert Lippert to supply program pictures to the market were duplicated by other theater chains, and the uneven release schedules of the major studios would give low-budget genre films open playdates in even deluxe houses, a fact that would be critical to the genre in the following years.

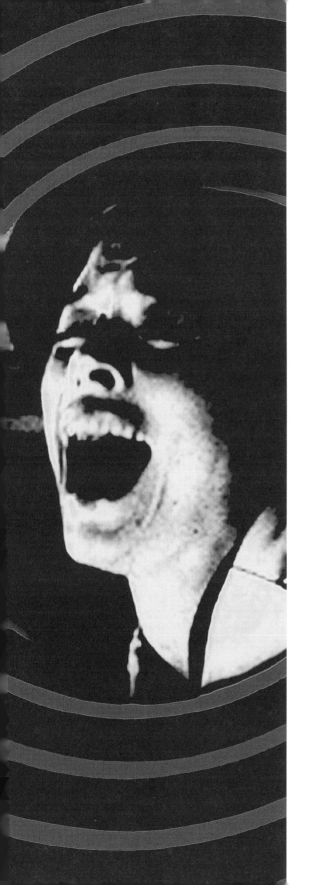

CHAPTER 3

"Look into the

Hypnotic Eye!"

Exhibitor Financing

and Distributor Hype

in Fifties Horror

Cinema

"HypnoVista! It actually puts YOU in the Picture. Can you stand it? SEE—The Vat of Death! SEE—The Fantastic Binocular Murder! FEEL—The Icy Hands! FEEL—The Tightening Noose!"—Poster copy for AIP's *Horrors of the Black Museum*

Whereas studio films such as *House of Wax* and *Creature from the Black Lagoon* had been promoted to showcase technological advances in movie presentation, later horror programmers from independents such as *The She Creature* (1956), *I Was a Teenage Werewolf* (1957), *Macabre* (1957), *The Screaming Skull* (1958), and *Horrors of the Black Museum* (1959) were publicized with an unusual emphasis on their topical or horrific content. These shrill come-ons were a direct consequence of the marginal or at least secondary role these films played in the exhibition marketplace. Both trade journals and popular magazines of the time noted this carnival-barker element of genre film distribution, and several accounts of the business practices of AIP and others make repeated references to "Merlins," "mountebanks," and "the carny come-on."

The changes taking place in motion picture exhibition and distribution were crucial to the small but consistent success of the genre features. These changes included the shortage of year-round product from the major studios, the rise of the youth audience, and the reappearance of the double feature. The product shortage that affected both first-run houses and subsequent-run neighborhood theaters led to calls for exhibitors to finance production to ensure a year-round supply of product, and several regional and national circuits attempted to enter production. Because of demographic changes in the film audience as well as perceptions within the industry that its own advertising and promotional techniques were behind the times, the 1950s saw the growth of ad campaigns, exploitable titles, and poster art that preceded the casting or even scripting of the films. These efforts were the result both of the industry's desperation to recapture a dwindling audience staying at home in increasing numbers and of the need to draw a more downscale but still lucrative audience of juveniles and adolescents. The twin trends of advertising gimmicks and exhibitor financing are illustrated by Howco Productions's 1958 release *My World Dies Screaming*, which attempted to capitalize on the current controversy surrounding subliminal advertising.

At the same time that theater circuits such as ABC-Paramount and Houck were moving into production, several studios that had survived the upheavals of the fifties by supplying low-budget genre product to fill out double features in multichange houses and drive-ins attempted to move into the lucrative but risky distribution of more expensive "A" product. One of the most notable examples of this trend is Allied Artists, which attempted to offset the high-risk move into big-budget films with the consistent and predictable returns of genre pictures both from its own production units and from independents. Indeed, genre films played a crucial role in the efforts of the studios to upscale their product: one 1960 Allied Artists release, *The Hypnotic Eye* (1960), aptly demonstrates how the horror film fit into these broad trends.

One of the most important trends that contributed to the success of the low-budget genre cinema in the 1950s was the curtailment of production from the major studios. The majors began to produce fewer features every year, and more of these films were expensive blockbusters showcasing technology such as widescreen, stereo sound, and color. Production fell steadily from 479 features in 1940 to 379 in 1950 to 271 in 1955, finally reaching an all-time low of 224 in 1959.[1] The efforts of exhibitors to withstand this period of fewer releases and declining attendance included strategies as diverse as cultivation of the youth audience, exhibitor financing of production, sensationalist advertising, and an appeal to the government for the arbitration of film rentals. The product shortage hit the smaller neighborhood theaters particularly hard. The unavailability of first-run product combined with the studios' practice of "bunching" major releases together at the late summer and holiday seasons meant that many smaller theaters and even some large circuits would face a chronic shortage of product for much of the year. "While some first-run exhibitors complain of difficulty in finding suitable bookings," wrote *Motion Picture Herald* publisher Martin Quigley in 1954, "the chief burden of the decrease in Hollywood output has fallen on the smaller operations with multiple program changes during the week."[2]

Low-budget genre films were important to the survival of the small theater. A steady supply of product throughout the year was critical to these theaters: even a marginal or unsuccessful box-office performance kept the doors of the theater open and enabled the snack bar to help finance the operation's mortgage and payroll.[3] "It's necessary to provide the exploitation type B pictures that many double feature and two change houses need," a Massachusetts exhibitor told *Motion Picture Herald* in 1955.[4] As Harry Brandt, president of the Independent Theater Owners of America, told the Senate Small Business Committee in 1956:

> We buy all the companies. We need all of the product that is made. Particularly the small neighborhood theater. The small neighborhood theater, particularly in double feature areas, of which there are [over] 5200, [are] reported to be in the red . . . Ninety five per cent of those must be in the double feature three-times-a-week change. That means they need six pictures a week. That means they need 312 pictures a year. If the industry is producing 270 at the present time, obviously there isn't enough to go around.[5]

An example of a three-change-a-week theater that came to specialize in genre double bills was the Fans Theater in Philadelphia. Located at 40th and Market Streets, the Fans was a neighborhood house in a predominantly African American neighborhood in west Philadelphia near the University of Pennsylvania. The Fans played films in subsequent run anywhere from eight to twelve weeks after their first-run premieres at the downtown houses, charging an adult price of 25 cents for matinees and 50 cents in the evening. The Fans ran subsequent-run engagements of preconstituted double bills from AIP, Allied Artists, and other companies, genre double features that the theater programmed itself from different distributors, and reissues. Its audience was similar to the nabe audience described to the Senate Committee by North Central Allied's Benjamin Berger, "low wage earners, school children, pensioners, and the unemployed."[6] The horror double bill was a staple at the Fans and was often given the prime Thursday through Saturday run. For example, the week of September 16, 1955, the Fans ran the subsequent-run double feature *Cell 2455, Death Row* and *Chicago Syndicate* Sunday through Tuesday, the years-old westerns *Hondo* and *Man Behind the Gun* on Wednesday, and Columbia's preconstituted horror double bill *It Came from Beneath the Sea* and *Creature with the Atom Brain* on the weekend about two months after the Columbia package's initial run downtown. Other prime showcasing of horror features at the

Fans included a double feature of Universal's reissue of *Frankenstein* and *Dracula* in the last weekend of May 1956 and a Thanksgiving weekend run of *Curse of Frankenstein* and the youth-crime programmer *No Time to Be Young* in 1957.

"Theaters don't close because of a lack of 'B' pictures," read a 1955 *Motion Picture Herald* editorial. "The public can get all they want of this outmoded product, on their television receivers in their own homes."[7] However, the postwar ticket-buying public had changed from a general audience to one consisting largely of teenagers, and they didn't want to stay at home and watch TV. In *Teenagers and Teenpics*, Thomas Doherty traces several demographic and economic trends that contributed to this transformation.[8] The fifties was the first time in American culture that the teenager possessed sufficient discretionary income to be a targeted market for the products of the culture industry. Comic books, rock and roll music, and movies were all successful in reaching the teenage market, and each of these was met with a backlash from parents, teachers, clergy, and civic authorities. This controversy was to continue unabated for another twenty years and would form an important discourse in the youth rebellion of the sixties.

In a related development, sociologists, parents, and the criminal justice system drew on the literature of adolescent development and recast the problem of youth crime in its discourse of the maladjusted "juvenile delinquent." Not surprisingly, the Senate Judiciary Committee hearings on juvenile delinquency chaired by Estes Kefauver in 1953 and 1955 devoted a significant amount of time to the role that media consumption played in the postwar phenomenon of juvenile delinquency. These two trends, the courting of the teenage dollar and America's fear of its own children, would have an incalculable and irreversible effect on the horror film as the figure of the monstrous adolescent and the demonic child became staples of the genre in films such as *I Was a Teenage Werewolf* (1957), *Village of the Damned* (1960), *The Innocents* (1961), and many others (see chapter 8).[9]

By summer 1957, movie attendance by people over twenty-five had drastically declined. A poll conducted by Alfred Politz Research, Inc., and presented in *Motion Picture Herald*, revealed that "52.6 per cent of those who attend movies once a week or more are 10 to 19 years of age." The same survey concluded that the statistically "typical frequent movie-goer" was "a teenager in high school, who comes from a family that is financially well-off, and perhaps which intends to send him (or her) to college."[10]

James Nicholson and Sam Arkoff of American International Pictures pointed out to *Motion Picture Herald* in 1957 that the films offered to the youth audience "must not ever, under any circumstances, seem to have been especially chosen for them, conditioned to their years, or equipped with special messages."[11] Thus, the formula for the AIP programmer was to refine already established B picture genres such as the horror film, science fiction thriller, or action-adventure. With the notable exception of the company's hugely successful *Teenage Werewolf* and *Teenage Franken-stein* pictures, most AIP horror efforts like *The Screaming Skull* or *It Conquered the World* did not feature adolescent protagonists.

As director Terence Fisher's comments cited in the previous chapter acknowledge, the growing sophistication of this young audience is underscored by its ability to maintain an ironic distance from the horrific content of the films: the social ritual of horror movie attendance was often an occasion for laughter. In a 1958 forum between New York film critics and teenage members of the high school press, the current cycle of horror films was a frequent topic of conversation and prompted the observation from a teenage boy that fright films "usually failed in their purpose" and provoked laughter instead of fear: "They're comedies," he said.[12] Herbert Swope of Twentieth Century-Fox echoed these sentiments: "Any grown up, who has attended a children's matinee, can recall the hoots of derision greeting any hint of 'phony' romanticism, overdone ghoulishness or hammed up acting."[13]

The ascendance of the double feature was also a result of the increased importance of the youth market. A 1956 survey by the divorced Fox theater circuit, National Theaters, revealed that 72 percent of teenagers polled preferred double bills to single features. Of this trend, Sam Arkoff observed, "the age group from 12 to 21 doesn't want to stay home all the time."[14] A double feature provides a group (or a pair) of teenage moviegoers with a reason to stay out for the evening. As Doherty put it, "the double bill had culture and biology on its side."[15]

In his discussion of the rock-and-roll and horror teenpics, Doherty points out that deliberate alienation of the older audience was a crucial part of the aesthetic changes undergone by the horror film in the fifties and sixties. Increasingly, horror films like *Curse of Frankenstein*, *The Tingler* (1959), *Psycho*, and *The Hypnotic Eye* began to stretch the permissible limits of violence and gore. This ascendancy of the cinema of attractions at the expense of the cinema of narrative integration was also to affect traditional aesthetic norms of narrative plausibility, character consistency, and verisimilitude in acting as well (see chapter 4 on

Vincent Price). These features, all with roots in the cinema of attractions, would continue to be the strongest markers of genre film's low cultural status. The carnival barker, for a time banished to the sidewalk outside the theater, was about to take over the director's chair.

The courting of the youth audience corresponded with a crisis in the film industry over how to use advertising most effectively to counter declining attendance.[16] The importance of trailers in the successful promotion of features was underscored by national polls undertaken in 1957 and 1958 by public relations firm Al Sidlinger and Co., which found that, in a nineteen-week period, 35 percent of the filmgoers surveyed in 1957 and 43 percent of those surveyed in 1958 cited the trailer as the primary reason they had attended a particular feature.[17] As an exhibitor wrote to *Motion Picture Herald*, "Trailer advertising is No. 1 in my book for publicizing a picture. It reaches the eye of those you've hooked as movie patrons."[18]

This wishful reference to mind control and addiction is not coincidental. By the end of the decade, exhibitors and trade journals were calling on advertising to bring the insights that Madison Avenue had gleaned from clinical psychologists to bear on the moviegoing public. Of particular interest to several exhibitors and trade publications was motivation analysis, a growing field of research that attempted to both uncover the psychological motivations behind a person's consumption habits and to design advertising campaigns to appeal to these desires. In 1956, the Theater Owners of America hired promotional consultant Claude Mundo as an administrative assistant to the organization. At the owner's annual meeting in Los Angeles, Mundo asserted that "mental manipulation is what the industry's showmen need."[19]

Some distributors even attempted to promote moviegoing as therapeutic. In 1957, the advertising manager for MGM addressed the alumni association of Post Graduate Hospital in New York and suggested that moviegoing should be part of the pharmacopoeia. According to theater manager Walter Brooks, "he stressed the therapeutic value of going out to the movies, and urged the doctors to recommend the tranquilizing screen and to prescribe pictures instead of pills."[20]

The publicity and hype developed by the low-budget genre cinema in response to declining movie attendance brought to mind another type of prescription, namely, the exaggerated entreaties of the nineteenth-century patent-medicine showman. The carny barkers of the movie business were described by the popular press in similar terms. A 1960 *Time* magazine article refers to Nicholson and Arkoff of AIP as "the leading magicians in the field" at conjuring images of fright for public consumption. Nicholson, Arkoff, and *I Was a Teenage Werewolf* producer Herman Cohen are "the three Merlins."[21]

The carnivalesque attractions of the low-budget horror films of the fifties overwhelmed their narrative pretext. In fact, they were the first elements of the films to be conceived. As AIP's Cohen told *Time* magazine in 1958, "I always think of the title first. The story comes last. After the title come the advertising ideas—the gimmick, the illustrations [and presumably, the trailer], for these are what get the kids into the theater. *Then* comes the story—and every drop of blood and graveyard shudder must be as advertised."[22] This approach stands in marked contrast to the 1955 comments of Frank Whitbeck, head of the trailer department at MGM. Whitbeck had claimed that he and his department followed a film through all of its phases, writing, shooting, and editing, and when the film reached the rough cut stage, he "[sat] down with the staff and kick[ed] the picture around. How are we going to sell it to the public?"[23] Nicholson and Arkoff wore the mantle of the mountebank showman proudly, defending their advertising policy with the assertion that "the film industry is a carnival business, and it must deal therefore in carnival terms."[24]

In addition to the crisis in advertising, exhibitors also faced a crisis in the shortage of product. This situation became so acute that soon there were periodic calls across the industry for exhibitors to finance the production of features. In April 1954, Allied States Organization announced that it had entered into an agreement to underwrite one feature per month for twelve months that independent producer Hal Makelim would produce and for which 2,500 Allied theaters would guarantee playdates at a predetermined flat rental. However, Makelim produced only two western programmers, *The Peacemaker* (1956) and *Valerie* (1957), which were released by United Artists.[25] As Richard Hincha points out, the Makelim plan is part of a general failure of exhibitors to commit to production financing.[26]

This was soon to change. In May 1957, Edward Hyman, vice president of American Broadcast–Paramount Theaters (AB-PT) (the result of the purchase by the American Broadcasting Company of Paramount's divorced theater circuit), announced the formation of AB-PT Pictures Corporation, a production arm of the company designed to fill the playdates of its theater chain. "Shortage of product is the basic reason for going into production and we anticipate making good quality product," announced AB-PT production chief Irving Levin. The company stressed that it was going to "develop new actors, writers, directors, and producers" and that many of its features would be released in combination packages.[27] These two statements were broad hints to the industry that the company would focus its efforts on low-budget program features, which was exactly what happened. An agreement by AB-PT was arranged with Republic to place the AB-PT packages into general distribution after their playoff in the chain's theaters.[28]

In the slow season of June 1957 the company released its first combination, *Beginning of the End*, a giant insect sci-fi picture produced by Bert Gordon, and *The Unearthly*, a transplant mutation horror film modeled on similar mad-scientist shockers (derived from *Island of Lost Souls*) currently in release, notably United Artists/Bel-Air's *The Black Sleep* (1956). The trade press took notice of the films' low production values and speculated about their future. Of *Beginning of the End*, *Variety* wrote: "Based on its low cost, its protected haven in the AB-PT houses, and its susceptibility to exploitation, the film can conceivably wind up as a modest money-maker." *The Unearthly*, according to the weekly, was characterized as "fodder for a very unsophisticated market . . . There's nothing to recommend this one beyond its cheapness."[29]

The package opened in a saturation campaign at 244 theaters in the Midwest and South,[30] and the rural and neighborhood audiences at whom the AB-PT films were aimed received a second package in the slow winter season when *Girl in the Woods*, a country melodrama, and *Eighteen and Anxious*, a teenage melodrama about pregnancy and car racing, appeared in February 1958. Like its predecessor, the combination achieved moderate success, but the company's long-term plans never materialized. The direct production of features by AB-PT ceased, although it did provide financing for C. J. Tevlin's 1959 Allied Artists horror programmer *The Bat*, which starred Vincent Price and Agnes Moorehead and was directed by *House of Wax* screenwriter Crane Wilbur.[31] Just two years after the release of the first combination, AB-PT Pictures was spun off from its parent company and became Atlas Pictures Corporation.[32]

Although it was the largest, AB-PT was not the only exhibitor-financing project that resulted in genre films for theaters to book during slow periods in the release calendar. Several regional exhibitors made product for their theaters, which were then placed into general release on a state's rights basis. Gordon McLendon, head of the ten-theater Tri-State chain in Texas and owner of a hugely successful six-station radio group, formed McLendon Radio Pictures in 1959 because of the tremendous reciprocal potential of radio advertising and theater ownership in tapping the youth market. "If we can sell pictures, we can make pictures," McLendon told *Variety*.[33] McLendon's first and only package was inspired by the first AB-PT combination and featured *The Giant Gila Monster* and *The Killer Shrews*. The films were released in a territorial saturation in Dallas and Fort Worth to a successful tally,[34] but the package failed to catch on in national distribution. The films eventually found their way into heavy rotation on late-night television after AIP, which had bought them from McLendon, sold the TV rights to syndicator Screen Entertainment in 1963.

In 1951, J. Francis White, owner of the Consolidated Theater chain of thirty-one houses in North Carolina, South Carolina, and Virginia, along with Joy Houck, owner of the twenty-nine house Joy's Theaters chain in Arkansas, Louisiana, and Mississippi, formed Howco Productions to contract with Hollywood independents for features to fill their theaters' schedules and for eventual national distribution. Howco's productions throughout the decade included the western *Kentucky Rifle* and Ed Wood Jr.'s gangster melodrama *Jail Bait* (both 1954); the science fiction drama *Mesa of Lost Women* (1956) (made, according to *Variety*, "on the premise that product-hungry theaters would be forced to book anything");[35] the youth-pic double bill *Teen Age Thunder* and Corman-helmed *Carnival Rock* (1956); and the alien-possession horror film *Brain from Planet Arous* (1958). The latter featured former "Mr. Shirley Temple" John Agar, who was beginning his long alcohol-fueled slide from supporting roles in John Ford westerns to "starring" roles in zero-budget TV films like *Zontar, The Thing from Venus* and *Curse of the Swamp Creature* (both 1966; see chapter 7).[36] Has-been stars continued to be a marquee staple for Howco releases: in 1960, Howco attempted to cross over into the foreign and exploitation market with *Night of Love*, a World War II drama starring Brigitte Bardot.

Also in 1958, Howco released a double feature of the showbiz melodrama *Lost, Lonely, and Vicious* and the William Castle–derived shocker *My World Dies Screaming*. The latter was an attempt to capitalize on the controversy surrounding subliminal perception in advertising, and it claimed to feature the process of Psycho-Rama: single-frame, "hidden" images such as skulls, knives, and spelled words like "death" designed to trigger the audience's emotional responses. The images were advertised to the trade press as the Precon process, which was supposedly an outgrowth of experiments in subliminal perception by psychologists and advertisers.

Sheila, the female gothic protagonist of *My World Dies Screaming*, suffers from memory blackouts and plans to leave Switzerland to go back to the United States with her new husband, Phillip. The nameless dread

My World Dies Screaming (G. William Jones Film and Video Collection, Southern Methodist University).

from Sheila's past, buried deep in her unconscious, mirrors the subliminal "imprints" that will remain below the level of consciousness of the film viewer, supposedly causing a palpable but unexplainable dread and horror. The two return to Phillip's ancestral home in Florida, and Sheila is paralyzed with fear when she discovers that Phillip's house is the house from her nightmare. There she sees many apparitions, and the caretaker is murdered. At the end of the film, Phillip is revealed to be a benign hypnotist, having brought Sheila back to the house where she witnessed the ax murders of Phillip's siblings while a small child, committed by Phillip's half-brother, who was initially presented as the gothic heroine's helper and confidante.

The film's investigation of Sheila's unconscious thus provides her with an unknown "past life" to which she can regress under the threatening but beneficent eyes of Phillip. The audience is, supposedly, subjected to a series of emotional jolts via the "subliminal" Precon images, a process similar to the two trancelike manipulations to which Sheila is subjected by the film's male authority figures: the hypnotic pull of Phillip's ancestral mansion and the psychiatrist's vortex wheel that begins the film's present-day narrative. *My World Dies Screaming* mirrors the subliminal messages aimed at the viewer with its therapeutic investigation of the protagonist Sheila. In *My World Dies Screaming*, the plot to drive the female protagonist insane serves as a link between the supposedly hypnotic tropes of advertising and the narrative and stylistic structures of the horror film itself.

Of course, Precon and Psycho-Rama were pure hype and huckster-

ism, and *Motion Picture Herald* had, a month earlier, sarcastically predicted that it would soon be possible "for a showman to tell his patrons
they are seeing a second-feature picture unconsciously, at the same time
they are seeing the top-feature consciously . . . Look how much film
rental, and running time, a showman could save that way."[37]

While the film's Psycho-Rama stunt was distinctive, *My World Dies
Screaming* was hardly alone in its plot of hypnosis and regression. Many
horror plots of the mid-fifties contained the central motif of reincarnation or regression of the protagonist into monstrosity. This was a
hideous dystopic version of the myth of the "magic elixir," given secu-
lar form through a thin veil of psychopharmacology. Here the sadistic
patriarchal hypnotist was an updated version of the sorcerer or warlock of folklore. The immediate source for this plot was the best-selling
The Search for Bridey Murphy, which recounted the supposed regression of a young woman to a past life.[38] *The Search for Bridey Murphy*
was brought to the screen by Paramount in 1956, and many topical
exploitation films adopted the reincarnation motif. Even prestige pictures like *Vertigo* (1958) contained elements of the *Bridey Murphy* motif
(derived, in this case, from its literary source, *D'entre les morts* by Boi-
leau/Narcejac). *Bridey Murphy* elements were used by AIP in *The Undead*,
She Creature, and *I Was a Teenage Werewolf.* The roles of the psychiatrist
in each of these narratives were loosely derived from the evil hypnotist/
conjurer Caligari.

The late 1950s was a time of almost unprecedented concern with the
seemingly hypnotic powers that advertisers wielded over the public. The
same year that Whit Bissell's mad hypnotist Dr. Brandon injected teenage werewolf Michael Landon with regression serum saw both the publication of Vance Packard's *The Hidden Persuaders* and the controversy
surrounding subliminal advertising. Packard topped the 1957 best-seller
lists with his exposé of the advertising industry's cynical manipulation
of consumers through techniques learned from psychology and psychia-
try. It was the use of "depth psychology," the study of preconscious and
unconscious fears and desires, that provided the scientific basis for motivation analysis.[39] According to Packard, advertisers had realized immediately after the war that the increased standardization of manufac-
tured goods and the conversion of the American economic base from
production to consumption made necessary a rigorous scientific management of consumer demand.[40] Further, experiments in market research had demonstrated that consumers' self-reported consumption
habits were often at variance with their actual behavior.

By the early fifties, advertising agencies and marketing firms had

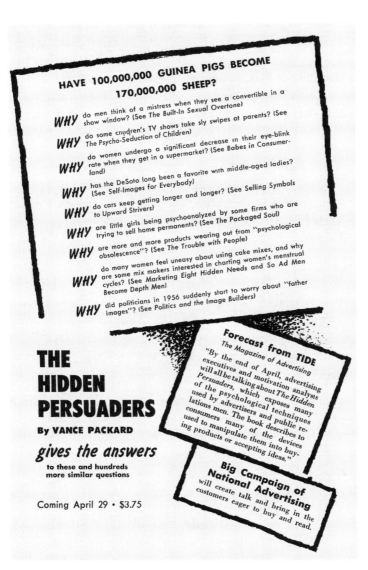

David McKay and Company's 1957 trade ad for Vance Packard's *The Hidden Persuaders*. Note the similarity of the reiterated "WHY's" to the "three SEE's" approach of contemporaneous film publicity (*Publishers' Weekly*).

begun to retain large numbers of clinical and academic psychologists as consultants in their efforts to develop ad campaigns that bypassed the consumer's rational and critical faculties and zeroed in on their hidden fears and desires. Packard's portrayal of depth psychologists and advertising executives lording over a modern Bedlam is more than metaphoric: early in the book he describes a "research director of a major ad agency, a tense tweedy man [who had] once worked as an aide in an insane asylum!"[41]

In Packard's own demonology of Caligari-like hypnotists, the main villain of his book is Dr. Ernest Dichter of the Institute for Motivational Research, Inc., one of the so-called fathers of depth analysis. Packard portrays Dichter's lair as a gothic castle, complete with a panopticon worthy of Fritz Lang's Dr. Mabuse:

> His headquarters, which can be reached only by going up a rough winding road, are atop a mountain overlooking the Hudson River, near Croton-on-the-Hudson. It is a thirty-room field-stone mansion where you are apt to see children watching TV sets. The TV room has concealed screens behind which unseen observers sometimes crouch, and tape recorders are planted about to pick up the children's happy or scornful comments.[42]

By the late fifties, the sorcerer, the fairground hypnotist, the mad scientist, and the ad man had condensed into one threatening and many-headed monster in the collective imagination. One of the most baroque appearances of this figure in low-budget horror would emerge from a studio attempting to make the risky move into big-budget, A film production, Allied Artists.

By the end of the decade, genre films were serving a number of functions for distributors. Exhibitor-backed companies such as Howco and McLendon were primarily interested in filling out playdates in their own theaters. Major studios including Columbia, Twentieth Century-Fox, and Paramount contracted with independent producers to ensure a year-round supply of product, releasing these films, often in double-feature packages, to downtown houses between major films or directly to neighborhood theaters.

Former Poverty Row studio Monogram was also an important supplier of genre films to the nabe market. After changing the company name to Allied Artists (AA) in 1953, president Steve Broidy attempted to move the company from a supplier of programmers and supporting features to the ranks of A film producers and distributors. Because of the high risk and huge capitalization required by this move, AA relied on its program features and exploitation films to provide a stable and predictable income to offset the ups and downs of its new blockbuster policy. Allied Artists had approached the product shortage of the mid-decade as an opportunity to expand its production schedule, and it almost immediately announced an increase in the number of A features it planned to produce.[43] In 1954, Broidy announced the production of AA's two most ambitious features, William Wyler's *Friendly Persuasion* and Billy Wilder's *Love in the Afternoon*, both to star Gary Cooper.[44]

The following year, Broidy went to fourteen key cities to meet with exhibitors to convince them to allot the new AA blockbuster films prime playing time.[45] In his meetings with the exhibitors, Broidy stressed the new company policy as a critical response to the product shortage, and he announced the release of several "top caliber attractions" including *Wichita* and *The Big Combo* in the slow "orphan period" of spring 1955.[46] Broidy's strategy was to "break through the magic circle" and use the A films with major stars to secure playdates in the deluxe houses, and he appealed to exhibitors to give the studio's product "as good dates and in as good situations as those given to the majors."[47] To secure engagements in the deluxe downtown houses, Wyler's *Friendly Persuasion* was released in the slow season of November 1956 and the Technicolor-CinemaScope import *Hunchback of Notre Dame* was issued in November 1957.

Allied Artists financed its transition to A film production by racking up sizable debts. The company's report for fiscal year 1957 showed a loss of almost $1.2 million, with domestic and Canadian film rentals down 20 percent from the previous year.[48] By summer 1958, Broidy told a group of exhibitors that "AA had neither lost nor made money" on *Friendly Persuasion* and *Love in the Afternoon* and that the company "had learned a lot from them."[49] What the company had learned was to focus its A film production on the international market and to exploit the domestic market with television sales and program features like low-budget genre films and double bills. Of the before-taxes profit of $684,000 announced by AA in May 1955, $527,000 of the company's gross income was derived from the sale of its old Monogram titles to TV.[50] Of the company's $12 million in gross income for fiscal 1955, over one-third was revenue from AA's subsidiary Interstate Television.[51] At a stockholder meeting in late 1955, Broidy told investors that "expansion in foreign operations and additional profits from that source" would be the most lucrative area for the company in the year to come.[52]

In 1957, the company signed an agreement with Rome's Lux Film for the distribution of Allied Artists product in Italy,[53] and the company established a similar arrangement with Associated British-Pathé. These moves resulted in consistently rising grosses for Allied Artists from the international market as revenue from domestic rentals continued to decline.[54] A successful marketing test in Argentina led to the company's search for French and Italian product to be marketed in the increasingly lucrative Latin American market.[55] Of the company's proposed top releases for 1960, at least three, *Billy Budd*, *The Capri Story*, and *Marco Polo*, appeared tailored for international distribution.[56] The following season, AA had acquired eleven films from Italy for distribution in Latin America,[57] and of the company's $13 million in income for 1961, more than one-third was from foreign rentals.[58] The Samuel Bronston–produced epics from Spain, *El Cid* (1961) and *55 Days at Peking* (1963), were also part of AA's concentration of its A film production toward the international market.[59]

Back at home, AA enjoyed consistent and predictable box-office returns from both in-house fare such as the Bowery Boys comedy series and from program features coproduced with independents. Atlanta circuit chief E. D. Martin remarked that "many of the best consistent-profit pictures have come from Allied Artists, which always had the small town exhibitor at heart."[60] By spring 1957, Robert O'Donnell, head of the powerful Texas Interstate chain, told a meeting of Texas exhibitors that "it is vitally important to us to keep Allied Artists in business to assure us of their steady supply of pictures." He stressed the particular importance of the allocation of playing time to the company's "secondary product."[61]

Independent production was crucial to AA's efforts to supply this product to exhibitors. By 1957, eighteen of the company's thirty-six planned releases were made by independent producers.[62] Broidy and the company attempted to mine the program market through an expanded release schedule, and the company's production slate for winter 1957–1958 shows a preponderance of genre pictures coproduced by AA with independents. These films included Archie Mayo's *The Beast of Budapest*, Corman's *Cry Baby Killer*, Woolner Brothers's *Teenage Doll*, and Adrian Weiss's *Bride and the Beast*.[63] Broidy later remarked that "apart from the blockbusters, pictures like *Macabre* and *The Fly* have shown that showmanship is far from dead and that the public will respond to something different."[64] In fact, AA was able to move back into the black the following winter primarily on the strength of two genre features, Castle's independently produced *House on Haunted Hill* and the in-house Burrows-

Ackerman production *Al Capone*, starring Rod Steiger. According to Broidy, these films were grossing higher than AA's previous box-office champions.[65] *Al Capone* topped the company's releases in 1959 with $2.5 million in rentals, followed by *House on Haunted Hill* with $1.5 million.[66]

Success in the program market was the goal of most of AA's releases in the late fifties, and the company's release schedules showed a wide array of genre films of which horror and science fiction were only a part. The reviews of these films in *Variety* are replete with references to "program mellers," "action-house fare," "lowercase bookings," "smaller situations," and "less discriminating audiences." Youth pics were represented by *Hot Rod Rumble*, *Speed Crazy* (both 1957), and *Cry Baby Killer* (1958). Allied Artists released many films in the mid-fifties cycle of violent urban thrillers, including *Night Freight*, *Sudden Danger*, *Finger Man*, *Murder Is My Beat*, and *The Big Combo* (all 1955). Location shooting served both low budgets and increased "realism" for true-crime dramas in both contemporary settings (*Riot in Cell Block 11* [1954], *The Phoenix City Story*, and *Las Vegas Shakedown* [both 1955]) and in the Prohibition era (*Al Capone* [1959] and *The Purple Gang* [1960]).

The true-crime genre was even expanded to encompass political tyrants in *Beast of Budapest* (1958), *Operation Eichmann* (1961), and *Hitler* (1962). The war genre was covered by *Screaming Eagles*, *Hold Back the Night* (both 1956), and *Surrender—Hell!* (1959). The company also released many topical or exploitation films, such as *I Passed for White* (1960), *Angel Baby*, and *Look in Any Window* (both 1961), and presold properties like the television-based feature *Crime in the Streets* (1956); *Saturday Evening Post* exposés like the drug-abuse drama *Death in Small Doses* (1957); and the Mafia thriller *Underworld USA* (1961). A serialized Jack Finney story from *Saturday Evening Post* also provided the source for Walter Wanger's production of *Invasion of the Body Snatchers* (1956).

The latter was among the most successful of AA's genre releases of the mid-fifties. Much has been written about this film, particularly the various interpretations of the takeover of humanity by emotionally voided "pod people." Peter Biskind has claimed that the film is a right-wing allegory that upholds the primacy of the individual vision against the collective center.[67] Matthew Bernstein, in contrast, has situated the film in a tradition of liberal social criticism, which was characteristic of producer Wanger's other films from the decade, *Riot in Cell Block 11* and *I Want to Live!* (1958).[68]

In addition to these two approaches, there is another light in which the film can be viewed, one that preserves rather than resolves the sug-

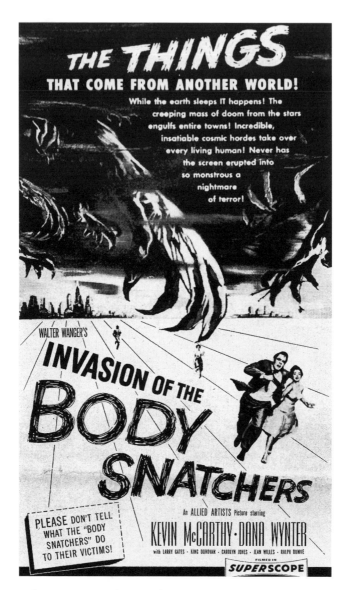

Walter Wanger's production of *Invasion of the Body Snatchers*
(1956) was one of Allied Artists's most successful genre releases of
the mid-fifties (Wisconsin Center for Film and Theater Research).

gestive ambiguity of many viewers' experiences of the film. During the middle to late fifties, several psychological thrillers told stories of hypnosis or brainwashing, and some of these films suggested a continuity between indoctrination by Red propaganda and hypnosis by Madison Avenue. Just five months after the premiere of *Body Snatchers*, Kevin McCarthy appeared in the United Artists release *Nightmare*, in which he plays a young jazz musician who has a recurring dream that he has murdered a man in a roomful of mirrors. The climax of the film reveals that he had been hypnotized to commit the murder by an old antagonist. *Time Limit* (1957) is a military courtroom drama in which a soldier on trial for treason is slowly revealed to have been brainwashed in a prison camp in Korea. Finally, *The Fearmakers* (1958), directed by Jacques Tourneur, features Dana Andrews as a Korean War veteran who comes home from years in a Chinese prison camp. He becomes a partner in a public relations firm and soon discovers that the firm has been taken over by an extensive Red Front conspiracy. His business partner is murdered, and the new partner, played by a cold and emotionless Dick Foran, begins altering polling data in the service of the conspiracy.

Director Tourneur and star Andrews had told an almost identical story in a British setting months earlier with Columbia's horror thriller *Curse of the Demon*. In this earlier film, the massive conspiracy uncovered by the initially skeptical Andrews was not political but supernatural, with warlock and Aleister Crowley-like magician Niall McGuiness at the center of a series of murders committed by an ancient demon he has invoked through a mysterious parchment.

The Hypnotic Eye (1960), a gruesome hybrid of the horror and noir thriller genres, was an attempt to capitalize on both the gimmicks innovated at AA by William Castle (see chapter 4) and the cycle of hypnosis and mind-control films described above. Near the end of the film a five-minute sequence shows the evil stage hypnotist, Desmond (played by Jacques Bergerac), hypnotizing both his live audience and presumably, by staring directly into the camera during his incantations, the movie audience as well. The name Allied Artists used to promote this gimmick, Hypno Magic, condenses the motifs of hypnosis and sorcery into a single phrase.[69] The film was independently produced by screenwriter William Read Woodfield and agent Charles Bloch for less than $400,000, with Allied Artists's Ben Schwalb (producer of the long-running Bowery Boys series) serving as line producer and studio liaison. In a 2000 interview with film historian Tom Weaver, Woodfield jokingly situated the film's "Hypno Magic" audience hypnosis stunt in the context of late-fifties film hype and publicity.

The evil Desmond in *The Hypnotic Eye* (Warner Communications).

> I'd been a magician in my youth. One day, I was driving down the highway looking at the white line, and I thought, "You could make a movie about this." People would come into the theater . . . the picture would start . . . and it's just a white line. A voice would say, "All right, everybody—just relax. Keep your eye on the white line." And we would hypnotize the audience . . . Ultimately we'd tell them it was the greatest movie they ever saw in their life and to tell all their friends. The post-hypnotic suggestion would be, "Talk it up!"[70]

In *The Hypnotic Eye*, the Great Desmond places attractive women in a trance onstage. These women later mutilate themselves at home in gruesome "accidents": one woman rinses her hair in the gas burner instead of the sink, another lowers her face into an electric fan, and a third washes her face with sulfuric acid.[71] Police detective Dave Kennedy and his partner, Phil Hecht, a criminal psychologist from the department, investigate the mutilations. Meanwhile, the detective's girlfriend, Marcia, conducts an investigation of her own when her best friend is disfigured after appearing onstage with Desmond.

Like *My World Dies Screaming*, *The Hypnotic Eye* was one of several horror films from the period whose promotional strategies actually featured a hypnotist/monstrateur figure in the films beyond the diegesis, in advertising or prologues. *Horrors of the Black Museum* (1960) and *Dementia 13* (1961) by AIP and Fairway-International's *The Incredibly Strange Creatures Who Stopped Living and Became Mixed-Up Zombies* (1964) all purported to cast a hypnotic spell over the audience at various points. It appears that the terror all of these movies attempted to instill in their audience was as much the fear of the dissolution of personality as the horror of bodily mutilation or death. As in the *Bridey Murphy* and regression films, the hypnotist or evil psychiatrist is a modern sorcerer, turning his victims into animals or zombies.

Writing three years before *The Hypnotic Eye*, Vance Packard told the story of a study undertaken by social-psychologist-turned-adman James Vicary to investigate why women had drastically increased the rate of impulse buying in supermarkets. Vicary used hidden cameras to observe the eye-blink rate of women as they shopped in order to measure their level of anxiety. Packard describes the results:

> Their eye-blink rate, instead of going up to indicate mounting tension, went down and down, to a very subnormal fourteen blinks a minute. The ladies fell into what Mr. Vicary calls a hypnoidal trance, a kind of light trance that, he explains, is the first stage of hypnosis . . . Many of these women were in such a trance that they passed by neighbors and old friends without noticing or greeting them. Some had a sort of glassy stare. They were so entranced as they wandered about the store plucking things off shelves at random that they would bump into boxes without seeing them.[72]

The female victims of Desmond in *The Hypnotic Eye* bear a close resemblance to Packard's popular image of women under the hypnoidal spell of consumerism. In the film's sexual and moral economy, the women's acts of self mutilation by fire, acid, and blades are monstrously disproportionate punishments for the very vanity, hope, and fear implanted in them by the advertising industry.

The film's precredits sequence introduces many of the motifs that will recur throughout the film. After the Allied Artists logo, swirling woodwinds play a minor musical theme generically coded to signify dizziness or disorientation, and a blonde woman in a black slip walks toward the camera in medium shot, looking almost into the lens as she rubs a shampoolike substance into her hair. She smiles like the "Breck girl" in the ads then playing, and her hand is shown in close-up turning the knob on a gas stovetop. The camera looks up from under the iron pot rest of the burner, which forms concentric circles on the image. The stove ignites, and through the ring of fire we see the woman lower her head into the flames, scrubbing her now-flaming hair as if rinsing herself in cool water. Suddenly, she stands bolt upright, her hair aflame, and stares wide-eyed into the camera as she screams in terror and pain. Her screams segue into the wail of a siren as a police car speeds along the freeway at night.

This opening passage of *The Hypnotic Eye*, along with all of the violent mutilation sequences in the film, resembles a grisly parody of a 1950s television commercial for cosmetic products. Like many of the horror films from this period, the images and icons in *The Hypnotic Eye* that suggest the horror of mind control and the dissolution of personality are strikingly similar to tropes of hypnosis and thrall that characterize both advertising's trade discourse and the warnings about them in *The Hidden Persuaders*.

A similar strain of imagery characterizes a 1962 trade ad in *Variety* by the CBS television network. The ad shows a young woman peering out from a television screen as she applies mascara to her left eye. In front of the television set we see a young woman with an identical hairstyle applying mascara to her right eye in perfect symmetry and synchronization with the woman onscreen, as if she were looking into a mirror. The ad's tag line reads, "A reflection of television's power over women."[73] Two of *Hypnotic Eye*'s most striking later images, the acid-scarred Dodie looking into the mirror recognizing the damage done by the acid, and the entranced Marcia looking into the mirror at Desmond approaching her from behind, will use an identical composition.

The introduction of the character of Phil points to a strategy that several horror-thriller hybrids would use in the early sixties, the doubling of the killer with a benevolent psychiatrist who explains the action to the police and to the audience. This figure is a recurring stock character in the noir thriller genre, featured in such films as *The Sniper* (1952) and *The Couch* (1962) and reaching an apotheosis in the epilogue of *Psycho*. In *The Hypnotic Eye*, the pipe-smoking bachelor Phil Hecht is presented as something of an odd-duck academic: he lives alone in a sumptuously furnished apartment—heroine Marcia later compliments him on his interior decor—in which he serves coffee from an elegant service set and plays classical piano in his silk bathrobe as his shaggy white dog sits at his side. These character traits, coded as effete or even effeminate to the film's original audience, place him on a continuum inbetween the regular-guy detective Dave and the suave, continental, and odious Desmond, whose actions and techniques he is called on to explain.

Late in the film, after Desmond has hypnotized Marcia and Dave and Phil have pieced together the clues pointing to Desmond and his mistress/stage assistant Justine, *The Hypnotic Eye* returns to the theater, where Desmond is performing onstage. The next several minutes feature Desmond looking directly into the camera (as had the paddleball-wielding carny barker in *House of Wax*) while the narrative comes to a complete stop.[74] In a medium shot, Desmond announces that members

Self immolation at the gas stovetop in *The Hypnotic Eye*
(Warner Communications).

A reflection of
television's power
over women

A 1962 CBS trade ad in *Variety* (New York Public Library).

The acid-scarred Dodie in *The Hypnotic Eye* (Warner Communications).

The Hypnotic Eye: Desmond and the hypnotized Marcia (Warner Communications).

The flashing light in *The Hypnotic Eye* (Warner Communications).

of the audience will now have the opportunity to "cross the dark, mysterious threshold of your own subconscious mind." Looking past the camera, he asks, "May I have the house lights, please?" At this point, the projectionist in the theater showing *The Hypnotic Eye* is to turn up the house lights to a dim ambiance. Each of Desmond's ensuing demonstrations feature a reaction shot from the crowd, which serves to set up a planted female scream in the auditorium, the final element of the Hypno Magic stunt.

Each of the following subsegments will engage the audience in highly repetitive motions with their eyes fixed on the screen in an attempt to instill dizziness before a strobing hypnotic eye is flashed onscreen. Next, Desmond instructs audience members to take out the "hypnotic eye balloon" they were given on entering the theater. Like the characters in the film, each viewer blows up the balloon and ties it off. Out of breath from blowing up the balloon and dizzy from repetitive motion, audience members place the balloon in their lap and are instructed to lean forward under the pretense of being told that "You cannot pick it up, you cannot!" by the deafening echo of Desmond's voice. When the audience is cued to sit up straight, in a condition of complete lightheadedness, the house lights rapidly go down and Desmond intones, "Now . . . if you dare, look into the hypnotic eye!" Suddenly, he produces the flashing light, which is shown in extreme close-up, strobing on and off and creating a vertiginous flickering in the auditorium as a spectral soprano voice warbles on the soundtrack.

Suddenly, a planted woman in the audience screams in unison with an unseen member of the audience in the film, and both the crowd on the screen and, presumably, the crowd in the movie theater look nervously around for the fainted woman. Finally, the narrative is rapidly reestablished with a close-up of Marcia, staring ahead under Desmond's spell. Up on the screen, Dave and Phil rush into the theater and attempt to storm the stage. Desmond trains the eye on Dave, who is shown in extreme close-up staring into the camera with the light flashing into his face. Regaining his senses, he jumps onto the stage to confront Desmond with his police revolver.

Meanwhile, Justine leads Marcia up a flight of stairs backstage toward a catwalk in a shot economically filmed near the ceiling of the Allied Artists soundstage. When Dave looks up, Desmond wrests the gun away from him, but Phil draws his own gun on Desmond and Dave picks up the dropped pistol. Justine rips off her latex mask, revealing her hideously scarred face like the Phantom of the Opera or Henri Jarrod. She throws the mask down at Phil and screams, "Kill him, Desmond!" In the struggle, Phil shoots Desmond and an anguished Justine screams her slain companion's name, spreads her arms, and calmly swan dives to her death on the stage floor, reprising the serene self-destruction of her victims.

Up on the catwalk, Marcia hangs by her fingernails over the stage. Phil awakens her from her trance as Dave rushes up the stairs to the catwalk, which swings wildly on its chains as he attempts to pull her up. Breathing a sigh of relief, Phil walks out from behind the curtain and addresses the audience in both the theater within the film and the 1959 movie house:

> Ladies and gentlemen, a word of warning. Hypnosis, although an important and valuable medical tool, can be extremely dangerous when used by untrained or unscrupulous practitioners. Therefore never allow yourself to be hypnotized by anyone who is not your doctor or who has not been recommended to you by your doctor [he turns to look directly into the camera], not even in a motion-picture theater. Thank you.

The film fades to black, and "The End" appears over the Allied Artists logo. This moment of direct address is a final gesture of stylistic and narrational self-consciousness characteristic of the cinema of attractions. Also, it brings the movie full circle back to the frontal close-up that had introduced Desmond's victim in the film's first shot. Of course, Dr. Phil Hecht's warning is also a disclaimer by Allied Artists for any untoward effects of the Hypno Magic stunt. The review of the film in *Variety* pointed to "exploitation gimmick which may be somewhat dangerous."[75] Nonetheless, the film's onscreen warning was ignored by the manager of the RKO Golden Gate Theater in San Francisco, who ran a local radio contest in which winners appeared onstage at the film's opening to challenge a stage hypnotist to entrance them.[76]

The role programmers such as *The Hypnotic Eye* played in the movie market led that film's producers to concoct a deranged premise and an even more bizarre promotional stunt in the hopes of differentiating their film from a host of competitors in the thriller and true-crime genres. The film's threadbare production values, graphic violence, hypertrophied use of direct address, and the hypnotism motif were all markers of an exploitation film designed to make a bigger-than-average splash in neighborhood theaters and action houses.

In addition to the supposedly hypnotic powers of the carny come-on in films such as *My World Dies Screaming* and *The Hypnotic Eye*, the "star shortage" of the late fifties further abetted the rise of the exploitation film. Sensational content and wild promotional gimmicks such as Psycho-Rama and Hypno Magic were effective strategies to deal with the absence of stars in the films.[77] Even though one of the ten points suggested by the AB-PT production proposal was the development of new stars,[78] none of the genre pictures produced by the company were designed to launch younger performers into star status. Doherty quotes an "unnamed ad man" who told *Variety* in 1958 that he enjoyed designing campaigns that were "pure punch, with no dilution"; this source also expressed relief that the campaigns on which he worked did not feature stars, who were usually the focus of a film's publicity.[79] Soon this would change with the arrival of a new generation of stars from overseas and the genre's ability to showcase the talents of aging stars and contract players. The most important figure in this trend would be waxworks monstrateur Vincent Price.

CHAPTER 4

"A Sissified Bela Lugosi":

Vincent Price,

William Castle, and

AIP's Poe Adaptations

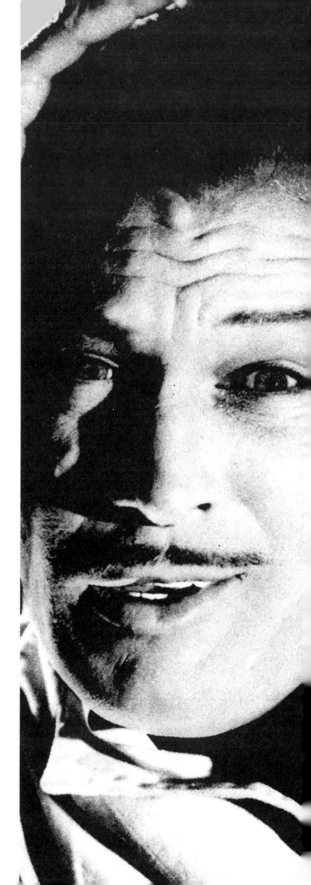

C rucial to the success of the studio-era horror films such as *The Raven* (1935), *Son of Frankenstein* (1939), and *The Wolf Man* (1941) receiving their television debut in the late fifties was the stable of stars associated with the genre, particularly Boris Karloff, Bela Lugosi, and Lon Chaney Jr. During the golden age of Hollywood, stars on long-term contracts became one of the most powerful means of product differentiation for the individual studios, who often instituted genre cycles to showcase the carefully nurtured personalities of their contract players. After the *Paramount* decision and with the curtailment of production by the major studios, many of the stars from the studio era became freelance performers. Major stars including John Wayne, Burt Lancaster, and Kirk Douglas started their own production companies, but the less popular horror personalities became increasingly visible (and increasingly well paid) in downscale, low-budget attractions acquired by the majors from independent producers or produced by in-house B units of the studios.

While technological innovations such as 3-D and distributors' gimmicks such as Hypno Magic were often the focus of publicity for the low-budget programmers produced by both smaller distributors and the major studios, the presence of a recognizable star was still a huge asset to a film seeking to cross over beyond the genre audience. The late fifties and early sixties saw a proliferation of trade sources bemoaning the "star shortage," industry shorthand for the lack of younger stars to replace the aging roster of studio personalities.

Like other independent producers of the fifties, William Castle was able to take advantage of the cutback of B film production by the majors. Castle rented studio space from Allied Artists and Columbia to shoot his series of gimmick shockers beginning with *Macabre* in 1957. Similarly, Roger Corman mastered the art of shooting low-budget genre features at breakneck speed and releasing them through Allied Artists, AIP, or his own company, Filmgroup.

Both Castle in the late fifties and Corman in the early sixties realized that breakout success would be possible only through securing the services of a star. The cycle of films that enabled them to do this featured the performer that would become one of the icons of the genre for the next fifteen years: former Fox contract player and insane wax sculptor Vincent Price, star of Castle's Columbia release from 1959, *The Tingler*, and of Corman's 1961 Poe adaptation, *Pit and the Pendulum*, released by AIP.

During the 1950s, very few distributors would employ in-house producers who specialized in genre fare. Universal-International, one of the decade's few exceptions to this trend, released no independently produced features: a survey of 1957 production by the major studios listed Universal-International alone as producing all of its releases direct,[1] and their William Alland–produced cycle of "weirdies" that began with *It Came from Outer Space* and ended with *The Mole People* was unique in the fifties cycle of science fiction and horror. By the mid-decade, all of the major studios had released many of their long-term salaried personnel and were functioning, in Tino Balio's phrase, primarily "as bankers supplying financing and landlords supplying studio space. Distribution was now the name of their game."[2] United Artists board chairman Robert Benjamin told *Motion Picture Herald* in 1955 that most major studios were incapable of bringing in a so-called low-budget picture for less than $750,000 because of overhead costs. An independent, on the other hand, could bring out an almost identical film for $350,000 with an excellent chance of recouping the negative cost even if the film was a second feature.[3]

Early in the fifties, Columbia saw independent production as a means of increasing its market share during the acute product shortage. The studio announced a plan to provide $10 million to finance independent production at its West Coast studios and offered technical resources and contract personnel to interested indies.[4] Except for United Artists, of all the major studios Columbia led the industry in 1957 with forty-two independent productions.[5] Indie producer Sam Katzman's Clover Productions provided Columbia with supporting features from a wide range of B genres including horror pictures (the double bill *Zombies of Mora-Tau* and *The Man Who Turned to Stone* [1957]), true crime (*Miami Exposé* [1956]), rock and roll (*Don't Knock the Rock* [1956]), troubled youth (*Going Steady* [1958]), and combat drama (*The Enemy General* [1960]).

Katzman's horror films were often released as part of saturation-booked double bills with features of fellow indie Charles Schneer's

Morningside Productions, which showcased the monster effects of stop-motion pioneer Ray Harryhausen: Katzman's *The Werewolf* was released with Schneer's *Earth vs. the Flying Saucers* in 1956, and *Creature with the Atom Brain* was released with Schneer's *It Came from Beneath the Sea*.[6] In addition, Columbia purchased one-half interest in Hammer Films's Bray studios in England to keep program product flowing through its distribution pipeline and to invest in British production as a means of unblocking Columbia box-office revenues frozen there by protectionist trade policies (see chapter 2).[7]

Like Sam Katzman's Clover Productions at Columbia, Robert Lippert's Regal Films maintained a long-term relationship with Fox. Lippert owned a circuit of thirty-one theaters in Northern California and Oregon, almost all of them drive-ins, including the highly successful Starlight chain.[8] An independent producer and distributor since 1943, Lippert oversaw production companies that were named, successively, Action Pictures, Screen Guild Productions, and Lippert Pictures.[9] In 1956, Lippert's distribution company was renamed Associated Film Releasing and placed under the control of Lippert Pictures's president E. J. Baumgarten; soon after, it was renamed Regal Films and began to produce pictures for release by Fox. Regal Films licensed the name Regalscope from Fox for its widescreen releases, and for the second half of the decade Regal produced as many as twenty films per year for release by Fox, with Lippert acting as liaison between the two companies from his office on the Fox lot.[10]

The company produced a wide range of genre films, from the western *Massacre* (1956) and the noir crime drama *Plunder Road* to the youth-pic tandem *Rockabilly Baby* and *Young and Dangerous* (all 1957). Many of Regal's films were given an artistic patina beyond their meager budgets by the effective musical scores of Albert Glasser. Regal produced several horror double bills that were part of the multiple-opening/saturation-advertising trend begun by Warner with *Beast from 20,000 Fathoms* and *Them!* Western director Charles Marques Warren helmed both halves of September 1957's *Unknown Terror* and *Back from the Dead* package, and for Halloween Fox issued a double bill of two of Regal's runaway programmers: *The Abominable Snowman* and *Ghost Diver*.

Why were horror films released at Halloween? In addition to the obvious reason, a wide range of genre films from an array of distributors turned up in both neighborhood theaters and larger downtown showcase houses because of the uneven seasonal distribution of top features by the majors. In winter 1955, a North Carolina exhibitor complained to *Motion Picture Herald* that "too many good films are released around the holidays [generally Christmas week and Easter] and in July and August, too few in the [mid-]winter, [late] spring and fall."[11]

Samuel Arkoff and James Nicholson of AIP understood this, and their heavily promoted genre combinations were often released during the most arid seasons for the exhibitor.[12] This policy continued from the early days of the company[13] to the years of international coproductions in the early sixties.[14] *The Undead* and *Voodoo Woman* package was released in March 1957, *Blood of Dracula* and *I Was a Teenage Frankenstein* in November of 1957 (making its bow in Texas at some of Interstate's premiere first-run houses), *The Bonnie Parker Story* and *Machine Gun Kelly* in May 1958, *The Spider* and *The Brain Eaters* in October 1958, and *Bucket of Blood* and *The Giant Leeches* in October 1959. Of course, AIP did not refuse to issue films during peak seasons: their most successful package, *I Was a Teenage Werewolf* and *Invasion of the Saucermen* bowed in June 1957. Most distributors, however, issued their genre double bills during off-peak periods. For example, Allied Artists released Corman's *Not of this Earth* and *Attack of the Crab Monsters* package in March 1957, William Castle's *Macabre* in March 1958, *War of the Satellites* and *Attack of the Fifty-Foot Woman* in April 1958, and *House on Haunted Hill* in January 1959.

The successful opening of major venues such as the Stanley Warner chain and Texas Interstate to the product of AIP, Allied Artists, and others led to complaints by exhibitors and critics. In Philadelphia, twenty-five blocks away from the Fans Theater's Thanksgiving 1957 sub-run of *Curse of Frankenstein*, the 1,500-seat Stanley Warner Stanton first-run house at 16th and Market Streets began the week-long run of Allied Artists's combination of *Cyclops* and *Daughter of Dr. Jekyll*, and a week later the same showcase house was running a double bill of *Eighteen and Anxious* and *The Weapon*. The Stanton continued to be the favored Philadelphia showcase house for the orphan-period first runs of genre films, including AIP's *House of Usher* (1960), Columbia's *Homicidal* and AIP's *Black Sunday*, *Pit and the Pendulum* (all 1961), *Premature Burial*, and *Burn, Witch, Burn* (both 1962). The film critic for the *Philadelphia Inquirer* sniffed, "Definitely a cause for the numerical boom in pictures over the previous season is the sorry fact that so much downright trash has found its way into downtown theaters. Double horror, double science fiction bills have become a habit, even with houses which, in the past, would have scorned such fare."[15]

Also, two genre pictures with exploitable titles were an effective centerpiece for saturation advertising, and the horror film proved particularly amenable to exploitation in this way. On one level, the saturation genre package was an answer to exhibitors' complaints about expanding production budgets and dwindling allotments for advertising: *Variety* pointed out that "the coin saved in the production is added to the exploitation campaign."[16] Walter Brookes wrote to his fellow exhibitors in *Motion Picture Herald* in 1957:

> We have never held any particular brief for "horror shows"—and, perhaps, two are better than one, for if you go for it, you might as well go double. But with a certain finesse—the particular handling that identifies both your program and your policy. You can always go along with a gag—and not commit yourself to a community ideal, whatever it may be. Maybe your folks LIKE "horror shows"—and maybe they're right.[17]

Massive radio and television advertising for these premieres also worked in tandem with exhibitor "gags" and stunts. Universal's package of *Curse of the Werewolf* and *Shadow of the Cat* was timed for regional multiple openings to coincide with the end of the 1961 school year, not coincidentally the "orphan" period of May/June.[18] The RKO Keith Theater in Washington, D.C., publicized the opening with a "werewolf wanted" sign in front of the building. Prospective applicants were screened, and the winner was changed into a werewolf by a local make-up artist in front of the theater on opening day. He then rode around town in a convertible accompanied by a black-masked "cat girl," also selected from a pool of applicants.[19] Finally, the manager of the Rustic Starlight drive-in in Effingham, Illinois, circulated handbills and published ad copy in the newspapers that tied in his 1961 "Rock-A-Shock all shook up show" of horror films and teen musicals with several highly publicized grave robbings in surrounding communities.[20]

Because relatively few exhibitors were able to exploit the activities of local necrophiles to sell movie tickets, stars remained vital to film industry promotion during this period. The aging actors from the studio era were only slowly being replaced by younger performers with box-office appeal for younger audiences. This "star shortage" was seen as a critical component of the "product shortage" of the fifties,[21] because without a star name even a moderately budgeted film was treated like a programmer in the marketplace. Further, the abandonment of B film production by the majors eliminated the main source for the careful nurturing of new talent.[22] As Trueman Rembusch, former president of National Allied told the Senate Small Business Committee in 1956:

> The lifeblood of the motion picture theater has always been the introduction of new personalities that attract hordes of fans. Limiting the pro-

duction of pictures prevented the development of new talent and has brought on, since 1947, the spectacle of the grandma and grandpa entrenched stars acting like youngsters, to the distaste of the important teen-age patron group. As my 18-year-old daughter says, "Clark Gable and Joan Crawford acting like young lovers. Ugh!"[23]

One of the most fascinating aspects of the middle-bracket horror film in this period is its ability to capitalize on the "ugh!" expressed by younger viewers when the once alluring, now aging actors and actresses walked on screen. In fact, the very star mentioned by Rembusch, Joan Crawford, would repulse audiences for years in a series of highly successful "menopausal horror" pictures whose misogynist narratives often capitalized on her former flapper and fallen woman personas. Films in this cycle include *What Ever Happened to Baby Jane?* (1962), *Straight Jacket* (1964), *I Saw What You Did* (1965), and *Berserk* (1967).[24] The horror genre was particularly well suited to showcasing aging players in roles of villains, deformed servants, or abject victims.

The highly successful middle-period career of gimmick schlock-meister William Castle can be situated within all of the trends outlined here. Beginning his career as a dialogue director at Columbia in the forties, Castle directed several films in the studio's "Whistler" series of B detective films. He received good reviews for his 1944 thriller *When Strangers Marry*, produced Orson Welles's *Lady from Shanghai* (1948), and directed one of Columbia's early 3-D releases, *Fort Ti* (1953). The success of independent producers like Katzman and Lippert at developing long-term relationships with the major distributors led Castle to become an independent producer-director in 1957. Castle formed Susina Associates, a partnership with novelist Robb White, for the production of five pictures in the $100,000 to $300,000 budget range. The films became *Macabre* (1957), *House on Haunted Hill* (1958), *The Tingler* (1959), *13 Ghosts* (1960), and *Homicidal* (1961). The company set up headquarters at the offices of Bel-Air Productions,[25] an independent production company that had been releasing genre programmers through United Artists. Bel-Air president Edwin Zabel was also vice president of the huge National Theater chain and general manager of Fox West Coast Theaters, and Zabel had guaranteed playdates for Susina's features. The company's first feature was *Macabre*, a premature-burial thriller shot in six days whose title and central plot twist were "inspired" by the previous year's import hit *Diabolique*. In a 1989 interview with historian Tom Weaver, White claimed that he put up *Macabre*'s $86,000 budget himself, with lab costs and payments to cast and crew deferred.[26] *Ma-*

cabre was released by Allied Artists with the first of Castle's gimmicks, a death-by-fright insurance policy for each ticket holder. The film was a huge hit.[27]

Castle had stated before the production of *Macabre* that "we'll use good actors — actors that don't look like actors — and if they happen to be stars, all well and good, but we'll be hiring performers to fit parts, never altering parts to fit the players."[28] In the time between *Macabre* and his Allied Artists follow-up *House on Haunted Hill* (1958), Castle could not have failed to notice the success of *The Fly* from Twentieth Century-Fox. A sumptuous and grisly sci-fi horror picture, *The Fly* sported a James Clavell script, a $500,000 budget, DeLuxe color, CinemaScope, and magnetic stereo sound. Vincent Price added marquee value as the scientist's brother, and the story was told in flashback by an ostensibly insane protagonist à la *Caligari* and *Curse of Frankenstein*. Lippert's former line producer Bernard Glasser told Tom Weaver in 1992 that *The Fly* was "totally in-house" at Fox even though many Regal technicians, including director Kurt Neumann, worked on the film.[29] Fox issued the film in summer 1958 in a package with Regal's *Space Master X-7* in the now-familiar saturation pattern with extensive radio promotions, theater stunts, and midnight horror shows. The film's four hundred West Coast openings in the choice July spot approached a $1 million gross and ran ahead of *Peyton Place* in many markets.[30]

It is highly unlikely that the role of Frederick Loren in *House on Haunted Hill* was not written with Vincent Price in mind. Price, once a second-leading man in films like *Laura* (1944), and a comic foil to Robert Mitchum in *His Kind of Woman* (1951), now continued the change in his persona that began with *House of Wax*, combining the villainy of his roles in *Shock* (1946) and *Baron of Arizona* (1950) with a fey, cuckolded sensitivity, prompting a 1960 *Time* magazine article to call Price "sort of a sissified Bela Lugosi."[31] *House on Haunted Hill* established the Susina production personnel that would continue throughout the series and provide a recognizable feel to the films that Castle could claim as an authorial signature: Robb White wrote the screenplay, Castle directed, and Von Dexter wrote the musical score.[32]

What Castle had done with *Macabre* and *House on Haunted Hill* was to combine the saturation advertising campaign perfected by Columbia and Universal in their Sam Katzman and William Alland packages with centralized and standardized publicity stunts and gimmicks that had previously been the purview of the local exhibitor. Where the New York Paramount had placed a "nurse" on duty in the lobby during *Curse of Frankenstein*, Castle and Allied Artists made *Macabre*'s insurance-policy gag part of the national advertising campaign. Where the Ritz in Ohio had placed a huge plastic fly in the box office under a livid green light, Castle and Allied Artists suspended a plastic skeleton over the heads of audiences everywhere for *House on Haunted Hill*. Castle was quite explicit about the independent producer's need to usurp the publicist's role heretofore monopolized by distributors and theater owners. "We can no longer expect the distributor to create the excitement needed to sell tickets," he told *Variety*. "We must do it ourselves."[33]

After *House on Haunted Hill*, Price made the Allied Artists follow-up *The Bat* (1959), financed by AB-PT, which played on a double bill with sub-run engagements of the Castle film. Meanwhile, Castle and White had set up a distribution deal with Columbia for their next feature, *The Tingler*. The outrageous premise of *The Tingler* is the search for the physiological origins of fear by a pathologist who discovers a centipede-like parasite monster that lives in the spinal cord of humans. Straight-faced publicity for the film asserted that the story "actually has its roots in ancient Greek and Roman attempts find the exact location of the soul."[34] In what must be the ultimate direct audience address, the monster is turned loose in a movie theater at the film's climax as the actual theater seats begin to vibrate from small motors installed under many of the seats. Castle named this new process of audience assault Percepto.

A saturation opening for *The Tingler* was impossible because of the needs of the Percepto stunt at the center of the film's publicity, including surround speakers at the rear of the theater and the tremendous cash outlay for the vibrating motors. After August and September prerelease "screamiere" engagements in Baltimore, Boston, and Detroit,[35] the film was released into downtown houses during the slow Halloween season of 1959, capitalizing on the holiday, the orphan period, and the national publicity for the gimmick.

The Tingler is the story of pathologist Warren Chapin (Price), who discovers the tingler while examining the shattered spines of electrocuted criminals. The tingler grows from microscopic size to three-feet long in mortally terrified victims. Only a terrified scream can paralyze the monster once it grips a person's spine. Warren's adulterous wife, Isabel, expresses contempt for his work and later attempts to let loose on him the crawling parasite as he lies drugged on the couch. Their loveless and claustrophobic marriage is echoed in that of Ollie and Martha Higgins, a middle-aged couple who run an impoverished silent-movie revival theater. At the film's midpoint, the deaf-mute Martha dies of fright as she witnesses a series of terrifying apparitions but is unable to scream. At the end of the film, Ollie is revealed to have frightened Martha to death

Allied Artists's newspaper ads for *House on Haunted Hill* prominently featured Price, but the star of the show was the Emergo gimmick featured at select first-run engagements (Wisconsin Center for Film and Theater Research).

for insurance money, and Warren confronts him, as Martha's tingler escapes from a steel box and threatens both the patrons of the silent movie house and the theater where *The Tingler* is playing in 1959.

The Tingler begins with a long shot of a theater screen. William Castle walks to the center and faces the audience. He introduces himself, then begins a spoken prologue that prepares the audience for the eventual onslaught of Percepto. He speaks in the ominous tones of the carnival barker (indeed, his autobiography was titled *Step Right Up!*) "I feel obligated to warn you," he says, "that some of the sensations, some of the physical reactions which actors on the screen will feel will be experienced, for the first time in motion-picture history, by certain members of the audience. I say certain members because some people are more sensitive to these mysterious electronic impulses than others." In fact, he says "certain members" because Columbia had arranged for the wiring of every tenth seat. He continues:

> These, uh—unfortunate sensitive people will at times [he smiles] experience a strange, tingling sensation. Others will feel it less strongly. But don't be alarmed, you can protect yourself. At any time that you are conscious of a tingling sensation you may obtain immediate relief by screaming. Don't be embarrassed about opening your mouth and letting it rip with all you've got, because the person in the seat next to you will probably be screaming too. Remember, a scream at the right time may save your life!

The most fascinating subplot of *The Tingler* concerns the silent-movie theater above which Ollie and Martha live. By the late fifties, impoverished sub-run theaters seeking a market niche impervious to the product shortages and exorbitant rentals of current films sometimes turned to silent films and other reissues. The thankless and poorly paid work of a small theater owner, detailed at length in the trade journals of the time, provide the motivation for the film's major plot twist of Ollie's efforts to frighten his wife to death and escape his hopeless life. Ollie tells Warren of the incessant cleaning involved in maintaining the theater, again echoing common exhibitor complaints that, even with color, widescreen, and stereo sound, the movies of 1959 are no better than those of thirty years before.

The performance of Judith Evelyn as Martha is the centerpiece of the film, and her neurotic pantomime (screenwriter White gives her a full range of obsessive and phobic tics) sets her off from all of the other characters in the film. She is, in the words of critic Tim Lucas, "truly a silent character in a sound movie,"[36] and her association with the silent-movie

Price on a bad LSD trip in *The Tingler* (Wisconsin Center for Film and Theater Research).

theater establishes a narrative justification for both her ultimate death by fright and her tingler's eventual "escape" into the theater to set up the Percepto stunt. The motif of the silent theater and the terrified, mute heroine was "borrowed" by screenwriter White from *The Spiral Staircase* (1946).

A scene that often fascinates modern viewers is one in which Warren injects himself with the then newly discovered drug LSD in order to summon his own tingler. He doubles the recommended dose and records his reactions on reel-to-reel tape. The LSD trip that follows functions beyond the scope of the narrative to provide Price with an opportunity to display the stylized and exaggerated performance style that would become increasingly foregrounded in the later Poe adaptations. Chromatic scales accompany Warren's growing dizziness, and his eyes shift suspiciously from side to side as he describes "a feeling of definite unease and apprehension." As he grows increasingly terrified, Warren loosens his tie thinking himself unable to breathe, then opens the window but believes it to be nailed shut. A hanging skeleton appears to walk toward him; the walls seem to close in. After struggling with the urge to scream, Warren becomes overwhelmed with fear, his back stiffens, and he cries out, much like the electrocuted prisoner from the beginning of the film.

In addition to the attractions of Price and Percepto, the scene of Martha's death by fright stands out as a setpiece of the film. Back at her apartment above the theater, Martha wakes with a start and looks around suspiciously. The lights dim and then flicker on and off. A rocking chair begins to rock by itself in another echo of the electric chair, and a door closes by itself. Martha staggers toward the other bed and, seeing the bedclothes stir, rips off the sheet. Suddenly, a balding, putrefying corpse sits bolt upright, threatening to leap off the screen in an homage to the famous morgue scene in *House of Wax*. The corpse comes at her with a long machete, and Martha flees into the central room of the apartment. The lights go on and off again, and a hairy hand throws a hatchet into a table at her side. In the darkened apartment, the bathroom door opens of its own accord.

Inside the bathroom Martha flicks on the light, and her eyes widen as she sees red blood flowing from the bathroom faucet in an otherwise monochromatic shot. Brief color scenes were not uncommon in low-budget black-and-white horror films in the late fifties and were featured in AIP's *I Was a Teenage Frankenstein* and *How to Make a Monster*. Nonetheless, the ingenious but simply executed mixture of color and black and white in this scene is unique to Castle: the sets and makeup were carefully painted to simulate monochrome, and the scene was shot in color. These brief color shots were then spliced into the release prints.

A hideous gurgling sound is heard as a bright red, blood-coated hand reaches out of the pool of gore. Martha clutches at her bathrobe and gingerly reaches out toward the hand as if unable to believe her eyes. Her back stiffens, and an electric bass guitar throbs a single low note in imitation of a heartbeat. The medicine cabinet swings open, revealing Martha's already completed death certificate, which she reaches out to touch. "Cause of death: FRIGHT," it reads. Her back stiffens, and she collapses on the floor dead.

The Percepto stunt occurs about fifteen minutes before the end of the film. Warren confronts Ollie about his role in Martha's death, while downstairs in the silent theater *Tol'able David* is showing on the screen to a piano accompaniment. The two-foot-long, antennaed, centipede-like tingler has broken out of the steel box in which Warren had placed it after Martha's autopsy. Now loose in the theater, the slimy monster creeps along the floor of the theater in parallel and rhyming action with the unwelcome advances of a young man toward his sweater-clad girl-friend. Ollie and Warren walk through the inner lobby and begin creeping around the rear of the auditorium looking for the tingler as the young woman moves away from her date to escape his groping. The tingler slithers down the aisle to where she is now seated alone and crawls onto her leg. She lets out a blood-curdling scream, and Warren turns on the house lights to the silent-movie auditorium.

At this point in the showing of *The Tingler*, a planted female in the auditorium screams in sync with the woman in the film, and the projectionist turns up the house lights as the image goes black. Further, the soundtrack is switched to the surround speakers at the rear of the house and ushers run down the aisle and place the "fainted" woman onto a stretcher. From the surround speakers, which correspond with Warren's position at the rear of the theater within the film, comes Vincent Price's warning: "Ladies and gentlemen, there is no cause for alarm. A young lady has just fainted and she is being attended to by a doctor and is quite all right, so PLEASE remain seated. The movie will begin right away." The house lights go back down as back onscreen Warren is shown turning the light switch in the film. *Tol'able David* begins again, and the tingler crawls through the porthole of the projection booth as Ollie and Warren search the floor between the seats in the theater. Suddenly, the film for both *Tol'able David* and, presumably, *The Tingler*, breaks, the soundtrack goes silent, and the screen goes white. The shadow of the tingler crawls across the screen, seemingly loose in the projection booth where the 1959 film is showing. The image goes dark, the house lights go completely down, and the sound is again switched to the rear speakers. Vincent Price's voice is heard for a second time from the rear of the house, along with ambient sounds of panicked moviegoers. "Ladies and gentlemen, do not panic but SCREAM, scream for your lives! The tingler is loose in this theater. If you do not scream, it may kill you!" The exhibitor's manual for *The Tingler* instructs the projectionist at this point to "give two pushes in rapid sequence" to the vibrating motors under the seats.[37] From the rear speakers moviegoers now hear the voices of terrified patrons shrieking, "Look out, it's under the seat!" "It's over here!" "It's on me! It's on me!" Vincent Price's voice breaks in again announcing, "Ladies and gentlemen, the tingler has been paralyzed by your screaming. There is no more danger. We will now resume the showing of the movie."

Warren and Ollie rush to the projection booth, where the tingler is choking the projectionist with its antennae. He cries out in terror, and the monster falls to the floor. The film then moves rapidly toward its conclusion. Warren captures the tingler in a 35mm film can, carries it upstairs, and replaces the tingler inside Martha's corpse. He accuses

Ollie of murdering Martha as surely as if he had shot or stabbed her. Warren walks out of the apartment, and the cowardly Ollie is unable to shoot him as he leaves.

After Warren has left, Ollie moves toward the bedroom door in an effort to leave, but the door slams in his face. Martha sits up in bed, the blood drained from her face except for black pools around the eyes, which stare straight ahead in a trance. At this point the projectionist's instructions read, "When the wife raises up from under the bedsheet, keep pushing the [buzzer] control until the end of the picture." While the auditorium seats vibrate, Ollie is paralyzed with terror. He stares wide eyed into the camera like the condemned prisoner from the beginning of the film. The image fades to black as we hear the collapse of his shattered corpse onto the floor. In a return to Castle's onscreen warning at the beginning of the film, the rear speakers boom once more with the extra-diegetic voice of Vincent Price, which intones, "Ladies and gentlemen, just a word of warning. If any of you don't believe you have a tingler of your own, the next time you are frightened in the dark — don't scream."

The admonition of Vincent Price/Warren Chapin at the end of *The Tingler* brings the film full circle to the snide "warning" provided by William Castle before the opening credits. This final bit of direct address also recalls Henri Jarrod's words to his patrons in *House of Wax*. These spoken words in the darkened theater served as a parting shot from the mountebank showman as the shaken fairgoer leaves the darkened tent and makes her or his way back to the open air of the carnival midway. American International Pictures and director Roger Corman would soon use this increasingly extravagant Price persona as a linchpin in their move to middle-bracket genre releases in color and widescreen.

The AIP Poe adaptations such as *House of Usher* (1960) and *Pit and the Pendulum* (1961) were not the first releases of Nicholson and Arkoff's company in widescreen. Corman's *Day the World Ended* was released in the SuperScope process in winter 1956. Introduced in the middle of the small-exhibitor backlash against expensive technological upgrades, SuperScope was a variable anamorphic system that had been praised by a watchdog committee of exhibitors' group Allied States Organization as an affordable system for the small operator.[38] The manufacturers of the system sold the lens outright to large circuits, made it available for rental, and in "hardship cases" actually provided it to the exhibitor at no cost.[39] The excursion into widescreen by AIP that followed was even more well suited to the parsimonious exhibitor. The Superama system provided a 2:1 aspect ratio on standard 35mm by using a process similar to the "printing down" of wide-gauge film to 35mm and required no extra projection equipment. *Machine Gun Kelly* and *The Bonnie Parker Story* were released by AIP in Superama.[40]

For the first several years of the company's existence, AIP released its films in preconstituted double features like 1957's *I Was a Teenage Werewolf* and *Invasion of the Saucer Men*, which were marketed to drive-ins, neighborhood theaters, and, in the slow seasons, deluxe downtown houses. The company realized that it could not demand the rental terms of a major studio blockbuster from exhibitors. As James Nicholson told *Variety*, "We can put out a package for $400,000, then offer it to a theatreman for the same terms he would receive for one middle-bracket picture. This way, he's saved the trouble of going out and finding a second feature.[41]

By 1960, the major studios had mastered the art of the saturation-booked preconstituted double feature and were able to place their product in a wide variety of situations. In 1958, Paramount hired director Gene Fowler Jr. to duplicate the success of his *I Was a Teenage Werewolf* with *I Married a Monster from Outer Space*, which went out on a double bill with indie Jack Harris's *The Blob*. In 1960, Paramount released Hitchcock's *Psycho*, the film that completely changed the standard for the low-budget, black-and-white shocker. At the other end of the industry, companies like Astor Pictures and Crown International were releasing quickie films like *Frankenstein's Daughter* and *Bloodlust* (both 1959) that would make even the penurious Arkoff blush. The continued success of AIP would have to be based on distinguishing their product from what *Motion Picture Herald* called "catch-penny opportunists who seek to take fly-by-night advantage of an era of scarcity by whipping out on minimum money a film that has little but running time to fill a desperate theater exhibitor's screen and marquee."[42] Nicholson told *Variety* that the films that smaller companies were making in imitation of the AIP product were "poorly written, brutal for sensationalism alone, and dishonestly advertised."[43]

Even long-time budget producer and chain exhibitor Robert Lippert had moved away from an exclusive roster of low-budget programmers. In 1960, he formed Associated Producers, a company designed to provide middle-bracket films inbetween major studio fare and Sam Katzman–style programmers. One of Lippert's most notable early productions at Associated Producers was an attempt to combine elements of horror and the psychological thriller with Alain Resnais–derived alienation: *Psycho*'s Robert Bloch scripted Lippert's 1962 widescreen remake, *The Cabinet of Dr. Caligari*, returning the horror genre to its original source.[44]

Back at AIP, Nicholson and Arkoff realized that in order to graduate to the realm of the middle-bracket picture, AIP needed to secure the services of a recognizable star. They must have noticed that color, CinemaScope, and the performance of Vincent Price were crucial elements of the success of *The Fly* in 1958, and that Price's presence had given a minimal respectability to the outrageous Castle films.

In December 1959, Arkoff announced AIP's plans to release fewer films with higher budgets as part of the company's attempts to become the industry's "ninth major."[45] AIP's *Pit and the Pendulum* (1961), the second film in the Corman Poe cycle after *House of Usher* (1960), represents the studio's new approach to distribution and more upscale films in color and widescreen. *Pit and the Pendulum* was produced and directed by Corman, and although the film is copyrighted under his Alta Vista Productions it is clearly an attempt by Nicholson and Arkoff to seek a better seat at the distribution table. Pathé Labs, which had underwritten several of AIP's earlier productions[46] and owned a percentage of Alta Vista in exchange for deferrals, was a natural choice for AIP's lab work. The widescreen Panavision cinematography, lush color, prestigious (but public domain) literary source, period sets and costumes in imitation of the English product, and presence of Vincent Price in the role of Don Nicolas Medina all signal a move to the "middle-bracket picture" advocated by many in the distribution and exhibition branches of the industry. Further, the Poe adaptations would increasingly be released during peak periods of the year, signaling AIP's growing confidence regarding its role in the competitive distribution marketplace.

The Poe adaptations also represent a new phase in the Vincent Price star persona, and they recast motifs from both *House of Wax* and the Castle films such as *House on Haunted Hill* and *The Tingler* against the background of an increasingly stylized performance. Price's acting style would come to suggest both nineteenth-century melodrama and popular notions of "highbrow" or "Shakespearean" stage performance. *Pit and the Pendulum* is a combination of two sets of motifs that had come to coalesce around its two stars: the *Bridey Murphy* doppelganger motif had motivated Barbara Steele's dual role in AIP's import hit *Black Sunday* (1961) (see chapter 6), and the cuckolded husband and the plot to drive the protagonist insane is derived from *House on Haunted Hill*.

Richard Matheson's screenplay for *Pit and the Pendulum* provides Poe's short story with a labyrinthine backstory of family horror derived from AIP's *House of Usher* of the previous year. Francis Barnard (John

Kerr) comes to the Spanish castle of Don Nicolas Medina after learning that his sister, Medina's young wife, Elizabeth (Barbara Steele), has died suddenly. Suspicious of the secrecy of Nicolas about Elizabeth, Francis presses Nicolas, his sister, Catherine Medina, and Nicolas's best friend, Dr. Charles Léon, for details of the family's shameful past. He discovers that Nicolas's father was the dreaded inquisitor Sebastian Medina and that Elizabeth may have been accidentally buried alive.

The film begins with an abstract wash of colors across the Panavision frame, liquid rivulets that resemble the oil transparencies used in acid-rock light shows later in the decade. On the soundtrack, Les Baxter's atonal score features electronically altered pizzicato strings and crashing percussion. The colors coursing across the frame, waves of yellow, red, and purple, then yellow and blue, and finally red, purple, blue, and green, will be the colors to which the entire image becomes tinted later in the film's scenes of torture, madness, and murder. A lone carriage is drawn along the beach taking Francis Barnard to the castle of Don Medina. Like *House of Usher*, *Pit and the Pendulum* begins with a lone young man arriving at the gloomy ancestral castle over which the grieving and neurotic Vincent Price presides. The coachman refuses to carry Francis further, and, like Jonathan Harker in countless screen adaptations of *Dracula*, the young man proceeds on foot.

In contrast to Hammer Films's tiny but meticulously dressed period sets, Daniel Haller's cavernous sets are sparsely decorated with often outsized props and provide the film's most self-consciously upscale mise-en-scène. The front door leads into the enormous central hall. Dinner is served at the ornate banquet table, which fills the entire Panavision frame as the camera peers through the flames of the huge fireplace. An ornamental gate in the hall leads to the network of corridors which lead through increasingly fortified metal gates into both the torture chamber and the mausoleum. As in *House of Wax* and *Curse of Frankenstein*, transgression of these boundaries leads to smaller spaces still: behind the wall of the mausoleum is Elizabeth's crypt, inside of which is the stone vault and the wooden coffin, and the torture chamber contains both the iron maiden and the upright human cage into which Elizabeth will be locked. Behind another locked door is the final forbidden secret, the cavernous room which contains the castle's ultimate horror, the pit and the pendulum.

One of the film's most distinctive elements is the interaction of Price with the decor. Although Price's well-publicized expertise in gourmet cooking had added a sizable avoirdupois since his role as the gaunt Roderick Usher the year before, blowsy robes and a mane of curly hair create a neurasthenic, epicine appearance for Nicolas Medina. The character moves from room to room in an almost swooning caricature of grief and distraction. Elizabeth's bedroom, kept just as she left it like the bedroom of the first Mrs. DeWinter in *Rebecca*, is full of fetishized props, including a large portrait for Price to emote over. The torture chamber is the inverted mirror image of the eroticized space of Elizabeth's bedroom: like Henri Jarrod's chamber of horrors, the space of this room channels sexual impulses into sadism and mutilation. In words that could be taken from a nineteenth-century dime novel, the mouth of a carnival barker, or a horror-film one sheet, Nicolas reveals that the torture chamber was his father's inner sanctum: "This was my father's world, Mr. Barnard . . . Was he not my father? Am I not the spawn of his depraved blood?" He leans on the upright cage that will twice imprison Elizabeth, and continues: "Suffice it that the blood of a thousand men and women were spilled within these walls, limbs twisted and broken, eyes gouged from bloody sockets, flesh burned black."

Later, in a flashback told by Nicolas's sister, Catherine, we see Nicolas as a boy, wandering into his father's torture chamber and examining the hideous instruments inside. When he hears his parents' voices, he hides in an alcove and observes his father, Sebastian, played in the flashback by Vincent Price, leading his mother, Isabel, and his Uncle Bartolome into the room. Sebastian, a hunchbacked, sneering figure seemingly based on a ham actor's conception of Shakespeare's Richard III, leads his wife and brother through the torture chamber in the manner of a fairground showman. In a red-toned image, Sebastian, waving a smoking hot poker in the air, suddenly strikes a savage blow to the neck of his brother, Bartolome. The mother, her image anamorphically distorted as if in a fun-house mirror, screams in terror in a yellow-tinted close-up. "Then, he turned on her, accusing her of vile acts of debauchery," Catherine explains, and Sebastian's face is refracted wildly out of shape in another red-toned close-up. Before the viewer can see any of the sexual torture that follows (this is not an Italian film, after all), the film cuts to a close-up of the weeping Catherine saying, "In front of Nicolas's eyes, our mother was tortured to death. Ever since that day, Nicolas has been unable to live as other men." This thinly disguised reference to Nicolas's impotence continues the cuckolded effeminacy that ran through the Castle films and Jarrod's chamber of horrors and would become increasingly foregrounded in the Vincent Price persona as the Poe series and its spin-offs continued in the decade.

For the rest of the film, many elements, most notably camera movement, color, music, and the performance style of Price, become increasingly stylized and self-conscious. After discovering a female corpse that had been buried alive in Elizabeth's coffin (is it his mother's? as in *Psycho*, we never find out "who's that buried" there) Nicolas is so unhinged that he pulls out a pistol from the dresser to commit suicide, but before he can shoot he is stopped by Catherine, who then leads him off to put him to bed. In his bedroom, he places his hands on his head and agonizes over his own possible insanity. Later, in the catacombs, he walks to Elizabeth's tomb and looks inside. Her bloody hands suddenly reach out and clutch at the sides of the vault. Nicolas is paralyzed with fear in this scene, which is a virtual replay of Mrs. Higgins's confrontation with the grasping hand in the bathroom in *The Tingler*. He flees in terror as a backlit Elizabeth follows him down the hall. Suddenly, Elizabeth is shown in close-up, her beautiful, cadaverous face is wide-eyed with a broad and evil grin. "Nicolas!" she screams in triumph.

With her adulterous partner, Doctor Léon, at her side, Elizabeth torments her husband with a catalog of his suffering: "So, my darling Nicolas, we've broken you at last . . . Is it not ironical, my love? Your wife, an adulteress? Your mother an adulteress? Your uncle an adulterer? Your best friend an adulterer?" Nicolas, his eyes blank, begins to laugh distractedly as the soundtrack plays his childhood theme. He struggles to his feet, and begins to address them as Isabel and Bartolome. "How do you like my workshop?" He begins to walk in his father's crippled shuffle. "I thought the two of you would enjoy the novelty of it. Come. Let me show you about a bit." He hits the doctor with a poker, who then falls to his death in the pit, and grabs Elizabeth. "Before the day is over, you will beg me to kill you to relieve you of the agony of hell into which your husband is about to plunge you."

Francis is also mistaken for Bartolome by the insane Nicolas and is knocked unconscious. He awakens tied to a slab in the enormous chamber that houses the pit and the pendulum. Price's acting style now reaches new heights of delirium, and Richard Matheson's lines, characterized by *Variety* as "the fruitiest dialog heard on the screen in a couple of decades,"[47] are a high-water mark of hysterical pseudoerudition:

Do you know where you are, Bartolome? . . . You are about to enter Hell, Bartolome. *Hell!* The nether world, the infernal regions, the abode of the damned [here the film cuts between images on the walls with every phrase], the place of torment, pandemonium, Abath, Totht, Gehenna, Naraka, *The Pit!*—and the pendulum, the razor edge of destiny. Thus the condition of man, bound on an island from which he can never hope to

Amour fou à la AIP: a swooning Price is tormented by the evil Barbara Steele in *Pit and the Pendulum* (Wisconsin Center for Film and Theater Research).

The climax of *Pit and the Pendulum* showcased both Price's delirium and Daniel Haller's expressionistic torture chamber set (Wisconsin Center for Film and Theater Research).

escape, surrounded by the waiting pit of Hell, subject to the inexorable pendulum of fate, which must destroy him finally.

The pendulum begins to swing, and in an oblique and foreshortened composition Francis lies on a gray slab, dressed in a white shirt, black pants, and black boots. The only splash of color is the red handkerchief in his mouth. After Catherine summons the servant Maximilian to help her break into the chamber, an optically printed grainy close-up of Francis's terrified eyes recall the sinister glares of the portraits of Sebastian and Elizabeth. The colors that washed under the credits and tinted the flashback sequences now dominate the image. A close-up of Nicholas is tinted red, and canted-angle shots of the charcoal inquisitors are tinted green, blue, yellow, and blue again as they are cut in time to the whoosh of the swinging pendulum. The blade begins to cut into Francis's chest, and the swath of blood echoes the red handkerchief in his mouth.

After a struggle with Maximilian, Nicolas falls to his death in the pit. Catherine and Maximilian are then able to stop the gears and raise the now-bloody pendulum from Francis's chest. As Francis, Catherine, and Maximilian leave the room, the camera cranes down into the pit, past the body of the doctor and into Nicolas's bloody and sightless death stare. Outside, the three mount the stairs of the torture chamber, and as Catherine looks down into the room before closing the heavy wooden door, she says, echoing Nicolas's earlier line, "No one will ever enter this room again." Suddenly, a whip pan right reveals a close-up of the terrified staring eyes of the caged Elizabeth, struggling to scream through her gagged mouth, her bloody fingers protruding through the bars of the cage.

Pit and the Pendulum was a huge commercial success, reaching the number-five position in rentals for the month of September 1961, and its two-week engagement at the Stanton in Philadelphia grossed over $26,000.[48] By year's end, the film had amassed $1.2 million in domestic rentals, and sub-run engagements promised another $800,000.[49] The success of *Pit and the Pendulum* underscored several trends that Corman and AIP would continue to exploit successfully over the next few years. The collaboration with Pathé Labs would help AIP switch the preponderance of its yearly releases to color, and Pathé would provide the initial financing for Corman's Poe follow-up, *The Premature Burial*, as well as for Corman's only box-office failure, the civil-rights drama *The Intruder* (1962). The release schedule for AIP would continue to feature fewer films, higher production values, and more releases in color and widescreen: *Pit and the Pendulum* was the centerpiece of the company's "New Horizons Project 61" release plan, which Nicholson described as "a blockbuster a month."[50]

In order to fill this release schedule, AIP would increasingly rely on both the acquisition of features produced abroad and coproduction deals with studios in England and Italy. Two of AIP's biggest successes of 1960 were its U.S. releases of two horror films from England's Anglo-Amalgamated, Ltd., *Circus of Horrors* and *Horrors of the Black Museum*. At the same time, the later films in the Poe cycle, particularly *Masque of the Red Death* (1964) and *Tomb of Ligea* (1965) both produced in England, would be characterized by the increasing influence of the international art cinema in their overt symbolism, stylized color, and flashback narrative structure. The confluence of genre cinema and art cinema would characterize much of the horror film for the rest of the sixties, and this change points to the growing international market for the genre film. This, along with the efforts of filmmakers, distributors, and exhibitors to exploit a period of relaxing censorship, would permanently alter the landscape of American horror cinema.

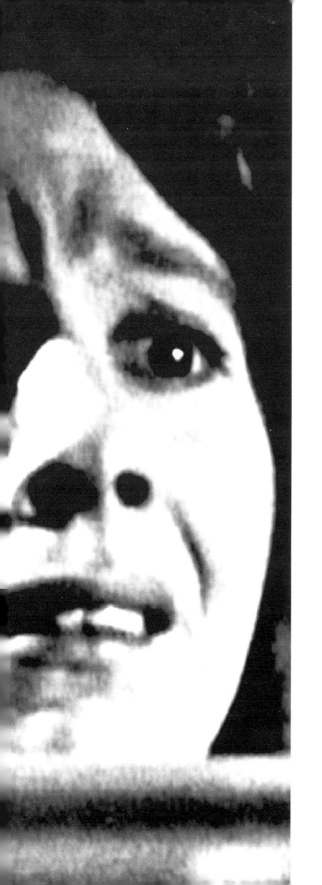

CHAPTER 5

Grind House or

Art House? Astor Pictures

and *Peeping Tom*

In her writing about the early-sixties growth of American neighborhood theaters specializing in foreign films, Joan Hawkins recounts the story of a 1960 protest by residents of Fort Lee, New Jersey, when a local theater converted to an "art house" programming policy. She cites a *Variety* article in which a local pastor stated that "it is a known fact that many of the foreign films are without a doubt detrimental to the morals of the young and old."[1] Throughout this period, movies imported from abroad such as *Wages of Fear* (1952), *And God Created Woman* (1957), and *Diabolique* (1955) contained nudity, violence, or other images forbidden by Hollywood's Production Code and thus carried both highbrow and lowbrow associations. The appearance of these films on American screens was made possible by the recession and retrenchment of the American film industry: in 1960 the combined releases of the American majors numbered only 226 films,[2] which sent neighborhood theaters on a wild scramble for product irrespective of country of origin.

These films from abroad were often marketed to both the "lost audience" of older, educated moviegoers and the downscale urban audience that frequented theaters designated by the business as "skin palaces" and "action houses." In addition to these crossover films, some distributors divided their release schedule into art-film and exploitation categories. According to a 1961 article in *Variety*, "The same guy who may gamble his shirt to acquire and promote an avant-garde pic about Uruguayan social conditions may also, with another subsidiary, be distributing a nudie epic titled *Falling Fig Leaves*."[3]

Long-time importer and distributor Astor Pictures attempted to capitalize on many of these developments in distribution and exhibition. After changing ownership in 1959, the company began an intensive expansion campaign. In 1961 Astor scored big with its American release of Fellini's *La dolce vita* on the strength of a highly successful crossover to a general audience. Less known is the distributor's handling of a number of horror and exploitation films from both the United States and abroad.

One of the company's least successful of these releases was a film that is today considered one of the most accomplished works in the history of the horror genre, Michael Powell's *Peeping Tom* (1960), which Astor released simultaneously to the genre, art-house, and exploitation markets in 1962. *Peeping Tom*'s hybrid status as art film and horror-exploitation entry had its roots in the efforts of both its English production company, the Archers, and its American distributor, Astor Pictures, to create a film that would appeal to the established programmer market as well as serve as a prestige item for its handlers. *Peeping Tom*'s abject failure on both counts points to several often-ignored parallels between the genre and art-film markets in the United States.

While former subsequent-run houses like the Fans Theater in Philadelphia were relying on the moderate but consistent audience for genre films, other theaters were responding to the retrenchment of the postwar period by converting to art houses and showcasing foreign and offbeat American films. "After the *Paramount* decision, throughout the late 1940s and the entire 1950s, many a theater owner began to seek an alternative to closing," writes Douglas Gomery. "Long under the thumb of the power of the Hollywood circuits, [they] struggled to find profitable niches in the new post-war filmgoing culture."[4] As Harry Brandt of the Independent Theater Owners of America stated in congressional hearings in 1956: "There is a great move on foot to import pictures from other nations. And some of those are being shown on the screens of your home town and mine."[5] These independent theaters were walloped by the movie industry recession, which increased competition for the fewer and fewer films released by the majors. In late 1954, Edward Hyman of the divorced American Broadcast-Paramount Theaters circuit suggested that even the smallest subsequent-run houses, with their three-times-a-week program changes, consider booking imports midweek.[6] With this prospect, the exhibitor had the opportunity both to bring the "lost audience" of older, more educated consumers back into the nabes by offering a product clearly different from television fare[7] and to cross foreign films over to a general audience. A 1956 survey of exhibitors revealed that an average of 76 percent of all theaters, including 64 percent of small-town theaters, had booked at least one broadly defined foreign picture during the 1955–1956 season.[8]

The growth of the art theater is yet another result of the product shortage of the late fifties. As Barbara Wilinsky notes, many of the art theaters that appeared after the war were former subsequent-run houses that had suffered from the extended first-run playoffs and high rentals of

Hollywood product.[9] By 1957, Philadelphia had twelve houses listed as art theaters in the *International Motion Picture Almanac*, with five instituting the art programming policy full time.[10] In addition to the upscale World, Trans Lux, and Arcadia art houses in the Center City section of Philadelphia, the rest of the art theaters in the city were neighborhood houses for whom the art policy meant different things. On Philadelphia's near west side, which encompasses both the University of Pennsylvania and Drexel campuses, the Eureka, like the downtown arties, played a full compliment of English and European imports as well as American independents. Other upscale art theaters were located in (then) wealthier neighborhoods, such as the north Philadelphia Wayne Theater, the Green Hill in Overbrook, and the Wayne Avenue in northwest Philadelphia.

Some nabe art houses, such as the Locust and the Spruce, located in predominantly African American west Philadelphia, and the Studio, located on the near east side of town, became increasingly reliant on domestic and imported exploitation films to fill their playdates. Throughout the sixties, these theaters, the Studio in particular, adopted an adults-only policy and became the primary showcases for domestic "nudie cuties" like *The Immoral Mr. Teas* (1959) and *Eve and the Handyman* (1960) and imported nudist-camp films like *As Nature Intended* (1962). These theaters, and many others like them in other cities, would also book more conventional imports and promote them with sensational advertising. Wilinsky notes that

> because of the connection between foreign films and risqué entertainment, "grind houses" specializing in exploitation films . . . also showed foreign films. Grind houses, predominantly run by independent operators, searched, like art houses, for inexpensive films to fill their screen time. Foreign films offered these theaters, like art houses, a practical alternative. Not surprisingly, these theaters tended to promote the sensational attractions of art films.[11]

Distributors were quick to respond to this development. In the middle of the fifties, distributors as varied as Italian Film Export's distribution arm, IFE Releasing, and Columbia subsidiary Kingsley International would attempt to move their product beyond the art theater and into general release as dubbed supporting features. To this end, Kingsley's 1954 release schedule included the Graham Greene adaptation *Brighton Rock*, retitled *Young Scarface*, which highlighted its gangster genre elements, and Max Ophuls's *Le plaisir*, retitled *House of Pleasure*, which helped its bookings in some adults-only houses.[12]

In 1957, the huge success of Kingsley's release of the French import *And God Created Woman* was not the result of an art-film "auteur" status of director Roger Vadim; rather, audiences flocked to theaters to witness the unrestrained sexuality and onscreen nudity of the twenty-three-year-old (but "barely legal" appearing) Brigitte Bardot. Kingsley promoted the film with arch newspaper ads describing the film as "a study in rounded surfaces." *Variety* soon concluded that the increased popularity of foreign product in U.S. theaters was largely due to "the expanding volume of European production aimed at the US exploitation market."[13] In 1956, Columbia paired its release of *1984* with another import, the mind-control sci-fi programmer *The Gamma People*, which shared more with Hammer's *Quatermass II* than with George Orwell.[14] And in 1962 United Artists import subsidiary Lopert Pictures gave Georges Franju's *Les yeux sans visage* the new title of *The Horror Chamber of Dr. Faustus*, teamed it with the low-budget programmer *The Manster*, and dumped it into limited release in theaters that specialized, according to Carlos Clarens, "in nudist and sadist fare."[15] The most famous sequence in *Les yeux sans visage*, a gruesome facial skin graft taken from an unwilling and drugged female victim, shown in unflinching close-up, was excised for the film's American release.

Hawkins sees the release of this package as an example of the fluid and ambiguous categories of horror and art cinema. She points out that

> posters and ads for the double bill stress both high- and low-culture connections. The copy for *The Manster*—"See the two-headed killer creature," "Half Man-Half Monster," "Invasion from the Outer World By a 2-Headed Creature-Killer"—links the "Master Suspense Show!" to carny freak shows, tabloid journalism, and B horror flicks. But the copy for *Horror Chamber of Dr. Faustus*—"worthy of the great horror classics of our time," "selected for special showings at the Edinburgh film festival," "a ghastly elegance that suggests Tennessee Williams"—stresses that film's connection to the sacralized world of legitimate theater and international film festivals.[16]

In Philadelphia, the *Dr. Faustus* and *The Manster* combination opened at the Stanley Warner Palace Theater on Market Street in fall 1962. This action house, located several blocks east of Center City near Chinatown, became the downtown showplace for genre films in the Philadelphia market. In a sure sign of the theater's downscale status, newspaper ads prominently proclaimed that the theater was "open all night." Featured double bills at the Palace would begin their "grind" early in the morning, around eight A.M., and continue uninterrupted until the theater

Lopert Pictures's newspaper ad for the *Horror Chamber of Dr. Faustus* and *The Manster* double feature package (Wisconsin Center for Film and Theater Research).

closed around three or four A.M. A genre or exploitation film would play for several days at the Palace as a sort of "first-run engagement," then be released to neighborhood theaters in multiple openings the following week. After its run at the Palace, the Lopert horror package opened at twelve neighborhood theaters, some of which, like the Midway, the Savoia, and the Leader, were also part of the Stanley Warner circuit.

An entire distribution network evolved to provide product for theaters like the Palace and its neighborhood offshoots. Like Howco, McLendon, and AB-PT in the exploitation field, these firms were often financed by chain exhibitors. The efforts of Continental Releasing, Distributors Corporation of America, and Astor Pictures to place their imports into both art houses and neighborhood theaters were often part of an operation that also included supplying program pictures to the genre market. According to a 1954 article in *Variety*, many successful foreign imports served the function of compensating for the decline in B movie production by the majors rather than expanding the market for the art film.[17]

This could lead to interesting cross-marketing. In 1961, respected art distributor Janus Films's huge push to establish crossover popularity for its Ingmar Bergman catalog included an aggressive courting of the drive-in market for the Academy Award–winning *Virgin Spring* ("We strongly recommend this film for adults only") and the retitled *Secrets of Women* and *The Devil's Eye*.[18] Later, Janus released to low-end art theaters several exploitation films catering to the nudie audience, including the British *Some Like It Cool* in 1962.[19] Some art distributors set up subsidiaries to handle exploitation product, such as Times's subsidiary Victoria Films, which released such titles as *Beat Girl*, *Pretty but Wicked*, *Scintillating Sin*, and *Lollipop*.

Often, distributors would attempt to cross over art and exploitation markets with a single film: United Motion Picture Organization's hugely successful 1956 release of Henri-Georges Clouzot's thriller *Diabolique* and Allied Artists's release of *The Hunchback of Notre Dame* the same year are notable examples of this trend.[20] In 1960, both Paramount's planned release of *Blood and Roses*—Roger Vadim's lesbian vampire gothic based on Sheridan LeFanu's *Carmilla*—and Janus's release of Bergman's *The Magician* were initially aimed at both the art and horror markets. Vadim's film received limited release as an adult art film because of its unsuitability to the juvenile horror market.[21]

Janus saw the sex-free *Magician* as a vehicle for breaking down the boundaries between mass and class entertainment in a wide release for Halloween 1959. Their newspaper ad for the film included a satanic-

VARIETY

Fifth Avenue Cinema (R&B)
[250-] $1.20-$1.80) — "Magician"
(Janus) (3d wk). Second round for
this Ingmar Bergman Swedish import is seen chalking up a record
$12,000 with N. Y. film critics tout-
ing pic as a classic. Initial stanza
was sock $10,500 with Invitational
premiere.

THE MAGICIAN

"A MASTERPIECE . . . nothing
short of miraculous." —The New Yorker·

"A jeweled horror tale" —N. Y. Mirror

ENGLISH VERSION AVAILABLE IN DECEMBER

Janus Films attempted to cross over Ingmar Bergman's
Magician to both the art-film and horror markets (New York
Public Library).

looking Max Von Sydow gazing at the viewer from the right margin
while bats flew across the top of the ad. The words "The Magician" appeared in ragged block letters identical to those used by the art depart-
ments of AIP and other distributors to promote horror movies. Trade ads
for the film quoted the *New York Mirror*, which called the film "a jeweled
horror tale."[22] Janus dubbed the film into English and obtained several
circuit bookings. *Variety* explained that "the reason Janus execs picked
. . . *The Magician* [instead of *Wild Strawberries* to distribute] is because of
what they describe as [the film's] 'horror-melodramatic' qualities. They
see it, in effect, as a sort of high-class *Tingler* and plan to exploit it as
such."[23]

Several of the distributors associated with the international art
cinema played a significant role in the release of horror films and other
genre pictures to the market in this period. Two of the most important of
these were Joseph Levine of Embassy Pictures and Walter Reade of Continental Distributing. Before forming Embassy and enjoying the commercial success of Vittorio De Sica's *Two Women* in 1961, Levine had successfully released the first two Hercules pictures starring Steve Reeves
and the Americanized version of Toho's *Godzilla* in the late fifties.[24] Like

Levine's Embassy, other art-film distributors were exhibitor-backed in this period of product drought. Continental Distributing, which would later balance its art-house releases with horror and science fiction programmers (see chapter 9), had been founded in 1954 by Theater Owners of America president Walter Reade.[25] Reade owned the Baronet Theater in New York and several more art houses and neighborhood theaters in the area.[26]

A company that handled theatrical distribution of several films later acknowledged as classics of either the art cinema or lowbrow genre cinema was Distributors Corporation of America (DCA), which was formed in 1954 by owners of the New York–area Century Circuit of thirty theaters. The company turned to foreign film distribution the next year with its acquisition of Henri-Georges Clouzot's *Wages of Fear*, an intense drama set in South America about a grueling cross-country trek in trucks filled with nitroglycerine.[27] Here DCA was trying to cross over between the art-house and action markets. *Wages of Fear* was almost certain to be denied a Production Code Seal because of its profanity and violence and thus would be readily booked only into art theaters that self-instituted an "adults-only" admissions policy. In an effort to market a film considered too ponderous for action houses, yet too violent for art theaters, DCA removed nineteen minutes from the film and found itself with little to market.[28] The following year DCA's British import *I Am a Camera*, the centerpiece of its 1955–1956 release schedule, was denied a seal because of dialogue about lesbianism and the main character's abortion.[29] President Fred Schwartz of DCA appealed the board's decision,[30] but the appeal was denied. As a result, DCA was unable to gain wide bookings for the film.[31]

For the remainder of the decade, DCA attempted to fill out its release schedules with foreign product, genre films from American independents, and reissues. In 1956, the company released the rock-and-roll programmer *Rock Rock Rock* and acquired the rerelease rights to a double feature of the noir classics *Brute Force* (1947) and *The Naked City* (1948).[32] In 1957, DCA announced that it would divide its release schedule into "top quality pictures, . . . exploitation package shows . . . [and] the best from the foreign market."[33] The company was able to deliver the exploitation packages it had promised. Negative pickups from abroad or from American independents kept the pipeline functioning at a relatively low cost. A package of the Toho import *Half Human* and the British *Devil Girl from Mars* was released by DCA in 1955, and the American indie *Monster from Green Hell* was teamed with Toho's *Rodan* in 1957. With $1.25 million in rentals, *Rodan* was DCA's biggest box-office

Ed Wood's *Plan Nine from Outer Space* (G. William Jones Film and Video Collection, Southern Methodist University).

success of the decade.[34] The company also released the imported duo of *Crawling Eye* and *Cosmic Monsters* in 1958 and a double bill of the British *Teenage Bad Girl* and the German *Teenage Wolfpack* in 1959. Later that year, DCA made film history when it released Ed Wood's *Plan Nine from Outer Space* on a double bill with a reissue of a previous Wood/Lugosi effort, *Bride of the Monster* (1955).

But because it was plagued by undercapitalization, DCA struggled to provide a steady flow of top-caliber releases. In 1961, company president Schwartz sought financing for its more ambitious plans through The Scranton Corporation, a Pennsylvania-based manufacturer that was making strong moves into diversification.[35] Soon an overextended Scranton Corporation faced reorganization under bankruptcy laws.[36] In 1962, with financing from Sig Shore's Vitalite Films, Schwartz bought the remnants of DCA from Scranton's trustees and formed Valiant Films,[37] which released the now-familiar mixture of art imports like the British *Angry Silence* and the Mexican Buñuel drama *The Young One*. Other releases included exploitation imports like the Peter Cushing melodrama *Mania*, a film based on the legend of nineteenth century graverobbers Burke and Hare,[38] and the Philippine-lensed horror film *Terror Is a Man*.[39] In 1961 Vitalite interests took over complete control of Valiant Films and continued to handle a wide range of art and exploitation product.[40] Much of the DCA catalog was sold to television in the sixties by program syndicator Flamingo Films (see chapter 7),[41] and Schwartz moved to MGM as head of special distribution projects, including art films, reissues, and pictures acquired abroad.[42] *Variety* pointed out that the purpose of this unit was "to sell what almost might be called castaway product," and Schwartz's experiences at DCA proved prescient: the biggest success of his tenure at MGM was the 1963 release of the imported horror combination of the British *Corridors of Blood* with Boris Karloff and the Italian programmer *Werewolf in a Girl's Dormitory*.[43]

Astor Pictures had been in business as an importer and distributor of supporting features since 1933. Like Embassy and Continental, Astor had attempted to exploit the seasonal product shortages that plagued neighborhood theaters.[44] Like DCA, it released both foreign imports earmarked for art houses and second-feature runs and AIP-like genre double bills. For example, Astor handled several Eady-subsidized British productions with American stars, releasing them in slow seasons, including the cloak-and-dagger drama *The Master Plan* (February 1955) starring Wayne Morris;[45] *Fear* (May 1956) starring a banished Ingrid Bergman;[46] *Passport to Treason* (May 1956) starring Rod Cameron;[47] and Hammer Films's *Men of Sherwood Forest* (September 1956) starring Don

Taylor.[48] In addition, in May 1953 Astor imported the Terence Fisher–directed *Four-Sided Triangle*, an android science fiction drama that anticipated the doppelganger theme and laboratory mise-en-scène of Fisher's later *Curse of Frankenstein*. The selling point of *Four-Sided Triangle* was, according to Astor trade ads, "the luscious Barbara Payton,"[49] and newspaper ads for the film used the "four SEEs" approach soon to be refined by Nicholson and Arkoff.[50] In the middle of the 1957 science fiction/horror boom, Astor contracted with American independent producer Marc Frederick for four "exploitation pictures with first consideration to entertainment values," according to Frederick.[51] The four were released in two combination packages, *She Demons* and *Giant from the Unknown* in March 1958,[52] and *Frankenstein's Daughter* and *Missile to the Moon* in October 1959.[53]

In 1959, company president Robert Savini died, and Astor, including its television subsidiary Atlantic Television, was bought by George Foley, public-relations executive, and Franklin Bruder, financier and executive vice president of City Stores, a successful retail chain that, like the Scranton Corporation, was seeking to diversify.[54] "It wasn't the Astor library which particularly interested Mr. Foley," according to a contemporary account in *Motion Picture Herald*, "It was rather the franchised dealers and distribution network which the company had established."[55] Foley and Bruder hoped to tap into an expanding market for the foreign film, taking advantage of the conditions in the film marketplace that were making imports more attractive to exhibitors[56] while using television promotion and music tie-ins, such as soundtrack albums, to highlight exploitable elements in their films for a class-to-mass crossover.[57]

Astor's most spectacular success with this strategy was its 1961 release of Fellini's *La dolce vita*, a coproduction of Italy's Riama Film and Cineriz. *La dolce vita* had been shopped around to the majors, and Columbia bought the rights for Great Britain and Latin America but declined to distribute it in the United States because the film's scenes of modern urban decadence, including sexual party games with a sadomasochistic flavor, were certain to result in the film's being denied a Production Code seal.[58] Astor paid Cineriz $625,000, an unheard of sum for an import (particularly from an independent distributor), for the U.S. rights to *La dolce vita*, and another $350,000 for its other major release of the 1961 season, Visconti's *Rocco and His Brothers*.[59] The company announced that it would release the subtitled Fellini film in key cities as a roadshow, a high-admission, reserved-seat engagement (also known as a "hardticket" booking) in deluxe downtown houses.

These engagements began in the orphan period of April 1961, and a dubbed print was announced for general release during the following summer.[60] In New York, *La dolce vita* played on a roadshow policy at the Henry Miller Theater, and the Michael Todd Theater was the site of the film's hardticket premiere in Chicago.[61] In Philadelphia, *La dolce vita* played a roadshow engagement at the Stanley Warner Boyd Theater downtown at a $2.75 admission and racked up over $17,000 in its first week.[62] By September, the film was playing in 162 theaters nationwide, including nine roadshow engagements.[63] Astor backed the film with massive radio and TV advertising, a soundtrack album from RCA, and a paperback novelization of the screenplay from Ballantine Books.[64] Despite receiving a "condemned" rating from the Legion of Decency, which threatened Catholic moviegoers with excommunication if they bought a ticket, hard or soft, *La dolce vita* succeeded beyond even Astor's wildest expectations: the film brought in $2.8 million in first-run rentals; reached the number-twelve spot in *Variety*'s list of 1961 releases; and enjoyed estimated total box-office receipts of $6 million after sub-run engagements well into 1962.[65]

Astor's releases in 1961–1962 can be broadly divided into two categories. The first category contained art imports such as *La dolce vita*, *Rocco and His Brothers*, Fellini's *Il bidone*, Alain Resnais's *Last Year at Marienbad*, Roger Vadim's *Les liaisons dangereuses*, Antonioni's *Il grido*, and Truffaut's *Shoot the Piano Player*. These films were designed for high-profile release in deluxe downtown houses backed by extensive promotion, including trade ads that featured portraits of the films' celebrity auteurs.[66] Some of these, particularly *La dolce vita* and *Les liaisons dangereuses*, could be exploited because of their sexual content and their lack of a Production Code seal. Astor's second category of films, "in the low-budget exploitation category," according to *Variety*,[67] could be handled through the company's established franchise dealers and distribution network and passed on to many of the houses that had been booking Astor product before the Foley/Bruder takeover. Here Astor was attempting to capitalize on the better terms and circuit bookings available in 1962 for foreign product able to cross over into the action and genre market.[68] Some of these films were imports and could be simultaneously promoted with art-house trappings and marketed to drive-ins, such as the Brazilian imports *Sun Lover's Holiday* and *The Girl in Room 13*. Other releases, such as *Yellow Polka-Dot Bikini* and *Festival Girl*, were earmarked for supporting-feature status in the art houses that had come to specialize in domestic nudie cuties and imports often misrepresented for the nudie market. Astor's efforts to cross over these markets with a single film helps to explain the strange fate of one of their 1961 releases, Michael Powell's *Peeping Tom*.

Peeping Tom was produced in 1959 by Powell's company, the Archers, which had retained that name after the departure of Powell's partner of many years, Emeric Pressburger. Powell and Pressburger had been responsible for many of the most critically acclaimed and popular British films of the forties, including *The Life and Death of Colonel Blimp* (1943), *A Canterbury Tale* (1944), *Black Narcissus* (1946), and *The Red Shoes* (1948). *Peeping Tom* was scripted by Leo Marks, a former code breaker during World War II who had a lifelong fascination with psychoanalysis. The film was director Powell's first British film after a two-year hiatus in Spain and was budgeted at $560,000.[69] Powell shot the film at Pinewood Studios with financing from distributor Anglo-Amalgamated, and he described *Peeping Tom* to the British trade press as a "Freudian thriller."[70]

The film tells the story of Mark Lewis (Carl Boehm), a voyeur and psychotic, whose now-deceased scientist father had subjected him to sadistic experiments as a child, including filming and taping his grimaces and cries of fear while torturing him with reptiles and sudden noises in the middle of the night. As an adult, Mark works as focus puller in a film studio by day, moonlights by taking pornographic pictures, and prowls the street at night with a hidden camera, murdering women with a bayonet affixed to his tripod while he films their faces in final agony. We later discover that the women are forced to watch their own death grimaces in a mirror attached to the camera. His first two victims are Dora (Brenda Bruce), a prostitute, and Vivian (Moira Shearer), an extra at the film studio.

Mark struggles against his compulsion and takes the first, halting steps toward friendship and romance with his downstairs tenant, Helen Stephens (Anna Massey), in spite of the objections of her sightless mother (Maxine Audley), who finds Mark secretive and stealthy. After murdering pinup model Millie (Pamela Green) during a photo shoot, Mark returns home to find that Helen has discovered his secret home theater and his homemade murder movies. As the police frantically attempt to break down the door to his studio, Mark commits suicide in front of Helen with his own weapon as preset still cameras record his death throes. The film ends with a shot of Mark's now-dark movie screen, while on the soundtrack we hear a taped exchange between the child Mark and his father, which ends with the child's tremulous, "Good night, Daddy. Hold my hand."

Forty years after its release, *Peeping Tom* remains an astonishing and eccentric concoction of highbrow and lowbrow elements. Screenwriter Marks and director Powell draw on both the cinema of attractions and the art cinema, and the film careens wildly between norms of fifties horror cinema and the tropes of self-reflexivity then current in the international art film. Mark Lewis, the tortured artist, possesses a lineage that includes both Max Von Sydow's Albert Emmanuel Vogler of *The Magician* and Vincent Price's Henri Jarrod of *House of Wax*. Mark's commercial work as focus puller in a film studio is paralleled in his more self-expressive work as a pornographer and, in his ultimate form of self-expression, his homemade snuff films. Like Jarrod, only total realism will satisfy him: at "Shepperfield Studios," hack director Arthur Baden is incapable of eliciting even the most rudimentary emotion from leading lady Pamela Shields. By contrast, Mark's adept direction of the bored pinup model Millie (he tells her "Look at the sea, please" to elicit a surprised expression) is mirrored in his compulsive search for the "perfect" face of fear captured forever on the screen of his private theater. In fact, Mark choreographs Pamela's swoon of terror when he arranges for the body of Vivian to be discovered on the set as he surreptitiously films her with his camera. "The silly bitch!" rasps the uncomprehending Baden, "She fainted in the wrong scene!"

The film also appropriates elements of psychoanalysis in its dizzying system of doublings and displacements. In one of the first images after the film's opening credits, Mark films the police taking Dora's body away on a stretcher through Newman Passage, site of one of Jack the Ripper's most famous murders. He is approached by a balding, mustached Cockney observer who looks a great deal like Michael Powell. Framed in Mark's viewfinder, he looks directly at the viewer and inquires, "What paper are you from?" Later, Powell actually appears onscreen in one of the home-movie flashbacks. Walking toward the stationary camera, Mark's father springs into focus and is revealed to be director Powell. The film provides Mark with another bald and mustached surrogate father figure, Mr. Peters, owner of the newsagent's shop and for whom he takes pornographic pictures. The film systematically associates these oedipal patterns with the self-reflexive trope: Peters is, through a narrative parallel, linked to studio head Don Jarvis who, like Peters, oversees the creative work of his minions while complaining of the money that their delays are costing him.

The cinematic "masterpiece" of Professor Lewis is an event we do not see, the on-camera goodbye kiss from Mark on the corpse of his mother. As Mark shows Helen his father's home movies, we see only her reaction. Also, we never see the projected image of Mark's mother. Why? The answer lies, I think, in the film's attempt to avoid an oedipal dimension that would have seemed almost laughably obvious: with his strawberry blond hair and round face, Mark seems to resemble his father very little. Further, while showing his home movies to Helen, Mark reaches for the living woman at the precise moment that he as a child reaches for his mother's lifeless arm on the movie screen. It seems safe to assume that the red-haired Helen (and the similarly hued Mrs. Stephens and Vivian) resemble Mark's mother; the prostitute Dora and pinup model Millie on the other hand resemble the evil stepmother, "her successor." After failing with Dora, Vivian, and Millie, Mark is unable to witness his own masterpiece, the look of abject terror on Helen's face when she inadvertently watches the filmed murder of Millie in Mark's absence — fairground-conjurer Powell allows us this privilege in a long and unbroken close-up take of her reaction to the film-within-the-film — and when he discovers her in his workshop, aware that she knows his secret, he turns his head away and pleads, "Don't let me see you frightened."

Peeping Tom ends, as does *The Tingler*, with a monster loose in the movie house (in this case, Mark's own private theater). It also ends, as does *House of Wax*, with the heroine trapped in the mad artist's lair. Mark turns both his camera and its fixed bayonet on himself and hurls Helen to the floor, knocking her unconscious before impaling himself. *The Tingler* ended with a blank screen and Vincent Price's admonition to the audience not to scream if they don't believe in the tingler. *Peeping Tom* ends with the same image, a blank theater screen and Mark's father speaking from beyond the grave, telling his son to "dry your eyes and stop." In the same way that Mark had turned a mirror on his victims and had turned his bayonet on himself, *Peeping Tom* turns back on Mark (and presumably the frightened audience as well) with his quivering, "Good night, Daddy. Hold my hand."

Peeping Tom was distributed in the United Kingdom by Nat Cohen and Stuart Levy's Anglo-Amalgamated, Ltd. of London and was one of three color horror films released by Anglo-Amalgamated in 1959. The others were the AIP coproduction *Horrors of the Black Museum* and the Independent Artists–produced *Circus of Horrors*. Although produced by different studios, the three Anglo horror releases of 1959–1960 have been called "the Sadean trilogy" by David Pirie, and are all obsessed with voyeurism, fetishized images of female disfigurement, and sadistic, Caligari-like patriarchal figures.[71] Unlike its Anglo companions, which were dismissed as mere genre programmers unworthy of seri-

Peeping Tom: "What paper are you from?" (Criterion Collection).

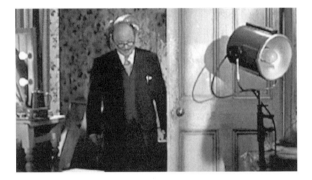

Peeping Tom: Mr. Peters, newsagent and pornographer (Criterion Collection).

Helen (Anna Massey) in *Peeping Tom* (Criterion Collection).

ous consideration, *Peeping Tom* received scalding reviews from an outraged British middlebrow press. However, contrary to director Powell's later statements and the received wisdom of film historians, the film was a modest commercial success in the United Kingdom, largely because of the highly publicized nude scene with famous pinup model Pamela Green.[72] Still, the film was not as successful as *Horrors of the Black Museum* and *Circus of Horrors*. Even those films lagged far behind the most successful films from Anglo during this period, the puerile *Carry On* sex comedies from producer Peter Rogers. *Carry on, Nurse* had topped the British box office in 1959.[73]

At this time, Anglo's Cohen and Levy were aggressively expanding both their handling of U.S. films in Britain and their forays into the U.S. market.[74] They had established a quid pro quo distribution deal with James Nicholson and Samuel Arkoff in which Anglo distributed AIP product in Great Britain. In exchange, AIP both released Anglo's films in the United States and financed coproductions in England that were eligible for government subsidies under the Eady plan. AIP distributed both *Horrors of the Black Museum* and *Circus of Horrors* in the United States in 1960. *Peeping Tom* briefly appeared on AIP's release chart in summer 1959, scheduled for release in summer 1960, but disappeared soon after.[75] It seemed that American distributors were skeptical of *Peeping Tom*'s ability to satisfy audiences that had flocked to see horror releases from Hammer, Castle, and AIP: *Peeping Tom* went begging for the entire 1959–1960 season.[76] Cohen and Levy's October 1959 trade ad showed its roster of five *Carry On* films in U.S. distribution from Governor Films and its two horror pictures from AIP. At the bottom of the ad is their entreaty to contact them for rights to two still-unsold properties from 1959, *Peeping Tom* and Joseph Losey's *Concrete Jungle*.[77]

Astor Pictures announced the American release of *Peeping Tom* to the trade press a year and a half later in July 1961. The film was initially listed as one of their prestige attractions and described as the "tentatively-titled Moira Shearer starrer produced and directed by Michael Powell for fall release."[78] Soon, however, star and auteur disappeared from Astor's trade publicity for the film, and genre elements were pushed into the foreground. A December ad in *Variety* reprinted a letter written to Astor sales rep George Josephs from the heads of the Interstate and Texas Consolidated circuits, which read: "We have just screened Astor's new horror movie, PEEPING TOM. With it's (*sic*) new approach, this English-made film is different, and was well received in our screening room. The photography and color were excellent, making it a very playable picture in our circuits."[79] In this ad, with its telling use of the word "different" and its praise for the film's color and photography, rare for horror film promotion, Astor was already hedging its bets on the film.

One can hardly blame them. The film departed from norms of the horror film in its disconcerting longeurs and in its emphasis on psychological rather than physical terror, making it likely to alienate horror fans used to Hammer and AIP product. On the other hand, it radically departed from the portrayal of "Britishness" familiar to postwar American art-film fans, from the Ealing comedies' middle-class eccentrics such as those played by Alec Guiness in *The Lavender Hill Mob* (1951) to the later "angry young man" roles such as Laurence Harvey's in *Room at the Top* (1959). The Catholic Legion of Decency gave *Peeping Tom* a B rating ("morally objectionable in part for all") and gave a clinically accurate description of its "voyeurism, developed in an atmosphere of sadism."[80]

From this point on, Astor's publicity for the film was heavily derived from Paramount's campaigns for *Psycho* and the Levine import *Jack the Ripper*. Newspaper ads for *Peeping Tom* screamed, "WARNING! Don't see "PEEPING TOM" unless you are prepared to see the screaming shock and raw terror in the faces of those marked for death! SEE IT FROM THE BEGINNING!" The ad showed the prostitute Dora getting undressed and a seminude model in profile, each with the tripod spike pointed at their throat. Above these pictures, framed against a brick wall (suggesting these women were streetwalkers), the ad read, "Marked for death by PEEPING TOM—TO LOOK MEANT DANGER / TO SMILE MEANT DEATH!"[81] These ads suggested yet another possible market for the film, nabe art houses that had instituted a policy of sexploitation films.

The Philadelphia release and playoff of *Peeping Tom* reflects its hybrid status as horror film, art film, and sexploitation entry. In September 1962, the film premiered on a double bill with another British thriller, Colorama's *Murder on the Campus*, at Philly's "showcase grind house," the Stanley Warner Palace on Market Street.[82] After an unusually unsuccessful two-day run (most engagements at the Palace ran five to seven days), *Peeping Tom* did not receive the expected multiple opening at the nabes the following week: it turned up in early October at the Ridge Pike drive-in in Conshohocken on a double horror bill with the four-year-old *Frankenstein—1970*.[83] The following week, *Peeping Tom* played a weeklong engagement at the Art Spruce in west Philadelphia and the Devon on Frankford in northwest Philadelphia on a double bill with *Gina*, starring Simone Signoret.[84] These two downscale nabe art houses specialized in archly marketed imports that attempted to cross over between the art and exploitation markets. For example, the week following the

Peeping Tom and *Gina* double bill the Devon played *Carry on Constable*, and the Art Spruce played *Love and the Frenchwoman* and the Brigitte Bardot film *The Truth* (advertised with the line "See Brigitte Bardot bare all in THE TRUTH!"), a combination that also ran that week at the nudie house New Broadway Adult Sho-Place.

It was in its incarnation as a sex film that *Peeping Tom* would enjoy a measure of success in the Philadelphia market. Four months later, in February 1963, *Peeping Tom* played at the Studio downtown, a house that was in the first stages of its transition to a skin palace, on a double bill with the nature film *Naked Island*.[85] This combination was held over for a second week, and the engagement brought in over $10,000 at the box office.[86] *Peeping Tom* returned to the Studio twice, once in November 1964 in a combination with *Passion Holiday*, which brought in $4,000 ("good" box office for the 383-seat house, according to *Variety*),[87] and again in February 1966 on a combination with *FE-Mail Special Delivery* ("SEE IT ALL! In Glorious 'Skin-Tone' Color!"). By the time of the latter engagement, the ambiguous and disturbing "voyeurism in an atmosphere of sadism" of *Peeping Tom* had begun to be unapologetically embraced within a whole subgenre of violent soft-core pornography from companies such as Cambist Films, Distribpix, Boxoffice International, and Entertainment Ventures.[88] For this particular market, *Peeping Tom's* newspaper ad shows the gazing male eye from the first image of the film with the simple tag line, "He waited—and he watched."[89]

Back in New York, Astor kept trying to repeat the success of *La dolce vita*, most notably with its December 1961 release of the similarly decadent and Legion of Decency "condemned" *Les liaisons dangereuses*. *Motion Picture Herald* pointed to the affinities between the Fellini and Vadim releases from Astor but expressed the opinion that the characters in *Liaisons* "are so completely vicious and depraved that they make their counterparts in the Fellini effort look almost normal and chaste by comparison."[90] Unfortunately for Astor, critical outrage in the *Herald* and other conservative publications was not balanced with the excellent reviews that had provided the countervailing force to *La dolce vita's* "condemned" rating. This lack of critical support resulted in Astor's securing only three hundred bookings for the film, leading to a loss on *Les liaisons dangereuses* of half a million dollars.[91]

In the meantime, the bills from Astor's massive expansion undertaken during the giddy days of *La dolce vita* were coming due: in 1961, the company had paid $1.3 million for the worldwide rights to *La dolce vita* from the film's original backers;[92] signed several international co-production deals, including a $3 million investment with Cineriz for

Fellini's $8\frac{1}{2}$ and other features;[93] formed a music publishing company;[94] and bought Pathé-American Distributing Corporation, including eighteen features and Pathé-American's nine exchanges.[95] Like Scranton's moves in acquiring interest in DCA, Astor had, in the words of an industry financier, engaged in a "too-rapid, over enthusiastic expansion of overhead."[96]

In January 1963, a new company called Astor Productions was incorporated in Albany, New York, and secured the American rights for Orson Welles's *The Trial*. The following month, Astor Pictures filed for Chapter 11 bankruptcy protection in New York Federal Court.[97] The reorganization and eventual demise of the company took another two years. In the fire sale held to pay Astor's creditors, the American theatrical rights to the English-language versions of *La dolce vita* and *Rocco and His Brothers* were eventually sold to another exploitation film company with international aspirations, the company that passed on the distribution of *Peeping Tom*: American International Pictures.[98]

CHAPTER 6

American International
Goes International:
New Markets,
Runaway Productions,
and *Black Sabbath*

The names of AIP's James Nicholson and Samuel Arkoff are usually absent from lists of importers of foreign art films in the 1960s. Arkoff, in particular, carefully polished his image as the crass, cigar-chomping philistine contemptuous of the pretensions of both art films and their audiences. In a 1974 interview, he complained of being surrounded by "so many goddamn artie-farties and pseudo-intellectuals in this business . . . Our whole civilization, unfortunately, has become one half-baked people . . . [And the audience is composed of] the intellectuals—there are about three in the whole country—the pseudo-intellectuals, of which there are a lot more, and the artie-farties, who are universal."[1]

In fact, AIP attempted to branch out into the art-film market in 1961 with their stateside handing of two British films, *Beware of Children* and *Portrait of a Sinner*. Also, in 1966 the company hoped to capitalize on the prestige of a possible Academy Award nomination for Sidney Lumet's *The Pawnbroker* by buying from distributor Allied Artists the rights to a circuit release of an edited version of the film.[2] These forays were not successful, partly because the company had no specialized advertising and publicity department to handle such releases.[3]

The successful international operations of AIP were the result of its capitalizing on trends in the international film industry that fit both its established corporate image and its efforts to increase both the number and quality of its annual releases. First, negative pickups, the outright buying of completed films, and coproductions with British and Italian studios enabled distributors Nicholson and Arkoff to add to their American release schedule features with production values far beyond what could be made for the same amount of money in Hollywood. Imports by AIP such as the Italian sword-and-sandal film *Sign of the Gladiator* (1960), and the Barbara Steele vampire film *Black Sunday* (1961), as well as coproductions such as *Horrors of the Black Museum* (1960) and *Black Sabbath* (1964) furnished product with sumptuous sets, costumes, and

technical artistry well beyond those of the company's in-house programmers. Second, international coproductions with England's Anglo-Amalgamated and Italy's Galatea and Italian International studios enabled
AIP's production arm to take advantage of government production subsidies and producers' rebates for the legally "British" and "Italian" films
partially financed by AIP. *Black Sabbath*, an international coproduction
by AIP, Rome's Galatea and Emeppi Cinematographica, and Paris's Société Cinématographique Lyre, is an example of Nicholson and Arkoff's
ability to differentiate its product from those by Hammer Films, William
Castle, and others by showcasing both the distinctive stylistic flourishes
of director Mario Bava and an increasingly recognizable AIP house style.

As part of the move into more upscale features such as the Poe adaptations in the early sixties, Nicholson and Arkoff realized, as had the
major studios before them, that profitable distribution of these higher-
budgeted features would require increased theatrical receipts from
abroad. Also, while seeking to expand its domestic release schedule,
AIP had observed Joseph Levine's purchase of foreign-made spectaculars
such as *Hercules* (1959) as well as horror films including *Jack the Ripper*
(1960), and they noted Levine's success at selling them to the American moviegoer. Finally, by 1960 all of the major studios had established
lucrative coproduction deals with studios in Great Britain and Europe.
These deals enabled Hollywood to use more of a film's budget on production values and less on labor and equipment costs while qualifying
for government subsidies as legally sanctioned "British" or "European"
productions.

American coproductions with the studios of Europe began shortly
after World War II as a result of the efforts of war-ravaged countries, including Italy and England, to block theater receipts from the major U.S.
studios in an effort to prevent large amounts of currency from leaving
their decimated economies. American companies could not take currency out of these countries in dollars, so coproductions were a way of
taking their earnings abroad in the form of motion pictures. Like most
smaller companies, AIP plowed virtually all of its earned money back
into production and could not afford to have its funds blocked in this
way. As a result, from 1954 to 1959 Nicholson and Arkoff concentrated
on the U.S. and Canadian box office. The overseas business of AIP was
largely confined to the open Latin American market.

Then, things began to change. Because of increased money available for international coproduction in Great Britain under the Eady plan
(see chapter 2), in 1957 AIP undertook in England its first coproduction

abroad (or "runaway" production), *Cat Girl*, which received Eady funding through coproducer Anglo-Amalgamated. For runaway productions like *Horrors of the Black Museum* and *Konga* (1961), Herman Cohen functioned as AIP's line producer working in England. Cohen and AIP put up half of the money, Anglo put up the other half (most of which came from the Eady Levy), and the rights were split: AIP received distribution rights in the Western Hemisphere (excluding the United Kingdom), and Anglo retained rights in the Eastern Hemisphere, where British colonial occupation had opened up a lucrative market for British films.[4]

Meanwhile, the easing of currency and import restrictions was underway in Italy. The Italian film trade organization, Associazione Nazionale Industrie Cinematographiche ed Affini (ANICA), eased both import restrictions and blocked currency throughout the fifties. Nicholson and Arkoff began their extensive operations in Italy in 1960, the year that blocked currency was ended. They escalated their activities in 1962, when ANICA, under the direction of its promarket director, Eitel Monaco, reached an agreement with Hollywood's Motion Picture Export Association to end the vestiges of the import quotas that had protected the Italian film industry throughout the fifties.[5] Both coproduction and expansion into the Italian theatrical market was initiated by AIP during this period. From its Italian operations, AIP would seek both inexpensive color theatricals for the American market and access to some of the money from the sizable Italian box office.

At first the company bought completed features including the Roman spectacle *Sign of the Gladiator*, a French-German-Yugoslav coproduction starring Anita Ekberg and Georges Marchal. While *Motion Picture Herald* announced that "*Sign of the Gladiator* now marks the company's entry into the big-budget, single-feature field," the film's publicity stressed the cinema-of-attractions "four SEEs" approach characteristic of its early genre pictures ("SEE The barbarian torture catacombs of horror!")[6] This is not surprising, because genre cinema accounted for more Italian product than the widely touted auteur cinema destined for American art houses. "Serious art house films are doing a constantly expanding business," wrote a trade journal in 1960, "but the major share of foreign earnings continues to go to the dubbed exploitation product."[7] In 1960 Joseph Levine's Warner release of *Hercules*, the Paramount-DeLaurentis *Tempest*, and AIP's two epic imports, *Sign of the Gladiator* and *Goliath and the Barbarians* accounted for over 90 percent of the $9.7 million earned by Italian imports.[8] The following year Italian imports earned $12.3 million, with dubbed spectacles accounting for at least two-thirds of this figure.[9]

In early 1960 all but a trickle of AIP's revenue came from the United States and Canada, and foreign marketing consisted largely of selling features outright to local distributors on a picture-by-picture basis. In February, Nicholson and Arkoff appointed William Reich as its first vice president in charge of foreign distribution.[10] Under his supervision and that of his successors Samuel Seidelman, Dave Horn, and Daniel P. Skouras, AIP would experience phenomenal growth during the sixties. By 1964, AIP was taking advantage of the decline in production from the majors by expanding its efforts in the world market, establishing operations in Japan, Hong Kong, South America, the Caribbean, the Philippines, Australia, and East Africa.[11]

In late 1960, AIP acquired another completed feature, Galatea's *La maschera del demonio*, which was, according to *Variety*, "a horror picture created for adult patronage."[12] Worldwide distribution rights (excluding Italy) were given to AIP for the "English-language" film (the actors had mouthed English on the set with all of the dialogue postsynchronized).[13] *La maschera*, the directorial debut of cinematographer Mario Bava, starred Barbara Steele in a dual role as both Princess Asa, a sixteenth-century vampire and satanist who had been burned at the stake, and her innocent nineteenth-century descendant, Katya. The film's plot, which concerned the resurrection of Asa and her vengeance on the dying noble family that succeeded her, bore a startling resemblance to the *Bridey Murphy* narratives of AIP's previous hits *The She Creature* and *The Undead* (both 1957), which feature regression and reincarnation. Armed with a product that fit well into production trends that the company had already successfully mined, AIP cut several scenes of extremely graphic violence and released the film in the slow season of February 1961 under the title *Black Sunday*. The film garnered both strong reviews and excellent box-office returns.[14] Star Barbara Steele, director Mario Bava, and the Italian horror film would all remain important to AIP's European activities.

Italy was not only a source of features, it also had a huge box office. In 1963, Italian moviegoers bought 740 million movie tickets,[15] which generated revenue of 132 billion lire—over $220 million.[16] Italy was both the largest national box office in Europe[17] (second only to the United States worldwide)[18] and the European country with the lowest cost line for American producers.[19] At the same time that AIP formed its arrangement with Anglo-Amalgamated in England, Globe International became the company's licensee in Italy.[20] It was under Globe's link with AIP that *Pit and the Pendulum*, through a huge local push by Globe, became an enormous hit in Italy in 1962.[21]

The codistribution arrangements were usually split by territory; Globe or another Italian company retained rights to Italy and AIP distributed the film elsewhere. In late 1964, AIP set up its own distribution organ in Italy, Sidis Cinematographica, financed by the American company but legally incorporated as an Italian firm. Problems had been encountered by AIP with extracting sufficient revenue from exhibitors and subdistributors due to underreporting of receipts (in the United States, Astor had bought the Pathé-America exchanges to bypass similar subcontractor hijinx). Next to Great Britain, Italy remained the biggest source of revenue for AIP. The formation of AIP's Sidis subsidiary marked the end of the deal with Globe, and later AIP even attempted to distribute through Sidis films coproduced with Italian partners.[22] In 1966, AIP would move its American International Pictures Export Corporation Headquarters from London to Rome. "The Italian capital," said AIP Export head Daniel Skouras, "is now the international marketplace for coproductions and sales," and Nicholson stated that most of the internationally produced films suitable for acquisition by the company were found in Italy.[23]

Why did a robust industry such as Italy continue to seek coproduction? First, American money kept film industry personnel employed. In addition, these coproductions were eligible for a number of plans designed to aid the local film industry. A united effort between the Italian government and the film industry had established incentives for both the exhibition and production of films legally classified as Italian. Out of the nationwide tax on theater tickets, exhibitors received postholiday rebates for showing Italian films and producers received a similar tax rebate for making films that earned local screen time.[24] The advantages of coproduction and cooperation were enumerated by ANICA president Eitel Monaco in 1960: "In exchange for liberal import, dubbing and distribution agreements here," he said, "we got low-cost financing, a lot of major U.S. pictures produced in our studios, U.S. participation in several major Italian spectacles, plus distribution of many of our pictures by major companies in the United States and throughout the world."[25]

The incentives for American companies to engage in coproduction were more obvious: 15 percent of federal admission taxes were rebated to the American coproducers. In the coproduction arrangements, the producers had to follow the strict rules of Italian nationality. This was accomplished by hiring a legally stipulated proportion of Italian crew and talent. Because of the lower wages paid to the Italian cast and crew, an American producer was capable of saving one-third of what an equivalent film would cost to produce in Hollywood.[26] Arkoff told *Variety* in

1966 that splitting territories with an Italian producer-distributor was a small price to pay: between the sum provided by the Italian studio and that available through the film aid law, "the amounts are often four times the sums provided when there is no co-distribution deal."[27]

AIP's most extensive and successful coproduction deal was with Fulvio Lucisano's Italian International Productions.[28] In a 1960 agreement, AIP contracted for ten films, two per year, in which AIP would provide two actors (these marquee names often counted for half the budget), the script, a supervisor for American dialogue, and an overall production supervisor. Lucisano provided the rest of the talent and production costs, while AIP retained distribution rights excluding Italy, France, and Belgium, which went to Lucisano.[29] This agreement produced *Warriors Five* (1962), Bava's *Planet of the Vampires* (1965) and *Dr. Goldfoot and the Girl Bombs* (1966), the espionage thriller *Spy in Your Eye* (1966), and Buster Keaton's last film, *War Italian Style* (1967).[30] By January 1962, AIP was alone among the American "major" studios and independents with more features being made abroad (fourteen) than in Hollywood (four).[31] In February 1963, AIP announced a deal with Galatea, original producers of the import hit *Black Sunday*, for a minimum of nine coproductions in the next eight years, with AIP retaining theatrical rights in English-speaking markets.[32]

Another crucial element of Italian/American coproduction was the star shortage in Italy. In Rome, proven box-office draws such as Sophia Loren, Gina Lollobrigida, Vittorio Gassman, and Marcello Mastroianni demanded salaries that only the major studios could afford. Thus, the Italian film industry became a second home for stars and featured players from America and elsewhere, and a 1960 *Variety* headline proclaimed, "half of Italy's stars [are] aliens."[33] One strategy that producers used to circumvent this star shortage was the episode film. In the episode film, three or more short narratives comprised the feature-length running time. This enabled producers, according to *Variety*, to "land marquee bait with minimum cash expenditure, [stars] only working for a few days on their cameos."[34] The most popular and successful of the episode films was *Yesterday, Today, and Tomorrow* (1963), which featured Sophia Loren in three roles. This trend continued through 1965 and included such films as *Compieiessi*, *Menage all' italiana*, and *Paranoia*. Another formula used by producers was the teaming of an up-and-coming or long-in-the-tooth American male with a young European ingenue, such as the tandem of Anita Ekberg and Georges Marchal in *Sign of the Gladiator*. These pairings came to characterize much of AIP's coproduction work in Italy, such as their 1964 release of the sword-and-sandal fantasy *Goliath and the Vampires*, featuring Gordon Scott and Gianna Maria Canale, and *Spy in Your Eye*, which teamed Dana Andrews with Pier Angeli.[35]

Another production trend, small but significant, in Italy in the early sixties was the horror film. By 1963–1964, many of the trade restrictions designed to protect the local film industry had been halted, and no comprehensive film aid law had been passed to take their place. By May 1963, several smaller Italian studios had folded, and financing from Italian banks was difficult to obtain without foreign guarantees.[36] As a result, money for film production was less readily available than in the previous two years. For local producers the more expensive sword-and-sandal pictures (which were beginning to saturate the U.S. market) gave way to horror films and westerns, which were less risky than spectaculars because they were relatively inexpensive to make and easy to sell for U.S. distribution, their primary market. In fact, Italian audiences disliked locally produced horror films so intensely[37] that the credits of Italian horror films were often Anglicized in the hope that moviegoers would think that they were British imports from Hammer or other companies.

The 1964 film *Black Sabbath* is an example of all of these trends: episode film, horror film, and the use of an imported male star and female ingenue as a response to the star shortage. For *Black Sabbath*, released under the title *I tre volti della paura* ("The three faces of fear") in Italy, AIP and Galatea retained director Mario Bava from *Black Sunday*, and AIP secured the services of marquee star Boris Karloff and leading man Mark Damon, who had been featured in the first of Corman's Poe adaptations, *House of Usher* (Damon's eight European films in eighteen months were cited as a record by *Variety*).[38] French cofinancing by Société Cinématographique Lyre brought the services of Michele Mercier and Jacqueline Perrieux (aka Jacqueline Soussard), and a key role was given to Galatea starlet Susy Andersen, later to appear in the AIP/Galatea *War of the Zombies* (1965). With this international cast, a key part of AIP's preproduction on the film included securing the services of Salvatore Billitteri of Titra Sound Corporation. Billitteri remained on the set throughout filming to supervise and plan the dubbing and, in the case of *Black Sabbath*, the transformation of the film for its American release.[39] This practice was in line with the growing awareness on the part of American producers that, in the English versions of European coproductions, English dialogue could no longer be mouthed phonetically but had to be executed in proper dramatic rhythm for its eventual looping by Titra and other specialists.[40]

In the first story of *Black Sabbath*, "The Drop of Water," an alcoholic and self-centered nurse (Jacqueline Soussard) steals a ring off the corpse of a recently deceased medium. Back at her shabby bourgeois apartment, she is haunted by apparitions of the dead woman and is found strangled the next morning, her own hands gripping her throat. The second story, "The Telephone," concerns a prostitute (Michele Mercier) who is taunted by phone calls from a man who claims to be a former client whom she knows is dead. Finally, "The Wurdulak" tells the story of a nineteenth-century Russian kulak family who finds that their patriarch, played by Boris Karloff, has returned to their home as a *wurdulak*, a vampire who lives on the blood of those he loves. Each of the episodes is introduced by Karloff in brief comic prologues in the manner of his NBC *Thriller* television series, which was placed into syndication while *Black Sabbath* was in preproduction.[41] *Thriller* was NBC's answer to the highly successful *Twilight Zone* and *Alfred Hitchcock Presents* anthology series, in which a sardonic and avuncular master of ceremonies introduced weekly stories of crime, suspense, and mystery. These spoken introductions, although common in television anthology dramas of the period such as *Bob Hope Presents* and *Dick Powell Theater*, were given a uniquely mordant twist through wordplay and deadpan gallows humor in the style of Henri Jarrod in *House of Wax*'s chamber of horrors and the crypt keeper in the E.C. horror comics of several years before.[42]

By the early sixties, the Italian horror film was substantially more violent, sexual, and downbeat than the carefully constructed Poe films that were forming the centerpiece of AIP's release schedule. Film historian and *Video Watchdog* publisher Tim Lucas has written a detailed account of the differences between *I tre volti della paura*, the version released in Italy and continental Europe, and *Black Sabbath*, the version handled by AIP in the United States, Canada, and Great Britain. Lucas points out that Bava and the personnel at Titanus Studios in Rome were following the contemporary practice of preparing different versions of the film on request of the coproducing studios, and that AIP insisted on several changes from the film's European version. First, Bava filmed Karloff introductions for AIP that would not appear in the European version: Karloff appears at the beginning of each episode in *Black Sabbath*, but *I tre volti della paura* contains only one introduction by Karloff after the main credits and a brief coda at the end with Karloff still in his wurdulak costume.[43] Second, the order of the three stories was changed for the U.S. version of the film. "Arkoff and Nicholson realized that young [American] audiences would demand a monster in the first story," writes Lucas, "and [thus] reassigned 'The Telephone' [which appeared first in

I tre volti della paura] to the middle position, in favor of 'The Drop of Water,' which featured the walking dead [in the first slot]. This strategy also withheld Karloff's 'Wurdulak' episode, the film's trump card, till last to send everyone out on a horrific high note."[44] Third, a couple of lingering close-ups of throat wounds and a severed head in "The Wurdulak" were shortened or masked.[45] Finally, the entire narrative of "The Telephone" was transformed through a complete rewriting of the dialogue track, as will be recounted below.

In *Black Sabbath*, Karloff introduces "The Drop of Water" reflected against a purple background on the surface of a pool of water. As he speaks, falling drops form foreshortened ripples on the surface of the water, commencing the visual and aural motifs that will structure the story to follow. Karloff calls the story a "tale by Chekhov," but Lucas cites a later interview in which Bava admits that the story was entirely his own, influenced by Dostoyevsky and Maupassant.[46] In addition, the story draws heavily on Martha Higgins's death by fright in *The Tingler*, as well as on motifs culled from *House on Haunted Hill* and *Psycho*. On a rainy night, nurse Chester sits at the window of her turn-of-the-century apartment, looking through the rococo-framed oval glass while an outside flashing light, advertising rooms to let, pulses huge pools of green light on her face. Nurse Chester's livid green pallor; the shape of the window, which recalls the ripples on the water in Karloff's introduction; and the flashing light, whose rhythm echoes the water drops, all continue motifs set up in the Karloff sequence. As the story progresses, she is called on the telephone to tend the body of Madame Zena, a psychic who has mysteriously died in her sleep.

At Madame Zena's decaying house, a cronelike servant opens the door and, chattering with fear, leads the nurse through a huge room. The two diminishing figures walk offscreen left, their continued movements visible through angled floor-to-ceiling mirrors as cats pace around the house and fill the air with their mewing. In one of his most distinctive (and cost effective) stylistic flourishes, director Bava uses colored gels on the architecture to create color zones in this and in the episode's final shots. The servant and the nurse enter Madame Zena's room, strongly backlit from the hall. The ornate decoration of these interiors and the highly detailed costumes and props are examples of the uniquely "European" production values that these coproductions were able to put up on the screen for AIP at a fraction of the cost of similar scenes in Corman's Poe adaptations.

The servant refuses to go any further, and the nurse walks up to Madame Zena's four-poster bed. Translucent veils are drawn around the bed, and a bedside candle flickers orange and purple lights on the nurse's face. Pulling aside the veil, the nurse encounters the hideous wide-eyed grimacing corpse of Madame Zena, brought into full close-up by a rapid zoom. This nightmarish face, a wax sculpture by Bava's father Eugenio,[47] is an even more frightening and misogynist vision than the mummified Mrs. Bates in the climactic scene of *Psycho*, and her unyielding waxen skin makes Madame Zena resemble the china dolls strewn about her bedchamber.[48] In an adjacent room, the two women prepare a white funeral dress to take to the death bed, and the servant tells a skeptical and hostile nurse Chester that Madame Zena died while in a trance during a séance and that everyone suspects she was killed by spirits of the dead. Later, the servant leaves Madame Zena's room to find a pair of shoes, and the nurse looks enviously at the corpse's ring. The bedside candle casts saturated orange and purple patterns on the nurse's face, and an unseen fly buzzes around the room. As another cat creeps into the bedroom, nurse Chester pulls the ring off of the corpse's finger with great effort, and it falls to the floor. Crawling on the floor looking for the ring, she is suddenly slapped by the dead hand of Madame Zena, which has slipped off the side of the bed. The nurse screams and knocks over a glass of water on the bedside table. She finds the ring on the floor next to yet another doll and hides it in her brassiere.

When nurse Chester returns to her apartment, all of the motifs associated with Madame Zena's death chamber invade the nurse's rented room. When she puts on the stolen ring and looks vainly at her own hand, a buzzing fly lands on her finger, and she is terrified and repulsed as it buzzes around her head. When the nurse hears dripping water behind the kitchen door, she goes to investigate and is further drawn from room to room by pounding and dripping sounds: outside in the foyer the shutter bangs open and shut as water from the rain drips onto the floor, and inside the apartment nurse Chester's own umbrella takes up the now-deafening rhythmic tapping pattern. The howling wind begins to take on the pitch and timbre of Madame Zena's mewing cats, and a sudden flash of lightning kills the electricity in the room. As nurse Chester is now intermittently bathed in green light, she is overwhelmed by a cacophony of sounds associated with the medium's corpse—the chattering of mewling cats, the buzzing of flies, the banging shutter, and the dripping of water. She trips and falls to the floor, and all sound stops.

Struggling to her feet, nurse Chester lights a candle and hears a high moan from behind the bedroom door. The sound is indistinguishable but echoes both the sound of the cats and the whistling wind heard earlier. She approaches the closed door, the central icon of the horror

Nurse Chester in *I tre volti della paura* (*Black Sabbath*)
(Image Entertainment).

The horrific death grimace of Madame Zena in *I tre volti
della paura* (*Black Sabbath*) (Image Entertainment).

genre, and turns the knob. Inside, lying on her bed, is the wide-eyed staring corpse of Madame Zena, and a rapid zoom-in highlights the other characteristic motif of horror, the corpse's dead but still-seeing eyes. A reaction shot shows nurse Chester similarly wide-eyed in terror. The corpse sits stiffly up in the bed like Count Orlock in *Nosferatu*, and the nurse flees into the living room only to find the doll-like Madame Zena seated in her rocking chair. The corpse smiles at her and rocks while holding a cat in her lap. Nurse Chester collapses on the floor, and then looks up to see Madame Zena floating above the floor toward her. In another shot, the hands of the corpse reach in from offscreen and gently place the nurse's own hand on her throat as she screams. A quick cut shows a black cat jumping onto the windowsill and mocking the nurse's scream with a loud screech.

The next morning, two police officers and the concierge look down at nurse Chester's lifeless body. The old woman's eyes move nervously about the room as she tells the police that no one has touched anything there, and rhyming close-ups alternate between the staring eyes of the nurse and the shifting glances of the concierge. The medical examiner points to the nurse's bruised and blistered finger, where a ring has been pulled off by force, and a huge close-up brings the concierge's eyes into the foreground. The camera zooms into the blue-lipped, staring face of the corpse, now looking just like Madame Zena[49] as the loud buzzing of a fly rises to deafening volume on the soundtrack.

"The Telephone," *Black Sabbath*'s second story, begins with an introduction by Karloff, not seen in European prints, which suggests that a modern ghost, unlike the fin de siècle Madame Zena, may use modern technology to haunt the living. The story features Michele Mercier as Rosie, an upscale call girl who is menaced by threatening phone calls from someone claiming to be Frank, a former client whom she knows is dead. Terrified, Rosie calls her friend Mary to spend the night with her. Believing Rosie to be suffering from delusions, Mary puts a tranquilizer into Rosie's tea and, while Rosie is asleep, is strangled to death by Frank with one of Rosie's silk stockings. Rosie awakens and, when likewise attacked by Frank, stabs him to death with a kitchen knife. After his body falls to the floor, we hear Frank's voice speaking through the unhooked telephone receiver: "Rosie! You can't kill me. I'll always be here. I'll be talking to you every night, no matter where you are. I'll be calling you. On the telephone!"

One of the features of several American coproductions abroad during this period is the preparation of more violent or sexually adventurous versions for Italian and French markets. Lucas recounts how the narra-

Rosie (Michele Mercier) in *I tre volti della paura* (*Black Sabbath*) (Wisconsin Center for Film and Theater Research).

tive of "The Telephone" was radically transformed from its version in *I tre volti della paura*, eliminating all references to Rosie and Mary's previous lesbian relationship and transforming Frank, the vengeful pimp and prison escapee, into a ghost who continues to haunt Rosie on the telephone after she has seemingly stabbed him to death. The European version, with its homophobic male fascination with lesbianism, gives a particularly fetishistic resonance to the murder of the icy Mary, who is strangled by the silk stocking of her beautiful femme lover Rosie. Mary struggles helplessly in medium close-up as Frank's powerful hands, extended from behind immaculately jeweled French cuffs, choke her to death. The original version ends with a long and languorous track and pan from Rosie's bed, where she cowers with the kitchen knife still in her hands, past the body of Frank, past the telephone off the hook, and coming to a stop on a voyeuristic view of the strangled Mary, whose eyes remain open in death like those of nurse Chester at the end of "The Drop of Water."

The final section of the film, "The Wurdulak," features Karloff as Gorka, a nineteenth-century Russian kulak patriarch who returns to his home after killing feared "Turkish bandit" Alibek. One by one, he infects the family with vampirism, beginning with his tiny grandson Ivan. He lures Ivan's mother Maria outside with the undead child's cries of "Mother! I'm cold!" Gorka's two sons, Peter and Gregor, are likewise infected, and the youngest daughter Zdenya, played by Galatea ingenue Susy Andersen, attempts to flee with the young male lead Vladmir, played by Mark Damon, who had a similar role in Corman's *House of Usher* (1960). The vampire family tracks the young couple to a deserted churchyard and attempts to reclaim their daughter as Vladmir sleeps. Awakening to find her gone, Vladmir later finds Zdenya back at the Gorka farmhouse. She stares vacantly into his eyes, kisses him passionately, and bites him on the neck as the family watches from outside the window.

"The Wurdulak" deploys many horror conventions in a very self-conscious and original way. The episode begins with the encounter between the young Vladmir and the mysterious house, and his initially hostile reception as well as the long buildup to the appearance of the marquee-name patriarch, continues the narrative motifs that characterize the AIP Poe films, which in turn draw on *Nosferatu* and other adaptations of *Dracula*. Gorka is introduced with a rapid zoom, almost a parody of the whip pans that had characteristically introduced Vincent Price in the Poe films. After Gorka returns to his home, the apprehensive family huddles around the stew pot on the blazing hearth, remembering Gorka's warning that he might return as a wurdulak. The interaction of the skeptical outsider Vladmir with the terrified peasants replays the countless generic scenes in Transylvanian taverns and inns, but in this domestic space the return of the patriarch is the source of fear.

One of the most unsettling aspects of "The Wurdulak," and one that anticipates the direction many horror films would take in the next fifteen years,[50] is its series of parallels between the values and rituals of patriarchal family life and the inexorable pull of abuse, incest, and vampirism. As Gorka sits in front of the fire, the flames play on his face just as they did on nurse Chester's at Madame Zena's deathbed, and his actions and commands grow increasingly frightening and abusive. When Zdenya brings him a plate of roast lamb, he knocks it to the floor in a rage. He demands to "fondle" tiny Ivan, and Maria reluctantly hands the child to him. Gorka commands Gregor to shoot the family's favorite dog to stop its offscreen howling (the gunshot and death shriek of the dog is timed with his kiss on the cheek of little Ivan). Finally, Gorka reaches into his saddlebag and pulls out the severed head of Alibek, which he demands be hung on the outside door (AIP trimmed a few seconds of this gruesome shot for the film's American release).

Nowhere are the distinctive Italian elements of mise-en-scène more present than in the churchyard, where the vampire family returns to claim Zdenya. The gothic ruins are presented as a highly stylized series of arches lit to emphasize the blues and earth tones that have dominated the palette of "The Wurdulak." In an obvious bit of foreshadowing, the young lovers descend into the crypt to find a place to sleep safely until sunrise. Vladmir leads the way through the cobwebbed subterranean passage past a grimacing skeleton laid out on a table, much like the corpses of Ivan and Peter in the house. As Zdenya cries in Vladmir's arms, horses approach the ruins.

As Vladmir sleeps, Gorka walks into the ruins; suddenly, Zdenya wakes and slowly walks, wide-eyed and mesmerized, out of the crypt and to her father. Karloff's dual role in *Black Sabbath* as vampire/hypnotist and host/monstrateur is underscored as he speaks to Zdenya in the heavily reverberating tones that had characterized his introduction to the film. "Why did you leave us?" he demands. "He loves me," pleads a terrified Zdenya. In the film's most undisguised allusion to the claustrophobic terror of the incestuous family, the old man soothingly replies, "No one can *love* you as much as *we* do. You know that." The scene unfolds using the stylistic motifs that have characterized *Black Sabbath* from its opening moments: seemingly disembodied heads float out of the darkness into patches of colored light, fixing their object in a serpentine stare. Each of the adult family members now advances out of the darkness, floating forward into pools of green and blue light. "Why?" whispers Peter, Maria, and Gregor, blood dripping from the wounds on their throats as Gorka hypnotically intones "Why did you leave us? . . . Why did you leave us? Why did you leave us?" This heavy reverberation, a feature of radio horror programs such as *Inner Sanctum* and *Lights Out*, was an addition for the film's American release: In the Italian version, the floating vampires advance in eerie silence, like Madame Zena on the cowering nurse Chester.

The most subversive element of the episode is the ending, which completely overturns our expected return to heterosexual normality at the end of an AIP horror film. Zdenya's eyes grow wide in a mesmerizing stare and she whispers, "Embrace me, Vladmir." He is unable to move, his gaze fixed on her as she brushes his lips with hers and sinks her teeth into his neck. A rapid zoom into the window shows Gorka, Maria, and little Ivan hungrily watching Vladmir's initiation into the wurdu-

The vampire Gorka (Boris Karloff) in *I tre volti della paura*
(*Black Sabbath*) (Image Entertainment).

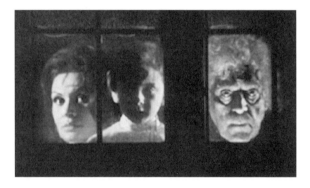

Three generations of the undead in *I tre volti della paura*
(*Black Sabbath*) (Image Entertainment).

AIP's newspaper ad for *Black Sabbath* (G. William Jones Film and Video Collection, Southern Methodist University).

lak family. Their faces, "the three faces of fear," according to Suzanne Liandrat-Guignes,[51] are bathed in a putrefying green light, echoing the first shot of "A Drop of Water," where nurse Chester stares out the window into the flashing light. Vladmir's horse flees in terror, and the film comes to an end.

Black Sabbath was released by AIP in May of 1964 on a double bill with another import directed by Mario Bava, *The Evil Eye*. The combination played the familiar downtown run of genre releases in the spring orphan period, showing at the Fox in Detroit,[52] the Center in Boston, the State in Chicago,[53] and the Paramount in Buffalo.[54] After the week-long downtown run, the package was released to neighborhood theaters and drive-ins. In Philadelphia, *Black Sabbath* and *The Evil Eye* played a week at the Stanley Warner Palace in late May,[55] then opened in twenty-three area theaters and drive-ins on June 3 and 5.[56] Of the twenty-three theaters that were part of the multiple opening of this double feature, fourteen were drive-ins. Drive-in theaters, which provided almost one-quarter of the annual U.S. and Canadian box office revenues, had become increasingly important in the multiple openings and modified saturation playoffs of many genre pictures,[57] as the Philadelphia run of *Black Sabbath* indicates. Drive-in managers were in virtual unanimity that color increased a drive-in feature's image resolution on larger screens and added to its commercial potential everywhere.[58] In addition, drive-ins with their multiple nightly features were a key market for smaller genre films, which could often be placed by their states-rights distributors on the same program with a combination from another distributor. For example, in 1968, Europix Consolidated used the AIP exchange in Philly to gain multiple bookings for Bava's *Kill Baby Kill* as part of a combination that included two German horror imports from Producers Releasing Organization, *The Phantom of Soho* and *The Monster of London City*.[59]

By 1963, despite a severe downturn in the Italian economy and the lack of investment capital for film production, the Italian film industry produced a record 270 feature films.[60] The figure would only slightly decrease over the next two years,[61] despite the unprofitability of many of the completed features that remained virtually unsold.[62] Meanwhile, the international branches of AIP and many other companies continued to acquire films from Italy and other countries throughout the decade. Even in Italy, with its huge domestic box office, a large number of these films were still being cofinanced by American interests or bought outright after completion. Clearly, lower production costs, access to production subsidies, and a steady product flow for a company's distribution outlets in the United States and abroad could not by themselves account for either Europe's inflated production schedules or the expensive switch to color on even the most modest genre films. At this point, all of the drive-in screens of America, each running dusk-to-dawn programs of genre films, would have been challenged to showcase all of the mythological, horror, science fiction, western, and espionage films being turned out by the European studios. What, then, was the reason that so many color genre films continued to roll out of European studios?

At the time of *Black Sabbath*'s release, *Variety* asserted that "one of the major factors in [the] continuing interest in the production of budgeters is the eventual revenue to be earned from feature-hungry TV stations."[63] In fact, one of Salvatore Billitteri's duties as AIP point man in Italy was the acquisition of Italian films for American International's growing TV syndication arm.[64] The switch to color signaled by the AIP Poe adaptations and the success of the Hammer imports point to long-range plans of production and distribution to exploit television syndication. Like the money saved and the markets opened by international coproduction, the sale of features to television provided much-needed capital for companies such as Astor Pictures, AIP, and Allied Artists to plow back into the production of more and costlier releases. The continuing aesthetic changes in the horror film brought about by the permanent switch to color were only one result of the growing interdependence between the international operations of increasingly diversified American distribution companies and the soon-to-be insatiable demand of television stations for feature films in color.

CHAPTER 7

Television Syndication and

the Birth of the "Orphans":

Horror Films in the

Local TV Market

Many baby boomers remember the first family on their block to own a color TV set. In my neighborhood in suburban Houston, the younger members of this lucky family experienced a sudden surge in popularity sometime in 1966, when I and other kids on the street would show up after school to watch *Bullwinkle*, just after supper to watch *Batman*, and on weekend afternoons to watch extremely violent adventure-and-spectacle movies such as *Brennus, Enemy of Rome* (1960), *Tyrant of Lydia against the Son of Hercules* (1963), and, my favorite, *Robin Hood and the Pirates* starring Lex Barker (1960).

Across town, managers of the local TV stations eagerly embraced these English-dubbed imported spectacle features, many of which had never enjoyed a U.S. theatrical release because they were a low-cost source of color programming. It was the same in TV markets all over the country: television syndication had become a highly lucrative sellers' market for distributors of feature films, and program suppliers at all levels of the industry attempted to exploit the shortage of feature films for American TV broadcast. Two technological trends, the rise of color TV and an increasing number of UHF stations, accelerated this process. In Europe and Japan producers who years before could never have dreamed of reaching the U.S. market were actively courted by program syndicators wanting to buy their features for syndication to hungry TV stations. Like the art-film market of a few years before, local TV often presented a strange mélange of art and exploitation, highbrow and lowbrow, in the same venue. The circulation of several feature film packages in the Philadelphia market in the mid-sixties shows the crucial role that horror and fantasy cinema and its purveyors played in this process.

Throughout the early fifties distributors of low-budget American films and import features had been syndicating film product to television, and by the mid-fifties the major studios had released huge numbers of pre-1948 features to network affiliates and independent stations, which usually broadcast these features in the afternoon and late at night. In 1961, agreements on residual payments between the major distributors and both the American Federation of Musicians and the Screen Actors Guild opened the way for the release of the post-1948 Hollywood product for broadcast by local stations and the major networks.[1] Because of the low-risk, presold quality of feature-film programming, stations began to fill increasing amounts of air time with movies, and this rising demand resulted in higher and higher prices by syndicators such as Columbia Pictures's TV subsidiary, Screen Gems, whose features-to-TV business resulted in extraordinary profits: the company posted record earnings in 1963, a year that saw the formation of music-publisher Screen Gems-Columbia Music, Inc. and record manufacturer Colgems Music Corp.[2] The success of early players including Screen Gems now spawned dozens of imitators as stations faced a feature-film shortage remarkably similar to that of the neighborhood theater ten years before.[3]

Genre films were a crucial part of the TV syndication of features from the very beginning. In 1957, Screen Gems contracted with Universal-International for a $20 million, ten-year lease on 550 pre-1948 Universal features, which were placed into syndication late in the year.[4] One of the first groups of these features that Screen Gems released was the "Shock!" package of fifty-two horror films from Universal's "golden age" of horror.[5] The package consisted of successfully rereleased box-office hits including *Frankenstein, Dracula*, and *The Mummy*, as well as program filler like *Chinatown Squad* (1935) and *The Spider Woman Strikes Back* (1947) (see the appendix for a complete listing alphabetically by company of the films in each feature package). The package was a huge success having sold before its October debut in over thirty markets.[6] Indeed, it proved to be a ratings winner on powerful stations such as WABC in New York,[7] KRON in San Francisco,[8] WCAU in Philadelphia,[9] and KTLA in Los Angeles.[10] Screen Gems's success spawned immediate imitation: Associated Artists Productions released its own fifty-two–feature horror package in late 1957[11] consisting largely of Monogram titles from the forties including *The Ape* (1940), *King of the Zombies* (1941), and *Face of Marble* (1946), and in May 1958 Screen Gems issued a second twenty-feature package, "Son of Shock," which included *Bride of Frankenstein* and other sequels and programmers such as *The Invisible Man's Revenge* (1944) and *House of Dracula* (1945).[12]

Throughout the next ten years, the price of feature-film programming continued to rise as the supply began to fall. In 1962, the major studios had a combined total of 3,350 films that were unsold to TV; by

when
WCAU-TV
gave
PHILADELPHIA
the

SHOCK
treatment

RATINGS.................*jumped* **85%** ....*to* **16.3**

AUDIENCE SHARE.....*soared* **58%** ....*to* **57.5**

SETS IN USE................*leaped* **12%** ......*to* **28.4**

*That's the amazing Philadelphia story...when
"SHOCK" premiered on a normally uneventful Tuesday*
night from 11:15 P.M. to 12:45 A.M.!

*WCAU-TV, the top rated station in this time period,
now enjoys an even more secure hold on its leadership
thanks to its scheduling the first run showing of the 52
greatest full length spine-tinglers ever filmed!*

<u>YOUR</u> AUDIENCE IS READY FOR A "SHOCK" TREATMENT

Call or wire

SCREEN GEMS *OCT. 1*
SOURCE: A.R.B. and Trendex

NEW YORK · DETROIT · CHICAGO · *Television Subsidiary of Columbia Pictures* · HOLLYWOOD · NEW ORLEANS

Screen Gems's 1957 trade ads for its "Shock" package reported its
overwhelming success in the Philadelphia TV market. Note the asylum
terrors lurking in the phrase "shock treatment" (*Broadcasting*).

the following year the number had plummeted to 1,400.[13] Syndicators were quick to capitalize on this trend. In 1963, the TV syndication market yielded a $100 million gross with features accounting for over 60 percent of the total,[14] and 1964 surpassed even this figure by generating $175 million, with features still topping two-thirds of the gross.[15] In 1961, *Broadcasting* magazine predicted that by 1967 the available feature film libraries would be completely played out.[16] Station owners complained about the rising costs but, according to *Variety*, "when it comes to choosing pix versus hour-long properties, or going 'live' with their own shows, most stations are scrambling for features, costs notwithstanding."[17]

This reticence on the part of stations to take risks with original programming was mirrored in the increasingly cautious attitudes of the program syndicators themselves, who had come to prefer the more stable demand for feature-film programming, and the preponderance of newcomers to the TV syndication field would place a major emphasis on what the trade called "vaulties," previously produced features and cartoon shorts. A 1963 newcomer to the ranks of television syndication was Screen Entertainment, formed by Harold Goldman, former National Telefilm Associates executive, and Hank Sapirstein, owner of UPA Pictures, which created the Mister Magoo TV cartoons. Goldman and Sapirstein had been partnered in the distribution of cartoons and half-hour telefilms since 1961, and they made their feature syndication bow with a $2 million deal for ninety-three post-1954 films, including sixty-nine that had been released theatrically by American International Pictures.[18] The AIP group included virtually the entire company backlog, from horror films such as *I Was a Teenage Werewolf* (1957) and *Horrors of the Black Museum* (1960) to juvenile delinquent films such as *Reform School Girl* (1957) and *High School Hellcats* (1958) to westerns such as *Five Guns West* (1955) and *The Gunslinger* (1956). The AIP package went into immediate release and found a showcase in the late-night slots that had come to specialize in horror and sci-fi genre fare since the initial success of Screen Gems's "Shock!" package and its many imitators.

It is no coincidence that James Nicholson and Samuel Arkoff negotiated this deal with Screen Entertainment at the moment they were moving into international coproduction and larger-budgeted features. To finance bigger releases such as the Jules Verne adaptation *Master of the World* (1961), AIP used the films in its vault for collateral in obtaining production financing,[19] but the company's $20 million outlay for twenty-four films in 1963 necessitated both the Screen Entertainment deal and a $2 million lease of AIP's sixty-nine features to the five ABC owned-and-operated stations the same month.[20] In order to make this deal, Nicholson and Arkoff had to buy out the interests of Roger Corman and others who had produced many of the sixty-nine films being sold.[21] For some, this was the first money they had seen since their initial producers' fees and/or promises of deferred payments. Edward Bernds, director of *High School Hellcats* and *Reform School Girl*, later told film historian Mark McGee, "I never made a dime on those pictures until they sold to TV. They said they never went into profit."[22]

American International Pictures was not alone in using this strategy. Astor Pictures and Allied Artists, two companies whose histories parallel AIP's in many ways during this period, used television sales to finance an expanded theatrical roster. Astor accompanied its expansion program of 1960–1962 with redoubled efforts to mine the assets of its TV subsidiary, Atlantic Television, and many of the titles that Astor had released theatrically over the previous twenty years were placed into circulation. The four Marc Frederick–produced horror/exploitation releases from 1958–1959, *Frankenstein's Daughter*, *Missile to the Moon*, etc., were released as part of Atlantic's "Six-Pack Special," and Monogram theatrical releases including *Spooks Run Wild* (1941) and *Bowery at Midnight* (1942) were part of an eleven-title "Thrills and Chills" package. The company became entangled in Chapter 11 bankruptcy proceedings in 1962–1963 (see chapter 5) at just the time that companies with control over their assets were enjoying unprecedented success in the television market. The four Frederick features were later bought by American International Television (AI-TV) and became late-night perennials in the late sixties.

Allied Artists had begun mining its catalog for TV income even earlier. The company's huge investment in its ambitious production program of A features in the late fifties was partially offset by the sale of features to TV by its subsidiary Interstate Television (see chapter 3). By 1962–1963, the company was still relying on the box-office success of saturation-booked genre double bills such as *The Black Zoo* and *Day of the Triffids* to offset the huge outlay for its prestige release of the season, *55 Days at Peking*.[23] In addition, Allied Artists's TV arm, now called Allied Artists Television, released a package of forty features to TV in its "Cavalcade of the 60s, No. 1" unit,[24] which included box-office hits such as *Friendly Persuasion* (1957), *Al Capone* (1959), and *Dondi* (1961),[25] and the company leased overseas TV rights to its catalog to Twentieth Century-Fox and Seven Arts for $1.2 million.[26] In addition, syndicator M and A Alexander, a division of early movies-to-TV giant National Telefilm Associates, bought the syndication rights to twenty-seven Allied Artists films, including *The Maze, Invasion of the Body Snatchers*, and *Riot in Cell Block 11*.[27]

As *Variety* noted, the company had "few prime vaulties" to sell,[28] so it capitalized on feature syndication's growing trend of thematic packaging. Bunching releases by theme or genre worked to the advantage of both syndicators and station programmers, providing a moderate but stable market for the distributor and a small but loyal audience for the station manager. As a result, horror and science fiction films had a significant rerun value on local stations. Said one syndication executive, "Dracula and his cape never ages."[29] Following the model of Screen Gems and "Shock!," Allied Artists released its twenty-two–feature "Sci-Fi for the 60s" package in August 1962.[30] "Sci-Fi for the 60s" contained most of the company's horror programmers from the previous decade, including *House on Haunted Hill, The Hypnotic Eye*, and *Not of This Earth*, as well as two pickups from Howco Productions, *The Brain from Planet Arous* and *My World Dies Screaming* (which was retitled *Terror in the Haunted House* for television).

The package was very successful, and several stations, including KMTV in Omaha and KTRK in Houston, gave them a regular showcase in the late-night weekend hours.[31] Just as "Shock!" had shown TV programmers the demand for horror films from the studio era, the Allied Artists package was the first of several collections of then-recent genre films to be released to television. In spring 1963 United Artists Associates (UAA), the television subsidiary of United Artists, released to TV its "Science Fiction-Horror-Monster" unit of sixty features. By far the most eclectic of the early-sixties horror packages, the UAA unit contained United Artists U.S. releases of the fifties such as *The Pharaoh's Curse* (1957) and *It! The Terror from beyond Space* (1958); the company's Hammer Quatermass films, *The Creeping Unknown* (1956) and *Enemy from Space* (1957); the Val Lewton and King Kong films from RKO; and two groups of pre-1948 films the company had acquired in its takeover of Associated Artists, Warner's horror films *Mystery of the Wax Museum* and *The Beast with Five Fingers* (1946), and Monogram programmers *The Ape* (1940) and *King of the Zombies* (1941). Not to be outdone, Allied Artists put out "The Exploitables," fifteen titles consisting largely of Filmgroup releases produced by Roger Corman such as *Beast from the Haunted Cave* (1958), *The Wasp Woman* (1960), and *Little Shop of Horrors* (1961). Screen Gems, the company that began the whole trend with "Shock!," weighed in with "X," a fifteen-feature package of recent Columbia releases including Japanese imports such as *Mothra* (1962), Hammer imports such as *Stranglers of Bombay* (1960), Sam Katzman's *Zombies of Mora-Tau*, and, the crown jewel of the package, *The Tingler*.

This syndicated tidal wave of recent horror and science fiction films guaranteed local stations a regular audience for weekly late-night horror showcases designed to broadcast these packages. For example, in Cleveland, wjw featured the aptly named show *Shock Theater* with host "Ghoulardi," which aired at 11:20 on Friday night; in Houston on KTRK a disembodied, reverberating voice introduced *Weird* on Saturday at 10:35 P.M.; and one of New York's most recognized celebrities was "Zacherle," host of WABC's own *Shock Theater*. These hosts were a comic inflection of the Caligari-monstrateur figure, and their introductions to the films often featured some of the same word play that characterized the masters of ceremonies from the E.C. horror comics a decade before.

As with the theatrical product shortage of the previous decade, the increased value of horror and exploitation films in this sellers' market was paralleled by a significant demand for pictures from abroad. In fact, before the agreement between the major studios and the guilds cleared Hollywood's post-1948 catalog for TV, major distributors such as UAA and smaller outfits such as Flamingo Telefilm Sales showcased recent films from Europe to which guild stipulations on residual payments to musicians and actors did not apply. Some of these films featured major stars such as Alec Guiness, Sophia Loren, Gina Lollobrigida, and Brigitte Bardot.[32] Other companies were able to take advantage of the so-called Monogram clause negotiated in 1953, by which a TV distributor could pay residuals to the Screen Actors Guild in the amount of 15 percent of the original cast cost of the film. This was impractical for major releases, but a distributor could easily afford these payments to distribute a low-budget programmer to local stations. This resulted in a flood of Poverty Row and exploitation films on television in the late fifties and early sixties.[33]

At the lower end of the business were the companies that found a place in the market supplying independent features and imports to local TV stations. Smaller companies provided the local TV market with eclectic packages of imports, pre-1948 features, and genre films. Flamingo Telefilm Sales was one of these companies. Flamingo was the syndication subsidiary of the diversified Buckeye Corporation of Ohio and owned syndication rights to the popular *Superman* TV series.[34] In 1960, the company bought, from Sig Shore's Valiant Films, TV rights to the DCA catalog from the 1950s (see chapter 5).[35] In addition, Flamingo acquired another twenty-five features from Essex-Universal and other companies,[36] and these sixty-three titles were grouped into two packages and placed into syndication in August. Their "Critics Award Package" of forty-six titles contained the characteristic DCA mix of art imports such as *I Am a Camera* and *Les Misérables* (1952), exploitation imports such as *Rodan* and *Teenage Wolf Pack*, and genre releases from American independents such as *Rock, Rock, Rock!* and *Plan Nine from Outer Space*.

It was a foregone conclusion that these and subsequent foreign-language films would be dubbed into English for their TV showings. Initially, stations were reluctant to show dubbed foreign product after seeing a number of hastily dubbed features from Cinécittà in Rome, but eventually film buyers throughout the country came to prefer European films dubbed into "American English" to British imports.[37] By 1964, virtually all films from abroad, whether Japanese sci-fi, Italian sword-and-sandal, or auteurist art film, would be syndicated in dubbed versions exclusively.

This "mass and class" approach to the TV sale of foreign films—or, in the words of one syndicator, "international pictures"—came to characterize the packages circulated by two of the larger importers, Embassy and Walter Reade-Sterling.[38] Embassy's first package of thirty-five features included sword-and-sandal hits such as two Hercules films with Steve Reeves, British comedy-mysteries like *What a Carve-Up!* (1961) (aka *No Place Like Homicide*), and art-house entries such as *Two Women* (1960) and *The Sky Above, the Mud Below* (1961). After merging with New York's Sterling Television in 1961,[39] Walter Reade's company— which now included part ownership in several production companies abroad, a circuit of over thirty theaters, and theatrical distributor Continental—released a package of forty Continental theatricals into TV syndication. The package included British comedies such as *The Smallest Show on Earth* (1957) and *School for Scoundrels* (1960); "angry young man" dramas such as *Expresso Bongo* and *Saturday Night and Sunday Morning* (both 1960); and imports from Europe and Asia including *General Della Rovere, Ballad of a Soldier* (both 1960), and *The Seven Samurai* (1954). Reade-Sterling courted controversy, not for the last time, by including in the package *Room at the Top* (1959) and *The Mark* (1961), both of which had run afoul of the Production Code Administration and the Catholic Legion of Decency (see chapter 9).

The demand for features became so acute and distribution of them so profitable that by 1963 many of the international pictures released to television were so-called orphans, which had never received theatrical runs in the United States.[40] Embassy released under the series title "Sons of Hercules" a series of thirteen Italian sword-and-sandal epics featuring muscle hero "Maciste," which sold very successfully,[41] and as the decade progressed the sellers' market would bring an avalanche of dubbed orphan pictures from abroad onto the airwaves. Of course, this trend was accelerated through the efforts of international film producers and distributors, who were well aware of the feature shortage on American television. Many art films were successfully syndicated, although these were usually films with the drawing power of a female star; Embassy's *Two Women*, for example, caused much knob fiddling and aerial bending by viewers seeking a clearer picture of Sophia Loren. The biggest demand was for action-adventure, western, and horror/science fiction movies.[42]

When some of these imports were accorded theatrical runs, the primacy of the TV market for genre releases was often noted by reviews in the trade press. *Variety* observed that the British horror film *Devil Doll* (1964) "was apparently . . . filmed with an eye to TV, depending heavily on close-ups, not just of the principals but almost everyone and everything in the film."[43] In 1968, the trade journal noted with some rancor that the U.S.-Spanish crime drama *Run Like a Thief* was typical of genre imports allotted only pro forma theatrical runs:

> Do they ever cease? [*Run Like a Thief* is another of the] mild action-adventure pix, filmed in Spain or Mexico or Italy with the actors mouthing English, turned out by indies for television syndication but accorded brief theatrical runs . . . In N.Y., they usually open as second features on 42d St.; perhaps one in 10 achieves a circuit run, and this only when RKO or UA Theatres or Loew's cannot obtain a programmer from any of the majors or important minors.[44]

One reviewer complained that the sets in the suspense import *The Destructors* were "too well-painted" in an obvious attempt to highlight their hues for the small color screen.[45] This comment points to the most significant development in the feature shortage that drove this entire branch of the industry: the explosion in color television. The NBC network, a subsidiary of color TV manufacturer RCA, had been heavily promoting color television since the early sixties with programming such as *Walt Disney's Wonderful World of Color*, *Bonanza*, and, most important for this study, *Saturday Night at the Movies*.[46] As early as 1963, program syndicators were making long-range plans to build an inventory of color programming for the boom in color TV that the entire industry knew was coming.[47] By the middle of the decade, color TV sales had outstripped the supply of available color programming. The year 1965 saw a doubling of the number of color sets sold to retail outlets, from 1.3 million to 2.7 million units, according to the Electronic Industries Association.[48]

The figure doubled again in 1966 with over 4 million sets sold, thereby placing color television in almost 20 percent of American households.[49] By the beginning of 1967, the Electronic Industries Association was predicting that annual color set sales could reach 7 million and put color TV in almost one-third of all American homes by the end of the year.[50] For this reason, television stations were beginning to think in terms of building a backlog of color programs[51] to attract the audiences needed to sell to advertisers.

However, in early 1966 only 10 to 15 percent of all syndicated programming was in color, and only about 2,300 color feature films were in active syndication.[52] Many of these features were part of packages sold to networks or large station groups in exclusive deals, making the number of color movies available to independent stations much smaller.[53] "A feature package which is wholly or largely made up of color product has a far greater chance of appealing to local programmers," Four Star Distribution vice president Len Firestone told *Variety*.[54] Program syndicators from ABC Films to King Features to American International Television began long-range plans to buy orphan features from abroad and, in the case of AI-TV, to produce low-budget color features for TV sale.[55]

A second major factor in the rising demand for feature films and other syndicated programs was the growth of UHF television stations in many American markets. Since the late thirties, RCA had been successful in its efforts to dictate technological standardization of TV equipment to favor its manufacturing patents. A crucial element of this process was the use by TV of the very high frequency portion, VHF, of the broadcast spectrum, between 44 and 216 megahertz. Ultrahigh frequency broadcasting, UHF, utilized an even higher frequency portion of the broadcast spectrum, above 300 megahertz, and had been proposed by CBS as an industry standard during FCC hearings in 1943 because of the wider bandwidth available for channel allocation and transmission. This wider bandwidth was highly favorable for the development of high-definition television and color broadcasting, areas in which CBS owned key patents. In order to avoid the widespread obsolescence of existing TV equipment, the FCC decided in favor of the VHF interests in 1947 and established channel allocations 2 through 13 in the VHF portion of the spectrum. Over the next twenty years, it was the VHF stations that became highly profitable network affiliates, and the small number of licenses granted to UHF stations, which operated on channels 14 through 84, were in markets that already contained successful VHF stations. This, coupled with the resultant low consumer demand for UHF receivers, ensured that these stations posed little threat to VHF affiliates.[56]

Eventually, market growth forced the FCC to support UHF expansion, and beginning in April 1964 all new TV sets shipped in interstate commerce were required by law to receive both VHF and UHF channels.[57] This enabled UHF to ride the wave of color television set sales throughout the decade.[58] The penetration by UHF increased nationally: from 21 percent of homes in 1965 to 33 percent in 1966 to 42 percent in 1967.[59] In addition, the FCC allowed UHF stations up to 5,000,000 watts of power while VHF stations were allowed between 100,000 and 316,000 watts. This dramatically increased both the area of coverage that a UHF station could enjoy and the potential audiences that could be sold to advertisers.[60]

By 1966, UHF stations were seen as the market of the future by program and feature film syndicators: of the $220 million in anticipated domestic syndication sales in 1967, UHF outlets were predicted to provide at least 10 percent of these sales.[61] At this point, several program syndicators, including Four Star, Embassy, and Walter Reade-Sterling, were already counting UHF sales of over 10 percent of their annual total,[62] and a 1967 article in *Broadcasting* pointed to the "change in competitive status of major three-VHF markets where U's have come up strong to compete." Mentioned are Philadelphia, Boston, and Cleveland, "which distributors in the past considered tight buyers' markets for features but which now are fast becoming sellers' markets."[63]

Many suppliers of programming attempted to capitalize on this burgeoning demand for feature film product. American International Television was formed in 1964 to exploit this product shortage in the same way that its parent company had sprung forth to provide pictures for product-hungry theaters ten years before. From the beginning, AI-TV concentrated its efforts in feature film programming. "Feature films are the mainstay of syndication," vice president Stanley Dudelson told *Broadcasting*, "Half-hour independent syndicated programs are dead, and so are syndicated daytime programs."[64] The first package of features that AI-TV distributed to TV was "Epicolor '64," a group of forty sword-and-sandal features that included three theatrical releases from 1960: *Sign of the Gladiator*, the Steve Reeves feature *Goliath and the Barbarians*, and AIP's condensed version of Fritz Lang's Indian diptych, *Journey to the Lost City*.[65] The vast majority of features in the "Epicolor" unit were orphans from Italy and Yugoslavia, such as *Slave Girl of Sheba* (1960) and *Brennus, Enemy of Rome*, titles that had been picked up by Arkoff and Nicholson through the efforts of their two Italian liaisons, Fulvio Lucisano and Salvatore Billitteri.

Packages of sword-and-sandal films enjoyed a brief period of intense

A tense moment in *The Mighty Ursus* (1962), one of dozens of Italian historical spectaculars lapped up by color-hungry TV stations in the mid-sixties (G. William Jones Film and Video Collection, Southern Methodist University).

popularity during the early phase of the color feature shortage on TV. Embassy's "Sons of Hercules" package was able to capitalize on the color shortage, with several stations ordering color prints of the Italian imports for their permanent library.[66] Similarly, in 1963 Medallion Pictures released to TV a thirty-film package of orphan spectaculars, titled "Spectacolor," which included *Son of Samson* (1960), *Last Glory of Troy* (1961), and Mario Bava's *Last of the Vikings* (1962).[67] Embassy, AI-TV, and Medallion were very successful with their color spectacle packages,[68] but by late 1964 a market glut had drastically lowered the demand for films in the sword-and-sandal genre.[69]

Nicholson and Arkoff went to great lengths to point out the difference between this orphan TV fare and their theatrical releases.[70] By 1964, the company was beginning to see its efforts to secure showcase bookings for its theatrical product pay off handsomely, and AIP tried hard not to alienate the great number of exhibitors who saw the diminishing TV clearance of theatrical features as a dire threat. After Allied and Theater Owners of America merged in 1965 to form the National Association of Theater Owners, the president of that organization expressed the fear that "we might wake up tomorrow to find ourselves playing day and date with television."[71] To calm exhibitors' fears, AIP inserted a non-retroactive clause beginning in 1963 into their exhibition contracts that stipulated that their theatrical releases would not be issued to TV within five years of their release date unless the film had failed to make back its negative cost.[72] Of course, this was not an entirely altruistic move: with the supply of features dwindling over the course of the decade, the longer that a syndicator held on to a moderate-to-successful theatrical release, the more money a network or station would be willing to pay. Partially because of the five-year window, AI-TV was able to negotiate a highly profitable deal with CBS for 1967 *Friday Night Movie* airings of *Beach Party* and *How to Stuff a Wild Bikini*.[73]

The company pressed on with its program of features acquired from abroad for TV distribution. In late 1964, AI-TV released "Amazing '65," a group of twenty features that included the theatrical imports *Black Sunday*, *Circus of Horrors*, and *The Hand* (1961); independent productions that had been released theatrically by AIP such as *Beyond the Time Barrier* (1960), *The Brain That Wouldn't Die* (1962), and *Night Tide* (1963); and orphan imports such as *The Blancheville Monster* (1962) and *Terror in the Crypt* (1964). This mixture of older theatricals and orphan imports continued with "Amazing '66," a package that included *The Man with X-Ray Eyes* (1963), *Dementia 13* (1961), and never-before-seen imports *Dr. Orloff's Monster* (1964) and *Attack of the Mushroom People* (1965).

Three packages of imports from Mexico's Azteca Studios were also released by AIP, some of which had been released theatrically by Saturday matinee distributor K. Gordon Murray. "Thrillers from Another World," volumes 1 and 2, contained black-and-white horror films in the Universal tradition, such as *The Vampire's Coffin* (1957) and *Man and the Monster* (1958); the uniquely Mexican myths of horror *The Brainiac* and *Curse of the Crying Woman* (both 1961); and the wrestling superhero features *Samson vs. the Vampire Women* (1957) and *Wrestling Women vs. the Aztec Mummy* (1965). "The Wonder World of K. Gordon Murray" was a package of thirteen color features of children's stories, such as *Hansel and Gretel*, *Little Red Riding Hood*, and *Santa Claus*, released in a weekly plan between early October and late December 1965 to coincide with end-of-the-year holiday excitement.

In 1966, AI-TV announced a new feature package, "Amazing Adventures '67," which was designed to exploit the color feature shortage and which included the theatrical hits *Black Sabbath* and *Master of the World*. Also in the package was a series of made-for-TV color features directed by Dallas-based filmmaker Larry Buchanan. The Buchanan films were extremely low-budget 16mm remakes of earlier AIP releases: *Zontar, The*

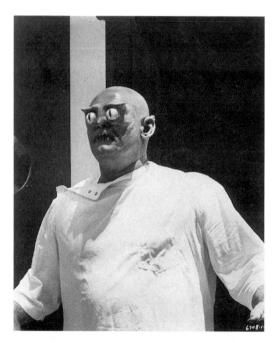

Larry Buchanan's *Curse of the Swamp Creature*
(G. William Jones Film and Video Collection,
Southern Methodist University).

Thing from Venus was a remake of *It Conquered the World* (1957), *Curse
of the Swamp Creature* was based on the screenplay of *Voodoo Woman*
(1958), and *The Eye Creatures* was a reworking of *Invasion of the Saucer
Men* (1957). Most of these films' meager budgets were spent on down-
on-their-heels Hollywood players such as John Agar, Les Tremayne, or
Tommy Kirk, who provided "marquee" value in the television listings.
Jeffrey Sconce has asserted that Buchanan's films "rank among the most
low-budget productions ever attempted in commercial filmmaking . . .
Mistakes in dialog, camera movement, and sound recording remain in
each film."[74] Still, Buchanan and his associates displayed ingenuity in
completing the films on their ridiculously low budgets, and almost every
film has moments of effectiveness, particularly *In the Year 2889*, the best
of the series. Other Buchanan films for AI-TV include *Mars Needs Women*,
It's Alive, and *Creature of Destruction*.

Other players in the effort to exploit the feature shortage were program syndicators who had branched out into the TV distribution of features. Desilu Sales was a company that was already sitting on several hot

syndication properties. In addition to a fabulously successful morning "strip" (one half hour each weekday) of *I Love Lucy* on CBS, the company was raking in the cash on three of syndication's most sought-after series, *The Untouchables, The Greatest Show on Earth,* and the prestige anthology drama *Desilu Playhouse,* all of which enjoyed immense popularity abroad as well as in the United States.[75] Desilu started feature film syndication in late 1964 when it entered a deal with Westhampton Film Corporation for forty-six of Westhampton's titles, including fifteen in color.[76] The "Westhampton Feature Package" consisted largely of titles released theatrically by Crown International. It was advertised in the trades as "first-run action packed feature films for television . . . all with the broadest audience appeal"[77] and included the low-budget exploitation films *Narcotic Squad* (1955) and *Secret File: Hollywood* (1961), science fiction films *Varan the Unbelievable* (1962) and *First Spaceship on Venus* (1963), and horror films such as the southern indie *Trauma* (1962); the Italian import *Mill of the Stone Women* (1963); and the skeleton in Robert ("Dad Brady") Reed's closet, *Bloodlust* (1959). Some of the features in the Desilu package, particularly the horror films and thrillers such as *The Girl Hunters* and *Anatomy of a Psycho* (both 1963), were unusually violent and gruesome for this period: TV prints of both *Bloodlust* and *Mill of the Stone Women* left intact scenes of onscreen human taxidermy, and *Bloodlust* had no fewer than three scenes in which characters struggled to remove leeches attached to their faces and chests.

Many of the distributors of these films to television were small operations formed exclusively to sell features to TV, and could not afford to acquire and hold on to name features until the price was right. These companies were often in serious need of ready cash with which to constantly expand their catalog.[78] Roberts and Barry was a feature film distributor that could be described by *Variety*'s phrase as an "office-in-hat operation." The company was run by Ben Barry, a syndicator who had been distributing programming to local TV stations since 1951.[79] Roberts and Barry, like Teleworld, Television Enterprises Corporation, Thunderbird, and many smaller distributors, relied on the thematic packaging of features in the absence of star vehicles or recognizable hits.

One of Roberts and Barry's contributions to genre programmers in the TV market was the distribution of thirty-three low-budget German thrillers produced in the early sixties and never shown theatrically in the United States. These films, part of a several-year cycle of *krimis* (crime dramas) based on the novels of Edgar Wallace, were one of the mainstays of the German film industry between 1960 and 1965.[80] Tim Lucas has argued that these stylized and often very violent thrillers, produced by West Germany's Rialto Film, form a parallel movement to the *giallo* mystery thrillers such as *Sei donne per l'assassino* (*Blood and Black Lace*) and *La ragazza chi sappeva troppo* (*The Evil Eye*) filmed in Italy during the sixties and seventies by Mario Bava and others. He goes on to add that perhaps they influenced the German genre to a significant degree. Rialto Film's Berlin rivals, CCC-Film, produced the series of Dr. Mabuse science fiction thrillers in the early sixties and produced a *krimi* cycle of its own with films based on the novels of Edgar Wallace's son, Edgar Bryan.[81] Roberts and Barry placed these films into syndication in 1965 under the package heading "Europa '33.'" The group contained both Edgar Wallace films from Rialto such as *The Squeaker* (1965) and Bryan Wallace adaptations from CCC-Film such as *Curse of the Yellow Snake* (1963) as well as the European James Bond knockoffs *Operation Hong Kong* and *Mission to Hell with Secret Agent FX 15* among others.

In addition, Roberts and Barry had acquired the rights to four of the European genre imports financed by Louisiana exhibitor Bernard Woolner. These were released in the "Woolner Four" package that contained Mario Bava's *Hercules in the Haunted World* (1963) and the Barbara Steele vampire film *Castle of Blood*, which was retitled *Castle of Terror* for TV. In 1967, Barry took many of the films in his catalog with him when he was signed on by the powerful Triangle station group to head its feature syndication arm, Triangle Program Sales.[82]

Another of the smaller syndication outfits was Thunderbird Films. Thunderbird was formed in 1965 as a subsidiary of a diversified manufacturing company, CBK Industries of Kansas City. The first feature package released by Thunderbird was "T-Bird I: The Exploitables," announced to TV in May 1965.[83] The twenty-six films in the package, eighteen of which were in color, represented a cross-section of the most successful categories of syndication imports. European stars Marcello Mastroianni and Jean-Paul Belmondo were featured in, respectively, *Ghosts of Rome* and *Web of Passion* (both 1961). By contrast *The Devil's Cavaliers* (1955) and *Revolt of the Barbarians* (1964) were historical spectaculars. In addition, the group contained Italian versions of popular genres such as the horror film *What!* (1963) and the youth pic *Beach Party, Italian Style* (aka *18 in the Sun*) (1965) as well as four films distributed theatrically by Times Films's Victoria subsidiary including the "shockumentary" *Mondo Cane* (1963). Like the eclecticism of art-theater programming of a few years before, this feature package (and many others like it) could be exploited in a range of programming situations and confounded distinctions between art and exploitation, highbrow and lowbrow, as I will show.

The circulation of many of these packages in the Philadelphia television market provides a representative case study of both demand and supply in the distribution of feature films in local syndication.[84] Philadelphia was fourth on *Broadcasting*'s 1966 list of the top hundred TV markets in terms of population and television penetration.[85] Second, the Philadelphia market topped even New York and Los Angeles in multiset homes.[86] By late 1966, the American Research Bureau estimated that 58 percent of the homes in the Philadelphia market were equipped with UHF television sets.[87] The sheer size of the market enabled virtually all of the feature-film packages from large, mid-size, and several small distributors to circulate through the city's television stations. Finally, the stations in Philadelphia represent a cross-section of economic and technological organization and include a network-owned-and-operated station, both network affiliates and UHF stations from powerful station groups, and independent UHF and educational stations.[88]

Three of the stations in the Philadelphia market did not program genre features to any extent. The city's National Educational Television affiliate, WUHY-TV Channel 35, was prohibited for both cultural and economic reasons from the use of feature films. In business since 1941, KYW-TV Channel 3 was the Philadelphia NBC affiliate and was a member of Westinghouse Broadcasting's Group W chain. NBC's prime-time feature showcases were a major source of movie programming for KYW, and its NBC affiliation and ownership by manufacturer Westinghouse made it an early pioneer in the colorcasting of both original programming and feature films in the Philadelphia market. Two of the most frequently used time periods for genre movies, the late-night slot and the afternoon hours, were taken up on Channel 3 by colorcasts, NBC's *Tonight Show*, and the Philadelphia-based *Mike Douglas Show* and other local programming, respectively.[89] Finally, WIBF-TV Channel 29, one of three UHF stations that commenced broadcasting in 1965, was an independent station owned by three Jenkintown business associates. In keeping with a common early strategy of UHF programming, Channel 29 relied heavily on local programming during its first three years in an effort to capitalize on local advertising, which had previously been priced out of the VHF advertising market.[90] Unlike the other UHF stations in the market, WIBF had no regular programming slots for thematically packaged feature films.

One of the CBS network's five owned-and-operated stations (or "O and O's" in the trade jargon) was WCAU-TV Channel 10, which commenced broadcasting in 1948. Channel 10 had aired the popular "Shock Theater" package from Screen Gems in 1957–1958, and the program's costumed host, John Zacherley as "Roland," later moved to New York and became hugely successful as *Shock Theater*'s "Zacherle." Enjoying the fruits of the network's buying power, WCAU-TV was part of a highly lucrative 1960 deal in which the five stations leased 275 films from Screen Gems.[91] These films were broadcast in late-afternoon *Early Show*, late-night *Late Show*, and overnight *Late Late Show* format, a common practice with CBS affiliates.[92] In 1960, WCAU began airing Seven Arts's package of 122 post-1948 Warner features that included major box-office hits like *Strangers on a Train* (1951), *A Star Is Born*, *Rebel without a Cause* (both 1955), and *The Searchers* (1956).[93] A number of genre releases were included in the package as well, including *Beast from 20,000 Fathoms* and *House of Wax*. Instead of premiering a horror program to showcase these latter titles (as they had done six years before with Screen Gems's "Shock" package), WCAU slotted them into the *Early Show/Late Show* programs as individual features. Similarly, Screen Gems's package of seventy-three Columbia "post-'48's," bought by the CBS O and O's in 1963, contained stray genre items such as Schneer's *Earth vs. the Flying Saucers* and Hammer's *Revenge of Frankenstein*,[94] but these, like the William Alland cycle of "weirdies" that included *Creature from the Black Lagoon* and *The Incredible Shrinking Man* released in a package of Universal "post-'48's" by Seven Arts,[95] were never given their own showcase on WCAU.

The ABC affiliate WFIL-TV Channel 6, broadcasting since 1947, was a member of the powerful group of stations owned by Triangle Publications, which also owned the *Philadelphia Inquirer*. In addition to the ABC network feature specials, WFIL ran a range of feature packages from both major distributors and independents. Channel 6 also aired a large number of "class" features in both prime time and late night: the station contracted with Walter Reade-Sterling for a package of features that included *Room at the Top* and features from the "Cinema 20" package, such as *La dolce vita* and *The Pawnbroker*, that Reade had bought from AIP.

In the mid-sixties, WFIL was the primary exhibitor of horror and science fiction films in the Philadelphia TV market. On Saturday nights after the eleven o'clock news, Channel 6 broadcast *Double Chiller Theater*, which featured most of the packages of "classic" and recent-vintage genre pictures from small to mid-size syndicators. The linchpin of *Double Chiller Theater* was Screen Entertainment's package of fifties AIP titles including *The Screaming Skull* and *The She Creature*. In addition, WFIL had contracted for films such as *The Hypnotic Eye* and *Daughter of Dr. Jekyll* in Allied Artists's "Sci-Fi for the 60s." When AI-TV released "Amazing '65" into the market, *Double Chiller Theater* began showing items from the package, including *The Brain that Wouldn't Die* and *Assignment Outer Space*. Two of AI-TV's follow-up packages, "Amazing '66" and the mostly color "Amazing Adventures '67," which included *Black Sabbath* and the Buchanan made-for-TV features, also bowed on *Double Chiller Theater*. In addition to the AI-TV, Allied Artists, and Screen Entertainment packages, WFIL also ran items from Screen Gems's "Shock" and "Son of Shock" packages such as *The Mummy* and *House of Frankenstein* as well as films such as *The Tingler* from the "X" group. The program also featured items like *Bloodlust* from Desilu's "Westhampton" package and Medallion's "20/20" like *Creature of the Walking Dead*.

Following *Double Chiller Theater* in the 1:00 A.M. slot was another feature showcase, *Hollywood's Best*, which usually ran programmers from the RKO, Warner, or United Artists library booked by UAA. For example, features on October 2, 1965, included a *Double Chiller Theater* of Mario Bava's *Hercules in the Haunted World* (Roberts and Barry) and Corman's *Creature from the Haunted Sea* (Allied Artists). *Hollywood's Best* followed, highlighting Universal's *Captive Wild Woman* (1943) from Screen Gems's "Son of Shock."

A member of the Kaiser Broadcasting group of stations, WKBS-TV Channel 48, showcased feature programming from some of the smaller packages from UAA as well as a group of mostly British imports from Walter Reade-Sterling. The station's horror programs were allocated to the Friday late-night and Saturday morning juvenile ghetto. *Beyond the Limits*, so named because it followed syndicated reruns of *The Outer Limits*, aired Fridays at 11:00 P.M. opposite the local news; and *Scary Tales* (later *Strange Tales*) ran Saturday at 8:00 A.M. and featured the movie from the previous week's *Beyond the Limits*. These horror programs drew from a much smaller library than WFIL's *Double Chiller Theater* and broadcast a combination of Lippert/Fox releases such as *The Unknown Terror* (1957) and *The Undying Monster* (1942) and independents such as *Invaders from Mars* (1953) from National Telefilm Associates, as well as a number of films from UAA's "Science Fiction-Horror-Monster" package including *The Pharaoh's Curse*, *Mark of the Vampire* (both 1957), and *Terror Is a Man* (1959). In search of color programming in 1966, the station entered the sword-and-sandal sweepstakes with *Gladiator Movie* on Friday nights at 8:30, which was supplied by Four Star's "Spectacular Showcase." In addition, the station premiered

Spy Man Movie at 8:30 P.M. on Saturdays in 1966 (opposite both NBC's *Get Smart* and CBS's *Mission Impossible*),[96] which showcased Four Star's "Superspy Action Group."[97]

Finally, WPHL-TV Channel 17, owned by Aaron Katz and Leonard Stevens, was the most ambitious of the three commercial UHF stations in the Philadelphia market. Indeed, Stevens would become an industry spokesperson for UHF and would try to organize a UHF splinter group within the National Association of Broadcasters in 1967.[98] The programming on Channel 17 headlined sporting events including National Hockey League games, professional soccer, and college basketball. Color, asserted co-owner Stevens, was "critically important" to the success of the station,[99] and sports increased the amount of programming in color desired by area advertisers. Because most of the major feature packages had been salted away by competing stations by the time WPHL began broadcasting in 1965, the station's movie programming emphasized foreign films from a range of independents and pre-1948 Hollywood classics. In 1966, with CBS affiliate WCAU running the unbeatable "mass" Wednesday-night lineup of *Lost in Space, Beverly Hillbillies, Green Acres, Gomer Pyle, USMC*, and *Danny Kaye*,[100] WPHL counterprogrammed a foreign film showcase at 9:00 P.M. that it called *For Adults Only*. In this slot the station ran features from an array of packages: *The Moralist* (1957) and *Hiroshima mon amour* (1959) from Video Artists's "Critics Choice" group; *The Sky Above, The Mud Below* (1961) and *Night Is My Future* (1948) from "Embassy Features"; and *The Tailor's Maid* and *The Lovemakers* (both 1958) from Trans-Lux's "Top Draw Group." Channel 17 added other import feature programs, including *Premiere Theater* on Monday nights at 9:00, *Wednesday Night Movie* at 9:00, and the *Foreign Film Festival* on Monday nights at 11:00. Films from a variety of packages were circulated through these slots, including *Web of Fear* (1964) from Comet's "Rainbow Feature Package" and *Waltz of the Toreadors* (1962) and *David and Lisa* (1963) from Reade-Sterling's "Cinema 90." Reade's "Cinema 90" was one of the packages in heavy rotation on WPHL.

The station also ran a weekly sword-and-sandal showcase, *The Heroic Movie*, on Fridays at 11:00 P.M., which was stocked by another Video Artists package, "11 Great Adventures," and by NBC Films's "Spectacolor" group. The horror broadcast by WPHL, *The Supernatural Movie*, aired Thursdays at 11:00 P.M. Channel 17's horror film library represented some of the most obscure orphans and theatrical features seen in the Philadelphia market. M and A Alexander Productions was able to place its "Chiller–Science Fiction Package" of *Hideous Sun Demon*

(1955), *Monster of Piedras Blancas* (1961), and two others on WPHL. The only AI-TV package played on WPHL was the "Thrillers from Another World" group of Mexican imports including *The Living Head* (1961) and *The Witch's Mirror* (1960).

One of the titles in Reade's "Cinema 90," *Hands of Orlac* (1960), turned up often on *The Supernatural Movie*. In fact, by 1967 a large number of feature packages contained a combination of mass and class features that could be slotted into very different movie showcases. For example, NBC Films's "Cinemagreats" group supplied *Cavalier in Devil's Castle* (1962) to *Heroic Movie*; *The Amorous Mr. Prawn* (1962) and *Doll That Took the Town* (1963) to *For Adults Only*; and *Horror Chamber of Dr. Faustus* and *The Invisible Dr. Mabuse* to *Supernatural Movie*. Similarly, Thunderbird's "T-Bird I" package provided to *For Adults Only* the films *Web of Passion* (1961) and *Mondo Cane* (1963), while *Heroic Movie* aired *The Devil's Cavaliers* (1958) and *Revolt of the Barbarians* (1964), and the mystery and horror slots highlighted *Frantic* and *Psychomania*.

One film in the Thunderbird package appeared frequently in the horror, mystery, and art-film showcases in 1966 and 1967: Mario Bava's *What!*, an Italian horror film from 1963. Produced by Vox Film in Rome, *La frusta é il corpo* (literally, "the whip and the body") was director Bava's first feature after the international hit, *I tre volti della paura* (*Black Sabbath*). *La frusta é il corpo* was retitled *What!* by tiny distributor Futuramic and given the briefest of American theatrical runs. *What!* tells the story of a nineteenth-century Russian aristocratic family whose disgraced eldest son Kurt (Christopher Lee) returns to the ancestral castle after months in exile to destroy the family and regain his patrimony. He resumes his affair with the masochistic Nevenka (Dahlia Lavi), now engaged to his brother. On a dark and stormy night, Kurt is stabbed to death with the same dagger with which the young servant Tania, pregnant with Kurt's child, had committed suicide. The balance of the film's ninety-minute running time concerns Nevenka's descent into madness as she may or may not be haunted by the ghost of her lover.

Why would an incest-themed, sadomasochistic Italian horror film starring Hammer's Dracula, Christopher Lee, be telecast as part of a "foreign film showcase"? First, like the art theaters of several years before, the independent television stations faced a shortage of product that could offer counterprogramming alternatives to their highly capitalized rivals (in this case, the major TV networks), and thus they needed to rely on eclectic programming strategies. Commercial standards of suitability for European films in the American TV market had drastically expanded as syndicators frantically attempted to feed the "voracious maw" of television (the phrase of Seven Arts chief Eliot Hyman). Second, the association of foreign films with eroticism and sophistication (hence WPHL's naming its feature program *For Adults Only*) led to the confounding of categories of art and exploitation, highbrow and lowbrow in programming decisions. Third, the painterly compositions and florid use of color in many European genre films, particularly the gorgeously saturated hues favored by former cinematographer Mario Bava, foregrounded the novelty of color television for viewers accustomed to monochrome TV fare.

Thunderbird chief Brad Marks attempted to allay the fears of local stations when it came to booking foreign product. "Many television men," he said, "don't realize that much of the sexiness in foreign movies is an added 'exploitation' that means nothing to the continuity of the movie." He asserted that Thunderbird's editing "made each movie fit our standards without shocking our sensibilities."[101] Thunderbird excised all of the whipping scenes and Nevenka's orgasmic writhings from *What!*, leaving the impression that the supposedly resurrected Kurt's nocturnal visits are prosaic vampirism.

What! is filled with eruptions of unmotivated color, particularly saturated reds and purples, and the pacing of the film is langorous, giving it an unmistakable "European" feel. In this, it was not alone: the curious art-film stylings of Italian genre pictures were noted by several frustrated film buyers for American syndicators. While putting together Four Star's "Superspy Action Group," company buyer Ed Cipes told *Variety* that "the main problem with the foreign spy vogue is that many are made like arties. They are 'dark' and lack the glamour and gloss that made the Bond films such hits."[102]

Still, someone was watching these films. Perhaps some of the people who were watching *Hiroshima mon amour* were also tuning in to *What!* and *Zontar, The Thing from Venus*. In fact, the explosion of feature films on television was having a significant effect on film culture. In a 1964 article, *Variety* pointed to the inclusion of Visconti's *Senso* (1954) in a Television Enterprises Corporation package for TV under the title *The Wanton Contessa*. The trade journal posited increasing instances of "really rabid movie buffs . . . learning to pay careful heed to the day-by-day TV log listings as well as the filmpage ads for those screen oddments, 'finds' and belated unveilings so relished by the cognoscenti."[103] Many of the baby boomer TV viewers who had grown up on the "Shock" package and costumed horror hosts of the early sixties were approaching college age and developing an omnivorous taste for nonmainstream films as the decade of the sixties wore on. Late-night telecasts of horror, science fic-

They Saved Hitler's Brain, one of many cult films aired as part of late-night movie showcases on local TV (G. William Jones Film and Video Collection, Southern Methodist University).

tion, and foreign films appealed to increasing numbers of insomniacs, pot smokers, and self-taught film critics who were beginning to develop an ironic, genre-literate approach to reading and enjoying these marginalized films in their marginalized time slots. Rock critic Lester Bangs later published an appreciation of this experience in 1976 in an essay called "Incredibly Strange Creatures."[104]

Jeffrey Sconce calls this mélange of art films and genre pictures "paracinema," and he praises it as a politics of film style offering a sort of parallel avant-garde for the discriminating initiate. Even the AIP films of Larry Buchanan, Sconce asserts, are praised for their "unique artistic vision . . . The films are unwatchable for most mainstream viewers, and consequently have assumed an exalted status among the 'hardcore' badfilm faction of paracinematic culture."[105] Of course, this meant that contemporary horror films shown in theaters had to be made of rather sterner stuff, and this development was not long coming to the horror film.

At the same time that local programmers were using orphan pictures from abroad and low-budget genre films as program filler, economies of scale in the TV distribution of features resulted in an increasingly centralized control of both the programming and distribution of movies on television. By the early seventies, the major companies like Seven Arts, Screen Gems, and National Telefilm Associates were controlling an even larger share of the most profitable sectors of the movies-to-TV business. Even genre programmers, once a defining element of the relationship between the independent syndicator and the local station's film buyer, became subject to this trend of centralization. This broad movement is evident in the relationship between Seven Arts's participation in Hammer Films's production financing and the CBS network's decision to enter late-night programming with *The CBS Late Movie.*

Canada's Seven Arts, Ltd. was one of the most successful of the larger companies that parlayed deals with the major distributors for the lease of their features to television. The company bought TV rights to Warner Bros. entire pre-1948 library in 1956[106] and acquired 122 post-'48 features from the same studio in 1960.[107] In addition, Seven Arts made deals for blocks of Twentieth Century-Fox post-'48's in 1961 and 1962[108] and bought 215 post-'48's from Universal, which that company had to unload as part of its takeover by Music Corporation of America in the early sixties.[109] The television distribution of these films was fabulously successful.[110] During the feeding frenzy of the 1966 sellers' market for feature syndication, Seven Arts posted an incredible 500 percent increase in seasonal earnings since 1964,[111] and the Canadian company bought Warner Bros. outright later that year.[112]

In 1962, Seven Arts Productions launched high-profile theatrical releases including *Whatever Happened to Baby Jane*, *Gigot*, and *Lolita*, but the company had been a silent partner in many of Hammer Film's horror productions since the fifties. Seven Arts provided funding for *Curse of Frankenstein*, *The Mummy*, and *The Man Who Could Cheat Death* (1959), which were released theatrically in the United States by Warner, Universal-International, and Paramount, respectively.[113] For Hammer, this provided production financing and—in addition to a separate deal with Columbia for features like *Revenge of Frankenstein* (1958) and *Stranglers of Bombay* (1960)[114] as well as picture-by-picture deals with other U.S. distributors—prevented a backlog of its films awaiting release with any single American major.[115] Hammer was free to negotiate theatrical distribution deals with the U.S. majors, and its mid-sixties distribution deal with Twentieth Century-Fox gave massive saturation advertising to Hammer dual combinations such as *Dracula, Prince of Darkness* and *Plague of the Zombies* and showcase releases including the Racquel Welch star-maker *One Million Years, B.C.* (all 1966).[116] For Seven Arts, participation in Hammer's films was a long-term investment that paid off handsomely: the rights to these films reverted to the Canadian company after several years. Further, because "Dracula and his cape never ages," Seven Arts was able to rerelease a combination of *Curse of Frankenstein* and *Horror of Dracula* in 1965 to a very successful tally.[117] More important, Seven Arts retained television rights to the films, which became more valuable as the decade progressed.[118]

By 1967, CBS was alone among the three networks in having no late-night programming. Programming by NBC and ABC in this slot was filled by *Tonight* and *The Joey Bishop Show*, respectively.[119] Contemplating the dwindling supply of vaulties from the major studios, CBS considered several possibilities for this slot and in 1969 premiered *The Merv Griffin Show*, which lasted only two years.[120] In early 1972, the network began *The CBS Late Movie*,[121] and Seven Arts, which had supplied features for CBS's prime-time movie slots for years,[122] was able to provide many of the Hammer Films releases, which it had kept out of syndication, to CBS as "first-run" network showings. The 1972–1973 season saw CBS showcasing a wide array of heavily censored TV prints of Hammer vaulties, including *Curse of Frankenstein, Dracula, Prince of Darkness, Frankenstein Created Woman, Two Faces of Dr. Jekyll* (which AIP had released as *House of Fright* in 1960), *Frankenstein Must Be Destroyed, The Mummy*, and *Dracula Has Risen from the Grave.*

The rebirth of the programmer through the television market was the result of several changes in the economics of production, distribution, and exhibition. The most significant elements in the continuing change of the horror genre throughout the decade would be the acquisition of the old studios by diversified corporations, the upscaling of the genre through its use in film adaptations of presold properties, and its growing use of more graphic violence and explicit sexuality.

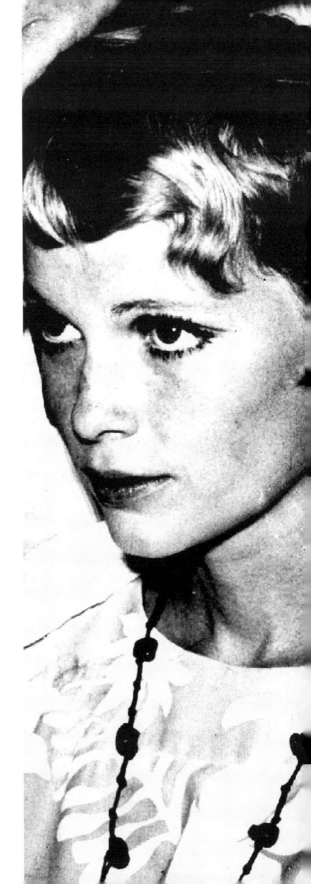

CHAPTER 8

Demon Children and

the Birth of Adult Horror:

William Castle,

Roman Polanski, and

Rosemary's Baby

By 1967 and 1968 a family night out at the movies, like a dinner conversation about current events, could be a fairly delicate business. Dad might want to go to the newly constructed suburban multiplex to watch John Wayne and Robert Mitchum rid a western town of bad guys in Howard Hawk's *El Dorado*; Mom might want to go see Robert Redford and Jane Fonda as newlyweds in *Barefoot in the Park*; and their college-age son would probably not want to be seen in public with them at all; indeed, he would be more likely to make plans with his friends to go see Roger Corman's *The Trip*, Peter Bogdanovich's *Targets*, or the political satire *The President's Analyst*. The family might just give up in exasperation and stay at home, depending on the night of the week, to watch *The Doris Day Show*, *Mannix*, or *Hawaii Five-O*.

Paramount Pictures was the producer or distributor of all of these movies and TV shows. The company was hardly unique among the Hollywood studios (or among record companies, for that matter) in its attempt to reach what had become a highly fragmented consuming public during a time of bewildering social change. By the mid-sixties, however, Paramount was struggling to overcome several years in which it had failed to anticipate many changes in the entertainment business. While companies like Seven Arts had parlayed its deals with the major studios into piles of money through lucrative TV syndication deals, Paramount had never released its post-1948 library into syndication. This made the unused assets on which the company was sitting much more valuable than the total market value of its stock, so Paramount became the next company to be swallowed up by a multinational corporation, Gulf and Western, in 1966.

Over the following two years, the newly diversified company attempted to negotiate several emerging trends in the film industry, including the growing importance of "horizontally integrated" merchandising tie-ins like soundtrack albums and novels. One of Paramount's many acquisitions during this period was former independent producer

William Castle, who signed on with the studio in 1966 in an effort to move out of programmers and into the production of more prestigious features. Another crucial area for Paramount's growing operations was an emphasis on Europe as both a production center and a key theatrical market. At the same time, one of Eastern Europe's most celebrated directors, Polish filmmaker Roman Polanski, was enjoying crossover success in both the genre and art-film markets with his first English-language film, the London production of *Repulsion* (1965). The fortunes of Paramount, Castle, and Polanski would come together in 1968 in the production of *Rosemary's Baby*, the Paramount adaptation of Ira Levin's best-selling novel of witchcraft and demonism.

By 1965 Paramount Pictures, the most successful of the major studios during the boom years of World War II, was near the bottom of a twenty-year slump. The studio had spun off its theater holdings because of the 1948 antitrust decision that bore the company's name and, in a move that bewilders business historians to this day, had in 1958 sold rather than leased its entire pre-1948 library to MCA in perpetuity.[1] Also, with rivals Warner, Universal-MCA, and Twentieth Century-Fox circulating hundreds of titles in local television syndication, Paramount was relying on network broadcasts for its television revenue and still holding back the lion's share of its film vault in a vain wait for pay TV, still almost a decade away. In the company's 1965 annual report to stockholders, it was revealed that only one of the company's releases, *The Sons of Katie Elder*, had enjoyed substantial profits on the basis of domestic theatrical rentals alone,[2] and stockholder Albert Zugsmith publicly accused the company of attempting to "mask and disguise" sizable losses in feature production by selling off residual rights to television clients.[3]

A year later, the company revealed that it owned almost two hundred post-1948 features that had never been televised. This gave Paramount, in the words of a trade journal, "the largest virgin library of any of the majors."[4] At this point, the value of the company's stock was growing at less than a third of the increase in market value of its post-1948 film library.[5] According to a contemporary account in *Variety*, it was only a matter of time before

> traders will realize that the potential of television sales is providing a secure source of income, virtually unaffected by audience whims. A film with a $1,500,000 budget, is presently assured of recouping all, or nearly all, its negative cost from television alone [and] roadshow release and TV potential can at least minimize the chance of disaster [in huge-budget

spectaculars] . . . Stock prices for such successful enterprises are bound to go up . . . and to share a measure of stability with the networks themselves.[6]

This made seemingly down-at-the-heels majors such as Paramount ripe for takeover by blocks of leveraged shareholders or huge multinational conglomerates. In 1965, two members of Paramount's board of directors, Herbert J. Siegel and Ernest Martin, acquired over 9 percent of Paramount's stock and threatened the company with a palace coup. Less than six months later, Paramount's board of directors, which now included Gulf and Western head Charles Bluhdorn—who had been acquiring a huge amount of stock in the company, including the interest of retiring Adolph Zukor[7]—bought out Siegel and Martin. This placed effective control of the company in the hands of Bluhdorn and Gulf and Western.[8]

The purchase of Paramount was part of a battery of acquisitions in communications and media for the oil conglomerate. Later that month Gulf and Western bought Muntz Stereo Pak, Inc., and in July Paramount was officially merged into Gulf and Western.[9] For years, the movie and TV business had been ripe for conglomeration: at the low end of the industry, diversified companies like Scranton in its takeover of DCA (see chapter 5) or CBK Industries in its attempt to enter TV syndication with Thunderbird Films (see chapter 7) had tried to acquire holdings in the entertainment field. Unlike these smaller, less capitalized companies, Bluhdorn's Gulf and Western, like Pepsi-Cola in its takeover of Columbia Pictures, had the resources to turn Paramount into a "conglomerate within a conglomerate" constituting a "leisure core" of theatrical films, television programs, cable television, leisure parks, music publishing, records, and theater ownership in Canada and Europe.[10] The latter aim was supported by a massive influx of cash from parent Gulf and Western into all levels of film production in Europe.[11] One of the results of this move would be Paramount's financing of baroque European genre films such as Roger Vadim's *Barbarella*, Mario Bava's *Danger! Diabolik*, and Sergio Leone's *Once upon a Time in the West*.

In May 1967, Bluhdorn officially assumed the reigns of president and board chairman of Paramount Pictures[12] and announced plans to revitalize the Paramount Music publishing firm, to purchase Dot Records, and to aggressively market soundtrack albums to Paramount releases on the company's own record label.[13] In addition, Gulf and Western moved decisively into television syndication with controlling stock in Desilu Productions in 1967.[14] A long-awaited off-network feature syndication arm was finally instituted, and the company released its "Portfolio I" and "Portfolio II" packages of films, which included *Psycho* (1960) and *The Man Who Shot Liberty Valance* (1962), to local TV stations.[15]

The massive restructuring at all levels of the company had left Paramount with very few feature projects in the offing, so the acquisition of one-time independent producer William Castle was a major asset, owing to his ability to turn out features in a hurry.[16] Since the release of the last Susina production in collaboration with screenwriter Robb White, the *Psycho*-derived *Homicidal* in 1961, Castle had continued his work as producer and director in a variety of successful projects. Late in 1961, Columbia released *Mr. Sardonicus*, a gothic mystery set in Eastern Europe featuring a disfigured protagonist whose paralyzed rictus recalled Conrad Veidt's Gwynplaine in *The Man Who Laughs* (1928). At the end of the film's penultimate reel, ushers passed out a "Punishment Poll" in which the audience ostensibly cast their ballot for either a happy or downbeat ending,[17] although no one has ever seen a print of the film in which the title character survives. In 1962, Castle and Columbia, who was heavily involved with England's Hammer Films in financing and distribution deals (see chapter 2), ventured into runaway coproductions à la AIP and Galatea in a deal with Hammer that provided for a series of "gimmick" horror releases to be financed wholly by Hammer and released worldwide by Columbia.[18] (The films had to qualify as "British" under the quota law in order to earn Eady production money.)[19] At this point, the Castle aesthetic fit in well with Hammer's then-current cycle of black-and-white psychological thrillers inspired by *Psycho*, such as *Taste of Fear* (1960) and *Maniac* (1962). Castle and Hammer's remake in 1962 of James Whale's *The Old Dark House* was prescient of his later projects in its emphasis on comedy.

The film was not successful, however, and Castle returned to the United States to sign a four-picture deal with Universal in 1964.[20] *Straight Jacket* starred menopausal-horror icon Joan Crawford as an ax murderess released from a mental hospital who is plagued by nightmares and hallucinations and around whom headless corpses begin to be discovered. *The Night Walker* (1964) starred Barbara Stanwyck as a widow haunted by terrifying dreams. *I Saw What You Did* (1964) was a story of a teenage girl whose prank phone calls lead a murderer to her house. Featured in a small role (but receiving top billing) was Crawford as the spiteful lover of the stalker who has murdered his wife.

The box-office success of Castle's Universal films, particularly *Straight-Jacket* and *I Saw What You Did*, spawned another cycle of Castle-inspired horror thrillers including a trio of Warner shockers, *Two on a Guillotine*, *My Blood Runs Cold*, and *Brainstorm* (all 1965), produced and directed by William Conrad, of the radio program *Lone Ranger* and, later, TV's *Cannon*. Castle moved to Paramount in 1966 in an attempt, according to *Variety*, "to broaden the producer's field."[21] A year later, Castle outlined his reasons: "There's no longer any room for programmers in today's market. They're making them for TV all the time. It's a new ball game and a new business, with exciting techniques and new subjects to be filmed."[22] At Paramount in 1967, Castle made the color and widescreen comedy thriller *The Busy Body*, starring Sid Caesar and Robert Ryan; *The Spirit Is Willing*, a ghost spoof also featuring Caesar; and *Project X*, a science fiction thriller featuring time travel and an amnesiac protagonist. Early in his tenure at Paramount, Castle bought the film rights to Ira Levin's *Rosemary's Baby* for a total of $150,000 after reading the galley proofs. The novel featured a plot device that Castle himself had successfully exploited in his Universal films: the narrative of a persecuted heroine who is either the victim of a sinister conspiracy or is descending into madness. When the book became a best-seller,[23] Castle was armed with a property with which he could "cross . . . an artistic Rubicon from successful exploitation shockers to class suspensers."[24]

In the years leading up to the appearance of Levin's novel, discourses on juvenile delinquency, the horror film, and other areas of popular culture became increasingly obsessed with the figure of the sociopathic or demonic child. The appearance of this motif was directly connected to the fear of the contamination of children by both permissive childrearing practices and products of the culture industry. William Paul, in his discussion of *The Bad Seed* (1955) and *Village of the Damned* (1961), asserts that the monstrousness of the children in these two films is a result of their precocious possession of adult traits like self-control and insight into the behavior of their elders. "Perhaps underlying the anxiety about too-adult children in both films," he writes, "is the increasing sense in the postwar period of childhood as distinctly separate from adult life rather than part of a continuum (as was most evident in the advent of youth culture). Parents were losing control not just of their children but of their ability to define the culture those children lived in."[25] Therefore, asserts Paul, efforts such as Frederic Wertham's 1953 crusade against comic books and the repeated script revisions of *The Bad Seed* at the insistence of the Production Code Administration were based "not so much [on] protecting the children from what they might see as [they were on] protecting the parents from what their children might become."[26]

Village of the Damned, with its narrative of blond-haired, alien-sired

The demon child and hypnosis horror motifs are on display in this newspaper ad for MGM's *Village of the Damned* from 1960 (Wisconsin Center for Film and Theater Research).

genius children, displaced the theme of hypnosis and thrall onto the children themselves. In the film, the children's eyes would go white as they hypnotized adults into compliance and self-destruction. The mesmerizing eyes of the children were highlighted in newspaper ads for the film. "Beware this stare" screamed the copy, "for behind the innocent eyes of this strange child lurk the demon forces of another planet."[27] The spell worked: *Village of the Damned* finished 1961 with over $1.3 million in rentals, with the film's total playoff reaching an estimated $1.5 million,[28] and, in a not entirely comforting development to parents concerned about "what their children might become," *Village of the Damned* proved wildly popular at kiddie horror matinees for the rest of the decade (see chapter 9).

After the further success of demon child films such as *The Innocents* (1961) and *Lord of the Flies* (1963), the motif became less characterized by the monstrousness of the child's precocity. These more baroque and stylized films invested motifs associated with children at play such as bouncing balls, lullabies, nursery rhymes, and china dolls with supernatural menace. *The Bad Seed* had achieved this effect through the recurrent motif of the child Rhoda's struggling piano rendition of "Claire de Lune," but two films from Italy, Bava's *Kill, Baby, Kill* (1966) and Fellini's "Toby Dammit" segment from *Histoires extraordinaires* (*Spirits of the Dead*, 1968), deployed the blonde curls, the girl's giggle, the discarded doll, and the bouncing ball to terrifying effect, often allowing the ball, offscreen giggle, and a dissonant sing-song melody on a music box to serve as metonymic markers of the vampire girl's unseen presence.

Many of these motifs can be found in *Repulsion*, the first English-language film of the other key player on *Rosemary's Baby*, Polish director Roman Polanski. Like the neurotic governess Miss Giddens in *The Innocents*, Carol Ledoux (Catherine Deneuve) is a repressed and tormented woman whose revulsion of sex along with a shameful childhood secret generate psychotic hallucinations. Her growing madness is repeatedly signaled by her hypnotic, whispering rendition of a childhood song. The film broadly hints at childhood sexual abuse as the root of her psychosis in its incessant return to a family portrait in which the eight-year-old Carol is already withdrawn into herself, gazing out away from the family. In addition, sounds such as the buzzing of flies around a putrefying skinned rabbit in the kitchen, the dripping of water in the bathroom that is echoed by the ticking of Carol's bedroom clock, and footsteps outside of her front door begin to signal the onset of her hallucinations of rapists and predators lurking in her apartment.

Carol's regression continues inexorably as she crawls on the floor like a child, wandering through the house with a wide-eyed stare as clutching hands reach for her around corners and even burst through the seemingly gelatinous walls. When her unwanted suitor Colin breaks into her apartment and begs her to tell him what is bothering her, she beats him to death with a candlestick and dumps his body into the bathtub. Later, when the landlord enters her apartment demanding the rent as well as clumsily trying to proposition her, Carol slashes him to death with a straight razor. At the end of the film she is found hiding under the bed staring fixedly into the air. If these motifs—the buzzing of the flies, the hallucinations in the apartment, and the final image of the sightless heroine's stare—sound familiar, a possible explanation is the hugely successful 1964 London run of *Black Sabbath* that neatly coincides with Polanski's arrival in London to work on the first draft of *Repulsion*'s screenplay.[29]

Unlike *Peeping Tom*, Hammer's *Never Take Candy from a Stranger*, and other horror-art also-rans, *Repulsion* was a huge international hit, and publicity for the film drew attention to both the film's horrific elements and the artistic excellence of Polanski's direction. Polanski's name even appeared above the title. Trade ads cited reviews that included phrases such as "masterpiece of the macabre," "luxurious shivers," and "well-done and extremely frightening."[30] The American distributor, Columbia subsidiary Royal Films, devised an ad campaign that combined images of the fatal straight razor and the genre's now-iconic golden-haired doll (which was being clutched by unseen hands) with quotes such as "'A tour-de-force of sex and suspense!'—*Life*" and "'A classic chiller of the 'Psycho' School!'—*Time*."[31] In the United States, the film premiered at art theaters, including the Baronet in New York and the Bala in Philadelphia, before opening wider in nonsaturation general bookings.

Virginia Wright Wexman asserts that *Repulsion* was an overtly commercial proposition designed to gain financial backing by Martin Ransohoff's Filmways for Polanski's next project, the more self-consciously absurdist art film *Cul-de-Sac* (1966).[32] After this film, a modest art-house success, Polanski began work on *Dance of the Vampires* for Filmways and MGM in 1967. The project was a disaster: Ransohoff, who retained the right of final cut in the version released in the United States,[33] claimed that during Polanski's watch, the budget of the film had expanded from $600,000 to over $2 million. Polanski claimed that the budget had gone from $1 million to $1.6 million.[34] When Ransohoff insisted that his version, which had been trimmed by twenty minutes and extensively redubbed, be entered at the Berlin Film Festival (at which Polanski had

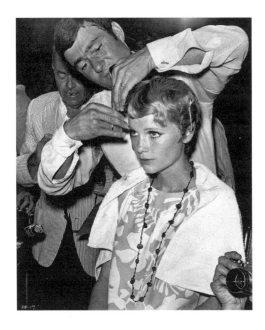

Vidal Sassoon cuts Mia
Farrow's hair in one of
William Castle's publicity
stunts for *Rosemary's Baby*
(Wisconsin Center for
Film and Theater
Research).

received the Grand Prize for two consecutive years with *Repulsion* and
Cul-de-Sac), Polanski made an unsuccessful attempt to take his name
off of the credits.[35] "I wanted to make a poetic fairy tale for kids, not the
vulgar burlesque he changed my film into," an enraged Polanski told
Variety.[36] The film was a miserable failure at the box office, but before
it was released in the United States under the title *The Fearless Vampire
Killers*, Polanski and his producer, Gene Gutowski, signed a multiple-
picture deal with Paramount.

Polanski's first project at Paramount was *Rosemary's Baby*, which
Castle would executive produce and Polanski would write and direct
while Gutowski waited for another project.[37] Castle was unsparing in
his public support for the director in an attempt to forestall any negative publicity that might accrue to their project, which was already in
production by the time *Fearless Vampire Killers* was withering in the sun-
light.[38] *Rosemary's Baby* went over budget, but Castle announced that
this was merely the result of bad weather during a stretch of the film's
New York location shooting.[39] To avoid a replay of Polanski's struggle
with Filmways, Castle guaranteed the director first preview cut approval
on *Rosemary's Baby*.[40]

Castle's fulsome praise for Polanski was mirrored in his promotion of
Mia Farrow as the star of the picture. Farrow, who was then in the public
eye with her role on ABC-TV's *Peyton Place* and her soon-to-fail marriage

to Frank Sinatra, had been voted number 7 in *Motion Picture Herald's* exhibitors' poll of "most promising new faces of 1966."[41] Mountebank conjurer Castle saw Farrow as another attraction in his arsenal, and he plunged himself into her creation with the enthusiasm he had once invested in Percepto and Emergo: "Instead of a tingler under the seat, a skeleton coming out of the screen, or issuing a 'fright attack' insurance policy on viewers' lives," Castle told *Variety*, "now I'm getting publicity by bringing over Vidal Sassoon to cut Mia Farrow's hair."[42] In addition to claiming that Ira Levin had told him that the character of Rosemary was written with Mia Farrow in mind, Castle convinced over fifty local news programs to run a special one-minute film story that showed Mia's haircut.

Paramount devised an effective ad campaign for the film that condensed the gothic heroine and demon child motifs into a single image without giving away the film's ending. Precariously placed on a rocky hilltop, an anachronistic baby carriage sits in front of a sunset that takes the shape of Mia Farrow's supine profile. She looks up in a trancelike stare in an obvious foreshadowing of her drugged rape by the demon on the coven's altar. Underneath this image, an elliptical text mimics both the attractions of the earlier "three SEEs" approach to the genre and the ersatz stream-of-consciousness often invoked by popular conceptions of art-cinema narration: "Rosemary . . . Guy . . . The Bramford . . . the girl . . . the dead girl . . . the neighbors . . . the friend . . . the dead friend . . . the nightmare . . . the doctor . . . the vicious nightmare . . . the other doctor . . . the truth . . . the baby . . . poor baby . . . whose baby? . . . pray for Rosemary's baby!"[43]

The final phrase, "pray for Rosemary's baby," circulated as a teaser on mini-ads and buttons the week of the film's release and provided Polanski with his only opportunity to express annoyance with Castle and Paramount with the way that *Rosemary's Baby* was being handled by the studio.[44] Trade and newspaper ads for the film followed the established pattern of accenting both the horrific and virtuosic elements for potential viewers: for example: "'A masterpiece of suspense and horror. Polanski is a master of the bizarre, erotic, and perverse.'— *Newsday*"; and "'Shivering and absorbing entertainment. Sly, stylish, and suspenseful film. A splendidly executed example of its genre.'— *Saturday Review*."[45]

The film version of *Rosemary's Baby* follows the events of the novel quite closely. Rosemary Woodhouse (Mia Farrow) and her husband Guy (John Cassavetes) move into the Bramford, a Manhattan high-rise apartment. They are befriended by an eccentric older couple, Roman and

The cinema of attractions meets the art-cinema stream of consciousness in this newspaper ad for *Rosemary's Baby* (Private Collection of Rick Worland)

Minnie Castavet (Sidney Blackmer and Ruth Gordon). After a horrible nightmare in which she is raped by a green-eyed demon, Rosemary finds herself pregnant. She begins to suspect a terrible conspiracy between Guy, the Castavets, and obstetrician Abraham Sapirstein (Ralph Bellamy). Her most paranoid suspicions are confirmed: she has been chosen by this coven of urban satanists to give birth to the Devil's son, and the film ends with her gently rocking the (unseen) demon spawn in his black-draped crib.

Certainly Polanski was attempting to show the Hollywood studios that he was capable of handling a successful property in a responsible way. In addition to this, however, the story gave him an opportunity to recast many of the motifs of *Repulsion* in a story in which all of the heroine's persecution fantasies turn out to be true and even worse than she had feared. Unlike Carol Ledoux, Rosemary is an educated, assertive, and socially aware woman: she reads constantly, owns copies of both volumes of Kinsey's *Sexual Behavior*, and, in an episode not in the novel, initiates sex with Guy on their first night in the new apartment with a brazen, "Hey—let's make love." The story is quite explicit about the means by which first Sapirstein and later Guy attempt to strip her of power and knowledge: both men insist that she throw away her books, which "only worry" her. Even with this assertive heroine, many of the motifs in *Repulsion* that characterized the psychotic Carol begin to coalesce around Rosemary. The long hallways of the apartment provide interior framings of half-unseen menaces, the ticking of the bedside clock accompanies her nightmares, she sees her distorted reflection in kitchen appliances, and she looks suspiciously through the peephole in her front door.[46]

Many of the more idiosyncratic elements of style and narration in *Rosemary's Baby* serve a number of functions in Paramount's "leisure core" of interrelated products and tie-ins that accompanied the film's release. From the opening images under the credits, the film provides the viewer with a series of cues that simultaneously create the film's characteristic unease and ambivalence about the supernatural in the modern world while foregrounding defamiliarizing elements that point beyond the film to the highly publicized novel tie-in and soundtrack album. Under the Paramount logo, a high organ drone and piano eighth notes set up the film's musical theme, an eerie lullaby in waltz time sung under the credits by a slightly off-key Mia Farrow. As the camera pans across the Manhattan skyline, Farrow's dissonant lullaby is accompanied by harpsichord fills in one of 1960s horror's most heavily coded bits of musical *stimmung*, a device that recurred throughout the decade in gothic horror films such as *Dementia 13* and *Pit and the Pendulum*. Farrow's halting delivery recalls both Rhoda's struggling rendition of "Claire de Lune" in *The Bad Seed* and the psychotic Carol's singsong melody in *Repulsion*. After the middle eight in the melody, the high strings take up the melody and weave in and out of Farrow's out-of-tune warbling.

This creepy and catchy melody subtly foreshadows much of the horror to come, including the sequence's recurrence at the end of the film, where the reprise of the melody is clearly intended to represent Rosemary's tremulous lullaby to her satanic offspring. In addition, the title theme to this major Paramount release sung by the star of the film is also a highlight of the Paramount Records soundtrack album.

As the music plays, the camera continues its leisurely pan left, moving across the verdant vista of Central Park, and suddenly catches the gothic spires of the Bramford building (in reality the Dakota, which would take on its own sinister connotations after the murder of John Lennon in 1980), an architectural motif that seems seriously out of place in Manhattan. Tilting down, we see its heavily pitched roof, high spires, and verdigris gables, all of which make it resemble less a New York apartment building than the establishing shot of a Hammer Dracula film set in the Carpathian mountains. The downright strangeness of the building is further accentuated by the distorted perspective lines that cinematographer William Fraker's wide-angle lens brings to the shot. This radically foreshortened high-angle view of the Bramford is in fact the mirror image of the cover of Random House's hardcover edition of Ira Levin's novel. On the dust jacket, we look up at the sinister building with its gables and spires, and arched across the top of the image is the cursive "Rosemary's Baby," which strongly resembles the typeface of the credits that we have just seen.

Throughout the film, the music of Chris Komeda who, as Krzysztof Komeda-Trzcinski, had scored all of Polanski's previous features except *Repulsion*, serves a wide array of narrative functions. The huge preponderance of the film's action takes place with no musical accompaniment at all: one strategy of *Rosemary's Baby*'s efforts to update the conventions of the gothic horror film consists of muting the outrageous stylistic excesses of editing, camerawork, mise-en-scène, and sound that had characterized the genre from *Son of Frankenstein* (1939) and *Rebecca* (1940) all the way through to *What!* (1963). This technique is balanced by a countervailing tendency that serves both generic and extratextual functions: when music is heard it is not deployed like the more traditional scoring of films in the classical system, which emphasized

Rosemary's Baby (Paramount Home Video).

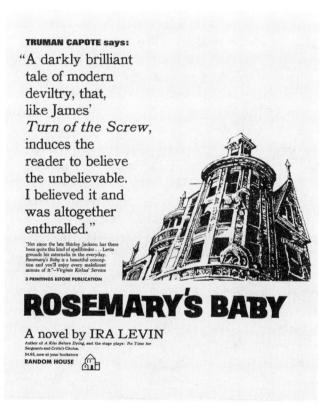

A Random House trade ad for the hardcover edition of Ira Levin's *Rosemary's Baby* (*Publishers Weekly*).

what music scholars have called "unheard melodies." Instead, Komeda's highly eclectic mix of free jazz, easy listening, horror-movie music of both the electronic *musique concrète* and Hermannesque high-strings variety tends to draw attention to itself. Jeff Smith has written of the changes in the commercial and aesthetic functions of film music in the sixties: as the studios that produced popular films became horizontally integrated into ancillary fields such as record and tape manufacturing and music publishing, musical soundtracks in the films began to draw attention to themselves.[47]

From the opening credits of *Rosemary's Baby*, Komeda's musical score serves three main functions. First, horror setpieces such as the demonic rape of Rosemary are accompanied by generic horror movie music punctuated with chromatic glissandi on the high strings, and the brief sequences featuring a bewildered Rosemary devouring nearly raw meat combine these motifs with the dissonant synthesizer music that would increasingly characterize horror music in the decade to come. Second, some melodies, such as the diegetic ivory-tickling jazz piano played on the Woodhouses's hi-fi set, as well as the nondiegetic six-eight flute melody heard under the montage of Rosemary's waiting for her friend Hutch at the Time-Life building, are coded as "contemporary" and serve an analogous function to the modish motifs in costume and production design provided by Anthea and Robert Sylbert. For example, the almost muzak-like easy-listening jazz that plays on the hi-fi set is heard twice, once while Rosemary attempts to spend the evening reading before being interrupted by a visit from Minnie Castavet, and a second time as the background for Rosemary and Guy's romantic evening *à deux* on "Baby Night." If this repeated melody is somehow missed by the audience, it becomes integral to the narrative when Rosemary asks Guy to "turn the record over" so she can hide the rest of the drugged mousse in her napkin, an action that motivates her awakening during the coven's invocation of the demon incubus.[48]

At times the music serves two or more functions simultaneously. During the film's most suspenseful sequence, the chase of the fleeing Rosemary through the Bramford by Guy and Sapirstein, the score turns into a wild free-jazz exploration for trumpet and quartet. In addition to the narrative functions served by Komeda's music, this wide range of stylings serves a third function as part of the attempt to provide "something for everyone" on Paramount Records's soundtrack album, which even included a psychedelic rock song heard briefly in the background during the Woodhouses's dinner party for their young friends.

Throughout the film we are restricted to what Rosemary sees, hears, thinks, and even dreams. After discovering the bloody and shattered body of Terry, the Castavets's "ward," on the sidewalk where she had apparently jumped to her death, Rosemary drifts into an uncomfortable sleep and, in the twilight between sleeping and waking, imagines "Terry's pulped face and one eye watching the sky" (in Levin's words)[49] and hears Minnie berating Roman through the thin apartment walls, bleating, "Sometimes I wonder how come you're the leader of *anything!*" At this moment Rosemary imagines Minnie's voice spoken from the mouth of a nun, who is holding a Bible in front of her in a graphic match to one of the ubiquitous self-help books on Rosemary's cinder-block bookshelf behind the bed. The camera pans right to a uniformed choir of Catholic school girls rehearsing a musical number in front of arched windows that are being bricked up by bored construction workers. The nun continues berating the camera in Minnie's voice, pointing accusingly at the windows and saying, "If you'd listened to *me*, we wouldn't have to do *that*! We'd have been all set to go now instead of having to start all over from *scratch!*"

This moment of great narrative depth and intense subjectivity is very unlike the understated suspense of most of the rest of the film: Rosemary's horror at Terry's suicide jump, symbolized by the bricking up of the windows, is conflated with the general malaise of shame from her Catholic school upbringing. By 1968, many Hollywood films had begun to include these "European-style" stream-of-consciousness passages, and their presence in *Rosemary's Baby* is a strong marker of the authorial signature of modernist film artist Roman Polanski. However, the opacity of the reference to Rosemary's childhood serves an additional function: without having read the original novel the viewer is unaware of the link between the two events in Rosemary's mind. In her dream, bricking up the windows at Our Lady school, a prank committed by the young Rosemary, kept the school from winning a "most-beautiful" competition run by an Omaha newspaper. In addition to creating a mood of unease—thus providing the film with a moment of art-cinema styling befitting a major-studio film by an important auteur, and preparing the viewer for the much more intense subjective sequence of demonic rape to follow—this brief passage invites the viewer to leave the theater and pick up a copy of the novel at the local bookstore to find out just what this sequence "means."

The same year of *Rosemary's Baby*'s release by Paramount, MGM issued the dazzling and sublimely confusing *2001: A Space Odyssey*. Timed with the release of the film was the paperback publication of Arthur C.

Clarke's screenplay novelization of *2001*, which in turn had been based on his short story "The Sentinel." The last thirty minutes of the Kubrick film, in which space travel by humans was placed into an elaborate philosophical and religious context, was perhaps the most opaque and abstruse sequence in the history of major-studio filmmaking. Clarke's novel became a sort of "bluffer's guide" for fans of the film.

The best-seller status of the novel *Rosemary's Baby* was crucial to the box-office success of Paramount's film, and vice versa. In fact, 1967–1968 saw the motion-picture industry coveting the success with which publishers were able to garner publicity and promotion for their products while, as *Variety* pointed out, spending a fraction of the studios' allotment for promoting movie releases.[50] Of course, this was jealousy of a most unflattering sort on the part of a movie industry that watched book publishers issue hundreds of titles every year, lose money on most of them, and press the envelope on censorship issues. Meanwhile, the studios waited in the wings for sifted-and-winnowed presold properties like *Rosemary's Baby*. In any event, Paramount, Random House, and Dell paperbacks were no doubt delighted about the reciprocal benefits that flowed to each in the marketing of *Rosemary's Baby* as a horror film, auteur work, and literary adaptation.

The second nightmare sequence of the film, Rosemary's drug-induced hallucinations and dim awareness of her impregnation by the conjured Devil, is in many ways the key to the disparate strands of influence that come together in *Rosemary's Baby*. In this sequence, a dizzy Rosemary lies on her bed and, after being disrobed by Guy, imagines her mattress floating on the ocean. Next, she is on a yacht with John F. Kennedy, Jacqueline Onassis, and adult incarnations of her Catholic school girlfriends. Finding herself nude, she looks up and sees the shelves in her linen closet mutate into the Sistine Chapel ceiling and stares at the image of God creating Adam. Back on the boat, she sees her friend Hutch on shore warning the ship of an imminent typhoon. Directed below deck by the boatswain, the Bramford's elevator operator Diego, Rosemary is tied to a bed in the center of a room while surrounded by a group of nude elderly people. Roman Castavet paints numbers and symbols on her body, and Guy crawls on top of her and begins sexual intercourse. Looking up into his eyes, Rosemary feels talons tearing into her shoulders and arms and sees a pair of yellowish feline eyes staring at her as the sex becomes painful. "This is no dream, this is really happening!" she screams before a black cloth is thrown over her face. Levin's novel is gruesomely explicit: "He repeated this exciting stroke again and again, his hands hot and sharp-nailed . . . Brutally, rhythmically, he drove his new hugeness. She opened her eyes and looked into yellow furnace-eyes, smelled sulfur and tannis-root, felt wet breath on her mouth, heard lust-grunts and the breathing of onlookers."[51]

Both the novel and film of *Rosemary's Baby* represent a highly self-conscious contemporary reworking of many of the oldest components of the female gothic. The entire story is told from the perspective of the young heroine who comes to live in a mysterious "castle"—in this case, the anachronistic Bramford/Dakota—with a history of madness and misery. In the film's first sequence, Rosemary and Guy are led on a tour of the building by the concierge Mr. Miklas, and they observe the disrepair in the halls and floor tiles. Inside the apartment of the recently deceased Mrs. Gardenia, the young couple see a collection of old furniture, a herbarium, and claustrophobic, almost-black varnished woodwork. The three are mystified by the oversize secretary that hides the linen closet, and Guy and Mr. Miklas are barely able to move the piece of furniture back to its original place. We later learn that a terrified Mrs. Gardenia had tried to block the secret passageway through which the Castavets and other members of the coven had been able to enter her apartment. Guy and Rosemary's first act on moving into the apartment is to paint the walls a dazzling white and to cover the bedroom walls with yellow flowered wallpaper, a pattern that echoes Rosemary's yellow dress in the early sequences of the film. As the film progresses, the ancient malevolence of the building begins to intrude on the apartment's mise-en-scène, with Terry's shattered face superimposed over the bright yellow wallpaper and Rosemary's face grotesquely distorted by her reflection on the metal toaster in a parallel image.

The "evil priests and nuns" of gothic novels are transformed into the elderly and eccentric group of satanists led by fellow tenants Roman and Minnie Castavet. The film's contemporary, middle-class American setting gives these stock characters a new lease on life. Hapless Roman, who is unable to mix cocktails without spilling them on the rug and who entertains Guy and Rosemary with a laundry list of cities in Alaska that he has visited, is later revealed to be the leader of the coven. The character of Minnie, played by Ruth Gordon in an Academy Award–winning performance, is the film's greatest dark-comic creation. Decked out in screaming aquas, oranges, and reds, she is a combination of Sophie Portnoy and Gladys Kravitz from TV's *Bewitched*, by turns cackling, mumbling, chewing with her mouth open, and turning over canned vegetables in Rosemary's apartment to check their price. The supporting cast of villains is equally rich. Ralph Bellamy plays Abe Sapirstein, the satanic Jewish obstetrician with the studio tan; Patsy Kelly plays the loud-mouthed, polyester-clad Laura-Louise; and, saving the best for last, the character of Mrs. Gilmore is played by Hope Summers, familiar to 1968 viewers as one of Aunt Bee's close friends on *The Andy Griffith Show*. "Hail Satan!" she sweetly beams, raising a glass of red wine in the film's final sequence.

There are many elements in *Rosemary's Baby* that draw on the cinema of attractions as exemplified by the horror film of the previous twenty years: the film deploys the motifs of the secret behind the door, present in the passageway that links the two apartments, and the menacing direct address, seen in the feline-eyed blazing stare of the demon incubus—and echoed in Guy's averted eyes, the blind eyes of Guy's rival Donald Baumgart, and the "piercing eyes" of Roman Castavet. In addition, fairground conjurer Castle remains a presence, both seen and unseen, throughout *Rosemary's Baby*. The film's first sequence, the tour of the new apartment, already reminiscent in the novel of the night porter scene in *Macbeth*, is given an extra charge by the presence of Elisha Cook Jr. in the role of Mr. Miklas. His role as monstrateur cannot fail to recall his similar function in Castle's *House on Haunted Hill*, where he had taken the skeptical party guests through the haunted house and shown them the knives, bloodstains, and acid vat used in all of the murders committed there. Further, the figure of Abe Sapirstein is the next in a long line of evil Caligari-like figures whose dominant position in the patriarchal world of the medical establishment invests him with powers of omnipotence and omniscience. It is the mere mention of his name that immediately discounts Rosemary's story of covens and conspiracy in the eyes of the young Dr. Hill, to whom Rosemary has fled late in the film. Sapirstein's voice reverberates with quiet menace as, just off-screen, he tells the betrayed Rosemary, "Any more talk of witches and we'll have to take you to a mental hospital."

As in *The Cabinet of Dr. Caligari*, this sadistic and evil doctor is doubled in the figure of the carnival showman, in this case William Castle himself. In a long sequence shot, Rosemary, having discovered that Sapirstein is a member of the coven, frantically telephones Dr. Hill from a phone booth on a sweltering June day. Waiting for his return call, she tries to hold the booth for as long as she can from a series of passersby. While on the phone with Dr. Hill, a middle-aged, grey-haired man approaches the outside of the booth and, facing away from Rosemary and the camera, waits at the right side of the Panavision frame for her to finish her call. She sees him, and her eyes grow wide with fright as the soundtrack shrieks with a Moog-synthesized frisson. The man turns around, and instead of a glaring Sapirstein, we are faced with a cigar-chomping William Castle, waiting to use the telephone in an uncredited cameo. Ivan Butler points to the "potentially sinister (and perhaps symbolic)"[52] appearance of Castle in this sequence, but in fact this is the third time that Castle has made his presence known, each one underscoring his role as string-puller and monstrateur: he also provides the voice of the newscaster narrating the Pope's visit to Yankee Stadium while Rosemary begins to collapse under the effects of the drugged dessert, and it is his voice again heard through the telephone as Mr. Weiss, the theatrical producer, calls Guy to offer him a key dramatic role after Donald Baumgart has gone blind.

One aspect of the publicity surrounding the release of the film was the attention paid by *Variety* and other trade journals to a moment in the film that is probably invisible to audiences twenty years after its release. When Minnie Castavet knocks on the door to present Guy and Rosemary with the drugged "chocolate mouse," Guy throws his napkin down on the table and mutters "Ah, shit!" as he gets up to answer the door. This use of language was a much-remarked-upon first in major-studio filmmaking, and it was part of a number of changes in permissible motion-picture content as Hollywood attempted to remain contemporary for late-sixties audiences, changes that would lead to the establishment of the aged-based film classification system by the MPAA later in the year. In *Rosemary's Baby*, the blasphemous story line,[53] explicit language, nudity of its female lead, and dialogue—which included discussion of menstruation, morning sickness, miscarriage, abortion, and necrophilia—was not matched by an increased level of onscreen violence. The major-studio horror film would take a few more years to move in this direction.

In Philadelphia, the film's release proceeded in three phases. Unlike the immediate saturation playoff of an exploitation double bill, *Rosemary's Baby* enjoyed, like *Repulsion* before it, the measured playoff of an art-film/horror crossover. *Rosemary's Baby* premiered in the prime late-June period at the deluxe, marble-inlaid Arcadia art theater, a six hundred seat house on Chestnut Street that was part of the Shapiro chain. After a $40,000 opening week,[54] the film's fifteen-week run brought in a total of $300,000.[55] Four weeks into this record-breaking run, a "special late show" was added on Friday and Saturday nights at 1:00 A.M., which discreetly recalled the midnight and late-night screenings of horror films such as *House of Wax* and *Curse of Frankenstein* but without tarnishing the engagement's upscale gloss.[56] At the time the late show was added, the film simultaneously opened at showcase houses in outlying areas including the Fox in Levittown and the Barn in Doylestown, as well as in drive-in theaters such as the Main Line in Philadelphia and the Tacony-Palmyra Bridge drive-in across the river in New Jersey.[57] After the film had enjoyed this wide playoff, it appeared at the Palace grind house in early November on a double bill with another Paramount release, the Italian crime thriller *Violent Four*. In the following weeks, it bowed in neighborhood theaters including the inner-city Nixon and the City Line Center as well as downscale drive-ins such as the Parkway in Woodbury, New Jersey, where it appeared with the surfer flick *Sweet Ride* and the British fantasy programmer *Vengeance of She*.[58]

Rosemary's Baby, along with *The Odd Couple*, was credited by *Variety* and other trade sources as signaling both Paramount's bounce back from the poor performance of 1966–1967 and the wisdom of its new parent, Gulf and Western.[59] *Rosemary* ended the year with $12.3 million in domestic and Canadian rentals, placing it at number 7 on *Variety*'s list of the top films of 1968. The film did not top Paramount's box-office charts that year, however: *The Odd Couple* earned $18.5 million,[60] and the two films were rereleased in an unlikely combination in early 1969.[61] This brought *Rosemary's* figures up to $15 million by the end of that year.[62] In addition, Dell's paperback edition of the novel, which was timed for concurrent release with the film and whose cover featured the baby-carriage-on-the-hilltop motif from the film's ad campaign, topped the best-seller lists for several months. In 1972, the film was shown on the ABC *Saturday Night Movie* series amid controversy, and it garnered high ratings for the network.

Many critics have seen in *Rosemary's Baby*, both in the novel and the film, the model for the next huge horror blockbuster, *The Exorcist* (1973). In the meantime, the motif of the demon child, the contemporary settings, and the downbeat endings would first be wedded to explicit violence in the next wave of low-budget horror films. Nowhere is this more evident than in the film whose engagement followed the multiple-house run of *Rosemary's Baby* in many 1968 movie theaters, the independently produced *Night of the Living Dead*.

CHAPTER 9

Family Monsters and
Urban Matinees:
Continental Distributing
and *Night of the*
Living Dead

For the second summer, Walter Reade Theatres in New York and New Jersey towns will play the annual Vacation Movie shows for children, under official school and Parent-Teacher Association sponsorship. Mr. Reade says the wonderful public and community relations that accrued from last year have made it easy to organize the series again. — *Motion Picture Herald*, May 15, 1954

Night of the Living Dead . . . casts serious aspersions on the integrity and social responsibility of its Pittsburgh-based makers, distrib Walter Reade, the film industry as a whole, and exhibs who book the pic. — *Variety*, October 16, 1968

The controversy surrounding the release of *Night of the Living Dead*, recounted in Jim Hoberman and Jonathan Rosenbaum's *Midnight Movies* and many other histories of the horror film, is now very well known.[1] Unleashed by the Walter Reade theater-chain subsidiary Continental onto unsuspecting kiddie matinee audiences in October 1968, the film was excoriated in *Variety* for hawking a "pornography of violence," as well as lambasted by Chicago reviewer Roger Ebert in a piece that was later reprinted in *Reader's Digest*. Ebert's essay, which is somewhat of a surprise for modern readers who are familiar with his defense of exploitation films and his screenwriting duties for nudie king Russ Meyer, begins with a description of the theater, the film, and the audience:

> It was a Saturday matinee in a typical neighborhood theater. There were a few parents, but mostly just the kids — dumped in front of the theater for a movie called *Night of the Living Dead*. There was a cheer when the lights went down. The opening scene was set in a cemetery (lots of delighted shrieks from the kids) where a teenaged couple are placing a wreath on a grave. Suddenly a ghoul — looking suitably decayed and walking in the official ghoul shuffle — attacks. The boy is killed, and the girl flees to a

nearby farmhouse. (More screams from the kids. Screaming is part of the fun, you'll remember.)

Ebert goes on to describe the film's escalation of outrages and to recount the stunned and terrified silence of the children in the theater at the end of the film after the film's hero is gunned down by the redneck vigilantes that have mistaken him for a ghoul. "I felt real terror in that neighborhood theater," Ebert writes. "I saw kids who had no sources they could draw upon to protect themselves from the dread and fear they felt . . . What are parents thinking," demanded Ebert, "when they drop their children off to see a movie called *Night of the Living Dead?*"[2]

A different question might be, "What were theaters thinking when they booked such a film into their afternoon matinee slot?" Many of the theaters that showed *Night of the Living Dead* were located in the inner city and served a predominantly African American audience. Like other nabe theaters, these houses were struggling against the chronic shortage of product, and they tried to fight back with an eclectic mix of programming that included subsequent runs, kiddie matinees, participation in huge multitheater saturation openings of genre films, and films from the nascent "adults-only" distribution network. The controversy surrounding the initial release of *Night of the Living Dead* was the result of Continental's misguided efforts to place the film in the inner-city nabe, horror matinee, and multiple-opening situations simultaneously. In the predominantly African American west Philly and northeast corners of the city, five neighborhood theaters—the Pearl, Fans, Uptown, Leader, and Nixon—exemplify the troubles faced by inner-city nabe operators in the late sixties. All of these theaters were part of *Night of the Living Dead*'s mass territorial first-run opening.

The controversy surrounding the release of *Night of the Living Dead* was only the most recent in a long series of skirmishes that Walter Reade and Continental had faced as they tried to carve out a profitable niche for themselves in the movie marketplace. While circuit owner and Theater Owners of America president Reade worked hard to establish good community relations for his houses and for the exhibition branch in general, in his role as head of Continental Distributing he sought to serve the market with product clearly differentiated from that of the major studios. Throughout the sixties, Reade asserted that the days were over for the movie with universal appeal and that distributors and exhibitors now had to tailor their product to one of a number of possible audiences.[3] In response to a 1960 *Motion Picture Herald* editorial lam-

Continental Distributing's ads for *Black Like Me* attempted to appeal to
audiences of both exploitation and social problem films (Wisconsin Center for
Film and Theater Research).

basting the trend of "sick" motion pictures imported by the majors and
independents, Reade wrote, "I am still of the opinion that our business
is not a mass business but a class business, and class business short
of pornography will always be successful . . . I am sure you will agree
that family pictures in the main have not been successful."[4] Continental
courted controversy with a series of challenging films for the class adult
audience, including a trio of films from the "kitchen sink" or "angry
young man" school in England. *Room at the Top* (1959) was condemned
by the Legion of Decency and banned in Atlanta,[5] *Expresso Bongo* (1960)
was condemned by the Legion,[6] and *Saturday Night and Sunday Morning*
(1961) was condemned by the Legion and banned in Kansas City.[7] One of
the company's most controversial releases was *The Mark* (1961), a drama
about a man released from the psychiatric ward of an Irish prison, after
serving time for child molestation, and his efforts to rebuild his life.

The success of Continental in importing features led the company
into limited partnerships in film financing. One of the company's efforts
in this area was *Black Like Me* (1963), the adaptation of John Howard
Griffin's autobiographical account of his travels in the South while dis-

guised as an African American. The film, shot on location with James Whitmore in the lead along with a cast of unknowns,[8] was part of a production trend in the early-to-mid sixties of low-budget, independently produced topical films about race relations in the United States. This trend also included Roger Corman's *The Intruder* (1961), Shirley Clarke's *The Cool World*, Ossie Davis's *Gone Are the Days* (both 1963), and Michael Roemer's *Nothing but a Man* (1965). These films were marketed at both neighborhood theaters in the African American community and at the wider market through appeals to the exploitation audience. An unnamed producer told a trade journal in 1963, "We are budgeting our picture so that, if necessary, we can recoup our costs in just the Negro market, even while aiming at as broad a market as possible."[9] Continental released *Black Like Me* in summer 1964 on a double bill with the horror import *The Hands of Orlac* (1960), which starred Mel Ferrer as a concert pianist who receives a hand transplant from a convicted killer and descends into homicidal madness. This metamorphosis narrative bore more than a passing resemblance to the plot of *Black Like Me*, and Continental opened the package in a multiple-run exploitation playoff. In Philadelphia, the *Black Like Me* and *Orlac* combination played a week at the Stanley Warner Palace grind house, following AIP's *Black Sabbath* and *Evil Eye* package, before opening wide at inner-city nabes and suburban drive-ins the following week.[10]

The history of the black motion-picture audience is particularly relevant to the emphasis in this study on the changing role of the neighborhood theater during the 1953 to 1968 period. The film industry was no different from other sectors of the culture industry in the sixties in its efforts to reach a growing market of African American consumers through specialized products and promotions of standard products. By 1967, *Variety* estimated that black moviegoers represented 30 percent of first-run movie patronage while numbering only 10 to 15 percent of the general population.[11] By the late sixties, the exhibition branch of the industry was finally learning to exploit the growing suburbanization of the white middle-class movie audience through new theater construction and changing distribution patterns. Thus the downtown picture palaces and the inner-city neighborhood theater enjoyed proximity to this large percentage of the black movie audience and developed a number of strategies to serve the communities near which they were located.

In these theaters, an African American supporting player often became the central attraction featured in a film's publicity. For example, the Leader Theater in Philadelphia featured ads for the 1965 sub-run engagement of *The Cardinal* by heralding "A Big Cast with Ossie Davis,"

The Pearl announced "Woody Strode in *The Professionals*" in 1967, and Simon of Cyrene became the Bible's biggest star when the Leader advertised "Sidney Poitier in *The Greatest Story Ever Told*" later that year.[12] Horror films were very popular with African American audiences. In fact, on the rare occasions when neighborhood theaters in African American neighborhoods in Philadelphia played films first run, it was often for mass openings of horror combinations such as Fox's releases of *Dracula, Prince of Darkness* and *Plague of the Zombies* in 1966 and *Frankenstein Created Woman* and *The Mummy's Shroud* in 1967. Some of these genre pictures provided second features for black-themed Hollywood and independent films in wide openings or sub-run in inner-city theaters. The Fans supported the 1962 sub-run engagement of AIP's *Premature Burial* with the backstage musical *Swinging Along*, which featured a brief performance by Ray Charles that was touted in the theater's newspaper ads. At the Pearl in 1965, *The Cool World* was cofeatured with the Bert Gordon sci-fi comedy *Village of the Giants* in 1965, the Leader supported *The Cool World* with Fox's *Curse of the Fly*,[13] and the Poitier western *Duel at Diablo* was paired at the Pearl in its multiple opening with the Amicus horror import *The Psychopath* in 1966.[14] Thus Continental's decision to issue *Black Like Me* on a double bill with *The Hands of Orlac* was prescient of double feature programming in the next several years.

In addition, there was heated debate in industry circles about whether films concerning "the race issue" were best sold as prestige social problem pictures or as exploitation items. For example, one of the films financed by Pathé-America's brief foray into feature distribution was Corman's *The Intruder*,[15] in which William Shatner played a racist agitator sent to a small southern town by a right-wing group to thwart desegregation. The film was unable to receive wide bookings until Alabama huckster M. A. Ripps retitled the film *I Hate Your Guts!* and issued it to the exploitation circuit through his Cinema Distributors of America in 1965.[16] Just five months after Continental's release of *Black Like Me*, Cinema V faced a similar quandary with its handling of Shirley Clarke's drama of Harlem life, *The Cool World*. Cinema V's initial publicity emphasized the action and exploitation angles, and the film played only in grind houses specializing in action fare and in theaters in African American neighborhoods in Washington, D.C., and Philadelphia. Unsolicited promotion from a San Francisco disc jockey helped the film cross over to both black and art-house audiences in its successful run at the Vogue. This integrated crossover success was elusive, however. Producer (and noted documentary filmmaker) Frederick Wiseman remarked that many theater owners were wary of black-themed topical films because "they think if they show a movie about Negroes, they'll have a riot on their hands."[17] Crossover success was also thwarted by racist anti-integration sentiments on the part of exhibitors themselves: theaters in Washington, D.C., were hesitant to book *Black Like Me* because, in the words of the film's incredulous producer, Julius Tannenbaum, they were concerned that "*Negro patrons might get into the habit of attending their theaters.*"[18]

At the same time that Continental was negotiating the often-conflicting demands of different markets for these race-themed social problem pictures, changes in the film marketplace were leading the company to broaden its roster of releases beyond art-house product into general-release films for a mass audience. Continental's parent company, the Walter Reade Organization, had merged with syndicator Sterling Television in 1961,[19] and the Reade-Sterling combination had enjoyed success in the TV market for several years (see chapter 7), but the roulette wheel of public whim was increasingly landing on the wrong color for Continental. In 1964, Walter Reade-Sterling posted a $491,000 loss largely due to "disastrous results from artie releases," according to *Variety*.[20] The following season, the company enhanced its release schedule with more overtly commercial items. Telling the trade press that "you can't take good reviews and awards to the bank,"[21] Reade and Continental issued *Agent 8¾*, a James Bond spoof that was very successful in a number of large-city bookings in the early summer. For the big turnaround, Continental followed the example of DCA's 1957 release of *Rodan* and issued the Japanese giant-monster import *Ghidrah, The Three-Headed Monster* in the orphan period of fall 1965 in a mass territorial opening pattern with saturation advertising. The "class-to-mass" strategy was highly successful: *Agent 8¾* racked up over $1 million in rentals, and *Ghidrah* surpassed $1.3 million and played many theaters that had never before showed a Continental product.[22]

The following year, Continental balanced the art-house entries, which Reade now called "specialized product," such as the Japanese art-house ghost story *Kwaidan*, Pasolini's *The Gospel According to St. Matthew* (a surprise hit, it turned out), and the Alberto Moravia adaptation *Time of Indifference*, with the more commercial releases such as the British science fiction import *Dr. Who and the Daleks* starring Peter Cushing, and the Japanese animated feature *Gulliver's Travels beyond the Moon*.[23] In a single year, video revenue and the increased rentals of the more conventional features rescued Reade's ledgers from a $500,000 loss in 1964, ushering in a similar-sized profit in 1965.[24]

Between 1965 and 1968, Continental pursued a number of strate-

Ghidrah, The Three-Headed Monster signaled Continental's move from "class" to "mass" in many of its annual theatrical releases (G. William Jones Film and Video Collection, Southern Methodist University).

gies in the increasingly competitive distribution marketplace. In 1968, Reade jumped on the diversification bandwagon by merging with the Rutland Corporation, a Vermont-based manufacturing firm. The new company, with a combined gross of over $23 million, provided Reade with more capital to invest in coproductions, feature acquisitions, and theater construction.[25] Meanwhile, Continental divided its release schedule into three categories: mass-appeal features destined for wide openings, "specialized product" for art theaters, and prestige attractions such as the Soviet import *War and Peace* (1968) or the James Joyce adaptation *Ulysses* (1967). In attempting to showcase films like *War and Peace* and *Ulysses* at roadshow engagements—that is, reserved seat bookings at high ticket prices—Continental was following a trend that the majors had successfully instituted with a number of very successful releases. The high ticket prices for Fox's roadshow engagements of *The Sound of Music* enabled the Julie Andrews musical to break the decades-old box-office record of *Gone with the Wind* as the all-time rental champion. In fact, the U.S. Department of Commerce asserted in 1967 that the increasing annual revenue of the motion picture industry was largely the result of higher admission prices, and it predicted that such increases in the future would continue to depend on the growing number of roadshow attractions released annually.[26]

At Continental, prestige programming was inextricably linked with Reade's efforts to fight censorship and age classification in both distribution and exhibition. The $3 million box-office success of *Ulysses*, partly the result of censor-baiting ballyhoo,[27] was necessary to compensate for the great disappointment of *War and Peace*, which was acquired from Mosfilm for an almost bank-breaking $1.5 million. The import feature was simply too long, at almost six hours (each unit of the two-evening program carried a $7.50 admission price),[28] to successfully cross over into mass success as a successful roadshow release.[29]

The thriving business of Continental's mass-appeal features *Ghidrah*, *Dr. Who*, and *Gulliver* in their saturation openings continued in what was one of the most important subsequent-run markets for horror and science fiction films of this period: the afternoon matinee circuit. In 1966, *Variety* noted that in the first half of the decade "the revenues from kiddie matinees have mushroomed and more than a dozen indie companies and several major distributors vie for prime playing time during the peak tot school season."[30] From the perspective of the local theater owner, these children's matinees provided programming that was supported by a large advertising push, the cost of which was amortized across a large number of theaters as well as lucrative concession sales.

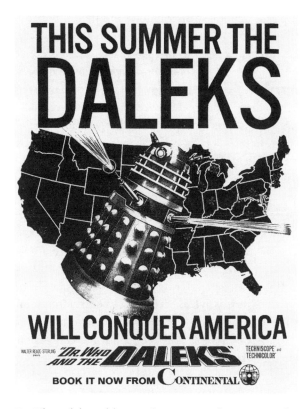

THIS SUMMER THE DALEKS

WILL CONQUER AMERICA

WALTER READE-STERLING "DR. WHO AND THE DALEKS" TECHNISCOPE and TECHNICOLOR

BOOK IT NOW FROM CONTINENTAL

Dr. Who and the Daleks was a huge success for Continental in both its 1965 first-run release and on the kiddie matinee circuit for the rest of the decade (Wisconsin Center for Film and Theater Research).

The three largest specialized kiddie matinee program suppliers were Edward Meyerberg's New Trends Associates, Inc.;[31] K. Gordon Murray, whose Mexican import feature *Santa Claus* was an enormous seasonal hit for over five years;[32] and Childhood Productions, whose success in the market led to runaway production and a public stock offering in 1967.[33] These three companies would arrange for a massive saturation advertising campaign in a major television market and open their films in as many as one hundred houses at a time. Murray's *Santa Claus* alone was earning $500,000 a week nationwide in the holiday season of 1964.[34] Murray, New Trends, and Childhood Productions demonstrated that with the children's matinee market "the normal 'hit-or-miss' rules of film distribution do not apply."[35] Indeed, these companies provided a type of film whose fantasy and fairy-tale qualities did not appear to date with the passing of time. In the words of a trade journal, "the 3-to-

10-year-old age group to which [these distributors] aim their product is being constantly replenished."[36]

In addition to the multiple openings of specialized kiddie product from Murray, New Trends, and Childhood Productions, nabe owners would often program double features of horror, fantasy, and science fiction films for a slightly older matinee audience of six-to-twelve year olds. Because this audience was also constantly turning over, and because the purpose of the Saturday matinee was for children to leave the house and get out from under the watchful eyes of their parents for a few hours, the actual films shown in these double features were often of secondary importance. Parents could drop off their children at the theater and enjoy a few hours of quiet around the house while the children shared an afternoon of scares, snacks, and laughter with members of their own age group. For the theater owner these matinee engagements were a very low-cost source of programming, often rented for a flat fee and shuttled between houses in a circuit-wide playoff over several weeks. A five hundred seat theater, charging thirty-five to seventy-five cents admission, could bring in over two hundred dollars at the box office (a small portion of which went to the distributor) and keep all of the concession profits for itself. For the distributor, these engagements represented pure profit, with prints circulating through local exchanges and generating income ten to twelve years after their initial theatrical run. Therefore, distributors such as AIP, Continental, Allied Artists, and some of the majors could keep almost-shredded prints of their already televised vaulties in circulation for hundreds of engagements every weekend.

For the young horror fans, the kiddie matinee was only one component of an explosion of horror-related media and merchandising in the mid-sixties. This included Aurora plastic model kits, trading cards, LP records of old radio horror shows, 8mm home-movie versions of the Universal classics, monster magazines, and reprints of fifties horror comics.[37] In Philadelphia it was possible to watch Channel 17's *Supernatural Movie* on Thursday night and Channel 48's *Beyond the Limits* on Friday night and *Strange Tales* early Saturday morning; spend the afternoon at a horror double feature at the local theater; then stay up Saturday night into the wee hours watching *Double Chiller Theater* and *Hollywood's Best* on Channel 6.

One of the crucial components of AIP's 1963 TV deal with both Screen Entertainment and the ABC owned-and-operated stations was James Nicholson and Samuel Arkoff's retention of theatrical rights to all of the films in the AIP catalog; consequently, their feature backlog remained a staple of the matinee circuit. Horror movies from the mid-fifties were still being shown at kiddie matinees in the late sixties: in spring 1966 the Towne Theater in Levittown, Pennsylvania, was playing a double feature of *The Screaming Skull* (1958) and *I Was a Teenage Frankenstein* (1957),[38] and two weeks later the inner-city Nixon was running Allied Artists's *Frankenstein 1970* (1958) and *Caltiki, The Immortal Monster* (1959). In May 1966 the audience at the inner-city Uptown was entertained by a double bill of the 1963 Jerry Lewis comedy *Who's Minding the Store* and Ed Wood's ten-year-old film *Bride of the Monster.* The fear expressed by the National Association of Theater Owners of opening "day and date" with television was often realized in the underbelly runs of the kiddie matinee and the all-night horror show. In July 1966, the Uptown ran a double feature of Allied Artists's *Castle of Blood* and *Monster from the Ocean Floor* when the latter had been on television just the previous Tuesday, and the Halloween spook show at the 309 drive-in in 1967 showed AIP's *Queen of Blood* twenty-four hours before it turned up on *Double Chiller Theater* under its TV title, *Planet of Blood.*

A number of other difficulties plagued neighborhood theaters subsisting on the eclectic mix of sub-runs, matinees, and exploitation films. A theater manager might have to hurriedly remove posters and lobby cards from the evening adults-only feature for the kiddie matinee and then replace them later while the ushers swept up the kids' popcorn to ready the house for the evening "raincoat crowd." Far from atypical was the weekend of June 11, 1966, when the Leader featured a kiddie horror matinee of *Blood of Dracula* and *The Magic Voyage of Sinbad.* In the evening the theater showcased Audubon Film's racial sexploitation drama *I Spit on Your Grave* and the mondo sexploiter *Ecco.* Six months later another inner-city house, the Pearl, showed as a matinee *I Married a Monster from Outer Space* and *Hey There It's Yogi Bear.* The kids were then ushered out of the theater before they crossed paths with evening patrons, there to see a double feature of *The Pink Pussycat* and *Unsatisfied.*

Some theaters attempted to cross over the same show at matinee that was playing in the evening. Where first-run multiple engagements of *King of the Grizzly* at the Pearl and *Fireball 500* at the Avenue (July 1966), Disney's *Bullwhip Griffin* at the center-city Broadway and the Norris in Norristown (March 1967), could easily perform fitting matinee service, other evening programs were a more problematic fit. The escalating levels of sex, violence, and profanity in even mainstream releases, coupled with the lack of an aged-based classification system for films, created confusion for theater managers, parents, and the juvenile audience itself. In March 1967, the Capital in west Philadelphia carried its engagement of the violent spaghetti western *For a Few Dollars More* into the matinee slot, and the Leader showed its regular evening feature, the brutal combat hit *The Dirty Dozen*, as the matinee the following September.

Later that September, the Nixon used its matinee to continue the regular first-run multiple opening of Fox's Hammer double feature *Frankenstein Created Woman* and *The Mummy's Shroud*. One of the reasons for this and other carryovers of the evening feature into the matinee slot was the increasing control that the major distributors were attempting to exert over the nabe box office. Both Myerberg of kiddie matinee distributor New Trends Associates and Marshall Fine of the National Association of Theater Owners lambasted the practices of distributors who insisted on exclusivity in the runs of their evening pictures. In other cases, distributors would insert clauses in the film rental contract entitling them to a percentage of the entire day's gross receipts. Both of these practices often had the unintended effect of forcing neighborhood theaters, in the rare cases where they were enjoying first-run status as part of a wide multiple opening, to show the adult-oriented evening picture as the matinee.[39]

At the same time that inner-city theaters such as the Nixon were trying to stay in business with their programming mix of subsequent-runs, matinees, and participation in saturation openings, Continental continued to court the African American audience that patronized the Nixon and other city nabes: in 1967 it released another black-themed topical, the screen adaptation of LeRoi Jones's play *The Dutchman*,[40] and a year later came the Theater Guilds's production of the Herbert Biberman–directed *Slaves* with Ossie Davis and Dionne Warwick, followed by a low-budget horror film from Pittsburgh with an African American protagonist, *Night of the Living Dead*.[41]

Night of the Living Dead recounts one night in the lives of seven people trapped in an isolated farmhouse while, outside, an amassing horde of recently dead, radiation-infected cannibal zombies attempt to break into the house. As the number of zombies outside increases, the internal struggles of the human survivors become more lethal. Ben, the African American protagonist, serves as protector to catatonic survivor Barbara, whose brother Johnny is murdered by a zombie in the film's opening scene. Ben and Barbara are mirrored by two other couples, Harry and Helen Cooper, a middle-aged married couple keeping watch over their zombie-infected daughter Karen, and Tom and Judy, a young teenage couple. The middle section of the film is devoted to bitter arguments between Ben and Harry about how to survive the zombie onslaught. After an attempt to flee the house leads to the fiery death of Tom and Judy— we see the zombies devouring their cooling entrails in the film's most famous scene—Ben shoots Harry Cooper in a struggle over the locked front door, the now-dead/undead Karen kills and devours her mother, and Ben boards himself in the basement, the very place Harry had insisted was their only chance of survival. Discovered by a redneck posse of zombie hunters in the morning, Ben is mistaken for a ghoul and shot in the head. The film ends with Ben's body being dragged into the morning light and incinerated in a bonfire with the very zombie that killed Johnny in the film's opening scene.

In *Night of the Living Dead*, Continental had a product that was suited to the well-tested playoff of the genre film: it was released at Halloween, during the slow fall season. Also, it was simultaneously booked into a large number of subsequent-run theaters and drive-ins and was supported by saturation advertising in newspapers, radio, and television. In Philadelphia, the wide release for the film utilized twenty neighborhood theaters and drive-ins, including the Leader and the two drive-ins often specializing in horror fare, the Airport drive-in in southwest Philadelphia and the Ridge Pike drive-in in Conshohocken. The ad campaign for the film used a gambit copied from the now-respectable William Castle: "IF 'Night of the Living Dead' Frightens You to Death," screamed the ads, "You are covered for $50,000!"[42] Further, the film contained elements from the company's successful combination of *Black Like Me* and *The Hands of Orlac* all in one package: the proven success of horror in the inner-city market was now enhanced by a film with an intelligent and resourceful African American protagonist. In addition, *Night of the Living Dead* featured a perfect "Mr. Charlie" foil to Duane Jones's Ben, the fidgety, balding middle-class patriarch Harry Baldwin.

The film marks a crucial turning point in the history of the low-budget horror film, and its tremendous influence makes some of its most startling elements invisible to modern viewers. *Night of the Living Dead*'s absence of stars and its marginal place in the network of 1968 horror film production and distribution led screenwriter John Russo and director George Romero to differentiate their approach to the genre by emphasizing graphic violence, bleak social commentary, and a downbeat ending. Neither critics nor audiences seemed to know what to make of this: critics were outraged, audiences were often alienated, and theaters sometimes experienced a backlash for booking the film. Of course, it was precisely the film's violence and bleakness that led to its critical recuperation as a visionary and subversive work several years later.

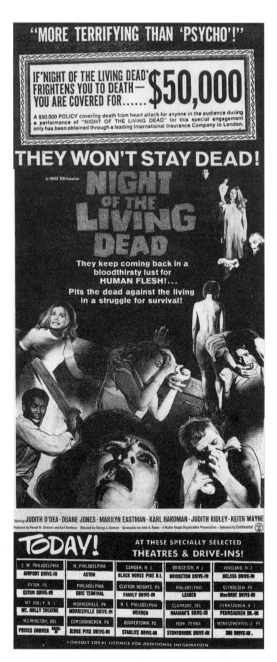

Newspaper advertisement for the 1968 Philadelphia release of *Night of the Living Dead* (*Philadelphia Inquirer*).

Night of the Living Dead combined graphic violence and late-sixties nihilism with motifs from fifties atomic sci-fi programmers such as Corman's 1954 *Day the World Ended* (Wisconsin Center for Film and Theater Research).

In 1968 theater owners hoped that *Night of the Living Dead* could be exploited in both horror-matinee and evening slots. In the afternoon, the film could be shown with a years-old AIP or Allied Artists black-and-white vaultie, with which the black-and-white, apocalyptic radiation-based invasion narrative shared a number of traits.[43] In the evening, it could be highlighted on a double bill with a second feature designed to appeal to the African American audience. At the Merben Theater on Frankford Avenue, *Night of the Living Dead* played its first-run engagement with the Poitier drama *For the Love of Ivy*. This combination showed up the following week at the Nixon and the Eric Terminal at 69th and Market, and the Eric in suburban Fairless Hills played Romero's film on a dual bill with the Jim Brown caper film *The Split*, while at the Astor Theater on Girard Avenue *Night of the Living Dead* played on the lowercase of the Dean Martin and Robert Mitchum western *Five Card Stud*. At the Mount Holly Theater just across the river in New Jersey, the film played a double feature with the Toho giant-monster import *King Kong Escapes*. At four of these venues, these double features were carried over into the matinee slot. The Nixon was the only exception; there, the management wisely substituted an AIP double feature of *Invasion of the Saucer Men* and *Circus of Horrors*.[44] The management's wisdom was born of bitter experience: in 1964, Nixon manager George Norcutt had been fined $1,000 by a grand jury for "giving and advertising an obscene show" and "contributing to the delinquency of minors" for featuring the "obscene, sadistic, and perverted" Herschell Gordon Lewis *Blood Feast* at an April Saturday matinee.[45] By 1968 the protracted scenes of zombie extras, some partially or completely nude, munching on chocolate-syrup-soaked entrails in the black-and-white *Night of the Living Dead* equaled or surpassed anything in Lewis's groundbreaking Eastmancolor gore classic.

It was under a similar set of circumstances that Roger Ebert witnessed the onslaught of *Night of the Living Dead* against its juvenile audience at the neighborhood theater in inner-city Chicago. Ebert's review gives a plot synopsis of the film and notes that the "pretty dull argument among the trapped people" was "popcorn time for a lot of kids." He points out that "apparently some sort of unearthly radiation" is responsible for the resurrected army of zombies. "It almost always is," he proffers. After the unexpected end of the second act, when the teenage couple and would-be protagonists Tom and Judy are incinerated and devoured by the ghouls, "the mood of the audience changed," according to Ebert: "Horror movies were fun, sure, but this was pretty strong stuff. There wasn't a lot of screaming anymore. The place was pretty quiet." At the end of the movie, Ebert states, the theater was silent:

> I don't think the younger kids really knew what hit them. They'd seen horror movies before, but this was something else. This was ghouls eating people—You could actually see what they were eating. This was little girls killing their mothers. This was being set on fire. Worst of all, nobody got out alive—even the hero got killed.[46]

At the end of his tirade, Ebert appeals to the recently adopted MPAA aged-based classification system and notes that the Walter Reade Organization and Continental did not subscribe to the ratings. Reade's theaters began using the MPAA classification system in late 1968, but the company steadfastly refused to submit Continental releases to the Board for classification.[47]

Despite its notoriety *Night of the Living Dead* did not meet Reade's expectations of a million-dollar gross in its first year of release. However, the unremitting success of the film at midnight screenings and in showings by campus film societies in the United States, paired with excellent box-office returns in Europe and Japan, meant that receipts far exceed that figure by the early seventies. Further, the film became a staple as a supporting feature at drive-ins for the next several years. A minor technical omission at the time of the film's release would haunt the filmmakers fifteen years later at the dawn of the video age: Continental's change of the film's title card (the film's working title had been *Night of Anubis* after the Egyptian goddess of the underworld) neglected to include a copyright notice, and to Romero's horror the film seemed to pass into the public domain after Continental folded in the seventies. By the mid-eighties dozens of video catalogs were offering cheap 16mm transfers of the film, with the original filmmakers receiving no royalties from these sales.

Night of the Living Dead's influence on the horror genre was incalculable, establishing onscreen cannibalism as *the* horror motif of the seventies and spawning two Romero-directed sequels and countless imitations in Europe. Homages to *Night of the Living Dead* can be found in films as disparate as *Pink Flamingos* (1972) and *They Came from Within* (1975), and it has been screened at the Museum of Modern Art. Its artistic elements anticipate many trends in the low-budget horror and blaxploitation genres of the seventies.

In 1968, however, it shared both generic traits and marketing elements with the horror and science fiction genre films of the fifties and the low-budget race-themed topical dramas of its time. These films were both crucial programming elements in the doomed efforts of theaters serving the inner-city neighborhood market to adapt to the changing movie marketplace. In the ensuing years, Hong Kong–produced martial arts films and the blaxploitation cycle of 1971–1974, which contained a strong current of horror genre hybrids such as *Blacula* (1972) and *Abby* (1974), created interest at the inner-city nabe box office. By the end of this cycle in the mid-seventies, however, Philadelphia's Pearl, Nixon, Uptown, and Leader theaters had closed their doors for good.

CONCLUSION

The Horror Film in

the New Hollywood

I n 1968, just months after the releases of both *Rosemary's Baby* and
Night of the Living Dead, the Motion Picture Association of America
scrapped the Production Code Administration and replaced it with
the age-based system of film classification, which remains to this day.
The ratings of G, M, R, and X were the final recognition that the general film audience of the studio era had been replaced by a multiplicity
of audiences, each with their favorite stars, genres, and related product
tie-ins.

The period between 1953 and 1968 coincided with the growth and
coming-of-age of the postwar baby boom generation. During this period, whole segments of the economy, the culture industry in particular, were reconfigured to separate this new group of consumers from
their discretionary income. For example, popular music completely re-
tooled itself to feed young people's insatiable demand for the rock-and-
roll music that their parents despised.

Thomas Doherty notes that the sheer repellence of a film title like
I Was a Teenage Werewolf (1957) was fodder for newspaper editorial writers and stand-up comics months before and after the film's release, and
that young people, particularly adolescent boys, came to embrace these
deliberately alienating and downscale cultural forms.[1] These teenagers
even came to see their choices in consumption habits as an important

means of self-expression. The horror comics of the 1950s and the monster and science fiction magazines of the 1960s were accompanied by reprints of the novels of H. P. Lovecraft, record albums of *Lights Out* radio broadcasts from the thirties and forties, and a huge number of other elements of a burgeoning culture of buffs and cognoscenti.

This was part of a much larger series of changes within the postwar consumer economy. By 1968 the Hollywood studios had been acquired by huge multinational corporations with a hand in an immense range of products and services. The next twenty-five years would see these firms exploit the consumer market in an increasingly sophisticated way. Companies in oil production and distribution; soft-drink sales; talent brokering for the film, television, and recording industries; and leisure and manufacturing were now in possession of the studio logos. A motion picture was now the hub in a vast array of products that could include everything from miniature figures, soundtrack recordings, T-shirts, and toys and posters to novelizations of the screenplay. Feature films could lead to a moneymaking franchise of several years' duration that could include as many as ten or twenty movies (for example, the James Bond films) and a dizzying proliferation of tie-ins.

Other changes in the movie industry that are associated with the 1953 to 1968 period continue to form a model for contemporary exploitation of the movie marketplace. First, the saturation booking pattern innovated by genre films during the fifties and sixties came to be associated with blockbuster releases from the major Hollywood studios: Universal's release of *Jaws* in this way was considered a landmark in the seventies, but this, like many other changes, was a more extensive and refined version of a process begun as early as 1953 with Warner's release of another giant-monster epic, *Beast from 20,000 Fathoms*. Also, the upscaling of the lowbrow monster film through major stars and a presold literary property exemplified by *Jaws* (and *The Exorcist*, for that matter) is a direct result of the changes in studio economics outlined in chapter 8 in relationship to Paramount and *Rosemary's Baby*.

Second, the growing importance of the international box office continued unabated through the nineties and beyond. As of this writing, over half of the annual box-office revenue for the Hollywood studios comes from abroad. Third, the various ancillary markets associated with viewing Hollywood features at home have actually supplanted box-office receipts in their generation of revenue: videocassette, DVD, cable, and broadcast TV now provide the lion's share of the American market.

Some changes are immediately visible in genre cinema itself. The formulas innovated by AIP and others—in particular the youth cycle of horror and exploitation films—are still in full swing in the *Scream, A Nightmare on Elm Street*, and *Friday the 13th* franchises. Paramount's *Friday the 13th* series follows the time-honored fifties and sixties tradition of a major studio knocking off the genre success of an independent production (in this case, John Carpenter's independently produced *Halloween*), and New Line's immense commercial growth in the eighties and nineties has its roots in the Astor/DCA model of a smaller distributor seeking a place in the market with a combination of eccentric art films and lowbrow genre items.

The cinema of attractions, which reached a sort of apotheosis in 3-D and the gimmicks and exploitation campaigns of producers such as William Castle, has come to displace the cinema of narrative integration in the genre picture as increasingly sophisticated special effects in films like *American Werewolf in London* (1981), *Hellraiser* (1987), and *The Mummy* (1998) threaten to overwhelm the movies in which they appear. In fact, the new "stars" of the horror genre are often special-effects technicians such as Rick Baker, Tom Savini, Rob Bottin, and the staff of Industrial Light and Magic, whose virtuosity is often highlighted in the preponderance of publicity surrounding the release of a new genre film.

At the intersection of the rating system and the increasing importance of special effects, we find the genre's most well known and widely discussed legacy from the fifties and sixties: the continuing escalation of onscreen gore. Despite what we might hear on morning talk shows and the bluster of right-wing politicians around election time, most American films pale into chaste rectitude next to their Asian or European counterparts in terms of gore. It is unthinkable that an American studio would release, let alone produce, movies as shocking as Herman Yau's repulsive cannibal horror film *Human Porkbuns*, aka *The Untold Story*, (1992) or the simulated necroporn of Nacho Cerda's *Aftermath* (1996). Still, the two dominant models for the narrative deployments of onscreen violence can be found in the films examined in the final chapters of this volume.

Rosemary's Baby represents the more upscale version: here we see big-name stars, a story based on a best-selling novel, and attempts to offset its increasing levels of mayhem with some kind of religious, philosophical, or literary gloss. *The Exorcist* (1973), *The Omen* (1976), *Silence of the Lambs* (1990), and *Seven* (1995) are additional examples of this trend. *Night of the Living Dead* provides the model for another kind of film: the leaner, energetic, regionally produced independent feature that came to constitute the richest artistic vein in seventies and eighties horror in films such as *The Texas Chain Saw Massacre* (1974) and the early work of Wes Craven, Larry Cohen, and David Cronenberg.

The years addressed in this book also coincided with an unprecedented interest in movies by the intelligentsia. Because of the rise of the postwar art theater and successful marketing of "daring" and "controversial" films from abroad with new stars, the international art cinema became commercially viable in the United States, and European directors became "stars" themselves who were capable of selling a film to distributors and the public. Popularized versions of criticism found in *Cahiers du Cinéma* and other European film journals resulted in closer attention to the aesthetic dimensions of American films. In addition, the wide availability of 16mm equipment enabled a culture of oppositional and avant-garde cinema to flourish. In New York, first Amos Vogel's Cinema 16 and later Jonas Mekas's Filmmakers Cinemateque showcased the work of Maya Deren, Kenneth Anger, Jack Smith, Andy Warhol, Shirley Clarke, Mike and George Kuchar, and John Cassavetes. While Deren, Cassavetes, and others viewed their work as diametrically opposed to the genre fare offered by Hollywood, filmmakers like Anger, Smith, Warhol, and the Kuchars inherited from the surrealists a rapt fascination with the mass-produced popular fantasies of genre film. In *Allegories of Cinema: American Film in the Sixties*, David James writes of the Kuchars's appropriation of elements of Douglas Sirk and Roger Corman such that

> the Corman Z movie . . . stands in something of the same relation to the films of the major studios that a Kuchar film stands in relation to the Z movie. Since the sixties this critical double bind has provided the basis for a self-consciously produced genre of "bad" movies, and for a reevaluation of older directors like Edward D. Wood, Jr. and Oscar Micheaux which has elevated them from bad to "bad."[2]

Here James, despite his supercilious attitude toward filmmakers as fascinating as Wood and Micheaux, is making a crucial historical link between the converging streams of the genre and avant-garde cinemas of the sixties. Indeed, filmmakers such as Mike Kuchar, in the sci-fi and comic book elements of *Sins of the Fleshapoids* (1965); Kenneth Anger, in the appearance of Caligari's Cesare in *Inauguration of the Pleasure Dome* (1954) and the pop music score of *Scorpio Rising* (1963); and Jack Smith, in the vampire film iconography of *Flaming Creatures* (1963), draw as much on elements of lowbrow popular culture as they do on high modernism and the avant-garde.[3]

The reciprocal relationship between the art cinema and the horror film is further evident in films of the period, ranging from *Peeping Tom* to *Rosemary's Baby*. The auteurist readings performed by sixties critics on the films of directors such as Fellini, Bergman, and Antonioni were soon deployed by other writers to find authorial signatures in the films of Bava, Corman, and Terence Fisher. Both of these phenomena, as well as the self-conscious appropriation of lowbrow elements in the underground films of Smith, Warhol, and the Kuchars, have been analyzed by Joan Hawkins in *Cutting Edge: Art-Horror and the Horrific Avant-Garde*.[4] Hawkins draws important parallels between the cultural and economic status of lowbrow body genres such as horror and porn and the increasing tendency of the avant-garde to treat similar motifs. In some cases, such as the radically changing critical reputation of Tod Browning's *Freaks* (1932) or the production and release of Paul Morrissey's *Flesh for Frankenstein* (1973), the only difference between these two institutions is the context of reception.

This aesthetic and cultural ambivalence reached its ultimate extension in the midnight cult cinema of the seventies. Here was a film movement of "exploitation films for art theaters," in John Waters's phrase.[5] Many art theaters remained open throughout the seventies on the strength of box-office receipts generated by eccentric hybrids like Waters's own *Pink Flamingos*, which borrowed as heavily from Fellini, Genet, and Pasolini as it did from William Castle and Herschell Gordon Lewis; *The Texas Chainsaw Massacre*, which combined grueling visceral horror with eccentric stylistic flourishes and non sequiturs from the art film and New American Cinema; and the savage spaghetti western–derived violence in Alexander Jodorowski's *El Topo*, which was balanced with off-the-wall religious symbolism derived from Bergman and Buñuel.

The seventies boom in low-budget genre cinema, detailed extensively by Robin Wood, Tony Williams, and others, as well as the cult film phenomenon of the art theater, came to an end in the early eighties. This coincided with two irreversible trends: first, the upscaling of the horror and science fiction genre in films such as *Alien*, and, second, the success of home video, which put the final nails in the coffin of the drive-in theater, the sub-run grind house, and the art theater. Incredibly, home video resulted in the resurrection of many of the very films covered in this study, from zero-budget programmers like *Robot Monster* and *The Brain That Wouldn't Die* to a restored rerelease of *Peeping Tom* and, as James notes, their reappraisal in a completely different context.[6] By the mid-eighties, the Castle, Corman, and Hammer films were still under copyright to the multinational entertainment conglomerates operating

Ridley Scott's *Alien* (1979) appropriated elements of several
low-budget programmers of the fifties and sixties and
lavished them with post-*Star Wars* production design and
special effects (Twentieth Century-Fox).

under the names of the old studios, and were issued on video like trade
paperbacks of classic novels. Hundreds of the more obscure genre films
of the fifties and sixties—many of which had been released directly to
TV—had fallen into the public domain. This enabled independent video
companies such as Rhino, Something Weird, and most important, Sinister Cinema, to transfer 16mm TV prints of hundreds of genre programmers to video and sell them through mail order at popular prices.

The main conduit through which this product was delivered to its intended audience was advertisements in a new series of genre fan magazines like *Filmfax*, *Psychotronic*, and the more scholarly and impeccably
researched *Video Watchdog*. These publications were designed to appeal
to both aging baby boomers, for whom the films had nostalgia appeal,
and younger fans, the heirs to the tradition of the Kuchars and the sur-

realists.[7] This latter group, which had affinities with adjacent oppositional cultures such as punk music and body modification (indeed, the
movie zine phenomenon of the past few years has its roots in an earlier
movement surrounding punk and new wave), produced in 1986 a volume of criticism called *ReSearch #10: Incredibly Strange Films*, edited
by V. Vale and Andrea Juno.[8] A wide range of essays in the book recasts
the exploitation films of the fifties and sixties as an avant-garde *man-
qué*, and the back cover reprints Picasso's famous quote that "the chief
enemy of creativity is 'good' taste."

The aging baby boomers, of whom I must admit I am one, have parlayed the buff's interest and completist zeal of their teenage fan years
into a concern with issues of canonicity, influence, and restoration that
is more closely tied to the recuperation of popular culture by the intelligentsia than it is to the frisson of the films' original disreputability. We
have our masterpieces, too, and we are willing to make pilgrimages to
see them. In the late 1990s, the Internet was abuzz with the mail-order
availability of a virtually unwatchable video copy of the work print of
the fourth *Texas Chainsaw Massacre* film. The sheer indecipherability of
the video signal became a marker of the object's special, forbidden, and
sacred status.

In "'Trashing' the Academy," Jeffrey Sconce has written of a recognizable canon of art films and low-budget body genre films he calls "paracinema." These films, once shown in marginal venues such as art theaters and late-night television, are now almost exclusively available on
home video, often from mail-order video companies operating on the
knife's edge of copyright legality. Sconce draws on critics as varied as
Bourdieu, Gans, and Lester Bangs to bolster his central point that an
appreciation of paracinema, or lowbrow cinema, or trash films is insepa-
rable from a distaste for middlebrow culture and cinema and a delight
in offending the sensibilities of people who consume tasteful, literate
movies.[9] This is just about the only thing that can account for a video
catalog that contains entries for films as varied as Buñuel's *Criminal Life
of Archibaldo de la Cruz* (1955), Mario Bava's *Lisa and the Devil* (1972),
and Doris Wishman's *Keyholes Are for Peeping* (1971).

And offend sensibilities these and other wares do: cultural watchdogs
still prowl the carnival midway. At the time of this writing, concerned
parents (are there any other kind?) carry on the tradition of Frederic
Wertham and Vance Packard and are mounting increased attacks on
television programs, compact discs, and the Internet. As Mikhail Bakhtin has noted in his study of medieval France, *Rabelais and His World*,
the often-terrifying world of the carnival was an occasion for the tem-

porary inversion of cultural and moral values characteristic of a feudal hierarchy.[10] The democratized, consumerist American carnivalesque is viewed with a deep ambivalence by a Puritan sensibility that seeks both to restrain individual desires and to unleash them in consumption. Nowhere is this ambivalence more clearly expressed than in the cultivation of the young as a consumer group in the postwar period.

The horror film of the fifties and sixties, proffered to its young audience by mountebank snake-oil salesmen such as Samuel Arkoff and William Castle, was part of a huge shift in the way popular culture was financed, produced, distributed, sold, and received. The period of this study stretches from the days of a mature oligopoly to an age of international conglomeration in the media industry. It is a measure of the adaptability of the horror cinema and the cinema of attractions that these forms continue to fascinate and infuriate across a fifty-year technological and economic divide. The itinerant trickster and conjurer is still there, pulling back the tent curtain to invite us to enter the dream world of the attraction, revealing a frightening exhibition of freaks and curiosities, interstitial beings who cross categories that many still prefer to keep distinct. For the historian of popular culture, this mountebank is as important as the demons that hide in the darkness of his tent.

APPENDIX

Feature Film Packages in

Television Syndication,

1955–1968

M and A Alexander

CHILLER–SCIENCE FICTION PACKAGE (4 titles). Released to TV: early 1964

Cape Canaveral Monsters (1960)
* Flight of the Lost Balloon (1960)
Hideous Sun Demon (1955)
Monster of Piedras Blancas (1961)

Source: TV Feature Film Source Book—
Series, Serials, and Packages (spring 1964), p. FF-2.

American International Television

EPICOLOR '64 (40 titles). Released to TV: 3/9/64.

* Attack of the Moors (1960)
* Attack of the Normans (1960)
* Avenger of the Seven Seas (1960)
* The Black Invaders (1960)
* Brennus, Enemy of Rome (1960)

* The Burning of Rome (1960)
* Challenge of the Amazon Queen (1960)
* Colossus and the Gladiator (1964)
* Colossus and the Headhunters (1960)

*Throughout appendix, asterisk denotes a color feature

* Colossus of the Arena (1960)

* Duel of Fire (1960)

* Goliath and the Barbarians (1960)

* Goliath and the Dragon (1960)

* Hercules against Rome (1960)

* Hercules and the Black Pirate (1960)

* Hercules against the Barbarians
(1960)

* Hercules against the Mongols (1960)

* Hercules and the Masked Rider
(1960)

* Hercules of the Desert (1960)

* Journey to the Lost City (1960)

* King of the Vikings (1964)

* King of the Mongols (1964) aka
Genghis Khan and the Mongols

* The Masked Conqueror (1960)

* Mask of the Musketeers (1960)

* Musketeers of the Sea (1960)

* Messalina (1960)

* Prisoner of the Iron Mask (1960)

* Queen of the Seas (1960)

* Revenge of the Conquered (1960)

* Revenge of the Barbarians (1960)

* Revenge of the Musketeers (1960)

* Samson and the Sea Beast (1960)

* The Saracens (1960)

* 79 A.D. (1960)

* Sign of the Gladiator (1960)

* Slave Girls of Sheba (1960)

* Taur the Mighty (1960)

* The Ten Gladiators (1960)

* Thor and the Amazon Women
(1960)

* Women of Devil's Island (1960)

AMAZING '65 (20 titles). Released to TV: 9/2/64.

Amazing Transparent Man (1960)

* Angry Red Planet (1960)

* Assignment Outer Space (1962)

* Battle beyond the Sun (1963)

Beyond the Time Barrier (1960)

The Blancheville Monster (1962)

Black Sunday (1961)

The Brain That Wouldn't Die (1962)

* Circus of Horrors (1960)

* The Day the Earth Froze (1964)

The Hand (1961)

Invasion of the Star Creatures (1962)

The Invisible Creature (1960)

* Journey to the Seventh Planet (1962)

* Konga (1961)

Lost Batallion (1962)

Night Tide (1963)

Phantom Planet (1962)

Terror in the Crypt (1964)

Twist All Night (1962)

EPICOLOR '65 (20 titles). Released to TV: 9/2/64.

* Ali Baba of the Seven Saracens
(1964) aka Hawk of Baghdad

* Desert Raiders (1964)

* Erik the Conqueror (1964)

* Fire over Rome (1962)

* Fury of Achilles (1962)

* Giant of the Evil Island (1964)

* Goliath at the Conquest of Damascus
(1964)

* Guns of the Black Witch (1962)

* Hercules and the Tyrants of Babylon
(1964)

* Hercules, Prisoner of Evil (1964)

* Revenge of the Gladiators (1964)

* Rome 1585 (1962)
* Samson and the Seven Miracles of
    the World (1963)
* Samson and the Slave Queen (1964)
* Slave Queen of Babylon (1962)
* Sword of Damascus (1962)
* Sword of the Empire (1963)
* Valley of the Doomed (1963)
* War Gods of Babylon (1962)
* White Slave Ship (1962)

THRILLERS FROM ANOTHER WORLD (19 titles). Never released
theatrically in the United States. Released to TV: 9/65.

The Brainiac (1961)
The Bloody Vampire (1962)
Curse of Nostradamus (1960)
Curse of the Aztec Mummy (1965)
Curse of the Crying Woman (1961)
Curse of the Doll People (1960)
Geni of Darkness (1962) aka Blood of
    Nostradamus
The Living Head (1961)
Invasion of the Vampires (1961)
Doctor of Doom (1962)

The Monster Demolisher (1961)
Man and the Monster (1958)
Samson vs. the Vampire Women
    (1961)
Robot vs. the Aztec Mummy (1957)
The Vampire (1957)
Samson in the Wax Museum (1963)
The Vampire's Coffin (1957)
World of the Vampires (1960)
The Witch's Mirror (1960)

AMAZING '66 (22 titles). Released to TV: 9/65.

* Attack of the Mushroom People
    (1965)°
Burn, Witch, Burn (1962)
Castle of the Living Dead (1964)°
Cry of the Bewitched (1956)°
* Dagora, the Space Monster (1964)°
Dementia 13 (1963)
Dr. Orloff's Monster (1964)°
The Evil Eye (1964)
Face of Terror (1962)°
Invasion (1966)°

Man in Outer Space (1961)°
* The Man with X-Ray Eyes (1963)
The Mind Benders (1963)
Monster on the Surf (1964)°
Panic in the Year Zero (1962)
* Pyro (1963)
* Reptilicus (1962)
Space Monster (1965)°
* The Terror (1963)
The Unearthly Stranger (1963)

°Never released theatrically in the United States

TOP SECRET ADVENTURES (19 titles). Espionage/crime films produced in France and Germany; never shown theatrically in the United States. Released to TV: 9/65.

Agent of Doom (1963)
The Atomic Agent (1959)
The Black Monocle (1961)
Danger in the Middle East (1960)
† Dangerous Agent (1953)
† Destination Fury (1961)
† Headlines of Destruction (1955)
Killer Spy (1965)
Monsieur Gangster (1963)
Nest of Spies (n.d.)

Operation Abduction (1958)
Operation Caviar (1961)
Operation Diplomatic Passport (1965)
Operation Gold Ingot (1961)
The Scarlet Baroness (1959)
Secret File 1413 (1961)
To Catch a Spy (1957)
Walls of Fear (n.d.)
Whereabouts Unknown (n.d.)
X-Ray of a Killer (n.d.)

ADVENTURE '66 (22 titles). Released to TV: 9/65.

* Adventures in Indochina (1958)°
* Ape Man of the Jungle (1962)°
California (n.d.)
Desert Fighters (1954)°
Escapade (1957)°
Escape from Saigon (1963)°
Eyes of the Sahara (1960) aka Eye For an Eye
Incident at Saigon (n.d.)°
* Lost Treasure of the Aztecs (1964)°
* Marco Polo (1960)
Operation Bikini (1963)
Outpost in Indochina (1962)°

Sergeant X of the Foreign Legion (1960)°
Sins of Babylon (1963)°
* South of Tana River (1963)°
Stranger from Hong Kong (1963)°
* Swamp of the Lost Monsters (1965)
* Temple of the White Elephants (1964)°
Trapped by Fear (1960)°
Warriors Five (1962)
Wrestling Women vs. the Aztec Mummy (1965)
* The Young Racers (1963)

GROUP II—THRILLERS FROM ANOTHER WORLD (4 titles). Never released theatrically in the United States. Released to TV: 10/65.

Bring Me the Vampire (1965)
* The Living Coffin (1965)

100 Cries of Terror (1965)
Spiritism (1965)

† Stars Eddie Constantine   ° Never released theatrically in the United States.

THE WONDER WORLD OF K. GORDON MURRAY (13 titles). Release plan: program one per week from 10/3/65 to 12/31/65.

The False Prince (n.d.)

Frau Holly (1961)

Hansel and Gretel (1954)

The Littlest Angel (1966) aka
    Gregorio and The Littlest Angel

Little Boy Blue (n.d.)

Little Red Riding Hood (1960)

*Little Red Riding Hood and Her
    Friends* (1961)

*Little Red Riding Hood and the
    Monsters* (1960)

Mischief in Wonderland (n.d.)

Puss 'n Boots (1960)

The Queen's Swordsman (n.d.)

Santa Claus (1960)

The Table, the Burro, and the Stick
    (n.d.)

Source for all preceding American International Television packages: TV *Feature Film Source Book—Feature Packages* (spring–summer 1966), p. FF-7.

CINEMA 20 (19 titles). Many titles released theatrically by Allied Artists or Astor. Announced to TV: 3/66.

The Eleanor Roosevelt Story (1965)

The Fool Killer (1965)

The Girl in Room 13 (1961)

The Girl Getters (1966)

I Spy, You Spy (1966) aka *Bang Bang
    You're Dead*

King and Country (1964)

La dolce vita (1961)

Umbrellas of Cherbourg (1964)

Life Upside Down (1965)

Long Day's Journey Into Night (1962)

Ninety Degrees in the Shade (1964)

Rocco and His Brothers (1960)

The Pawnbroker (1965)

Rope around the Neck (1965)

Sands of Beersheba (1966)

The Servant (1963)

The Swindle (1955)

The Three Sisters (1966)

The Trial (1961)

Source: *Broadcasting*, 3/28/66, pp. 23–25.

AMAZING ADVENTURES 1967 (25 titles). Announced to TV: 3/66.

Apache Fury (1964)

Atragon (1963)

Black Sabbath (1964)

Curse of the Swamp Creature
    (1966) °

Death Pays in Dollars (1967) ° aka
    Death at Owell Rock

The Eye Creatures (1965) °

Hunter of the Unknown (1966) °

From Istanbul, Orders to Kill
    (1965) °

Go-Go Mania (1965)

The Hunt (1954) °

Wildcats on the Beach (1959) °

Lost World of Sinbad (1961)

Master of the World (1961)

° Never released theatrically in the United States

*MMM 83 (1965)°
*Operation Atlantis (1965)
*Operation Counterspy (1966)°
*Planet of Blood (1966) aka Queen of
   Blood
Portrait in Terror (1965)°
*Prisoner of the Jungle (n.d.)°
*Savage Gringo (1965)
*Special Correspondent (n.d.)°

*Tiger of the Seas (1962)°
Track of the Vampire (1966) aka
   Blood Bath
Voyage to the Planet of Prehistoric
   Women (1966)
*Zontar, The Thing From Venus
   (1966)°

Source: Broadcasting, 3/28/66, p. 27.

DOMINANT 10 (10 titles). Announced to TV: 3/66.

Commando (1964)
Conquered City (1962)
Desert War (1962)
*Killers Are Challenged (1965) aka
   Secret Agent Fireball
Wolves of the Deep (1959)
The Last Man on Earth (1964)

*Man from Cocody (1966)
Operation Warhead (1961)
Run, Psycho, Run (n.d.)
Torpedo Bay (1964)

Source: Broadcasting, 3/28/66, p. 27.

Allied Artists Television

SCI-FI FOR THE 60s (22 titles). Announced to TV: 2/62.

The Atomic Submarine (1959)
Attack of the Crab Monsters (1957)
Attack of the 50 Ft. Woman (1958)
The Bat (1959)
Caltiki, The Immortal Monster (1960)
The Cosmic Man (1957)
The Cyclops (1957)
#The Brain from Planet Arous (1958)
Daughter of Dr. Jekyll (1957)
The Disembodied (1957)
Frankenstein 1970 (1958)
From Hell It Came (1957)
The Giant Behemoth (1959)

House on Haunted Hill (1959)
The Hypnotic Eye (1960)
#Terror in the Haunted House (1958)
   aka My World Dies Screaming
The Indestructible Man (1956)
Not of This Earth (1957)
Spy in the Sky (1958)
*Queen of Outer Space (1958)
War of the Satellites (1958)
*World without End (1956)

Source: TV Feature Film Source Book—
Feature Packages (winter 1962–spring
1963), p. FF-5.

#Added to the package for 1963

THE EXPLOITABLES (15 titles). Released to TV: 2/63.

Atlas (1961)°

Beast from the Haunted Cave (1959)°

The Bride and the Beast (1958)

Creature from the Haunted Sea
   (1961)°

The Devil's Partner (1961)

#Fright (1957)

Hands of a Stranger (1962)

The Last Woman on Earth (1961)°

Little Shop of Horrors (1961)°

*Magic Voyage of Sinbad (1962)

#Manfish (1956)

#The Man without a Body (1957)

*Mermaids of Tiburon (1962)

*Pirate of the Black Hawk (1961)

The Wasp Woman (1960)

Source: TV Feature Film Source Book—
Feature Packages (spring 1964), p. FF-6.

Associated Artists Productions

HORROR FEATURE PACKAGE (52 titles; incomplete listing). Announced to TV: 10/57.

The Ape (1940)

Convict's Code (1935)

The Chinese Cat (1944)

Crime Smasher (1943) aka Cosmo
   Jones, Crime Smasher

Criminal Investigator (1942)

Riot Squad (1941)

Doomed to Die (1940)

Face of Marble (1946)

The Fatal Hour (1940)

Gang Bullets (1938)

Hidden Enemy (1940)

House of Mystery (1941)

The Jade Mask (1945)

King of the Zombies (1941)

The Living Ghost (1942)

Man from Headquarters (1942)

Meeting at Midnight (1944)

Midnight Limited (1939)

Monte Carlo Nights (1934)

Mr. Wong, Detective (1938)

Mr. Wong in Chinatown (1939)

Murder by Invitation (1941)

Mysterious Mr. Wong (1935)

Mystery of the 13th Guest (1943)

Mystery Man (1935)

Mystery of Mr. Wong (1939)

Phantom Broadcast (1933)

Phantom Killer (1942)

Police Bullets (1942)

Phantom of Chinatown (1940)

Revenge of the Zombies (1943)

The Scarlet Clue (1945)

The Secret Service (n.d.)

Shadow and the Missing Lady (1946)

Shadow behind the Mask (1946)

Shadow of Suspicion (1944)

The Shadow Returns (1946)

The Shanghai Cobra (1945)

Silent Witness (1942)

°Released theatrically by Filmgroup   #Added to the package for 1964

Strange Mr. Gregory (1945)
The 13th Man (1937)
Undercover Agent (1939)

Source: TV *Film Source Book—Series, Serials, and Packages* (winter 1962–spring 1963), p. FF-94.

Atlantic Television

"SIX-PACK" SPECIALS (5 titles). Released to TV: 1961.

Date with Disaster (1958)
Frankenstein's Daughter (1959)
Giant from the Unknown (1958)
Missile to the Moon (1959)
She Demons (1958)

Source: TV *Feature Film Source Book—Series, Serials, and Packages* (winter 1962–spring 1963), p. FF-8.

THRILLS AND CHILLS PACKAGE (11 titles). Released to TV: 1961.

The Black Doll (1938)
Black Dragons (1942)
Bowery at Midnight (1942)
Ghost Crazy (1944) aka *Crazy Knights*
Ghosts on the Loose (1943)
The Invisible Ghost (1941)
Lady in the Morgue (1938)

Spooks Run Wild (1941)
Rocket to the Moon (1954) aka *Cat Women of the Moon*
Voodoo Man (1944)
The Westland Case (1937)

Source: TV *Feature Film Source Book—Series, Serials, and Packages* (winter 1962–spring 1963), p. FF-9.

Comet Film Distributors

RAINBOW FEATURE PACKAGE #1 (14 titles). Announced to TV: 2/65.

*Angel on Earth (1961)
*Carnation Frank (1961)
*Casino de Paris (1960)
*Girl and the Legend (1962)
*Girl from Hong Kong (1963)
The Golden Patsy (1962)
*Meet Peter Foss (1961)
*Only a Woman (1962)
*Operation Delilah (1964)

*Scampolo (1959)
*The Ski Champ (1962)
Two Worlds (1959)
*Whiskey and Sofa (1961)
Web of Fear (1964)

Source: TV *Feature Film Source Book—Feature Packages* (spring–summer 1966), p. FF-49.

WESTHAMPTON FEATURES (41 titles). Released to TV: 10/63.

Anatomy of a Psycho (1963)

* Attack Squadron (1963)

* Ballad of a Gunfighter (1963)

Bloodlust (1962)

* Cavalry Command (1963)

* Dangerous Charter (1962)

The Devil's Hand (1962)

* East of Kilimanjaro (1962)

* First Spaceship on Venus (1963)

* The Girl Hunters (1963)

Go, Johnny, Go! (1958)

* Hey, Pineapple! (1963)

* I Bombed Pearl Harbor (1961)

Ivy League Killers (1962)

Journey into Nowhere (1962)

* Make Way for Lila (1962)

* The Mighty Jungle (1962)

* Mill of the Stone Women (1963)

Narcotic Squad (1955)

The Phony American (1962)

A Public Affair (1962)

Punishment Batallion (1964)

The Quick and the Dead (1964)

The Scavengers (1959)

Secret File: Hollywood (1961)

* Secret of the Telegian (1963)

The Seventh Commandment (1961)

Shell Shock (1964)

Spy Squad (1963)

Stakeout (1962)

* The Starfighters (1963)

The Tell-Tale Heart (1963)

Terror at Black Falls (1963)

Then There Were Three (1962)

3 Blondes in His Life (1963)

Trauma (1962)

* Trial at Kampili (1963)

Varan the Unbelievable (1962)

We Shall Return (1963)

When the Girls Take Over (1962)

Women and War (1964)

Source: TV *Feature Film Source Book—*
Feature Packages (spring–summer 1966),
p. FF-15.

Embassy Pictures

13 SONS OF HERCULES (13 titles). Available at feature length or as two
one-hour "cliffhangers." Released to TV: 1/64.

* Empress Messalina Meets the Son of
   Hercules (1963)

* Fire Monsters against Hercules
   (1962)

* Hercules against Maciste in the Vale
   of Woe (1962)

* Hero of Babylon (1963)

* Mole Men against the Son of
   Hercules (1962)

* Son of Hercules Returns (1963)

* Return of Hercules (1963)

* Triumph of Maciste (1962)

* Tyrant of Lydia against the Son of
   Hercules (1963)

Ulysses against the Son of Hercules (1962)

Ursus in the Land of Fire (1963)

Venus Meets the Son of Hercules (1962)

Vulcan, Son of Jove (1963)

EMBASSY FEATURES (32 titles). Announced to TV: 12/62.

Aphrodite (1962)

Atilla (1958)

The Bear (1963)

Bimbo the Great (1963)

Bluebeard aka *Landru* (1962)

Constantine and the Cross (1962)

David and Goliath (1961)

The Devil's Wanton (1962)

Divorce Italian Style (1962)

Fabiola (1951)

Fabulous World of Jules Verne (1961)

Face in the Rain (1963)

Fury at Smugglers' Bay (1962)

Gaslight Folies (n.d.)

Gentle Art of Murder (1962) aka
    Crime Does Not Pay

The Hellfire Club (1961)

Hercules (1959)

Hercules Unchained (1960)

Jack the Ripper (1959)

The Lovemakers (1962)

Love at Twenty (1963)

Madame (1963)

Morgan the Pirate (1961)

Night Is My Future (1963)

No Place Like Homicide (1961) aka
    What a Carve-Up!

O.K. Nero (1953)

The Passionate Thief (1962)

The Sky Above, the Mud Below (1962)

Strangers in the City (1962)

Thief of Baghdad (1961)

Two Women (1961)

Uncle Was a Vampire (n.d.)

Source: TV Film Source Book—Feature Packages (spring 1964), p. FF-23.

ADVENTURE 26 (26 titles). Adventure-spectacle films produced in Italy. Released to TV: 9/65.

The Black Archer (1959)

The Black Devil (1957)

Blood on His Sword (1961)

Cartouche (1954)

Conqueror of the Orient (1960)

Conquest of Mycene (1963)

The Devil of Paris (n.d.)

Fra Diavolo (1962)

Helen of Troy (1956)

Hero of Rome (1964)

Joseph and His Brethren (1960)

Journey Beneath the Desert (1961)

Lion of St. Mark (1963)

Maciste in King Solomon's Mine (1964)

The Mongols (1961)

Pia of Ptolemy (1958)

Robin Hood and the Pirates (1960)

Romulus and the Sabines (1961)

The Seven Revenges (1961)

Terror of the Black Mask (1962)

Terror on the Steppe (n.d.)

Tiger of the Seven Seas (1962)

Triumph of Robin Hood (1963)

The Trojan War (1962)

*Vengeance of the Three Musketeers (1961)

Vulcan, Son of Jove (1961)

Source: TV *Feature Film Source Book—Feature Packages* (spring–summer 1966), p. FF-17.

Flamingo Telefilm Sales

THE FESTIVAL PACKAGE (30 titles). Released to TV: 8/59.

Be Beautiful but Shut Up (1958)

A Bride for Frank (1957)

*Captain from Koepinick (1958)

Confessions of Felix Krull (1958)

The Crucible (1958)

Defend My Love (1958)

Dreaming Lips (1958)

Fernandel, the Dressmaker (1958)

Fugitive in Saigon (1957)

Gates of Paris (1958)

Guendalina (1957)

Hijack Highway (1957)

House on the Waterfront (1959)

Inspector Maigret (1958)

Julietta (1958)

The Last Bridge (1954)

The Little World of Don Camillo (1953)

The Most Dangerous Sin (1958) aka Crime and Punishment

Nights of Cabiria (1957)

Of Life and Love (1958)

The Orient Express (1953)

Papa, Mama, the Maid, and I (1956)

Photo Finish (1958)

The Proud and the Beautiful (1957)

Rigoletto (1959)

3 Feet in a Bed (1958)

There's Always a Price Tag (1958)

We Are All Murderers (1957)

Wheel of Fate (1953)

Woman in the Painting (1953)

Source: TV *Film Source Book—Series, Serials, and Packages* (winter 1962–spring 1963), p. FF-20.

CRITICS AWARD PACKAGE (46 titles). Released to TV: 1962.

At the Stroke of Nine (1957)

*Baby and the Battleship (1955)

Battle Hell (1956)

Bermuda Affair (1956)

The Devil's General (1956)

Folly to Be Wise (1949)

Frisky (1955)

Gold of Naples (1955)

The Green Man (1957)

Half-Human (1957)

Hell in Korea (1956)

The Holly and the Ivy (1953)

*Hunters of the Deep (1955)

I Am a Camera (1955)

Johnny One-Eye (1959)

Les Misérables (1952)

*Long John Silver (1953)

*Loser Takes All (1956)

Monster from Green Hell (1957)

Mr. Denning Drives North (1953)

Murder on Monday (1957)

My Outlaw Brother (1951)

No Orchids for Miss Blandish (1948)

Nothing but Blondes (1957)

Panic in the Parlor (1957)

Paper Gallows (1952)

Plan Nine from Outer Space (1959)

Please Mr. Balzac (1956)

Please Murder Me (1956)

Private's Progress (1955)

The Ringer (1950)

Rock, Rock, Rock! (1956)

* *Rodan* (1957)

Sail into Danger (1957)

* *Scandal in Sorrento* (1955)

The Silken Affair (1957)

Sudden Fear (1952)

The Surgeon's Knife (1957)

The Taming of Dorothy (1951)

Teenage Bad Girl (1957)

Teenage Wolf Pack (1956)

* *Three Men in a Boat* (1956)

Timelock (1957)

Who Goes There? (1948)

The Widow (1956)

The Wiretapper (1953)

Source: TV *Film Source Book — Series, Serials, and Packages* (winter 1962–spring 1963), p. FF-21.

Four Star International

SUPERSPY ACTION GROUP (11 titles). Never released theatrically in the United States. Released to TV: 3/65.

* *Agent Z55/Desperate Mission* (1964)

* *Agent 3S3/Passport to Hell* (1964)

Code Name: Tiger (1964)

The Deadly Decoy (1962)

Death of a Killer (1963)

Hit and Run (1958)

† *License to Kill* (1964)

The Monocle (1964)

None but the Lonely Spy (1964)

The Spy I Love (1964)

A Touch of Treason (1962)

SPECTACULAR SHOWCASE (21 titles). Never released theatrically in the United States. Released to TV: 8/64.

* *Avenger of Venice* (1965)

* *The Barbarian King* (1964)

* *Conqueror of the Desert* (1958)

* *Hercules and the Ten Adventurers* (1965)

* *Ivailo the Great* (1963)

* *Love of 3 Queens* (1963)

* *Nero and the Burning of Rome* (1955)

* *Night of the Great Attack* (1964)

* *The Old Testament* (1963)

* *Revolt of the Mamalukes* (1964)

* *Saladin and the Great Crusades* (1963)

† Stars Eddie Constantine

Samson and the Seven Challenges (1965)

Scheherezade (1963)

Spartacus and the Ten Gladiators (1965)

Terror of the Red Mask (1961)

Triumph of the Ten Gladiators (1965)

The Tyrant of Castille (1964)

The Violent Patriot (1959)

Vengeance of the Desert (1964)

Warning from Space (1963)

Zorikan the Barbarian (1960)

Source: TV *Feature Film Source Book—Feature Packages* (spring–summer 1966), p. FF-21.

Independent Television Corporation (ITC)

THE EXPLOITABLE 13 (13 titles). Never shown theatrically in the United States. Released to TV: 8/65.

Breakthrough (1963)

Golden Goddess of Rio Beni (1965)

The Last Charge (1964)

Love and Larceny (1962)

Mark of the Tortoise (1964)

Melody of Hate (1962)

River of Evil (1964)

Rocambole (1962)

Secret of the Sphinx (1964)

Terror Calls at Night (1962)

13 Days to Die (1965)

Vendetta at Sorrento (1963)

Voyage to Danger (1962)

Source: TV *Feature Film Source Book—Feature Packages* (spring–summer 1966), p. FF-25.

THE DELUXE TWENTY (20 titles). Never shown theatrically in the United States. Announced to TV: 8/66.

Affair at Ischia (1964)

The Balearic Caper (1966)

Black Eagle of Santa Fe (1966)

Blueprint for a Million (1966)

Captain from Toledo (1966)

The Devil's Choice (1963)

Formula C12/Beirut (1966)

Kill and Be Killed (1966)

James Tont: Operation Goldsinger (1966)

Kiss Kiss Kill Kill (1966)

The Last Tomahawk (1966)

Legend of a Gunfighter (1966)

The Man Called Gringo (1966)

Massacre at Marble City (1966)

Murder by Proxy (1966)

Mutiny in the South Seas (1966)

The Sand Runs Red (1965)

Serenade for Two Spies (1966)

Strangler of the Tower (1966)

Viva Juanito! (1965)

Source: *Broadcasting,* 8/22/66, pp. 12–13.

THE MAGNIFICENT 15 (15 titles). Never shown theatrically in the United States. Announced to TV: 9/67.

As Long as You Live (1964)

**Countdown to Doomsday* (1967)

**Death Is Nimble, Death Is Quick* (1967)

**Enter Inspector Maigret* (1967)

**Epitaph for a Fast Gun* (1967)

**Guns of Nevada* (1967)

**High Season for Spies* (1967)

**The Hunchback of Soho* (1967)

Killer with a Silk Scarf (1967)

**A Lotus for Miss Quon* (1967)

**Rebels on the Loose* (1967)

The Sinister Monk (1967)

**So Darling, So Deadly* (1967)

**Spy Today, Die Tomorrow* (1967)

**Trap for Seven Spies* (1967)

Source: ITC trade ad, *Broadcasting*, 9/18/67, pp. 11–12.

Medallion TV Enterprises

"20/20" PACKAGE (20 titles). Released to TV: 3/65.

Attack of the Mayan Mummy (1963)

Creature of the Walking Dead (1963)

Death on the Fourposter (1963)

Escape from Sahara (1963)

**The Fabulous Fraud* (1960)

48 Hours to Live (1960)

Four Fast Guns (1960)

I'll See You in Hell (1960)

**Jungle Girl and the Slaver* (1959)

**Love from Paris* (1961)

**Mistress of the World* (1959)

The Nylon Noose (1963)

Passport for a Corpse (1962)

Ring of Terror (1962)

The Shortest Day (1963)

Sputnik (1961)

Strike Me Deadly (1963)

The Two Colonels (1962)

Untamed Women (1952)

**Wall of Fury* (1962)

Source: *TV Feature Film Source Book— Feature Packages* (spring–summer 1966), p. FF-30.

CREEPING TERRORS, VOL. 3 (10 titles). Formerly distributed by Prime TV. Released to TV: 4/66.

The Crawling Eye (1958)

Crimes at the Dark House (1957)

Crimes of Stephen Hawke (1956)

Demon Barber of Fleet Street (1945)

Face at the Window (1953)

The Hooded Terror (1953)

The Man in Black (1950)

Murder in the Red Barn (1945) aka *Maria Marten*

Never Too Late to Mend (1951)

Room to Let (1950)

Source: *TV Feature Film Source Book— Feature Packages* (spring–summer 1966), p. FF-31.

KORDA CLASSIC THEATER (11 titles). Taken over by Medallion TV: 10/64. Reissued to TV: 2/63.

* Drums (1938)
* Elephant Boy (1937)
* Four Feathers (1939)
* Jungle Book (1942)
Knight without Armor (1937)
The Lion Has Wings (1940)

Man Who Could Work Miracles (1937)
Return of the Scarlet Pimpernel (1938)
Twenty-One Days Together (1938)
The Scarlet Pimpernel (1938)
Shape of Things to Come (1936)

FEATURES (35 titles).

Actors and Sin (1953)
Almost a Bride (1949) aka A Kiss for Corliss
Another Chance (1953) aka Twilight Women Bombay Waterfront (1952)
Breakdown (1952)
Caretaker's Daughter (1953)
Cover Up (1949)
Crooked Way (1949)
Don't Trust Your Husband (1948) aka Innocent Affair
Eye Witness (1950)
Fame and the Devil (1950)
The First Legion (1951)
Four in a Jeep (1951)
Gay Intruders (1958)
Ghost Ship (1953)
Hell Gate (1953)
* Island of Desire (1952)
Jungle Patrol (1948)
Let's Live Again (1948)

The Man Beast (1957)
Michael Strogoff (1937) aka Soldier and the Lady
Monster from the Ocean Floor (1954)
Project Moonbase (1953)
The Rebel's Son (1939) aka Taras Bulba
Robot Monster (1953) aka Monster from Mars
* She Devils (1953)
Serpent Island (1954)
The Silent Raiders (1954)
Summer Storm (1946)
Tough Guy (1953)
Undercover Agent (1953) aka The Slasher
The Vampire Bat (1933)
Wide Boy (1953)
Without Honor (1949)
Yesterday and Today (1954)

CREEPING TERRORS, vol. 2 (9 titles). Released to TV: 6/64.

The Crawling Hand (1963)
Curse of the Stone Hand (1964)
Invasion of the Animal People (1962)
Jungle Hell (1956)
Man in the Vault (1956)
The Slime People (1963)

Terror of the Bloodhunters (1963)
The Violent and the Damned (1963)
No Time to Kill (1963)

Source: TV Feature Film Source Book— Feature Packages (spring–summer 1966), p. FF-31.

CINEMAGREATS (50 titles). Many titles formerly released by Medallion Pictures. Announced to TV: 7/64, 10/64, 9/65.

Adventures of Mandarin (1960) aka
  Captain Adventure
The Amorous Mr. Prawn (1962)
* *Atlas against the Czar* (1964)
Bomb for a Dictator (1960)
* *Caribbean Hawk* (1963)
* *Cavalier in Devil's Castle* (1962)
* *Conqueror of Maracaibo* (1960)
The Defeat of Hannibal (1960)
The Devil's Agent (1961)
Doll That Took the Town (1963)
Down Memory Lane (1949)
* *Duel of Champions* (1962)
* *Executioner of Venice* (1963)
Fall Guy (1961) aka *Lisette*
* *Fighting Musketeers* (1963)
* *Gallant Musketeer* (n.d.)
* *The Golden Falcon* (n.d.)
* *The Great Deception* (1964)
Headquarters State Secret (1960)
Horror Chamber of Dr. Faustus
  (1962)
The Invisible Dr. Mabuse (1962)
Johnny Nobody (1961)
* *The King's Avenger* (1962) aka
  Hunchback of Paris
* *Knight of 100 Faces* (1960)
* *Knight without a Country* (1960)
* *Knights of Terror* (1963)
* *Knights of the Black Cross* (1960)
* *Lafayette* (1962)

* *The Last Rebel* (1956)
The Lion of Amalfi (1962)
Lipstick (1963)
Man or Beast (n.d.)
A Man Named Rocca (1961)
* *Marie Antoinette* (1960)
* *Marie of the Isles* (1961)
Murder by Two (n.d.)
* *Mysterious Swordsman* (1962)
* *Nearly a Nice Girl* (1963)
* *Rage of the Buccaneers* (1961) aka
  The Black Pirate
Rebel Flight to Cuba (1959)
Secret of Dr. Mabuse (1964) aka
  Death Ray Mirror of Dr. Mabuse
Testament of Dr. Mabuse (1962) aka
  Terror of the Mad Doctor
* *Slave of Rome* (1961)
Sins of Rome (1952) aka *Spartacus the
  Rebel Gladiator*
Victory at Sea (1959)
The Wastrel (1962)
Sweetheart of the Gods (1960)
* *Weapons for Vengeance* (1962) aka
  Arms of the Avenger
Strangler of Blackmoor Castle (1963)
Unholy Intruders (1956) aka *Strange
  Intrusion*

Source: TV *Feature Film Source Book—
Feature Packages* (spring–summer 1966),
p. FF-39.

SPECTACOLOR PACKAGE (30 titles). Formerly distributed to TV by Medallion Pictures 7/63. Acquired by NBC Films 9/65.

* *Alone against Rome* (1960)
* *Atlas against the Cyclops* (1961)
* *The Bacchantes* (1961)
* *Caesar the Conqueror* (1960) aka *Caesar, Conqueror of Gaul*
* *Cleopatra's Daughter* (1960)
* *The Desert Warrior* (1960)
* *The Fall of Rome* (1960)
* *The Fury of Hercules* (1961)
* *Giants of Thessaly* (1960) aka *The Argonauts*
* *A Girl against Napoleon* (1960) aka *The Girl from Granada*
* *Gladiator of Rome* (1960)
* *Goliath against the Giants* (1962)
* *Last Glory of Troy* (1961)
* *Last of the Vikings* (1962)
* *The Rebel Gladiators* (1960)
* *The Red Sheik* (1960)
* *Revenge of Ursus* (1960) aka *Vengeance of Ursus*
* *Rommel's Treasure* (1959)
* *Samson* (1960)
* *Samson against the Sheik* (1960)
* *Secret Mark of D'Artagnan* (1960)
* *Seven Tasks of Ali Baba* (1960) aka *Ali Baba and the Sacred Crown*
* *The Seven Swords* (1960)
* *Son of Samson* (1960)
* *Son of the Red Corsair* (1960)
* *Suleiman the Conqueror* (1960)
* *The Tartar Invasion* (1960) aka *The Tartar Girl*
* *Valley of the Lions* (1960) aka *Son of Atlas in the Valley of the Lions*
* *The Witch's Curse* (1960)
* *With Fire and Sword* (1960)

Source: TV *Feature Film Source Book — Feature Packages* (spring–summer 1966), p. FF-40.

National Telefilm Associates

SCIENCE FICTION/HORROR FEATURES (18 titles). All also available as part of other packages.

Back from the Dead (1957)
Chamber of Horrors (1940)
Dante's Inferno (1935)
Dr. Renault's Secret (1942)
Earthbound (1940)
Fire Maidens of Outer Space (1957)
Ghost Diver (1957)
Hell on Devil's Island (1957)
The Human Monster (1940)
* *Invaders from Mars* (1953)
Kronos (1957)

Lure of the Swamp (1957)
Man Who Wouldn't Die (1942)
Secret beyond the Door (1948)
She-Devil (1957)
The Undying Monster (1942)
The Unknown Terror (1957)
Whirlpool (1949)

Source: TV *Feature Film Source Book — Feature Packages* (spring–summer 1966), p. FF-45.

HORROR 5 (5 titles). Released to TV: 3/65.

The Awful Dr. Orloff (1964)
Devil's Messenger (1961)°
*Dungeons of Horror (1962)°
*Horrible Dr. Hichcock (1964)
Horror Hotel (1963)

Source: TV Feature Film Source Book—
Feature Packages (spring–summer 1966),
p. FF-44.

Prime T.V.

SCIENCE FICTION–HORROR FEATURES (6 titles).

The Ape Man (1943)
The Corpse Vanishes (1942)
†The Day the Sky Exploded (1958)
†The Incredible Petrified World (1958)
*Svengali (1955)
†Teenage Zombies (1958)

Source: TV Feature Film Source Book—
Feature Packages (spring–summer 1966),
p. FF-49.

Walter Reade-Sterling

CINEMA 100 (24 titles). Released to TV: 8/65.

Bebo's Girl (1964)
Black Like Me (1964)
A Coming Out Party (1962)
Day the Earth Caught Fire (1963)
*Doctor in Distress (1964)
*Father Came Too (1965)
*The 49th Parallel (1942) aka The
   Invaders
Heavens Above (1964)
High and Low (1964)
In the Doghouse (1964)
The Informers (1965)
A Jolly Bad Fellow (1964)
Ladies Who Do (1963)

Lord of the Flies (1963)
Luck of Ginger Coffey (1964)
Love and the Frenchwoman (1961)
No, My Darling Daughter (1964)
The Organizer (1964)
Prize of Arms (1965)
Rattle of a Simple Man (1964)
Seance on a Wet Afternoon (1964)
*The Singer Not the Song (1962)
This Sporting Life (1963)
*Tiara Tahiti (1963)

Source: TV Feature Film Source Book—
Feature Packages (spring–summer 1966),
p. FF-87.

°Never released theatrically in the United States
†Formerly distributed to TV by Teledynamics

CINEMA 98 (98 titles). Reissued to TV: 7/65.

Abroad with Two Yanks (1944)

Adam and Evalyn (1950)

Angel with a Trumpet (1950)

* Baby and the Battleship (1956)

Belles of St. Trinians (1954)

Black Magic (1944)

* Black Narcissus (1947)

The Blind Goddess (1948)

* Bonnie Prince Charlie (1947)

Breaking the Sound Barrier (1952)

Brief Encounter (1947)

Brewster's Millions (1945)

Bush Christmas (1947)

The Captain's Paradise (1953)

Carnival (1946)

* Cottage to Let (1941)

The Corsican Brothers (1941)

Crash of Silence (1953) aka Mandy

Cry, the Beloved Country (1952)

The Dark Man (1952)

Derby Day (1952)

Diamond City (1948)

Duke of West Point (1938)

Easy Money (1949)

Eight O'Clock Walk (1953)

* Emperor's Nightingale (1937)

Extra Day (1957)

Fire Over England (1947)

Forbidden (1947)

Front Page Story (1953)

Great Expectations (1947)

* Gibert and Sullivan (1953) aka The
   Great Gilbert and Sullivan

Green for Danger (1947)

The Green Man (1957)

The Green Scarf (1954)

The Happiest Days of Your Life (1950)

Heart of the Matter (1953)

A Hill in Korea (1956)

Home at Seven (1953) aka Murder on
   Monday

The Holly and the Ivy (1953)

Hotel Sahara (1951)

I Know Where I'm Going (1957)

Into the Blue (1951) aka Man in the
   Dinghy

The Intruder (1953)

* Ivory Hunter (1952) aka Where No
   Vultures Fly

* Jassy (1948)

Joe Palooka (1934)

* Josephine and Men (1955)

Kit Carson (1940)

Lady Godiva Rides Again (1953)

Lady with a Lamp (1952)

Last Days of Dolwyn (1949)

Last of the Mohicans (1936)

Lavender Hill Mob (1952)

* Loser Takes All (1956)

Madonna of the 7 Moons (1946)

Man in the Iron Mask (1939)

The Man Between (1954)

Mark of Cain (1948)

* The Mikado (1939)

Mr. Denning Drives North (1953)

Millions Like Us (1942)

Miss Annie Roonie (1942)

Mine Own Executioner (1947)

Mr. Emmanuel (1945)

My Son, My Son (1940)

Night without Stars (1953)

The Notorious Gentleman (1946) aka
   Rake's Progress

Odd Man Out (1947)

Orders to Kill (1959)

Outcast of the Islands (1954)

Poets Pub (1940)

Quartet (1949)

The Ringer (1950)
The Rockinghorse Winner (1950)
* *Saraband* (1949)
Seven Days to Noon (1950)
Small Back Room (1949) ·
Small Voice (1951) aka *The Hideout*
So Long at the Fair (1951)
Son of Monte Cristo (1940)
South Riding (1938)
* *Stairway to Heaven* (1947)
State Secret (1950)
Stranger's Hand (1955)
T-Men (1947)
* *Tales of Hoffman* (1953)
The Teckman Mystery (1954)

Teenage Bad Girl (1955) aka *My Teenage Daughter*
They Were Sisters (1945)
The Third Man (1950)
Trent's Last Case (1953)
Trio (1951)
Two Thousand Women (1944)
Vice Versa (1948)
Waterfront (1952) aka *Waterfront Woman*
Woman Hater (1949)
Wooden Horse (1950)

Source: TV *Feature Film Source Book— Feature Packages* (spring–summer 1966), p. FF-87, F-88.

CINEMA 90 (26 titles). Announced to TV: 8/63.

The Cheaters (1961)
Conspiracy of Hearts (1961)
David and Lisa (1963)
* *Doctor at Large* (1957)
* *Doctor in Love* (1961)
* *End of Desire* (1962)
Floods of Fear (1958)
Follow a Star (1941)
The Great Chase (1963)
Hands of a Strangler (1960) aka *The Hands of Orlac*
La belle americaine (1961) aka *What a Chassis*
League of Gentlemen (1961)
Loneliness of the Long-Distance Runner (1962) aka *Rebel with a Cause*

The Medium (1951)
My Uncle (1958) aka *Mon oncle*
Never Let Go (1962)
Oliver Twist (1948)
Operation Snatch (1962)
* *Sapphire* (1959)
* *Scott of the Antarctic* (1948)
The Silent Enemy (1958)
A Taste of Honey (1962)
Tiger Bay (1960)
* *Waltz of the Toreadors* (1962)
Wrong Arm of the Law (1963)
* *Your Shadow Is Mine* (1963)

Source: TV *Feature Film Source Book— Feature Packages* (spring–summer 1966), p. FF-88.

CINEMA 88 (54 titles). 1 new, 53 reissues.

The Adventuress (1947) aka *I See a Dark Stranger*
Against the Wind (1949)

Aku Aku (1961)
The Astonished Heart (1950)
* *Blanche Fury* (1948)

*The Blue Lagoon (1949)
The Blue Lamp (1951)
A Boy, a Girl, a Dog (1946)
*The Browning Version (1951)
Cage of Gold (1952)
The Calendar (1948)
Captain Boycott (1947)
Dark Journey (1937)
Dear Murderer (1947)
Devil and Daniel Webster (1941) aka
    All that Money Can Buy
Encore (1952)
End of the River (1947)
*The Eternal Waltz (1959)
Folly Be Wise (1949)
The Great Adventure (1954)
The Great Dan Patch (1948)
Hamlet (1948)
Highly Dangerous (1951)
In Which We Serve (1942)
An Inspector Calls (1954)
Kind Hearts and Coronets (1950)
Kon-Tiki (1951)
Life and Death of Rudolph Valentino
    (1960)
The Little Giants (1958)
Love Story (1944)
Madeleine (1950) aka The Strange
    Case of Madeleine

The Magic Bow (1950)
Man in the White Suit (1952)
Man of Evil (1942) aka Fanny by
    Gaslight
The Man Who Changed His Mind
    (1936) aka Brainsnatcher
Mr. Perrin and Mr. Traill (1945)
Passport to Pimlico (1949)
Private's Progress (1955)
The Promoter (1952)
*The Red Shoes (1948)
A Run for Your Money (1950)
The Secret People (1952)
The Seventh Veil (1946)
Sleeping Car to Trieste (1949)
Snowbound (1947)
Tawny Pipit (1944)
Three Cases of Murder (1953)
Tight Little Island (1949)
Train of Events (1952)
Waterloo Road (1945)
The Way to the Stars (1945)
We Dive at Dawn (1942)
*Wings of the Morning (1937)
The Young Caruso (1952)

Source: TV Feature Film Source Book—
Feature Packages (spring–summer 1966),
p. FF-88.

CINEMA 70 (75 titles). Released to TV: 10/60; acquired by RKO: 6/61; Walter Reade-Sterling distribution to TV: 5/62.

*Adventures of Arsene Lupin (1958)
*Andrea Chenier (1961)
Aparajito (1956) aka The
    Unvanquished
*Bachelor of Hearts (1959)
Ballad of a Soldier (1960)
Battle of the Sexes (1960)
Blue Murder at St. Trinians (1958)

*Bread, Love, and Dreams (1954)
Breakout (1954)
*The Bridal Path (1959) aka The
    Mating Game
Brothers-In-Law (1957)
*Call Me Genius (1961)
The City Stands Trial (1954)
Deadlier than the Male (1957)

The Entertainer (1960)
Expresso Bongo (1960)
* Follies Bergere (1957)
Four Desperate Men (1960)
The French, They Are a Funny Race (1957)
* Gate of Hell (1954)
General Della Rovere (1960)
* The Golden Demon (1956)
* Green Magic (1952)
Happy Is the Bride (1956)
The Heart of a Man (1959)
It Happened in Broad Daylight (1960)
Jungle Fighters (1961) aka The Long, the Short, and the Tall
Kanal (1961)
The Last Ten Days of Adolf Hitler (1956) aka The Last Ten Days
Law and Disorder (1957)
The Law Is the Law (1959)
Love in the City (1953)
Lure of the Sila (1949)
Make Mine Mink (1960)
Man in the Raincoat (1958)
A Man Escaped (1957)
Man to Man Talk (1958) aka Premier Way
The Man Upstairs (1959)
Man Who Wagged His Tail (1960)
The Mark (1961)
The Mistress (1959)
The Mirror Has 2 Faces (1959)
Nights of Rasputin (1960) aka The Night They Killed Rasputin

* A Novel Affair (1957)
Pather Panchali (1956)
Path of Hope (1950)
* The Phantom Horse (1956)
Pretty Boy Floyd (1960)
The Pure Hell of St. Trinians (1961)
* The Red Cloak (1961)
* Revolt of the Tartars (1960)
Riff-Raff (1961)
Room at the Top (1959)
The Roots (1957)
Saturday Night and Sunday Morning (1961)
The Schemer (1959)
School for Scoundrels (1960)
The Seven Samurai (1956)
The Slave (1958)
Smallest Show on Earth (1957) aka Big Operator
Too Late to Love (1959)
* The Truth about Women (1958)
Typhoon over Nagasaki (1957)
Ugetsu (1953)
Venice, the Moon, and You (1957)
A View from the Bridge (1961)
* Virgin Island (1960)
* Viva Revolution (1960) aka La Escondida
The Voice of Silence (1951)
The Wayward Wife (1952)
* Whirlpool (1959)
The Wide, Blue Road (1961)
Without Pity (1949)
* Woman of Evil (1955)
The World of Apu (1959)

MISCELLANEOUS GROUP (34 titles). Announced to TV: 8/63.

Bad Lord Byron (1948)
A Boy, a Girl, and a Bike (1949)
The Brothers (1947)

Caravan (1947)
The Clouded Yellow (1951)
The Cruel Sea (1953)

Curtain Up (1953)

Desperate Moment (1953)

Diamond City (1948)

Dr. Paul Josef Goebbels (1944)

Don't Take It to Heart (1945)

Fame Is the Spur (1946)

* Genevieve (1954)

Ghost Train (1943)

Good Time Girl (1948)

The Great Barrier (1937)

The Guv'nor (1947)

Hunted (1952) aka *Stranger In Between*

The Impersonator (1963)

Iron Duke (1934) aka *Wellington*

King Arthur Was a Gentleman (1942)

The Lady Vanishes (1938)

* London Town (1946)

Miranda (1948)

Mr. Hulot's Holiday (1953)

My Brother's Keeper (1949)

One Good Turn (1955)

A Place of One's Own (1945)

* A Queen Is Crowned (1953)

Theirs Is the Glory (1946)

Time Flies (1944)

* Titfield Thunderbolt (1953)

Uncle Silas (1948) aka *The Inheritance*

The Weaker Sex (1945)

Source: TV *Feature Film Source Book—Feature Packages* (spring–summer 1966), p. FF-89.

Roberts and Barry

PLUS 22 (4 titles). Announced to TV: 3/65.

* The Black Torment (1965)

The Brain (1965)

* Hercules against the Moon Men (1965)

Tomorrow at Ten (1964)

EUROPA "33" (33 titles). Announced to TV: 3/65.

The Avenger (1960)

The Black Abbot (1963)

Black Cobra (1963)

* Black Panther of Ratala (1962)

Carpet of Horror (1962)

* Coffin from Hong Kong (1963)

Curse of the Hidden Vault (1964)

Curse of the Yellow Snake (1963)

Door with Seven Locks (1962)

Fellowship of the Frog (1960) aka *Face of the Frog*

Forger of London (1961)

The Green Archer (1961)

Hong Kong Hot Harbor (1962)

The Indian Scarf (1963)

Inn on the River (1962)

The Inn on Dartmoor (1964)

Invisible Terror (1963)

* Last Ride to Santa Cruz (1963)

* Mission to Hell (1964)

The White Spider (1963)

Mysterious Magician (1964)

* Operation Hong Kong (n.d.)

* Pirates of the Mississippi (1963)

The Red Circle (1960)

The Red Hand (1960)

Room 13 (1964)

Secret of the Black Trunk (1962)

Secret of the Black Widow (1964)

Secret of the Chinese Carnation
  (1964)

Secret of the Red Orchid (1962)

The Squeaker (1965)

The Strange Countess (1961)

Terrible People (1963)

WOOLNER FOUR (4 titles). Announced to TV: 2/64.

Castle of Terror (1963) aka *Castle of
  Blood*

* *Hercules and the Captive Women*
  (1963)

* *Hercules in the Haunted World*
  (1963)

* *Pirate and the Slave Girl* (1962)

Source: TV *Feature Film Source Book—
Feature Packages* (spring–summer 1966),
p. FF-50.

KAMP FEATURES (5 titles). Released to TV: 7/64.

Fog for a Killer (n.d.) aka *Out of the
  Fog*

Man on the Run (n.d.) aka
  Kidnappers

Meteor Monster (1958) aka *Teenage
  Monster*

No Survivors Please (1963)

Operation Mermaid (1963) aka *Bay of
  St. Michel*

Source: TV *Feature Film Source Book—
Feature Packages* (spring–summer 1966),
p. FF-50.

Note: The "Europa 33" and "Kamp"
packages were acquired by *Triangle
Program Sales* and placed into
distribution in Winter 1967. Source:
TV *Feature Film Source Book—Feature
Packages* (winter 1967–1968
supplement), pp. FF-29, FF-30.

Screen Entertainment

AIP PACKAGE (69 titles). Announced to TV: 1/65.

Amazing Colossal Man (1957)

* *Apache Woman* (1955)

Astounding She-Monster (1959)

Attack of the Giant Leeches (1959)

Attack of the Puppet People (1958)

The Beast with a Million Eyes (1956)

Beware of Children (1961)

Blood of Dracula (1957)

The Bonnie Parker Story (1958)

The Brain Eaters (1958)

A Bucket of Blood (1959)
Cat Girl (1957)
The Cool and the Crazy (1955)
Daddy-O (1959)
The Day the World Ended (1956)
Diary of a High School Bride (1959)
Dragstrip Girl (1957)
Dragstrip Riot (1958)
Fast and Furious (1954)
* Five Guns West (1955)
Ghost of Dragstrip Hollow (1959)
The Giant Gila Monster (1959)
Girls in Prison (1956)
* The Gunslinger (1956)
The Headless Ghost (1959)
Hell Squad (1958)
High School Hellcats (1958)
* Horrors of the Black Museum (1959)
Hot Rod Gang (1958)
How to Make a Monster (1958)
I Was a Teenage Frankenstein (1957)
I Was a Teenage Werewolf (1957)
Invasion of the Saucer Men (1957)
It Conquered the World (1956)
The Jailbreakers (1960)
Jet Attack (1958)
The Killer Shrews (1958)
Machine Gun Kelly (1958)
Motorcycle Gang (1957)
* Naked Africa (1957)
Night of the Blood Beast (1958)
Oklahoma Woman (1956)

Operation Camel (1961)
Operation Dames (1959)
Paratroop Command (1958)
Reform School Girl (1957)
Road Racers (1959)
Rock all Night (1957)
Rock around the World (1957)
Runaway Daughters (1956)
The Screaming Skull (1958)
Shake, Rattle, and Rock (1956)
The She Creature (1956)
* She Gods of Shark Reef (1958)
Sorority Girl (1957)
The Spider (1958)
Submarine Seahawk (1958)
Suicide Battalion (1958)
Tank Battalion (1958)
Tank Commandos (1959)
Teenage Caveman (1958)
Terror from the Year 5000 (1958)
* Thunder over Hawaii (1957)
The Undead (1957)
Viking Women and the Sea Serpent
   (1957)
Voodoo Woman (1957)
War of the Colossal Beast (1958)
White Huntress (1957)
Why Must I Die? (1960)

Source: TV Feature Film Source Book—
Feature Packages (spring–summer 1966),
pp. FF-51, FF-52.

Screen Gems

"X" (15 titles). Announced to TV: 9/25/63.

* Battle in Outer Space (1960)
Curse of the Demon (1957)
* The H-Man (1959)

The Electronic Monster (1960)
The Giant Claw (1957)
Mein Kampf (1961)

Mothra (1962)
* *The Silent World* (1956)
Stranglers of Bombay (1960)
The Tingler (1959)
12 to the Moon (1960)

The 27th Day (1957)
We'll Bury You! (1962)
The Woman Eater (1959)
The Zombies of Mora-Tau (1957)

SHOCK PICTURES (52 titles). Released to TV: 8/57.

The Black Cat (1934)
Calling Dr. Death (1943)
The Cat Creeps (1946)
Chinatown Squad (1935)
Danger Woman (1946)
A Dangerous Game (1941)
Destination Unknown (1942)
Dracula (1931)
Dracula's Daughter (1936)
Enemy Agent (1940)
Frankenstein Meets the Wolf Man (1943)
Frankenstein (1932)
The Frozen Ghost (1943)
The Great Impersonation (1935)
Horror Island (1941)
House of Horrors (1946)
The Invisible Man (1933)
The Invisible Man Returns (1940)
The Invisible Ray (1936)
The Mad Doctor of Market Street (1942)
The Last Warning (1939)
The Mad Ghoul (1943)
The Man-Made Monster (1941)
The Man Who Cried Wolf (1937)
Night Key (1937)
The Mummy (1932)
The Mummy's Ghost (1944)

The Mummy's Hand (1940)
The Mummy's Tomb (1942)
Murders in the Rue Morgue (1932)
The Mystery of Edwin Drood (1935)
The Mystery of Marie Roget (1942)
The Mystery of the White Room (1939)
Night Key (1937)
Night Monster (1942)
Nightmare (1942)
Pillow of Death (1945)
The Raven (1935)
Reported Missing (1937)
Sealed Lips (1941)
Secrets of the Blue Room (1933)
Secrets of the Chateau (1934)
She-Wolf of London (1946)
Son of Dracula (1943)
Son of Frankenstein (1939)
The Spider Woman Srikes Back (1946)
The Strange Case of Doctor Rx (1942)
The Spy Ring (1938)
Weird Woman (1944)
Werewolf of London (1935)
The Witness Vanishes (1939)
The Wolf Man (1941)

Source: TV *Feature Film Source Book—Series, Serials, and Packages* (winter 1962–spring 1963), pp. FF-55, FF-56.   ·

SON OF SHOCK (20 titles). Released to TV: May 1958.

Before I Hang (1940)

Behind the Mask (1932)

Black Friday (1940)

The Black Room (1935)

The Boogie Man Will Get You (1942)

Bride of Frankenstein (1935)

Captive Wild Woman (1943)

The Devil Commands (1941)

The Face Behind the Mask (1941)

Ghost of Frankenstein (1942)

House of Dracula (1945)

House of Frankenstein (1945)

Invisible Man's Revenge (1944)

Island of Doomed Men (1940)

Jungle Captive (1945)

The Man They Could Not Hang
   (1939)

The Man Who Lived Twice (1936)

The Man with Nine Lives (1940)

The Mummy's Curse (1945)

Night of Terror (1933)

Source: *TV Feature Film Source Book—
Series, Serials, and Packages* (winter
1962–spring 1963), p. FF-64.

Television Enterprises Corporation (TEC)

REGENCY FEATURE FILM GROUP (28 titles). Announced to TV by TEC:
1/66.

Battle Inferno (1959) aka Inferno

*The Blackmailers (1960)

The Choppers (1962)

Deadwood 76 (1965)

Eeegah! (1962)

*Empire in the Sun (1956)

The Fall Guy (1963)

*Fight for Glory (1962)

Flight to Fury (1964)

Fourth for Marriage (1964) aka
   What's Up Front

Frozen Alive (1964)

*Furious Encounter (1962)

*Indian Paint (1964)

The Man with Two Faces (1964)

*Night Riders (1963)

Pattern for Murder (1964)

Pillar of Fire (1963)

*Pursuit Across the Desert (1961)

*A Queen for Caesar (1962)

*Shipwreck Island (1961)

*Spies-a-Go-Go (1965) aka Nasty
   Rabbit

Stronghold (1952)

*Sunscorched (1964)

Sword of Grenada (1956)

*Three and a Half Musketeers (1961)

*The Wanton Contessa (1954) aka
   Senso

Wild Guitar (1962)

*Wild Stampede (1962)

MONTGOMERY PACKAGE (5 titles). Announced to TV: 2/66.

Fortress of the Dead (1965)

*From Hell to Borneo (1964)

*Guerillas in Pink Lace (1964)

*Samar (1962)

*The Steel Claw (1961)

SCIENCE-FICTION PACKAGE (10 titles). Produced in Mexico. Announced to TV: 2/66.

H. G. Wells' New Invisible Man (1962)

Invasion of the Zombies (1963)

The Incredible Face of Dr. B (1961)

Neutron—The Black Mask (1963)

Neutron vs. the Death Robots (1961)

Neutron vs. the Amazing Dr. Caronte (1960)

Neutron vs. the Karate Assassins (1962)

Neutron vs. the Invisible Killers (1964)

Neutron—The Cosmic Bomb (1962)

Return from the Beyond (1961)

Source: TV Feature Film Source Book—Feature Packages (spring–summer 1966), p. FF-70.

Teleworld

INGMAR BERGMAN FESTIVAL (18 titles). Released to TV: 5/67.

*All These Women (1964)

Brink of Life (1957)

The Devil's Eye (1960)

Dreams (1955)

Lesson in Love (1954)

The Magician (1959)

Monika (1952)

Port of Call (1948)

Secrets of Women (1962)

The Seventh Seal (1956)

The Silence (1963)

Smiles of a Summer Night (1955)

Summer Interlude (1950) aka Illicit Interlude

Three Strange Loves (1949)

Through a Glass Darkly (1961)

The Virgin Spring (1959)

Wild Strawberries (1957)

Winter Light (1962)

GROUP II (14 titles). Released to TV: 5/67.

*The Big Blackout (1966)

Dead Eyes of London (1964)

Harlow (1965)

Kozara (1967)

*Marco the Magnificent (1966)

Marine Battleground (1966)

*Northwest Massacre (1966)

*Rat Trap (1963)

*Shoot to Kill (1966)

The Soldier (1965)

*Spies Strike Silently (1965)

*Via Maia (1961)

Who Killed Johnny R (1964) aka *Kill Johnny R*
Who Killed Teddy Bear (1964)

Source: *TV Feature Film Source Book—Feature Packages* (winter 1967–68, supplement), p. FF-28.

TELEWORLD 12 (12 titles). Released to TV: 11/66.

* *Blood of the Vampire* (1958)
Carnival of Souls (1962)
Corridors of Blood (1958)
* *Creation of the Humanoids* (1962)
Curse of the Voodoo (1965)
The Devil Doll (1964)
* *Fabulous Baron Munchausen* (1961)
Fiend without a Face (1958)

First Man into Space (1959)
The Haunted Strangler (1958)
* *Horror Castle* (1963) aka *Virgin of Nuremburg*
* *Slaughter of the Vampires* (1961)

Source: "Teleworld Licenses 32 Feature Films," *Broadcasting*, 11/14/66, p. 77.

Thunderbird Films

T-BIRD I: "THE EXPLOITABLES" (26 titles). Announced to TV: 5/65.

* *Adventures of Gil Blas* (1965)
Barrier of the Law (1950)
* *Beach Party Italian Style* (1965) aka *18 in the Sun*
† *Beat Girl* (1959) aka *Wild for Kicks*
* *The Blue Continent* (1960)
* *Daughter of Mata Hari* (1955)
Defiant Daughters (1961) aka *Shadows Grow Longer*
* *The Devil's Cavaliers* (1958)
* *The Dragon's Blood* (1963) aka *Siegfredo*
† *Frantic* (1961) aka *Elevator to the Gallows*
Frontier Wolf (n.d.)
* *Garibaldi* (1961) aka *Viva l'italia*
* *Ghosts of Rome* (1961) aka *Fantasmi a Roma*

†* *Mondo Cane* (1963) aka *A Dog's Life*
* *Island Princess* (1955) aka *Isola*
* *Napoleon II* (1964)
* *Of Flesh and Blood* (1965)
* *The Orientals* (1960) aka *Women of the Orient*
† *Psychomania* (1961)
* *Purple Moon* (1961)
* *Revenge of Ivanhoe* (1965)
* *Revolt of the Barbarians* (1964)
* *Ship of Condemned Women* (1963)
Train Robbery Confidential (1965)
* *Web of Passion* (1961)
* *What!* (1964)

Source: *TV Feature Film Source Book—Feature Packages* (spring–summer 1966), p. FF-73.

†These titles were released theatrically by Victoria Films, the exploitation subsidiary of Times Films. They were deleted from the Thunderbird package in winter 1967.

TOP DRAW GROUP (14 titles). Announced to TV: 7/63.

And the Wild Wild Women (1961)

Blonde in a White Car (1960) aka
    Nude in a White Car

The Case of Dr. Laurent (1959)

Close-Up (1948)

The Head (1961)

The Lovemaker (1958)

Man in the Moon (1961)

Open Secret (1948)

Passion of Slow Fire (1962)

Poor but Beautiful (1958)

Rocket from Calabuch (1958) aka *The
    Rocket*

The Savage Eye (1960)

Secrets of the Nazi Criminals (1962)

The Tailor's Maid (1958)

Source: TV *Film Source Book—Feature
Packages* (spring 1964), p. FF-98.

AWARD FOUR (4 titles).

*Dance Little Lady (1955) aka
    Dancing on a Dream

Hill 24 Doesn't Answer (1955)

La Strada (1956)

Lovers and Lollipops (1956)

Source: TV *Feature Film Source Book—
Feature Packages* (spring–summer 1966),
p. FF-72.

United Artists Associates

SCIENCE FICTION-HORROR-MONSTER FEATURES (58 titles).
Announced to TV: 5/15/63.

Alias John Preston (1955)

The Beast of Hollow Mountain (1956)

The Ape (1940)

The Black Sleep (1956)

The Beast with Five Fingers (1946)

Bedlam (1946)

The Body Snatcher (1945)

The Brighton Strangler (1945)

Cat People (1942)

The Creeping Unknown (1956)

Curse of Dracula (1958)

Curse of the Cat People (1944)

Curse of the Faceless Man (1958)

*Destination Moon (1950)

Donovan's Brain (1953)

Doctor X (1932)

Enemy from Space (1957)

Face of Marble (1956)

The Flame Barrier (1958)

The Four Skulls of Jonathan Drake
    (1959)

*Gog (1954)

Hound of the Baskervilles (1959)

I Bury the Living (1958)

I Walked with a Zombie (1943)
Isle of the Dead (1945)
It! The Terror from beyond Space (1958)
King Kong (1933)
King of the Zombies (1941)
Lady of Vengeance (1957)
The Leopard Man (1943)
The Living Ghost (1942)
The Lost Missile (1958)
* *Macumba Love* (1960)
The Magnetic Monster (1953)
Man from Planet X (1951)
Neanderthal Man (1953)
The Manster (1962)
Mark of the Vampire (1957) aka *The Vampire*
Mighty Joe Young (1949)
The Mysterious Doctor (1943)
Phantom of Crestwood (1932)

The Pharaoh's Curse (1957)
Red Planet Mars (1952)
Return of Doctor X (1939)
Revenge of the Zombies (1943)
* *Riders to the Stars* (1954)
The Seventh Victim (1943)
Son of Kong (1933)
The Strange Mr. Gregory (1945)
Stranger on the Third Floor (1940)
Svengali (1931)
Terror Is a Man (1960)
The Thing (1951)
Three Strangers (1946)
UFO (1956)
Voodoo Island (1957)
The Walking Dead (1936)
The Woman in White (1948)

Source: *TV Feature Film Source Book— Feature Packages* (spring–summer 1966), p. FF-75.

Video Artists

CRITICS CHOICE (12 titles).

Amelie (1961)
Anna (1952)
The Big Deal (1956) aka *Big Deal on Madonna Street*
Bitter Rice (1949)
Crazy for Love (1955)
The 400 Blows (1959)
Double Deception (n.d.)

Hiroshima, mon amour (1959)
Les Miserables (1943)
The Moralist (1957)
Rififi (1955)
White Nights (1959)

Source: *TV Feature Film Source Book— Feature Packages* (spring–summer 1966), p. FF-86.

11 GREAT ADVENTURES (11 titles).

The Angry Silence (1959)
The Executioners (1958) aka *Hitler's Executioners*
It Takes a Thief (1960)

* *King on Horseback* (1960)
Mania (1961)
Panic Button (1963)
* *The Sword and the Cross* (1959)

The Sword and the Dragon (1958)
Tamango (1958)
Theodora Slave Empress (1956)
The Youngest Spy (1962) aka My
    Name Is Ivan

Source: *TV Feature Film Source Book—
Feature Packages* (spring–summer
1966), p. FF-86.

SELZNICK MOVIE THEATER (16 titles). Reissued to TV: 9/62.

Adventures of Tom Sawyer (1938)
A Bill of Divorcement (1932)
The Farmer's Daughter (1947)
The Garden of Allah (1946)
I'll be Seeing You (1945)
Indiscretion of an American Wife
    (1954)
Intermezzo (1939)
Little Lord Fauntleroy (1936)
Notorious (1946)

The Paradine Case (1948)
Portrait of Jennie (1948)
Rebecca (1940)
Since You Went Away (1944)
Spellbound (1945)
The Spiral Staircase (1946)
The Wild Heart (1952)

Source: *TV Feature Film Source Book—
Feature Packages* (spring–summer
1966), p. FF-86.

Video Cinema Films

THIRTY-ONE FAMOUS FEATURES (31 titles).

Badman's Gold (1951)
Border Outlaws (1950)
Buffalo Bill Rides Again (1947)
Canadian Pacific (1949)
Cariboo Trail (1950)
Carnegie Hall (1947)
Cattle Queen (1951)
Fall of the House of Usher (1950)
Fighting Man of the Plains
    (1949)
Federal Man (1950)
The Fighting Stallion (1950)
The Forbidden Jungle (1950)
Fun on a Weekend (1947)
Genghis Khan (1953)
Hangmen Also Die (1943)

Heaven Only Knows (1947)
Hollywood Barn Dance (1947)
The Hoodlum (1951)
I Killed Geronimo (1950)
It Happened Tomorrow (1944)
Korea Patrol (1951)
The Long Night (1947)
Lured (1947) aka Personal Column
New Orleans (1947)
On Our Merry Way (1948) aka
    Miracles Can Happen
Scandal in Paris (1946) aka Thieves
    Holiday
A Song for Miss Julie (1945)
The Tiger and the Flame (1955)
    aka The Warrior Queen

Timber Fury (1950)
Voice in the Wind (1944)
The Young Widow (1946)

Source: TV *Feature Film Source Book—Feature Packages* (spring–summer 1966), p. FF-86.

NOTES

Introduction

1 For a summary of the industrial organization of Hollywood during the studio era, see Tino Balio, ed., *The American Film Industry*, rev. ed. (Madison: University of Wisconsin Press, 1985), pp. 253–84. A more detailed view of this period in American film history is Douglas Gomery, *The Hollywood Studio System* (New York: St. Martin's Press, 1986).

2 For an excellent discussion of this early-thirties production trend, during which the term "horror picture" was first coined, see David Skal, *The Monster Show: A Cultural History of Horror* (New York: Penguin, 1993), pp. 113–209; and Carlos Clarens, *An Illustrated History of the Horror Film* (New York: Capricorn Books, 1968), pp. 59–104. A brilliant rereading of horror films from 1931 to 1936 is Rhona J. Berenstein's *Attack of the Leading Ladies: Gender, Sexuality, and Spectatorship in Classic Horror Cinema* (New York: Columbia University Press, 1996). Berenstein carefully analyses censorship files, contemporary publicity, and press reception of many of classic horror's canonic texts and finds that historical and theoretical assumptions of horror as an unfettered playground for the sadistic male spectator is at best an oversimplification and at worst demonstrably false.

3 See Thomas Schatz, *The Genius of the System: Hollywood Filmmaking in the Studio Era* (New York: Pantheon Books, 1988), pp. 228–31.

4 In some small-town and rural theaters, however, a Poverty Row B-genre film, usually a western, was occasionally shown as the main attraction. In my father's hometown of Humble, Texas, the Jewel Theater on Main Street stayed solvent through the Depression by showing a regular pro-

gram of B westerns from Majestic, Republic, Monogram, and Grand National.

5 Eric Schaefer, *Bold! Daring! Shocking! True! A History of Exploitation Films, 1919–1959* (Durham: Duke University Press, 1999).

6 Balio, *The American Film Industry*, p. 401.

7 Barbara Wilinsky, *Sure Seaters: The Emergence of Art-House Cinema* (Minneapolis: University of Minnesota Press, 2000), pp. 65–77.

8 See Clarens, *An Illustrated History of the Horror Film*; S. S. Prawer, *Caligari's Children: The Film as Tale of Terror* (Oxford: Oxford University Press, 1980); and Nöel Carroll, *The Philosophy of Horror; or, Paradoxes of the Heart* (New York: Routledge, 1989).

9 See Robin Wood, "An Introduction to the American Horror Film," in *Movies and Methods*, vol. 2 ed. Bill Nichols (Berkeley: University of California Press, 1985); Carol Clover, *Men, Women, and Chain Saws* (Princeton: Princeton University Press, 1992); Skal, *The Monster Show*; Andrew Tudor, *Monsters and Mad Scientists: A Cultural History of the Horror Movie* (Oxford: Basil Blackwell, 1989); Tony Williams, *Hearths of Darkness* (New York: Associated University Presses, 1988); William Paul, *Laughing/ Screaming: Modern Hollywood Horror and Comedy* (New York: Viking, 1994); and Harry Benshoff, *Monsters in the Closet: Homosexuality and the Horror Film* (Manchester: Manchester University Press, 1997).

10 Gary Edgerton, *American Film Exhibition and an Analysis of the Motion Picture Industry's Market Structure, 1963–1980* (New York: Garland Publishing, 1983), p. 18.

11 Thomas Doherty, *Teenagers and Teenpics: The Juvenilization of American Movies in the 1950s* (Boston: Unwin and Hyman, 1988), p. 74 (emphasis in original).

12 Thomas Schatz, *Hollywood Genres: Formulas, Filmmaking, and the Studio System* (New York: Random House, 1981), pp. 36–41.

13 Mark Jancovich, *Rational Fears: American Horror in the 1950s* (Manchester: Manchester University Press, 1996).

14 Linda Williams, "Film Bodies: Gender, Genre, and Excess," in *Film Genre Reader II*, ed. Barry Keith Grant (Austin: University of Texas Press, 1995).

15 Tom Gunning, "The Cinema of Attractions: Early Film, Its Spectator and the Avant-Garde," *Wide Angle* 8, nos. 3–4 (1986), p. 65.

16 *Ibid.*, p. 60; and Tom Gunning, "Now You See It, Now You Don't: The Temporality of the Cinema of Attractions," *The Velvet Light Trap* 32 (fall 1993): p. 18.

17 Joan Hawkins, *Cutting Edge: Art-Horror and the Horrific Avant-Garde* (Minneapolis: University of Minnesota Press, 2000), pp. 53–64.

CHAPTER 1. Horror in Three Dimensions: *House of Wax* and *Creature from the Black Lagoon*

1 R. M. Hayes, *3-D Movies: A History and Filmography of Stereoscopic Cinema* (Jefferson, N.C.: McFarland and Co., 1989), pp. 215–18.

2 John Waters, "Guilty Pleasures" in *Crackpot: The Obsessions of John Waters* (New York: Vintage, 1987), p. 109.

3 "All-Time Wows," *Variety*, January 13, 1954, p. 10.

4 "Third Dimension: New Bait for Movie Box Offices," *Business Week*, November 8, 1952, p. 137; and "The Third Dimension: An Industry Changes Its Product," *Business Week*, July 25, 1953, p. 60.

5 See John Belton, *Widescreen Cinema* (Cambridge: Harvard University Press, 1992).

6 Richard Hincha, "Twentieth Century-Fox's CinemaScope: An Industrial, Organizational Analysis of Its Development, Marketing, and Adoption" (Ph.D. diss., University of Wisconsin—Madison, 1989), p. 155.

7 Belton, *Widescreen Cinema*, p. 134.

8 Ibid., p. 136; Hincha, "Twentieth Century-Fox's CinemaScope," pp. 190–91.

9 Hincha, "Twentieth Century-Fox's CinemaScope," p. 138.

10 Ibid., p. 193.

11 Hal Morgan and Dan Symmes, *Amazing 3-D* (Boston: Little, Brown and Co., 1982), p. 22.

12 See Hayes, *3-D Movies*, pp. 8–12.

13 Ibid., p. 23.

14 Ibid., p. 69.

15 "New Dimensions Perk Up Hollywood," *Business Week* March 14, 1953, p. 128.

16 "Natural Vision Ready for Public Showing," *Motion Picture Herald* (hereafter *MPH*), November 22, 1952, p. 38.

17 "Third Dimension," p. 134.

18 "'Bwana Devil' Breaks All Records at Philadelphia," *MPH*, January 10, 1953, p. 18.

19 "'Bwana': $5,000,000 Grosser," *Variety*, March 11, 1953, p. 3.

20 "Top Grossers of 1953," *Variety*, January 13, 1954, p. 10.

21 "Reappraisal of Film Rental Deals Looms as Direct Offshoot of 3-D," *Variety*, April 22, 1953, p. 7.

22 "High Costs of 3-D Prints New Industry Problem," *Variety*, March 25, 1953, p. 3.

23 "Strictly for the Marbles," *Variety*, March 11, 1953, p. 68.

24 "Polaroid's Stock Soars via 3-D," *Variety*, January 28, 1953, p. 7.

25 "Flash in the Pan?" *Time*, March 2, 1953, p. 90.

26 "3-D Costing Loew's 300G to Convert 31 N.Y. Theaters," *Variety*, February 4, 1953, p. 7.

27 "Lippert's 3-D Drive-In," *Variety*, April 15, 1953, p. 20.

28 "Depthies' Tix Tilt Upheaval," *Variety*, June 24, 1953, p. 3.

29 "Majors' 'Shortsighted' Policy on 3-D Exhibition Rapped at N.J. Allied Meet," *Variety*, July 15, 1953, p. 4.

30 "Public Responsibility Must Be Met: Barnett," *MPH*, October 10, 1953, p. 17.

31 "Exhibs' $110,000,000 Gamble," *Variety*, April 1, 1953, p. 27.

32 "F&M Seeking Ban on 3 Projectionists for 3-D," *Variety*, June 17, 1953, p. 15.

33 Earle M. Holden, "Letters to the Herald," *MPH*, September 19, 1953, p. 8.

34 "Exhibs Losing Coin on 3-D Setup; Customers Balk at Ticket Tilt," *Variety*, April 8, 1953, p. 2.

35 "Allied Theater Owners Will Blast 3-D's 50% Rentals at N.J. Meet Today," *Variety*, July 8, 1953, p. 4.

36 "Exhib Anger at 3-D Slowly Rising; Irked by Sales Terms, Quickies," *Variety*, June 17, 1953, p. 5.

37 "Myers Tells Senators: 3-D Is Weapon for Murder," *MPH*, April 18, 1953, p. 12.

38 See "Allied Demands War on Distribution Policies," *MPH*, August 28, 1954, p. 13. The 1955 figure is taken from Wesley A. Sturges, "Statement," U.S. Congress, Select Committee on Small Business, *Motion Picture Distribution Trade Practices 1956*, hearings before a subcommittee of the Select Committee on Small Business, 83d Cong., 2nd sess., 1956, p. 84.

39 For a discussion of the economics behind the ostensibly monopolistic practices behind the shift from "mass" to "class," see Wesley A. Sturges, "Statement," U.S. Congress, 1956 hearings, p. 73. Also, Hincha asserts that "increased film rentals, exhibition's favorite whipping boy, were responsible for only one-quarter of the average exhibitor's drop in profits between 1947 and 1953. The post-war rise in fixed and operating expenses for theater owners was far more of a burden than increased rentals" ("Twentieth Century-Fox's CinemaScope," p. 67).

40 "To Control or Not Is Big Allied Question," *MPH*, October 16, 1954, p. 12; "Allied Gets 'Weapon' in Control Bill Draft," *MPH*, October 23, 1954, p. 12. Again, Hincha points out that exhibitors' arguments here were often tendentious: "Exhibitors who had longed to move up in run status now expressed annoyance with their many colleagues who also sought to advance their situations, creating competition where none had existed before . . . Having argued stridently for years to let the forces of market pressures and the law, rather than oligopoly, control the licensing of pictures, they now found the adverse effects of those forces pushing them to support measures at odds with antitrust laws and natural market forces" ("Twentieth Century-Fox's CinemaScope," p. 71).

41 A crucial component of Cinerama had been its stereophonic sound, and Natural Vision became involved in the stereo race when Gunzburg formed Natural Sound Corporation to distribute exclusively the Kinevox stereo sound system to exhibitors for a cost of just over $5,000. See "Gunzburg to Distribute Stereophonic Sound Kit," *MPH*, May 16, 1953, p. 14.

42 RCA trade ad, *MPH*, March 28, 1953, p. 33.

43 "RCA 4-Track Reproducer to Be Ready in September," *MPH*, July 28, 1953, p. 23.

44 Warner trade ad, *Variety*, April 8, 1953, p. 29.

45 Warner trade ad, *MPH*, March 28, 1953, p. 15.

46 "Warner Plans 21 Films in 3-D," *MPH*, June 6, 1953, p. 20.

47 "'Lost Audience' Back, Temporarily, but Wary of 3-D Gimmick Cycles," *Variety*, April 29, 1953, p. 79.

48 "Crix Cackle at 3-D Trix, 'Cacophony' Sound; Public Doesn't Give 1-D Hoot," *Variety*, May 27, 1953, p. 1.

49 Ralph D. Goldberg, "Letters to the Herald," *MPH*, August 22, 1953, p. 8.

50 Bosley Crowther, "Picture of Hollywood in the Depths" *New York Times Magazine*, June 14, 1953, p. 14.

51 In 1953, Columbia featured Rita Hayworth in *Miss Sadie Thompson*, a re-make of *Rain*, the 1932 Somerset Maugham adaptation that had starred Joan Crawford. That studio's first film in its own polarized 3-D process, *Man in the Dark*, was a recasting of their 1936 thriller, *The Man Who Lived Twice*, with Edmond O'Brien in the role originally played by Ralph Bellamy. Warner released *A Star Is Born*, their 1954 musical reprise of the 1936 Selznick hit, with James Mason and Judy Garland in the roles earlier played by Fredric March and Janet Gaynor. By the time the film was in production, 3-D had been eschewed in favor of CinemaScope and Warner Phonic sound. After *The Robe*, Twentieth Century-Fox's second foray into CinemaScope was the color and stereo sound remake of the 1932 Joan Blondell vehicle, *The Greeks Had a Word for Them*, now titled *How to Marry a Millionaire* and starring Betty Grable, Marilyn Monroe, and Lauren Bacall. "With the novelty provided by the new systems being used, it's safer to stick to story material that offers the least likely risk and is best fitted to the requirements of individual systems," opined *Variety* ("Studios 'Play It Safe' with 3-D: Pix Themes Shun Offbeat Slant," *Variety*, August 12, 1953, p. 15).

52 André Gaudreault, *Du littéraire au filmique: Système du récit* (Paris: Méridi-èns Klincksieck, 1988), p. 23.

53 Ibid., p. 20.

54 "3-D Technique," *MPH*, February 28, 1953, p. 3.

55 "3-D Diagnosis," *Newsweek*, October 12, 1953, p. 98.

56 "Letters," *MPH*, June 27, 1953, p. 8.

57 Hollis Alpert, "SR Goes to the Movies," *Saturday Review*, April 25, 1953, p. 30.

58 Crowther, "Picture of Hollywood in the Depths," p. 64.

59 This scene is a comic representation of just the sort of "carny come-on" that would be the subject of constant industry debate for much of the rest of the decade and which will form the basis of much of the chapters that follow.

60 John P. Sisk, "Passion in a New Dimension," *Commonweal*, October 26, 1953, p. 64.

61 Parker Tyler, "The Era of the 3-D's," *New Republic*, May 18, 1953, p. 23.

62 "The Big Illusion," *Time*, April 20, 1953, p. 114.

63 Robert Kass, "Film and TV," *Catholic World*, June, 1953, p. 224.

64 "Cheaters Aren't the Answer," *New Yorker* April 18, 1953, p. 133.

65 Terry Ramsaye, "Terry Ramsaye Says . . . ," *MPH*, May 30, 1953, p. 14.

66 "3-D's Field Day for Film Biz," *Variety*, February 25, 1953, p. 1.

67 "Around the Clock 'Wax' Premiere," *MPH*, May 2, 1953, p. 40; "Round-The-Clock 'Spook' Preem for 'Wax' on Coast," *Variety*, March 25, 1953, p. 3.

68 "'Wax' Breaks More Records in Detroit and Chicago," *MPH*, May 9, 1953, p. 12.

69 "National Boxoffice Survey," *Variety*, May 20, 1953, p. 3.

70 "3-D Films Bolster May Biz in Keys," *Variety*, June 3, 1953, p. 4.

71 "'Wax' Running Out of 3-D Equipped Houses," *Variety*, June 17, 1953, p. 3.

72 "RKO Plans Saturation Campaign for 'Joe Young,'" *MPH*, June 20, 1953, p. 52.

73 "1422 'Beast' Dates Set," *MPH*, June 20, 1953, p. 53.

74 "Plan Fast Playoff for WB 'Beast,'" *Variety*, June 17, 1953, p. 5.

75 Warner Bros. trade ad, *MPH*, May 29, 1954, pp. 4–5.

76 See "Exhibs Eye Chances of Less Costly 3-D Modes: Nord, Vectograph, Norling," *Variety*, June 24, 1953, p. 3; and "'Naturama'—A Way to Print Two Subjects on One Reel," *MPH*, June 7, 1954, p. 18.

77 "National Film Has 3-D Glasses," *MPH*, March 14, 1953, p. 25.

78 "Polaroid vs. Depix Corp., Alvin M. Marks in Action on Patent Infringement," *Variety*, April 8, 1953, p. 3.

79 "Pola-Lite Co. Looks to 7,000,000 Specs Per Wk," *Variety*, August 19, 1953, p. 15.

80 "3-D Comeback," *Business Week*, December 12, 1953, p. 46.

81 "3-Developments," *Variety*, May 27, 1953, p. 7.

82 "L.A. 'Robot' Deal to Set Distrib Pattern," *Variety*, June 24, 1953, p. 3.

83 See Stephen King, *Danse Macabre* (New York: Viking, 1983), p., 137; and Harry Medved and Michael Medved, *The Golden Turkey Awards* (New York: St. Martin's Press, 1981), p. 89.

84 "Pic Industry Moves to Wed 3-D and Widescreen for Fusion of Effects," *Variety*, May 20, 1953, p. 21.

85 "3-D's New Wait-and-See Stance," *Variety*, September 30, 1953, p. 22.

86 "Single-Strip 3-D Spreading Steadily but Needs Product," *MPH*, August 7, 1954, p. 19.

87 "3-D Comeback," p. 46. See also "Moropticon Plan Offered," *MPH*, December 12, 1953, p. 12.

88 "Altec, RCA to Install Pola-Lite Equipment," *MPH*, June 5, 1954, p. 22.

89 Noël Carroll, "King Kong: Ape and Essence," in *Planks of Reason: Essays on the Horror Film*, ed. Barry Keith Grant (Metuchen, N.J.: Scarecrow Press, 1984), p. 219.

90 Ibid., pp. 221, 223.

91 Ibid., p. 237.

92 "Universal Sets 17 Saturation Openings for 3-D 'Lagoon,'" *MPH*, March 6, 1954, p. 18.

93 "Cite 32 New Installations For Pola-Lite 3-D System," *MPH*, May 8, 1954, p. 38.

94 "Finis to Favored 3-D Terms," *Variety*, July 29, 1953, p. 7.

95 See "Depix Loses to Polaroid on 3-D Film Viewers," *MPH*, March 5, 1955,

p. 21; and "Polaroid Backs 'Revenge' with Special Services," *MPH*, March 12, 1955, p. 34.

96 "Universal's 'Weirdies' Ain't Crazy; $8,500,000 since '54 a Lot of Clams," *Variety*, April 3, 1954, p. 3.

97 "Need Indie Producer Now to Fill Release Skeds in Flats Shortage: Dowling," *Variety*, April 2, 1954, p. 16.

98 "Mpls Boothmen 3-D Demands Another Headache for Nabe, Suburban Spots," *Variety*, September 23, 1953, p. 22.

99 Crowther, "Picture of Hollywood in the Depths," p. 66.

CHAPTER 2. The Color of Blood: Hammer Films and
Curse of Frankenstein

1 "Horror Remains a Major Commodity; and James Carreras Oughtta Know," *Variety*, May 28, 1958, p. 7.

2 See David Pirie, *A Heritage of Horror: The English Gothic Cinema, 1946–1972* (New York: Avon, 1974); Peter Hutchings, *Hammer and Beyond: The British Horror Film* (Manchester: Manchester University Press, 1993); and Howard Maxford, *Hammer, House of Horror: Behind the Screams* (Woodstock, N.Y.: Overlook Press, 1996).

3 Denis Meikle, *A History of Horrors: The Rise and Fall of the House of Hammer* (Lanham, Md.: Scarecrow Press, 1996), pp. 3–4.

4 Ibid., p. 6.

5 Ibid., pp. 7–10.

6 Maxford, *Hammer, House of Horror*, p. 18.

7 Thomas H. Guback, *The International Film Industry* (Bloomington: Indiana University Press, 1969), p. 154.

8 Maxford, *Hammer, House of Horror*, p. 33.

9 Allan Bryce, ed., *Amicus: The Studio that Dripped Blood* (Liskeard, Eng.: Stray Cat Publishing, 2000), pp. 8–15.

10 Denis Meikle, letter to the author, September 1, 2002.

11 Michael Carreras, internal memo at Hammer Film Productions, Ltd., n.d. I am very grateful to Dick Klemensen of *Little Shoppe of Horrors* for sharing with me a number of documents concerning Subotsky's Frankenstein script.

12 Meikle, *A History of Horrors*, pp. 32–33, 38.

13 Letter from James Carreras to Eliot Hyman, September 3, 1956. British Film Institute, Hammer Films Special Collections, Item 1(a).

14 Letter from Max J. Rosenberg to Michael Carreras, May 10, 1956, p. 1. My thanks to Dick Klemensen for providing me with a copy of the letter.

15 Letter from Eliot Hyman to James Carreras, August 28, 1956. British Film Institute, Hammer Films Special Collections, Item 1(a).

16 Meikle, *A History of Horrors*, p. 38.

17 Pirie, *A Heritage of Horror*, p. 8.

18 Ibid., p. 10.

19 Ibid., p. 143.

20 Ibid., p. 13.

21 Meikle, *A History of Horrors*, p. 43.

22 Quoted in Peter Evans, "My Night Out—with Frankenstein," *Kinemato-graph Weekly*, November 29, 1956, p. 22.

23 See "'I Don't Make Horror Films' Says Fisher," *Kinematograph Weekly*, March 26, 1959, p. 17.

24 Bill Edwards, "British Production—Losey All Set to Start Fifth British Feature," *Kinematograph Weekly*, December 18, 1958, p. 147

25 Ibid., p. 51.

26 Clarens, *An Illustrated History of the Horror Film*, p. 145.

27 "British Production—Black Magic Spells New Year's Work," *Kinemato-graph Weekly*, August 28, 1958, p. 23.

28 Pirie, *A Heritage of Horror*, p. 72.

29 See Allen Eyles, ABC: *The First Name in Entertainment* (London: BFI Publishing, 1993). See also "Warner Not to Sell Holding in ABPC—Official," *Kinematograph Weekly*, October 4, 1956, p. 1; and "ABPC Rumour Quashed," *Kinematograph Weekly*, October 4, 1956, p. 4.

30 See "1957 at the Criss Crossing Roads," *Variety*, January 8, 1958, p. 7.

31 See Skal, *The Monster Show*, p. 138.

32 "'The Curse of Frankenstein'—Make Money!" *MPH*, August 17, 1957, p. 32.

33 "Showmen in Action," *MPH*, August 3, 1957, p. 37.

34 "Paging All Horror Fans," *MPH*, October 19, 1957, p. 24.

35 "1957—At the Criss-Crossing Roads," p. 2.

36 "Hammer Will Remake UI Horror Films," *Kinematograph Weekly*, August 21, 1958, pp. 1, 6.

37 "Hammer Stresses Films at 'Middle' Spending," *MPH*, June 18, 1960, p. 23; and "Hammer Eyes New Production Deals," *Variety*, July 13, 1961, p. 14.

38 "Horror Remains a Money Commodity," *Variety*, p. 7. See also "New Partnership Will Double Bray Capacity," *Kinematograph Weekly*, October 30, 1958, p. 7.

39 "Spring, and B's Still Swarm," *Variety*, March 18, 1965, p. 3.

CHAPTER 3. "Look into the Hypnotic Eye!": Exhibitor
Financing and Distributor Hype in Fifties Horror Cinema

1 "Hollywood Today: Pictures and Their Makers," *MPH*, October 22, 1955, p. 13; and "Product Shortage—1960 Edition; 230 Features, Only 6 over 1959," *Variety*, September 14, 1960, p. 4.

2 "TOA's Production Project," *MPH*, November 13, 1954, p. 3.

3 For a piquant discussion of the importance of concessions to a theater's ledger, see Douglas Gomery, *Shared Pleasures: A History of Movie Presentation in the United States* (Madison: University of Wisconsin Press, 1992), p. 81: "The word around film industry conventions became: find a good location for a popcorn stand and build a movie theater around it" (81).

4 "More Product Crying Need but Exhibition Differs on Solution," *MPH*, March 26, 1955, p. 15.

5 Harry Brandt, "Statement," U.S. Congress, 1956 hearings, p. 239. Producer Sam Katzman was championing these multichange houses as outlets for independent features as late as 1960. See "Sam Katzman on Exhib Vagaries," *Variety*, September 28, 1968, p. 3.

6 Benjamin Berger, "Statement, U.S. Congress, 1956 hearings, p. 94.

7 "More Than Meets the Eye—This 'Product Shortage,'" *MPH*, April 16, 1955, p. 33.

8 Doherty, *Teenagers and Teenpics*, pp. 51–63.

9 William Paul in *Laughing/Screaming* devotes much of his perceptive analysis of the modern horror film to this trend.

10 "Politz Research Study Uncovers the 'Typical Frequent Movie-Goer' as Bright Teen-Ager," *MPH*, November 23, 1957, p. 15.

11 "AIP Heads Set Sights on Teenage Patron," *MPH*, May 25, 1957, p. 20.

12 "Youth Wants to Know about the Movies!" *MPH*, October 11, 1958, p. 21.

13 "Sex! Horror! Crime!" *MPH*, December 6, 1958, p. 18.

14 "Teens Tend to Double Bills," *MPH*, February 4, 1956, p. 18.

15 Doherty, *Teenagers and Teenpics*, p. 152.

16 Kevin Heffernan, "The Hypnosis Horror Films of the 1950s: Genre Texts and Industrial Context," *Journal of Film and Video* 54, nos. 2–3 (summer/fall 2002).

17 "The Power of Trailers," *MPH*, March 30, 1957, p. 7. "Say Trailers Attract 43%," *MPH*, January 11, 1958, p. 24.

18 Mrs. Anna Bell Ward Olson, "Letters to the Herald," *MPH*, August 24, 1957, p. 6.

19 "RX: Psychodynamics," *MPH*, April 21, 1956, p. 11.

20 "Return to Analytical Selling Is Needed," *MPH*, November 23, 1957, p. 35.

21 "Monstrous for Money," *Time*, July 14, 1958, p. 84. For Arkoff's humorous description of this process, see Richard Gehman, "The Hollywood Horrors," *Cosmopolitan*, (November, 1958), p. 40.

22 Ibid., p. 40.

23 Ernest Emerling, "An Appreciative Look at Movie 'Trailers,'" *MPH*, March 19, 1955, p. 39.

24 "Is Carny Come-On Necessary?" *MPH*, November 5, 1958, p. 15.

25 "Makelim Plan Abandoned; Seek Major Release for First Picture," *MPH*, May 26, 1956, p. 26; "Hal Makelim to Go Visiting Once Again," *MPH*, March 16, 1957, p. 14.

26 See Hincha, "Twentieth Century-Fox's CinemaScope," p. 58.

27 "Levin Cites AB-PT Aim in Producing," *MPH*, May 10, 1957, p. 30.

28 "Republic, AB-PT Deal," *MPH*, March 30, 1957, p. 5. "AB-PT Pictures to Be Released by Republic," *MPH*, June 15, 1957, p. 26.

29 *Variety*, review, July 3, 1957.

30 "AB-PT Films Open in 244 Theaters," *MPH*, June 8, 1957, p. 27.

31 "Reactivated Liberty Sets 'Bat' for Early Release," *MPH*, July 11, 1959, p. 20.

32 "Levin, Mandell Form Atlas Pictures Corp.," *MPH*, May 16, 1959, p. 11.

33 *Variety*, review, June 10, 1959, p. 3.

34 "McLendon Forms Own Distribution Company," *MPH*, July 11, 1959, p. 19.

35 *Variety, Mesa of Lost Women* review, October 17, 1956.

36 Agar died in 2002 after decades of sobriety through membership in Alcoholics Anonymous. He had spoken candidly about his former troubles and was active in a number of religious and community outreach groups. He is remembered by fans and interviewers (including this author) as an unusually gracious and generous man.

37 "Subliminal Absurdity," *MPH*, March 8, 1958, p. 7.

38 See "Zombie Pix Upbeat and Durable," *Variety*, May 9, 1956, p. 11; and Mark Thomas McGee, *Faster and Furiouser: The Revised and Fattened Fable of American International Pictures* (Jefferson, N.C.: McFarland and Co., 1996), pp. 54–55.

39 Vance Packard, *The Hidden Persuaders* (New York: David McKay and Co., 1957), p. 27.

40 Ibid., p. 21.

41 Ibid., p. 27 (punctuation in original).

42 Ibid., p. 31.

43 "Need 26 More 'A's: O'Donnell," *MPH*, June 5, 1954, p. 20.

44 "Allied Artists in High Gear: Rodgers Advisor," *MPH*, September 4, 1954, p. 17.

45 "Broidy Road Tour Boosts Allied Artists," *MPH*, March 12, 1955, p. 21.

46 "Allied Artists Cites Progress," *MPH*, March 26, 1955, p. 20.

47 "Allied Artists Sets 37 Films," *MPH*, April 2, 1955, p. 26.

48 "Allied Artists Cuts Loss To $1,189,688 for Year," *MPH*, October 18, 1958, p. 13.

49 "AA Plans 4 'Blockbusters' for 1958–59," *MPH*, August 2, 1958, p. 20.

50 "Allied Artists Profit Rises," *MPH*, May 28, 1955, p. 18.

51 "Allied Artists Plans 36 Releases in 1957," *MPH*, January 19, 1957, p. 20.

52 "Broidy Sees Upturn in A.A. Profits," *MPH*, November 19, 1955, p. 24.

53 "Allied Artists, Lux in Italian Deal," *MPH*, March 16, 1957, p. 12.

54 "Allied Artists Grosses Abroad at All-Time High," *MPH*, February 7, 1959, p. 15.

55 "A.A. Seeks Imports," *MPH*, November 2, 1957, p. 7.

56 "Allied Artists Skeds 14 Big Properties," *Variety*, May 4, 1960, p. 3. "Broidy Lists 14 Top AA Films in 1960," *MPH*, May 7, 1960, p. 10.

57 "Allied Artists O'seas Rentals Up 14%; Cuba Remains Worry," *Variety*, January 20, 1960, p. 15. "Allied Artists Acquires Films for Latin American Market," *MPH*, August 5, 1961, p. 16.

58 "Allied Artists' Net Profit Is $529,338 for 1961," *MPH*, February 15, 1962, p. 15.

59 "Income Down, as Allied Artists' Broidy Tells Stockholders of Upgraded Prod," *Variety*, October 18, 1961, p. 5.

60 "Allied Artists Cites Progress," p. 20.

61 "O'Donnell Asks Support for Allied Artists," *MPH*, April 20, 1957, p. 19.

62 "Allied Artists Plans 36 Releases in 1957," p. 20.

63 "Allied Artists Production Is Speeded," *MPH*, November 9, 1957, p. 21.

64 "AA Plans 4 'Blockbusters' for 1958–59," p. 20.

65 "Allied Artists Moving into the Black, Says Broidy," *MPH*, March 28, 1959, p. 11.

66 "1959—Probable Domestic Take," *Variety*, January 6, 1960, p. 34.

67 See Peter Biskind, *Seeing Is Believing: How Hollywood Taught Us to Stop Worrying and Love the Fifties* (New York: Pantheon Books, 1983), pp. 137–44.

68 Matthew Bernstein, *Walter Wanger, Hollywood Independent* (Berkeley: University of California Press, 1994) p. 243.

69 See Allied Artists trade ad, "You too will get the shock of your life when you see 'THE HYPNOTIC EYE,'" *MPH*, January 23, 1960, p. 18.

70 William Read Woodfield, interview with Tom Weaver, 2000. Published online at http://www.bmonster.com/horror26.html.

71 Herschell Gordon Lewis's *The Wizard of Gore* (1970) bears a striking resemblance to *The Hypnotic Eye* in its use of the hypnotist/monstrateur plot and in its Grand Guignol violence against the hypnotist Montag's female victims. It is unclear whether Lewis was influenced by the earlier film or whether he was making use of this figure, which, I have shown, predates the horror film proper and the narrative cinema itself.

72 Vance Packard, *Hidden Persuaders* (New York: David McKay and Co., 1957), p. 106.

73 CBS trade ad, *Variety*, July 25, 1962, pp. 44–45.

74 This scene, along with the interlude in the beatnik coffee house, was almost always excised by local television stations when Allied Artists put the film into syndication as part of its "Sci-Fi for the 60s" package in 1963.

75 *Variety*, review, January 20, 1960.

76 "Used Live Hypnotist to Promote 'The Hypnotic Eye,'" *MPH*, May 14, 1960, p. 691.

77 "Ordinary 'B' Kaput; It's Gimmick Today," *Variety*, March 22, 1961, p. 19.

78 "Goldenson Has Ten-Part Plan for Stimulating Box Offices" *MPH* January 21, 1956, p. 16 and "'Orderly Release' of New Faces," *Variety*, June 1, 1960, p. 25.

79 Thomas Doherty, *Teenagers and Teenpics: The Juvenilization of American Movies in the 1950s* (Philadelphia: Temple University Press, 2002), p. 27.

CHAPTER 4. "A Sissified Bela Lugosi": Vincent Price,
William Castle, and AIP's Poe Adaptations

1 "Independents Supplied 219 Films during Past Production Year," *MPH*, October 5, 1957, p. 11.

2 Tino Balio, "Retrenchment, Reappraisal, and Reorganization, 1948–" in Balio, ed. *The American Film Industry*, p. 419.

3 "'Fewer-Better' Is Not Answer, Four Insist," *MPH*, January 1, 1955, p. 23.

4 "Film Shortage Aid Looms from Several Directions," *MPH*, November 20, 1954, p. 12; "Hearty Yes Greets Columbia's Plan," *MPH*, November 13, 1954, p. 14. See also "Columbia to Finance Independents for Majority of Future Product," *MPH*, April 5, 1958, p. 14.

5 "Independents Supplied 219 Films During Past Production Year," p. 11.

6 See "Columbia, Schneer in Three-Film Deal," *MPH*, May 12, 1956, p. 42; and "Columbia Signs New Deal with Schneer," *MPH*, April 19, 1958, p. 23.

7 "Hammer Stresses Films at 'Middle' Spending," *MPH*, June 18, 1960, p. 23.

8 *International Motion Picture Almanac, 1957* (New York: Quigley Publications, 1956), p. 500.

9 Ibid., p. 165.

10 "20th-Fox Signs Regal to Make 27 in Year," *MPH*, August 3, 1957, p. 22; "Regal Starts 10 Pictures in Ten Months," *MPH*, November 23, 1957, p. 29.

11 "More Product Crying Need but Exhibition Differs on Solution," *MPH*, March 26, 1955, p. 15. See also "July to Boom—Not All Happy," *Variety*, July 6, 1960, p. 24.

12 See "AIP Heads Set Sights on Teen-Age Patron," *MPH*, May 25, 1957, p. 20; and "Lurid Titles, Harmless Tales," *Variety*, October 14, 1959, p. 3.

13 "Nicholson Finds Playdates Easier," *Variety*, March 30, 1955, pp. 3, 20.

14 "Amer-Int'l Prez Tires of Exhib Condescension; Raps Lazy Showmanship," *Variety*, October 11, 1961, p. 25.

15 Mildred Martin, "Foreign Films Win Spots among Year's Best Ten," *Philadelphia Inquirer*, November 8, 1957, p. 1D.

16 "Zombie Pix Upbeat and Durable," *Variety*, May 9, 1956, p. 11.

17 Walter Brooks, "Double Bills—They're In and Out," *MPH*, August 17, 1957, p. 31.

18 Sidney H. Rechetnik, "Universal Selling a Film Package: One 'Werewolf' and One 'Shadow,'" *MPH*, April 29, 1961, p. 17.

19 "Horror Stunts Boost 'Werewolf,' 'Cat' at RKO Keith's Theater, Washington," *MPH*, June 10, 1961, p. 154.

20 "He Shook 'Em Up for His Horror Show, Did Phil Hayes of Effingham Drive-In," *MPH*, August 15, 1959, p. 369.

21 "Indies Need for New Faces Cited," *Variety*, November 25, 1959, p. 17.

22 "Film Shortage Stems from Star Shortage," *MPH*, March 24, 1956, p. 26.

23 Trueman Rembusch, "Statement," U.S. Congress, 1956 hearings, p. 79.

24 Crawford's *Baby Jane* costar, Bette Davis, made this subgenre entirely her own in films like *Dead Ringer* (1964), *Hush Hush, Sweet Charlotte*, *The Nanny* (both 1965), *Madame Sin* (1972), *Burnt Offerings* (1976), and *The Dark Secret of Harvest Home* (1974).

25 "Castle Ideas Good Match with Ability," *MPH*, July 13, 1957, p. 23. The White/Castle partnership was also involved in the production of the television series *Men of Annapolis*. See Tom Weaver, "An Outspoken Conversation with Robb White," *Filmfax* (December/January 1989–1990): p. 60. It is very likely that the use of recognizable star names in Castle's low-

budget features was designed to make them more attractive in the ancillary market of syndicated television in the following years.

26 Weaver, "An Outspoken Conversation," p. 61.

27 See "Mad, Mad Doctors 'n' Stunts," *Variety*, July 23, 1958, p. 7; and "M: For Macabre and Mazuma," *Variety*, June 18, 1958, p. 7.

28 "Castle Ideas Good Match with Ability," p. 23.

29 See Tom Weaver, *Science Fiction Stars and Horror Heroes: Interviews with Actors, Writers, and Directors from the 1940s through the 1960s* (New York: McFarland and Co., 1994), p. 146.

30 "Fox Says 'Fly' Heads for $1,000,000 Gross," *MPH*, July 26, 1958, p. 33.

31 "Blood Pudding," *Time*, September 1, 1961, p. 50.

32 Hugo Friedhofer supplied the musical score for *Homicidal* using orchestration similar to Dexter's.

33 "Producers Smart to Do Own Sell, per Bill Castle," *Variety*, October 31, 1962, p. 3.

34 "Columbia's *The Tingler*—You—and Your Audience—Play Important Roles in Percepto," *MPH*, September 19, 1959, p. 19.

35 See "Testing the Tingle," *MPH*, September 19, 1959, p. 24.

36 Tim Lucas, "William Castle on Laserdisc," *Video Watchdog* 30 (1995), p. 59.

37 "Columbia's *The Tingler*," p. 20.

38 "Myers Calls SuperScope Today's Best Buy," *MPH*, April 3, 1954, p. 26.

39 "Tushinsky System to be Generally Available," *MPH*, February 27, 1954, p. 9.

40 "AIP to Shoot in Superama," *MPH*, March 15, 1958, p. 23.

41 "Don't Kill Thrill Chill Mill," *Variety*, March 26, 1958, p. 5; cited in Doherty, *Teenagers and Teenpics*, p. 151.

42 "Stop 'Bad' Production, Says Wilson," *MPH*, March 3, 1956, p. 25.

43 "Don't Kill Thrill Chill Mill," p. 5.

44 "Lippert Company Formed for Large Budget Films," *MPH*, July 29, 1961, p. 16.

45 "Arkoff Tells AIP's Blockbuster Plans," *MPH*, December 19, 1959, p. 17.

46 "AIP Plans 10 Features with New York Financing," *MPH*, March 28, 1959, p. 12.

47 *Variety*, review, September 7, 1961.

48 "Picture Grosses," *Variety*, September 20, 1961, p. 6.

49 "1961: Rentals and Potential," *Variety*, January 10, 1962, p. 58.

50 "Nicholson Promises Policy of 'Blockbuster a Month,'" *MPH*, April 1, 1961, p. 15.

CHAPTER 5. Grind House or Art House?: Astor Pictures and *Peeping Tom*

1 Hawkins, *Cutting Edge*, p. 22.

2 "TOA Sees Relief from Film Shortage," *MPH*, May 27, 1961, p. 6.

3 See "Who's Who of New York Importers," *Variety*, April 26, 1961, p. 171.

4 Gomery, *Shared Pleasures*, p. 181.

5 Harry Brandt, "Statement," U.S. Congress, 1956 hearings, p. 239.

6 "Product Shortage Relieved by Booking Imports," *MPH*, October 23, 1954, p. 55.

7 "Foreign Films Get New Lease on Theater Life," *MPH*, June 9, 1956, p. 19.

8 "Institute Panelists Study Price Scales and Product Shortage," *MPH*, April 21, 1956, p. 13.

9 Wilinsky, pp. 65–79. See also "Shortage: Showman's Chance; Majors Ape Former Statesrighters; Imports New Importance to Yanks" *Variety* May 25, 1960 and "Three More Turn to Art Policy in Pittsburgh" *MPH* May 3, 1958, p. 18.

10 *International Motion Picture Almanac, 1957*, p. 542.

11 Wilinsky, *Sure Seaters*, p. 124.

12 Hy Hollinger, "Foreign Pix Gain by Racy Tags," *Variety*, June 30, 1954, p. 5.

13 "Manhattan 'Art' Bottleneck—Importers May Have to Build," *Variety*, March 20, 1957, p. 5.

14 "Zombie Pix Upbeat and Durable," *Variety*, May 9, 1956, p. 11.

15 Clarens, *An Illustrated History of the Horror Film*, p. 155. In addition, some art theaters used a carnival-style ballyhoo to attract patrons to their films. In 1963, the Fine Arts Theater in Dallas employed local women and men to parade through the streets of town dressed in revealing costumes inspired by the harem sequence in *8½* to promote the Fellini film. Three years later, female drama students from a local college recreated the costumes from Fellini's *Juliet of the Spirits* in a similar downtown promenade. See "Bizarre Scene in '8½' Inspires Dallas Stunt," *MPH*, November 13, 1963, p. 36; and "Fellini 'Spirits' Get Fine Arts Treatment," *MPH*, July 20, 1966, p. 18.

16 Hawkins, *Cutting Edge*, p. 75.

17 "Dubbing of Foreign Pix Still a Moot Point among Distribs in U.S. Market," *Variety*, April 9, 1952, p. 13.

18 See Janus trade ad, "Bergman Spells Bonanza for Drive-Ins," *Variety*, August 16, 1961, p. 64.

19 "Updated Distrib Strategy; Angles on the Offbeat Films," *Variety*, February 7, 1961, p. 76. See also "Who's Who of New York Importers," *Variety*, April 26, 1961, p. 171.

20 "Foreign Films Get New Lease on Theater Life," *MPH*, June 9, 1956, p. 19.

21 See "Par May Duck Vadim's Lesbo 'Roses'; Doubt-or-Delay Brando's 'Jacks,'" *Variety*, August 10, 1960, p. 8; and "Par Strategy: 'Blood and Roses' for 1961," *Variety*, August 17, 1961, p. 3.

22 See Janus trade ad, "Ingmar Bergman Spells BIG Box Office," *Variety*, October 21, 1959, p. 20.

23 "Dubbed Swedish 'Magician' Watched as Clue to Circuits Taking Offbeaters," *Variety*, March 23, 1960, p. 14. These crossover attempts would eventually have a pronounced effect on the horror film in the sixties: *Psycho* would borrow as liberally from *Diabolique* and *Les yeux sans visage*

as it would from William Castle's horror melodramas, and Robert Lippert would remake *Caligari* in 1962 with a Robert Bloch script heavily influenced by Alain Resnais. A crucial figure in this growing syncretism between the genre and art cinemas, I will show, is Roman Polanski, who would successfully straddle the two markets with *Repulsion* in 1965. Paramount would lend art-film trappings to the Rock Hudson shocker *Seconds* in 1966 before producer William Castle would inaugurate a new chapter in both Paramount Pictures and the horror cinema with *Rosemary's Baby* (1968).

24 See "The Supercolossal, Well Pretty Good, World of Joe Levine," *Business Week*, (March 1964), p. 132.

25 "Importers Tight Race," *Variety*, December 22, 1954, p. 11.

26 "Foreign Pics' 'Now or Never'—NY Artie Outlets All Sewed Up?" *Variety*, August 24, 1955, p. 3.

27 "'Wages' Hints that Lorau Films May Go to DCA," *Variety*, June 2, 1955, p. 10.

28 For a synopsis of the censorship and marketing problems DCA faced with *Wages of Fear*, see "The Film You Won't See," *Nation*, August 6, 1955, p. 110.

29 "'I Am a Camera' and Candid DCA's Hot Tomato Amoral Heroine," *Variety*, June 22, 1955, p. 7; and "Code-Nixed 'Camera' Focuses on Same Subjects Okayed in Other Films," *Variety*, August 3, 1955, p. 1.

30 "Company Presidents and Johnston View 'I Am a Camera' on Appeal; See Test of Code, Legion Power," *Variety*, August 10, 1955, p. 3.

31 "Presidents Echo 'Camera' Decision," *Variety*, August 17, 1955, p. 5.

32 "To Reissue Two," *MPH*, June 9, 1956, p. 25.

33 "DCA Announces 23 Features for 1957," *MPH*, January 19, 1957, p. 24.

34 "Schwartz: Distribs Need Continuity or Face Exhib Balks," *Variety*, February 8, 1961, p. 62.

35 Ibid., p. 4.

36 "Scranton Corp (That Was) Okayed to Sell Roach Studio to Wenrob," *Variety*, March 7, 1962, p. 14.

37 "Schwartz: Distribs Need Continuity," p. 62. "50 Theaters Booking 'Mania'-'Thief' Combo," *Variety*, January 18, 1961, p. 19; and "Schwartz: Distribs Need Continuity," p. 62.

38 "50 Theaters Booking 'Mania'-'Thief' Combo," p. 19.

39 See "'B' Market Dates Today: 2,500," *Variety*, July 31, 1963, p. 5.

40 "Who's Who of New York Importers," *Variety*, April 26, 1961, p. 171.

41 "Flamingo's Trim; Pete Yeager Exits," *Variety*, July 12, 1961, p. 31.

42 "Fred Schwartz Joining MGM in September," *Variety*, July 8, 1961, p. 19.

43 "'Ghoul'-'Blood' Sweet BO Music via Corn—Macabre Barnum Bally," *Variety*, June 12, 1963, p. 26.

44 See "Film Shortage? Indie Distribs Say, 'Look to Us,'" *Variety*, September 5, 1962, p. 3.

45 See review, *MPH*, May 14, 1955, p. 68.

46 "Acquires Bergman Film," *MPH*, December 3, 1955, p. 29.

47 See review, *MPH*, July 14, 1956, p. 969.

48 See review, *MPH*, October 6, 1956, p. 98.

49 See Astor trade ad, *MPH*, June 6, 1953, p. 33.

50 One of Astor's ad slicks for the film is reproduced in Sinister Cinema's 1996 catalog, p. 27.

51 "Screencraft to Produce for Release by Astor," *MPH*, October 26, 1957, p. 28.

52 Review, *Variety*, March 19, 1958.

53 "Layton-Astor to Make 10 Films in Two Years," *MPH*, May 3, 1958, p. 23; and review of *Missile to the Moon*, *MPH*, November 21, 1959, p. 491.

54 "Astor Pictures to Bruder," *MPH*, December 12, 1959, p. 12. "Astor Pictures Sold to Franklin Bruder," *Broadcasting*, December 14, 1959, p. 96.

55 William Werneth, "Broadening the American Audience for Foreign Films," *MPH*, August 30, 1961, p. 5.

56 See "Supply Down, Terms Up, Exhibitors Suddenly Cordial to Indie Distribs," *Variety*, October 3, 1962, p. 5.

57 "'Sweet Life': Road Show 'If,'" *Variety*, January 25, 1961, p. 19.

58 "Col Has 'Dolce Vita' for Commonwealth Lands But Ducked U.S. Market," *Variety*, August 16, 1961, p. 19.

59 "Shock Therapy for NY Execs," *Variety*, August 16, 1961, p. 2.

60 Review, *MPH*, April 22, 1961, p. 100.

61 Astor trade ad, "How Big Is *La Dolce Vita* in America?" *MPH*, July 1, 1962, p. 17.

62 "Picture Grosses," *Variety*, July 1, 1962, p. 6.

63 "'La Dolce Vita,' with 200 Prints, Assumes Model Role for Linguals," *Variety*, October 18, 1961, p. 3.

64 Astor trade ad, "How Big Is *La Dolce Vita*?" p. 17–18.

65 "1961: Rentals and Potential," *Variety*, January 10, 1962, p. 13.

66 See Astor trade ad, "The *Big* Ones Go to Astor," *Variety*, May 2, 1962, p. 61.

67 "'Sweet Life': Road Show If," p. 19.

68 "Supply Down, Terms Up, Exhibitors Suddenly Cordial to Indie Distribs," p. 5.

69 Review, *Variety*, April 20, 1960.

70 Bill Edwards, "Production," *Kine Weekly*, November 19, 1959, p. 22.

71 Hutchings, *Hammer and Beyond*, p. 163.

72 Several theaters in London, for example, actually posted outside the theater as a carny come-on the excoriating reviews the film received from the British press. See Kevin Heffernan, "Michael Powell's *Peeping Tom*: A Film Maudit Reconsidered," forthcoming.

73 "Britain's Box Office Best for 1959," *MPH*, January 9, 1960, p. 32.

74 See "Cohen and Levy Sign New Five-Year Production Pact," *MPH*, January 9, 1960, p. 37; and "Cohen Comes to America for Distribution Talks," *MPH*, January 24, 1960, p. 14.

75 "Release Chart by Companies," *MPH*, July 1960, p. 705.

76 See "Product Digest: Release Chart by Companies," *MPH*, July 1959, p. 705.

77 Anglo-Amalgamated trade ad, *MPH*, October 10, 1960, p. 42.

78 "De Vecchi Reveals Astor's Multiple Product Deals," *Variety*, July 19, 1961, p. 54.

79 Astor trade ad, "Astor's 'Peeping Tom' a Real Eye-Opener," *Variety*, December 6, 1961, p. 16.

80 "'Peeping Tom,' 'Head' Are Rated 'B' by Legion," *MPH*, October 18, 1961, p. 23.

81 *Peeping Tom* newspaper ad, *Philadelphia Inquirer*, October 24, 1962, p. 36.

82 *Philadelphia Inquirer*, September 12, 1962.

83 *Philadelphia Inquirer*, October 8, 1962.

84 *Philadelphia Inquirer*, October 24, 1962.

85 "Picture Grosses," *Variety*, February 20, 1963, p. 8.

86 "Picture Grosses," *Variety*, February 27, 1963, p. 10.

87 "Picture Grosses," *Variety*, November 4, 1964, p. 9.

88 For a discussion of the exhibition and distribution context of the sexploitation film in the mid- to late sixties, see Eric Schaefer, "Gauging a Revolution: 16mm and the Rise of the Pornographic Feature," *Cinema Journal* 41, no. 3 (spring 2002): pp. 4–7.

89 *Philadelphia Inquirer*, February 25, 1966, p. 15.

90 Review, *MPH*, November 29, 1961, p. 365.

91 "Costs Cut, Astor Pictures Continues; Inland Credit Cancels That Auction," *Variety*, January 16, 1963, p. 5.

92 "'Dolce Vita' to Astor Globally for $1,350,000," *Variety*, March 14, 1962, p. 5.

93 "Astor Cineriz in Co-Production," *Variety*, May 30, 1962, p. 7.

94 "Wilson Is Astor Music Head," *MPH*, September 27, 1961, p. 16.

95 "Astor Pictures Buys Pathé-Amer. In Expansion Moves Embracing 18 Features," *Variety*, June 27, 1962, p. 4.

96 "Costs Cut, Astor Pictures Continues," p. 5.

97 "Astor Assets Exceed Liabilities," *Variety*, February 6, 1963, p. 3.

98 "Landau-Unger Exit AA 'Sales Agency'; Dicker Tie to American International," *Variety*, December 18, 1965, p. 3.

CHAPTER 6. American International Goes International:
New Markets, Runaway Productions, and *Black Sabbath*

1 Samuel Z. Arkoff interview with Linda May Strawn, in *Kings of the Bs: Working within the Hollywood System*, ed. Todd McCarthy and Charles Flynn (New York: E. P. Dutton, 1975), pp. 260–63.

2 See "American-International Aims at Arties Stressing It'll Carry MPAA Seal," *Variety*, January 18, 1961, p. 7; and "Exploiteer at All 28 AIP Branches," *Variety*, February 26, 1966, p. 27.

3 "AIP Abandons Artie Aspirations for Now, but May Try Again Later," *Variety*, September 6, 1961, p. 4.

4 "Clean Horror Harms No Kids-Herman Cohen," *Variety*, February 10,

1960, p. 5; and "Financing, Autonomy Cited in Foreign Filming Trend," *MPH*, March 11, 1961, p. 11.

5 "Italy Ends Quota, Blocked Lira," *Variety*, June 13, 1962, pp. 13, 39.

6 "AIP Launches Big Push for 'Sign of the Gladiator,'" *MPH*, October 3, 1959, p. 27.

7 "Foreign Films' U.S. Jackpot," *Variety*, April 20, 1960, p. 78.

8 Ibid., p. 1.

9 "How Foreign Product Scored in U.S.," *Variety*, April 26, 1961, p. 170. See also "Foreign Rentals in U.S.," *Variety*, April 29, 1964, p. 30.

10 "AIP Appoints Reich," *MPH*, February 20, 1960, p. 10.

11 "Income Rises in Foreign Parts for American Int'l," *Variety*, April 15, 1964, p. 17.

12 "American International Handling 3 Overseas, but Not Domestically," *Variety*, November 9, 1960, p. 4.

13 "Lionello Santi in NY; His Galatea of Rome Aimed 'Esther' at Yanks," *Variety*, December 7, 1960, p. 22.

14 Initially the film was to have been called *House of Fright*, one of dozens of copyrighted titles AIP kept on file at its offices for possible future releases. The title *House of Fright* was used in 1961 for their release of Hammer's *Two Faces of Dr. Jekyll*, on which Columbia had "relinquished U.S. rights when the seal was denied on homo angles," according to *Variety*. As with *Black Sunday*, AIP made the film more suitable for its juvenile patronage by editing some brief scenes and redubbing some of the dialogue. See "Hammer's 'Fright' Film: Have Shears, Will Cut for Shurlock and Little," *Variety*, May 10, 1961, p. 3.

15 "Admissions in Italy," *Variety*, May 8, 1963, p. 35.

16 Eitel Monaco, "Taxation, Television, and Finances Haunting Italy," *Variety*, May 8, 1963, p. 36.

17 Eitel Monaco, "Upsurging Italy and Its Further 'Growth' Factor," *Variety*, April 26, 1961, p. 64.

18 "Italo Film Biz Up to 2d Spot in World Market," *Variety*, February 10, 1960, p. 25.

19 "Italy's Film Production Costs; Cheaper than Britain, France, but Top Spain, Greece, Yugo," *Variety*, May 2, 1962, p. 36; and "Italy Holds Cost Line to '62 Levels; Still Less than Britain or France," *Variety*, May 8, 1963, p. 69.

20 Vincent Canby, "American-International Aims to Give Meaning to Foreign Half of Tag," *Variety*, April 13, 1960, p. 3.

21 "Globe Films, with A-I, Outlines Ambitious '62 Prod., Distrib Program," *Variety*, December 27, 1961, p. 12.

22 "American Intl. Sets Own Distribution in Italy; Part of Indie's Spreading Out," *Variety*, September 30, 1964, p. 4.

23 "AIP Chooses Rome for Base," *Variety*, November 2, 1966, p. 11.

24 "Rapture (Modified) of Italy," *Variety*, May 4, 1966, p. 93.

25 Eitel Monaco, "Italy: Sound Policies, Planned Growth; And Television Villain Failed," *Variety*, April 20, 1960, p. 67.

26 "AIP to Make More and Buy Less from O'seas Prods; Italian Ties," *Variety*, September 1, 1965, p. 5.

27 "Overseas Angles Essential to AIP," *Variety*, June 29, 1966, p. 17.

28 See "Widening Range of AIP Product; Also of Its New Trans-American," *Variety*, Feburary 9, 1966, p. 14.

29 "Demi-Gods but Not Muscle Bound; Nicholson on Beefcake Casting Problem, *Variety*, June 15, 1960, p. 20.

30 "More Yank Action in Italy," *Variety*, May 4, 1966, p. 124.

31 "Hollywood versus Other Places," *Variety*, January 10, 1962, p. 7.

32 "'We Got 10, and No Reissues,' Big Nicholson Stress," *Variety*, February 6, 1963, p. 4.

33 "Half-of-Italy's Stars Aliens; English as Big Business Asset," *Variety*, April 26, 1961, p. 63.

34 "Key to Bankers: A New Law; Italy Needs to Stop Coasting," *Variety*, May 12, 1965, p. 77; and "Bond, Sage Cycles Top Italy: Fatigue Yields to Public Whim," *Variety*, April 27, 1966, p. 29.

35 William Castle devised the most spectacular instance of this kind of sexist marketing when he signed ingenues from thirteen different countries for his *13 Frightened Girls*. Castle planned to promote each of the thirteen as the "star" of the film in her own country. See William Castle, *Step Right Up! I'm Gonna Scare the Pants Off America* (New York: Pharos Books, 1992), p. 176.

36 "As Romans Now Do, Carry On: Magic No More, Skills Prevail," *Variety*, May 8, 1963, p. 35.

37 "Least-Likely to Succeed at Italian Box Office," *Variety*, May 4, 1966, p. 92.

38 "Rome Crowded with Internationalists; Many Own Homes, Make Many Films," *Variety*, May 8, 1963, p. 35.

39 Tim Lucas, "*Black Sabbath*: The Unmaking of Mario Bava's *Three Faces of Fear*," *Video Watchdog* (May/June 1991): p. 43.

40 "Foresight Needed in Lingual Films; 'Dubbing Oughtta Start on Set,'" *Variety*, October 18, 1961, p. 24.

41 See Lucas, "*Black Sabbath*," p. 36; and MCA trade ad, "Now Available for Local Programming—*THRILLER*—your host and star, Boris Karloff," *Broadcasting*, April 9, 1962, p. 43.

42 In the case of Karloff, the connection with the horror comics would prove more than coincidental: in 1966, Gold Key Comics would begin publication of *Boris Karloff's Tales of Mystery*, a horror and mystery comic based in part on the E.C. comics.

43 Lucas, "*Black Sabbath*," pp. 36–37.

44 Ibid., p. 37.

45 Ibid., p. 51.

46 Ibid., p. 36.

47 Ibid., p. 52.

48 Suzanne Liandrat-Guignes, "La trois visages de la peur," in *Mario Bava*, ed. Jean-Louis Leutrat (Liège: Éditions du Céfal, 1994), p. 83.

49 Ibid., p. 83.

50　Lucas, "*Black Sabbath*," p. 51, sees "The Wurdulak" as prescient of the "venereal horror" subgenre that began its ascendance with David Cronenberg's *They Came from Within* in 1976.

51　Liandrat-Guignes, "La trois visages," p. 83.

52　"Picture Grosses," *Variety*, May 13, 1964.

53　"Picture Grosses," *Variety*, May 27, 1964.

54　"Picture Grosses," *Variety*, June 17, 1964.

55　*Philadelphia Inquirer*, May 27, 1964, p. 33.

56　*Philadelphia Inquirer*, June 3, 1964.

57　"More Drive-Ins as First Runs," *Variety*, April 27, 1960, p. 5.

58　"Film Pastures Reap Harvest," *Variety*, August 9, 1961, p. 5.

59　*Philadelphia Inquirer*, January 3, 1968, p. 16. For an explanation of the relationship between these small distributors and their use of local exchanges, see "Producers Releasing Org Outlets via AIP," *Variety*, March 15, 1967, p. 4.

60　"Production in Italy Hits Record 270 Films," *Variety*, August 21, 1963, p. 26; and "As Romans Now Do," p. 35.

61　"Key to Bankers: A New Law," *Variety*, May 12, 1965, p. 77.

62　"As Romans Now Do," p. 35.

63　"Spring, and B's Still Swarm," *Variety*, March 18, 1964, p. 70. See also "TV and O'seas Saving 'B' Films," *Variety*, February 9, 1966, p. 5.

64　"AIP to Make More and Buy Less from O'seas Prods, p. 5.

CHAPTER 7. Television Syndication and the Birth of the "Orphans": Horror Films in the Local TV Market

1　For a detailed account of the economic and labor-relations issues behind this phase of Hollywood's relationship with television, see Amy Schnapper, *The Distribution of Feature Films to Television* (Ph.D. diss., University of Wisconsin—Madison, 1975); and William Lafferty, "Feature Films on Prime-Time Television," in *Hollywood in the Age of Television*, ed. Tino Balio (Boston: Unwin and Hyman, 1990).

2　"Screen Gems Hits New Profit High," *Broadcasting*, November 11, 1963, p. 73.

3　An overview of this dilemma from the perspective of the television stations can be found in "Program Sources Drying Up?" *Broadcasting*, September 18, 1961, p. 19; and "Will First-Run Films Be Extinct?" *Broadcasting*, November 27, 1961, p. 27.

4　"Universal's 10-Yr Lease of 550 Pix to Screen Gems," *Variety*, June 12, 1957, p. 1, 86; and "Universal's Library Goes to Screen Gems," *MPH*, August 10, 1957, p. 15.

5　"SG Distribution Plans Revealed for 600 Pre-'48 Universal Films," *Broadcasting*, August 12, 1957, p. 60.

6　"SG Plans Frightening Results with New Horror Films Package," *Broadcasting*, October 21, 1957, p. 135.

7　Screen Gems trade ad, *Broadcasting*, October 21, 1957, p. 49.

8 Ibid., p. 51.

9 Ibid., p. 55.

10 Ibid., p. 57.

11 "Second 'Horror' Package Offered," *Broadcasting*, September 2, 1957, p. 79.

12 Screen Gems trade ad, *Broadcasting*, May 19, 1958, p. 25.

13 "Prices Soar for Post-48 Films," *Broadcasting*, July 22, 1963, p. 23.

14 "$100,000 Syndie Gross," *Variety*, January 1, 1964, p. 47.

15 "115,000 U.S. Syndie Gross," *Variety*, July 29, 1964, p. 25; and "Syndicators Confident of Future," *Broadcasting*, January 25, 1965, p. 68.

16 See "Will First-Run Films Be Extinct?" p. 27.

17 "Syndie Runs, Hits, & Errors," *Variety*, June 7, 1964, p. 31.

18 "Vaulties Buy Starts New Outfit," *Variety*, September 18, 1963, p. 17; and "TV Slated to Get 93 More Post-'54s," *Broadcasting*, September 16, 1963, p. 86.

19 "New Prod's Vaultie Values," *Variety*, April 19, 1961, p. 5; and "Only Hitchy Can Get Away with a Horror-Packed-with-Yocks Come-On," *Variety*, November 28, 1962, p. 3.

20 "American Int'l Budgets $20,000,000 for 24 Films; 9 Assured Hollywood," *Variety*, June 12, 1963, p. 4; and "Amer-Int'l Rents 1st 69 Pix to TV in $2 Mil-Plus Deal; All at Least 5 Yrs. Old in Keeping with Pledge," *Variety*, June 19, 1963, p. 13.

21 "Roger Corman in $627,000 Selloff of 16 AIP Pix," *Variety*, May 15, 1963, p. 3.

22 See McGee, *Faster and Furiouser*, p. 236.

23 "AA's 'Black Zoo' Grosses $260,000 in 60-House 13 Chain Gotham Spread," *Variety*, May 29, 1963, p. 13; and "Allied Artists Passes Dividend; Hopeful for Profitable New Films," *Variety*, May 29, 1963, p. 3.

24 "Allied Artists Sets 40 Feature Films for TV," *MPH*, October 4, 1961, p. 18.

25 Broadcast Information Bureau, *TV Film Source Book — Series, Serials, and Packages* (winter 1962–spring 1963), pp. FF-5–6.

26 "Allied Artists Nets $60,673 in Fiscal '63-'64; TV Sale Picks Up $1,218,425," *Variety*, October 21, 1964, p. 22.

27 "Post-50 Features to M & A Alexander," *Variety*, August 9, 1961, p. 23. See also Broadcast Information Bureau, *TV Film Source Book — Series, Serials, and Packages* (winter 1962–spring 1963), p. FF-2.

28 "AA Yens Big Pix; Selling Studio in Fiscal Tactic," *Variety*, September 12, 1962, p. 18.

29 "Old Pix (Good Ones) Never Die," *Variety*, June 5, 1963, p. 1; and "Savvy 'Mix Your Pix' Pattern," *Variety*, November 13, 1963, p. 31.

30 "UAA, NTA, Allied Cinematic and Hour Syndie Selloffs," *Variety*, August 15, 1962, p. 29.

31 See Allied Artists Television trade ad, "Pat," *Broadcasting*, May 13, 1963, p. 8; and "Sci-Fi and Horror Still Attracts 'Em," *Variety*, June 12, 1963, p. 31. See also "Film Sales," *Broadcasting*, August 13, 1962, p. 60; and

"More Stations Pact for Allied Artists Sci-Fi," *Variety*, September 5, 1962, p. 22.

32 "Post-'48's? 1000 of 'Em on TV," *Variety*, June 1, 1960, p. 29; and "Market's Brisk in Movie Imports for TV," *Broadcasting*, March 6, 1960, p. 78.

33 "'Monogram Clause' Cues Year of Low-Budget Features to TV," *Variety*, January 27, 1960, p. 24.

34 "Flamingo's Trim; Pete Yeager Exits," *Variety*, Juy 12, 1961, p. 31.

35 "Market's Brisk in Movie Imports for TV," p. 78.

36 "Flamingo Gets 25 Post-'53 Films for TV," *Broadcasting*, July 11, 1960, p. 24.

37 "Snubs Rub Dub Distributors," *Variety*, May 11, 1966, p. 39; and "Plenty of Dubbed Pix in TV Market; Breaking Through in Hinterlands," *Variety*, July 30, 1966, p. 35.

38 See "TV's 'Mass and Class' Features; Int'l Pix Get a Major Play," *Variety*, March 13, 1963, p. 33.

39 See "Walter Reade, Inc. with Sterling TV; 'Public' 1st Time," *Variety*, December 20, 1961, p. 1.

40 "TV Haven for Pix 'Orphans,'" *Variety*, November 25, 1964, p. 31.

41 "It's Not What but How You Slot 'Em; Study in Divergent Syndie Concept," *Variety*, November 25, 1964, p. 31.

42 "Pix Traffic across Atlantic; U.S. TV Famine No Secret O'seas," *Variety*, November 10, 1965, p. 39.

43 *Variety*, review, June 15, 1964.

44 *Variety*, review, January 17, 1968.

45 *Variety*, review, February 8, 1968.

46 "Can RCA Force Color Evolution?" *Broadcasting*, February 20, 1961, p. 97; and "Color Is Dealer's Gold at Rainbow's End," *Broadcasting*, October 30, 1961, p. 76.

47 "Syndication's Big Tint-Up," *Variety*, September 11, 1963, p. 31.

48 "2,860,000 Color Sets Now in Use," *Variety*, January 20, 1965, p. 30 (these figures according to NBC); and "Color Set Sales Doubled in '65," *Broadcasting*, March 7, 1966, p. 70. See also "Will Color Sales Pass 4 Million?" *Broadcasting*, January 3, 1966, p. 44.

49 See "Out of the Egg with a Bang," *Broadcasting*, January 3, 1966, p. 29; "Color Set Sales Up 88.4% in '66," *Variety*, October 26, 1966, p. 30; and "Color Sales Jump 88% in Eight Months," *Broadcasting*, October 31, 1966, p. 80.

50 "'67 Color TV Sales Put at 7,000,000," *Variety*, January 11, 1967, p. 29. The U.S. Census Bureau released much more conservative figures in November 1967, asserting that as of June 1967, 19.3 percent of households owned a color TV. See "Major Gains Continue in UHF, Color Set Counts," *Broadcasting*, November 13, 1967, p. 46.

51 "Syndication's Big Tint-Up," p. 31.

52 "Color Only Small Part of Total Film Backlog," *Variety*, January 3, 1966, p. 88.

53 "Color Tones Up Syndication Sales Picture," *Broadcasting*, March 21, 1966, p. 69.

54 "Stations Want Features in Color; Growing Trend Affects Distribs," *Broadcasting*, October 14, 1964, p. 34.

55 "Color Tones Up Syndication Sales Picture," pp. 73–74. For a discussion of AI-TV's cycle of made-for-television features from Dallas-based filmmaker Larry Buchanan, see McGee, *Faster and Furiouser*, pp. 236–41.

56 For a discussion of the role of the UHF/VHF dispute and its eventual effects on the economic structure of network television, see William Boddy, *Fifties Television: The Industry and Its Critics* (Urbana: University of Illinois Press, 1992), pp. 42–51.

57 "All-Channel Sets on Rise," *Broadcasting*, June 24, 1963, p. 97.

58 "Syndies' 'U Are My Sunshine,'" *Variety*, June 18, 1966, p. 33.

59 "New Penetration Heights for Tint, UHF, 2-Set Homes," *Variety*, November 17, 1965, p. 25; "Color in 13%, UHF in 33.8% of All U.S. Homes," *Broadcasting*, December 19, 1966, p. 4; and "Major Gains Continue in UHF, Color Set Counts," *Broadcasting*, November 13, 1967, p. 46.

60 "Dan Overmyer's Empire-Building Visions on UHF's Wide Open Range," *Variety*, March 24, 1965, p. 47.

61 "Syndies' 'U Are My Sunshine,'" p. 33.

62 "U's Newest Syndicator Prospect," *Broadcasting*, November 14, 1966, pp. 31–32.

63 "Impact of U's," *Broadcasting*, December 18, 1967, p. 5. See also "A U-Turn Creates Traffic for NTA, MGM-TV," *Broadcasting*, December 19, 1968, p. 64.

64 "Color Tones Up Syndication Sales Picture," p. 72.

65 See "AI-TV's Bundle of 'Spectacolor' Pix," *Variety*, March 11, 1964, p. 30.

66 "Embassy Tint Sprint," *Variety*, July 22, 1964, p. 52.

67 "Those Direct-to-TV Pix Imports," *Variety*, July 22, 1964, p. 52.

68 "See AI-TV's 'Sandals' Fiscal Hotfoot," *Variety*, September 9, 1964, p. 31.

69 "Sword & Sandal: Tough Sale," *Variety*, September 23, 1964, p. 67.

70 "Teenpix Wave Over-Done, Arkoff Tips (Doesn't Detail) Switch of Format," *Variety*, May 26, 1965, p. 4.

71 "Exhibitor Scores Films Rush to TV," *Broadcasting*, December 12, 1966, p. 63.

72 "'Film Biz a Self-Feeding Cannibal'; Nicholson-Arkoff First to Promise No TV Selloff Inside Five Years," *Variety*, March 27, 1963, p. 7; and "Sales to Television Prime Target for Exhibitors; AIP Sets 5 Year Clearance," *MPH*, April 3, 1963, p. 7.

73 "CBS Buying 30 Pix from 7 Arts at $525,000 Per," *Variety*, June 15, 1966, p. 27; and "Two For AI-TV," *Broadcasting*, September 12, 1966, p. 74.

74 Jeffrey Sconce, "'Trashing' the Academy: Taste, Excess, and an Emerging Politics of Cinematic Style," *Screen* 36, no. 4 (winter 1995): p. 390.

75 See "Desilu Sales Whopping $5,000,000 Syndie Gross; O'seas Markets Hot," *Variety*, May 29, 1963, p. 27; and "Desilu Sales Spurt in Slack Season," *Variety*, November 11, 1964, p. 35.

76 "Features-to-TV Biz Today's Big Lure; Desilu Latest to Fall in Line," *Variety*, August 26, 1964, p. 25.

77 Desilu trade ad, *Variety*, August 26, 1964, p. 35.

78 "TV's Increasing Appetite for Features (Either Post or Pre-'48)," *Variety*, July 15, 1964, p. 29.

79 See "Triangle Distributes 19 Mystery Films," *Broadcasting*, August 14, 1967, p. 64.

80 See "60 to 94 German Films on '63-'64 Program but B.O. Quality Dubious; Main Trend to Cheap Crime Yarns," *Variety*, July 20, 1964, p. 25.

81 For an excellent overview of the stylistic and commercial history of the *krimi* and its primary auteur, the prolific Alfred Vohrer, see Tim Lucas, "Dial 'W' for Wallace! The West German 'Krimis,'" *Video Watchdog* (November/December 1989). Reprinted in *The Video Watchdog Book* (Cincinnati: Video Watchdog, 1992), pp. 138–61. See also "German Film Outlook Hazy," *Variety*, September 20, 1962, p. 11; CCC-Film trade ad, *Variety*, May 2, 1962, p. 112; and "Edgar Wallace Big in Germany, Less So in U.K.," *Variety*, April 26, 1967, p. 132.

82 "Triangle Distributes 19 Mystery Films," p. 66.

83 "Thunderbird Films' First Feature Package," *Variety*, May 19, 1965, p. 58.

84 The data for this case study was compiled from the daily television listings in the *Philadelphia Inquirer* from 1962 to 1968. Because my focus is the circulation of feature packages, not individual titles, I have not cited individual broadcast dates for films.

85 "6 CATV's Backed for Philadelphia," *Broadcasting*, December 5, 1966, p. 46.

86 "Philly TV Heads Up Multi-Set Parade," *Variety*, November 22, 1967, p. 19.

87 "ARB Lists Color and UHF Sets," *Broadcasting*, December 26, 1966, p. 36.

88 A complete rundown on the ownership, management, and technical specifications of the stations in the Philadelphia market can be found in *Broadcasting Yearbook 1966* (New York: Broadcasting Publications, 1966) pp. 314–35.

89 KYW-TV did run Embassy's "Sons of Hercules" package in summer 1966.

90 For an explanation of this strategy, see "Dan Overmyer's Empire-Building Visions," p. 58.

91 "CBS O & O's Lease 200 Columbia Films," *Broadcasting*, December 5, 1960, p. 82.

92 "TV Features' Sound Economy," *Variety*, August 31, 1960, p. 25. Individual stations showcasing *The Late Show* were even provided with a catchy theme jingle, familiar to an entire generation of baby boomers, which was customized for the station's channel allocation.

93 "Warner Bros Trip Their Toes," *Broadcasting*, September 26, 1960, p. 58.

94 See Broadcast Information Bureau, *TV Feature Film Source Book—Feature Packages* (spring–summer 1966), p. 54-FF.

95 Ibid., pp. 62–63.

96 Tim Brooks and Earle Marsh, *The Complete Directory to Prime-Time Network and Cable TV Shows, 1946-Present* (New York: Ballantine, 1995), p. 1187.

97 See "FSD Cinematics in Sales Spurt," *Variety*, May 26, 1965, p. 34.

98   "UHF's Organize Outside of NAB," *Broadcasting*, May 29, 1967, p. 41.

99   "Indie Operators Put on a Happy Face Describing the Joys of UHF," *Variety*, March 30, 1966, p. 66.

100 See Brooks and Marsh, *The Complete Dictionary*, p. 1187.

101 "Sex and the Single Standard," *Variety*, October 27, 1965, p. 38.

102 "'Make Like Bond' Cues Big Pix Prowl," *Variety*, May 26, 1965, p. 43.

103 "TV Haven for Pix 'Orphans,'" *Variety*, November 25, 1964, p. 31.

104 Lester Bangs, "Incredibly Strange Creatures," reprinted in *Psychotic Reactions and Carburetor Dung* (New York: Vintage, 1988).

105 Sconce, "Trashing the Academy," p. 390.

106 "Warners Film Library Sold," *MPH*, March 10, 1956, p. 14.

107 "Warner Post-48 Films Sold," *Broadcasting*, September 12, 1960, p. 80.

108 See "20th-Fox Sells 88 Post-48's to 7-Arts," *Broadcasting*, April 3, 1961, p. 78; and "Seven Arts Acquires Rights to Fox Films," *Broadcasting*, February 19, 1962, p. 64.

109 "7 Arts in $21,500 U Buy; 10-Year Deal on 215 Post-'48s," *Variety*, July 17, 1963, p. 49; "Fancy Package," *Broadcasting*, July 1, 1963, p. 7; and "Seven Arts Buys 215 from U-I for TV," *MPH*, July 10, 1963, p. 1.

110 See "Warner-7 Arts TV Upsurge; Major Changes on Broad Front," *Variety*, November 15, 1967, p. 29.

111 "Seven Arts Net Up 500% in Six-Month Period," *Broadcasting*, February 14, 1966, p. 62; and "7 Arts Up Five Times Year Ago; Enough Film for 2d Big TV Deal?" *Variety*, February 16, 1966, p. 5.

112 For an account of the economic background to this takeover, see Robert Gustafson, "'What's Happening to Our Pix Biz?' From Warner Bros. to Warner Communications, Inc.," in *The American Film Industry*, rev. ed., ed. Tino Balio (Madison: University of Wisconsin Press, 1985), pp. 575–76.

113 "Seven Arts' $30,000,000 Stake in Pix; Already in TV, Eyeing B'way 'GWTW,'" *Variety*, September 14, 1960, p. 1.

114 See "Hammer to Increase Output for Columbia," *MPH*, June 4, 1960, p. 14; and "Hammer Stresses Films at 'Middle' Spending," *MPH*, June 18, 1960, p. 23.

115 "Shock Shop on Carreras Shoots a Sumptuous 'She,'" *Variety*, July 15, 1964, p. 20.

116 See "Carreras in Gotham; Talks More Hammer Pix for 20th Century Fox," *Variety*, September 24, 1967, p. 13; and "Hammer Establishing New Ties for Its Line of Fright Wig Epics," *Variety*, February 21, 1968, p. 24.

117 "Seven Arts Adopts Self-Sell," *Variety*, September 23, 1964, p. 3; "Lesson for Theatre Men: How to Scare Patrons," *MPH*, February 17, 1965, p. 27; and "'Shock Treatment' Provided in Horror Show Campaign," *MPH*, March 17, 1965, p. 26.

118 "Family Holdbacks: TV Gravy; 7 Arts, Levine Retain Rights," *Variety*, July 29, 1964, p. 3.

119 See "Possibility of CBS-TV Entering Late-Night Derby with Feature Films, Wearing 'Em Out for Syndication," *Variety*, April 19, 1967, p. 69; and

"80% of CBS-TV Affiliates Favor Late-Night Show," *Broadcasting*, July 24, 1967, p. 51.

120 Brooks and Marsh, *The Complete Directory*, p. 673.

121 Ibid., p. 149.

122 See "26 Titles in W7 Package for CBS," *Variety*, May 29, 1968, p. 27.

CHAPTER 8. Demon Children and the Birth of Adult Horror:
William Castle, Roman Polanski, and *Rosemary's Baby*

1 See "Paramount Completes Sale of Pre-'48 Features to EMKA," *Broadcasting*, March 3, 1958, p. 83.

2 "Bless-Our-Television-Clients Implicit in Par 1965 Figures," *Variety*, April 15, 1966, p. 3.

3 "Zugsmith Grabs Torch Dropped by Herb Siegel; Raps Par Statement," *Variety*, April 20, 1966, p. 3.

4 Ibid.

5 For a discussion of the huge impact that this simple ratio would have on the motion picture industry, see Gustafson, "'What's Happening to Our Pix Biz?'" p. 575.

6 "New Era of Film Security; Video Deals Cheer Wall St.," *Variety*, October 12, 1966, p. 30.

7 "Industrialists Ruttenberg, Bluhdorn Replace Par's Zukor, 93, Griffis, 79," *Variety*, March 30, 1966, p. 3; and "Siegel & Martin Scram Par; Bluhdorn Key in Company Win," *Variety*, April 20, 1966, p. 3.

8 Ibid., p. 28.

9 See "Paramount to Retain Own Name in Merger," *MPH*, July 13, 1966, p. 5; and "'What's with Our Picture Biz?'" *Variety*, October 26, 1966, p. 1.

10 "Bluhdorn: Shadow and Shape; Biz Eyes Par as 'Leisure Core,'" *Variety*, March 8, 1967, p. 23.

11 "European & Hollywood Expansion of 'New' Par; Goal 36 Features," *Paramount*, January 18, 1967, p. 4 and "New Par Deals in O'seas Sites; 'Toll' Up Again," *Variety*, February 1, 1967, p. 3.

12 "Par Toppers Seen Complete," *Variety*, May 17, 1967, p. 3.

13 "Gulf & Western to Shuffle Par's Music, Disc Cos. to Beef Up Their Operations," *Variety*, December 21, 1966, p. 43.

14 "With Stock, G & W Will Wholly Control Famous ($30-Mil), Desilu ($17-Mil)," *Variety*, February 15, 1967, p. 4.

15 See Paramount trade ad, *Broadcasting*, September 25, 1967. p. 27; "Par Exec Teams & 'Vibrancy,'" *Variety*, November 8, 1967, p. 22; and "Paramount Starts Film Syndication," *Broadcasting*, April 4, 1967, p. 114.

16 "Par's Alter Ego Exec Setup," *Variety*, November 16, 1966, p. 7.

17 See Columbia trade ad, "The Picture with the Punishment Poll," *MPH*, September 15, 1961, pp. 38–39.

18 "Hammer Offering Financing for 'Gimmick' Film Ideas," *MPH*, Decem-

ber 20, 1961, p. 18; and "Hammer Films Spending $4,200,000 on 6 Films," *Variety*, January 24, 1962, p. 12.

19   "Carreras and Castle to Produce Jointly," *MPH*, September 13, 1961, p. 15; and "Hammer Eyes New Production Deals," *Variety*, December 13, 1961, p. 14.

20   "William Castle and Staff Plight Three-Year Troth with U for Pix, Video," *Variety*, August 5, 1964, p. 3.

21   "Bill Castle's Contract: 4-in-2 Years for Par," *Variety*, October 12, 1966, p. 22.

22   "Bill Castle's Low-Budgeter Ballyhoo Takes on $5-Mil Sophisticated Look," *Variety*, September 6, 1967, p. 15.

23   Ibid.

24   Review of *Rosemary's Baby*, *Variety*, May 29, 1968.

25   Paul, *Laughing/Screaming*, p. 282.

26   Ibid., p. 277.

27   MGM ad mat for *Village of the Damned*, 1961.

28   "Rentals and Potential," *MPH*, January 10, 1962, p. 58.

29   The film also made a strong impression on a young teenage musician from London who, under the stage name Ozzy Osbourne, would name a soon-to-be-famous rock band after Bava's masterpiece. See Maurizio Colombo and Antonio Tentori, *Lo schermo insanguinato: Il cinema italiano del terrore 1957–1989* (Rome: Marion Solfanelli, 1990), p. 63.

30   See Royal Films trade ad, *Variety*, June 20, 1965, p. 17.

31   Newspaper ad mat, *Philadelphia Inquirer*, November 3, 1965, p. 30.

32   Virginia Wright Wexman, *Roman Polanski* (Boston: Twayne Publishers, 1985), p. 33.

33   "Polanski: Metro's Teeth in My Neck, and Please Take Me Off 'Vampire,'" *Variety*, November 15, 1967, p. 7.

34   "U.S. Showman vs. 'Artist'; Roman Polanski in Hate 'n' Love," *Variety*, February 7, 1968, p. 3.

35   "Polanski Informs Bauer that 'Vampire' Slashing Much Distresses Him," *Variety*, July 5, 1967, p. 7.

36   "U.S. Showman vs. 'Artist,'" p. 18.

37   "Polanski, Gutowski Pair Go to Paramount," *Variety*, March 15, 1967, p. 4; and "Gutowski-Polanski Prep 4-Pic Slate," *Variety*, April 19, 1967, p. 67.

38   "U.S. Showman vs. 'Artist,'" p. 18.

39   "Bill Castle's Low-Budgeter Ballyhoo," p. 15.

40   Ibid.

41   "Most Promising New Faces of 1966," *MPH*, February 2, 1966, p. 6.

42   "Bill Castle's Low-Budgeter Ballyhoo," p. 15.

43   See Paramount trade ad, *Variety*, June 12, 1968, p. 23.

44   "A Teaser Prayer for 'Rosemary' Is Creating Palaver," *Variety*, July 3, 1968, p. 7.

45   See Paramount trade ad, "Praise for *Rosemary's Baby*," *Variety*, June 19, 1968, p. 9; and newspaper ad, *Philadelphia Inquirer*, June 28, 1968, p. 23.

46 Ivan Butler, in *The Cinema of Roman Polanski* (New York: A. S. Barnes and Co., 1970), notes many of these parallels.

47 Jeff Smith, *The Sounds of Commerce: Marketing Popular Film Music* (New York: Columbia University Press, 1998).

48 This plot device was used in the novel, although Levin had provided the Woodhouses with an album of Ella Fitzgerald singing Cole Porter for their amorous evening. See Ira Levin, *Rosemary's Baby* (New York: Random House, 1967), p. 81.

49 Ibid., p. 43.

50 "Pix Envy Book Pubs 'Breaks'; Literati Paid Ads No Factor," *Variety*, May 17, 1967, p. 5.

51 Levin, *Rosemary's Baby*, p. 89.

52 Butler, *Cinema of Roman Poplanski*, pp. 172–73.

53 For an account of the controversy that *Rosemary's Baby* created on this account, see *Films 1968: A Comprehensive Review of the Year in Motion Pictures* (New York: National Catholic Office of Motion Pictures, 1969), p. 138; "Catholic Dogma vs. Screen; 'Rosemary' Poses Fear of Mockery," *Variety*, June 19, 1968, p. 3; and "'Sacrilege' or 'Blasphemy' Make Boggy Grounds; 'Rosemary's Baby' Recalls 'Miracle' Reversal," *Variety*, June 19, 1965, p. 24.

54 "Picture Grosses," *Variety*, June 26, 1968, p. 9.

55 "Picture Grosses," *Variety*, June 26, 1968–October 9, 1968.

56 *Philadelphia Inquirer*, July 26, 1968.

57 *Philadelphia Inquirer*, July 12, 1968.

58 *Philadelphia Inquirer*, November 13, 1968 and November 20, 1968.

59 See "Par Near B.O. Turnaround," *Variety*, May 29, 1968, p. 7.

60 "Big Rental Films of 1968," *Variety*, January 8, 1969, p. 15.

61 See Paramount trade ad, "What's Bigger Box Office? One Smash Hit Like THE ODD COUPLE? Or One Smash Hit like ROSEMARY'S BABY?" *Variety*, January 8, 1969, pp. 11–13.

62 See "All-Time Box-Office Champs," *Variety*, January 7, 1970, p. 25.

CHAPTER 9. Family Monsters and Urban Matinees:
Continental Distributing and *Night of the Living Dead*

1 See Jim Hoberman and Jonathan Rosenbaum, *Midnight Movies* (New York: Harper and Row, 1983), p. 110; Robin Wood, "George Romero: Apocalypse Now," in *Hollywood from Vietnam to Reagan* (New York: Columbia University Press, 1986), p. 115; Andrew Tudor, *Monsters and Mad Scientists: A Cultural History of the Horror Movie* (Oxford: Basil Blackwell, 1989); and David J. Skal, *The Monster Show: A Cultural History of Horror* (New York: Penguin Books, 1993), pp. 307–9.

2 Roger Ebert, "Just Another Horror Movie—Or Is It?" *Chicago Sun-Times*, January 5, 1969, p. C1.

3 Walter Reade Jr., "Recipe for Getting and Maintaining the Film Audience," *MPH*, April 3, 1963, p. 9.

4   See Martin Quigley Jr., "Sick Pictures = Sick Industry," *MPH*, November 24, 1960, p. 3. Reade's response is in "Sick Pictures Editorial Stirs Tide of Reaction across the Industry," *MPH*, October 8, 1960, p. 13.

5   See "Continental Plans to Refile Damage Action on 'Room,'" *MPH*, May 20, 1961, p. 12.

6   "Legion of Decency Condemns 'Expresso,'" *MPH*, May 7, 1960, p. 13.

7   "Legion Condemns 'Saturday,'" *MPH*, May 13, 1961, p. 15; and "Britain's 'Saturday Night' Banned in Kansas City," *MPH*, July 1, 1961, p. 16.

8   See "$273,000 Budget on Reade-Sterling 'Black Like Me,'" *Variety*, July 17, 1963, p. 3.

9   "Race to Film Race Issues," *Variety*, July 17, 1963, p. 20.

10   *Philadelphia Inquirer*, June 3, 1964, p. 31, and June 10, 1964, p. 30.

11   "One Third of Film Public: Negro," *Variety*, November 29, 1967, p. 3.

12   *Philadelphia Inquirer*, October 11, 1965, January 21, 1967, and March 25, 1967.

13   *Philadelphia Inquirer*, September 28, 1965.

14   *Philadelphia Inquirer*, June 25, 1966.

15   "Pathé-America's 1962 Financing of 12-to-18 Indie Features," *Variety*, December 27, 1961, p. 3.

16   "Let 'Em Ripps: Dixie & Pixie; Fink, Trash, Guts as Typical Sell," *Variety*, August 4, 1965, p. 5.

17   "Puzzle Re Clarke's 'Cool World,'" *Variety*, November 11, 1964, p. 23 (emphasis in original).

18   "Dixie Shy of 'Black Like Me,'" *Variety*, February 17, 1965, p. 7.

19   See "Reade, Sterling TV in Merger," *Broadcasting*, December 25, 1961, p. 47.

20   "Nice Notices Not Negotiable; Reade's Policy Now Hard-Nosed," *Variety*, September 15, 1965, p. 7.

21   Ibid.

22   "Bettered Outlook at Continental Co.," *Variety*, November 8, 1965, pp. 5, 21.

23   See Continental trade ad, *Variety*, January 8, 1966, p. 87; and "Pasolini's 'St. Matthew' for Reade; New Range of Product Ups Quarter," *Variety*, November 24, 1965, p. 7.

24   "Reade-Sterling Turns Around from 491G Loss in '64 to 505G Profit," *Variety*, May 4, 1966, p. 12; and "Walter Reade/Sterling Shows 1965 Fiscal Profit," *Broadcasting*, April 20, 1966, pp. 78–79.

25   "Reade Merges Rutland Corp.; See a Combined Gross of $23,000,000," *Variety*, August 14, 1968, p. 19.

26   U.S. Department of Commerce, Business and Defense Services Administration, *U.S. Industrial Outlook 1968* (Washington, D.C.: U.S. Government Printing Office, 1967), pp. 85–86.

27   See "Reade in L.A.; Non-Theater Pix Up; Ulysses at $3-Mil; TV Insures 'War & Peace,'" *Variety*, November 20, 1968, p. 26.

28   "Showmanship Links U.S.–U.S.S.R.; Soviet and Reade on 'War & Peace,'" *Variety*, April 17, 1968, p. 5.

29 "Reade's 'W & P' Sell: Tix Going by Installments," *Variety*, July 5, 1968, p. 7; and "Saxton Strong on Reade Regardless of Rutland Deal," *Variety*, October 30, 1968.

30 "Woes of Special Matinees; Kids Dates Hit, Indie in Blast," *Variety*, April 13, 1966, p. 24.

31 Ibid.

32 "Source of U.S. Kidpix: Mexico," *Variety*, December 16, 1964, p. 7.

33 "Kiddie Matinee Economics; Timeless Pics, with Pitfalls," *Variety*, October 25, 1967, p. 13.

34 "Source of U.S. Kidpix," p. 24.

35 "Kiddie Matinee Economics," p. 13.

36 Ibid.

37 In *The Monster Show* Skal devotes an entire chapter to this phenomenon, which he calls "The Graveyard Bash."

38 Engagement periods for the films given here and on the following pages were taken from issues of the *Philadelphia Inquirer* on the following dates: May 21, 1966, June 25, 1966, May 28, 1966, July 30, 1966, October 13, 1967, June 11, 1966, February 4, 1967, June 18, 1966, July 23, 1966, March 25, 1967, March 18, 1967, March 25, 1967, September 2, 1967, and September 16, 1967.

39 "Theatres Warned to Retain Matinee Rights for Kidpix," *Variety*, April 27, 1966, p. 7; and "Woes of Special Matinees," p. 13.

40 "After Gamy 'Ulysses,' It's Inter-Racial 'Dutchman' for Reade Distribution," *Variety*, February 1, 1967, p. 24.

41 See Continental trade ad, *Variety*, October 9, 1968, p. 18.

42 See *Philadelphia Inquirer*, October 23, 1968, p. 27.

43 For a detailed elaboration of *Night of the Living Dead*'s deployment of motifs from fifties horror and science fiction films, see Kevin Heffernan, "Inner-City Exhibition and the Genre Film: Distributing *Night of the Living Dead*," *Cinema Journal* 41, no. 3 (spring 2002): pp. 59–77.

44 *Philadelphia Inquirer*, November 1, 1968.

45 "'Blood Feast' Arrest; Hold House Manager on 'Delinquency' Angle," *Variety*, April 1, 1964.

46 Ebert, "Just Another Horror Movie," p. C1.

47 See "Sans Allies, Reade Complies," *Variety*, December 18, 1968, p. 3.

Conclusion: The Horror Film in the New Hollywood

1 Doherty, *Teenagers and Teenpics*, p. 84.

2 David James, *Allegories of Cinema: American Film in the Sixties* (Princeton: Princeton University Press, 1989), p. 144.

3 Juan Antonio Suarez, *Bike Boys, Drag Queens, and Superstars: Avant-Garde, Mass Culture, and Gay Identities in the 1960s Underground Cinema* (Bloomington: Indiana University Press, 1996).

4 Hawkins, *Cutting Edge*, pp. 141–203.

5 John Waters, *Shock Valve* (New York: Thunder's Mouth Press, 1997) p. 23.

6 James, *Allegories of Cinema*, p. 341.
7 Kristin Thompson and David Bordwell provide a brief discussion of this trend in their treatment of "connoisseurs of 'weird movies.'" See *Film History: An Introduction* (New York: McGraw-Hill, 1994), pp. 404–5.
8 V. Vale and Andrea Juno, eds., *Re/Search #10: Incredibly Strange Films* (San Franscisco: Re/Search Publications, 1986). There is even a cult film equivalent to reference perennial Leonard Maltin's *Movie and Video Guide*, Michael Weldon's *Psychotronic Encyclopedia of Film* (New York: Ballantine Books, 1983). Weldon updated this work in 1997 with more references and shorter entries as *The Psychotronic Video Guide* (New York: Vintage, 1996).
9 Sconce, "'Trashing' the Academy," pp. 374–75.
10 Mikhail Bakhtin, *Rabelais and His World*, trans. Helene Iswolsky (Bloomington: Indiana University Press, 1984), p. 15.

BIBLIOGRAPHY

Archives and Private Collections

G. William Jones Film and Video Collection. Dallas, Texas.
Hammer Films Special Collection, British Film Institute. London, England.
Shirley Clarke Papers, Wisconsin State Historical Society. Madison, Wisconsin.
Terence Fisher Special Collection, British Film Institute. London, England.
University of Delaware Microforms Collection. Newark, Delaware.
Wisconsin Center for Film and Theater Research. Madison, Wisconsin.

Published Works

Aguirre, Manuel. *The Closed Space: Horror Literature and Western Symbolism.* Manchester: Manchester University Press, 1980.
Arkoff, Sam, with Richard Trubo. *Flying through Hollywood by the Seat of My Pants: From the Man Who Brought You "I Was a Teenage Werewolf" and "Muscle Beach Party."* New York: Birth Lane Press, 1992.
Armstrong, Michael. "Some Like It Chilled." *Films and Filming* 17 (February 1971): 32–37; (April 1971): 37–42; (May 1971): 77–82.
Baker, H. L. "Children of the Night: The History of Evil Children in Film." *Bizarre* 4 (1975): 54–65.
Bakhtin, Mikhail. *Rabelais and His World.* Trans. Helene Iswolsky. Bloomington: Indiana University Press, 1984.

Balio, Tino, ed. *The American Film Industry*, rev. ed. Madison: University of Wisconsin Press, 1985.

——, ed. *Hollywood in the Age of Television*. Boston: Unwin Hyman, 1990.

Bangs, Lester. *Psychotic Reactions and Carburetor Dung*. New York: Vintage, 1988.

Barker, Martin, ed. *The Video Nasties: Freedom and Censorship in the Media*. London: Pluto Press, 1984.

Barth, Jack. "Fanzines." *Film Comment* 21, no. 2 (April 1983): 24–30.

Baumgarten, Paul A., Robert H. Montgomery, and Paul Sawyer. *Motion Picture Industry: Business and Legal Problems*. New York: Practicing Law Institute, 1972.

Bazin, André. "L'ogre en proie à l'enfance." *Avant-Scène du Cinéma* 282/283 (February 15-March 1, 1982): 87–88.

Belton, John. *Widescreen Cinema*. Cambridge: Harvard University Press, 1992.

Benshoff, Harry. *Monsters in the Closet: Homosexuality and the Horror Film*. Manchester: Manchester University Press, 1997.

Berard, Yves. "Les morts-vivants." *Avant-Scène du Cinéma* 187 (May 1, 1977): 23–38.

Berenstein, Rhona J. *Attack of the Leading Ladies: Gender, Sexuality, and Spectatorship in Classic Horror Cinema*. New York: Columbia University Press, 1996.

Bernstein, Matthew, *Walter Wanger, Hollywood Independent*. Berkeley: University of California Press, 1994.

Beylie, Claude, Jacques Goimard, and Michel Capdenac. "Fantastic Story." *Écran* 17 (July–August 1973): 2–22.

Birkhead, Edith. *The Tale of Terror: A Study of the Gothic Romance*. New York: Russell and Russell, 1963.

Biskind, Peter. *Seeing Is Believing: How Hollywood Taught Us to Stop Worrying and Love the Fifties*. New York: Pantheon Books, 1983.

Bleum, A. William, and Jason Squire, eds. *The Movie Business: American Film Industry Practice*. New York: Hastings House Publishers, 1972.

Boddy, William. *Fifties Television: The Industry and Its Critics*. Urbana: University of Illinois Press, 1992.

Bordwell, David. *Narration in the Fiction Film*. Madison: University of Wisconsin Press, 1986.

Bordwell, David, Janet Staiger, and Kristin Thompson. *The Classical Hollywood Cinema: Film Style and Mode of Production to 1960*. New York: Columbia University Press, 1985.

Braudy, Leo. "Genre and the Resurrection of the Past." In *Shadows of the Magic Lamp: Fantasy and Science Fiction in Film*, ed. George Slusser and Eric S. Rabkin. Carbondale: University of Southern Illinois Press, 1985.

Broadcast Information Bureau. *TV Film Source Book: Series, Serials, and Packages, 1962–1967*.

Broadcasting Yearbook 1966. New York: Broadcasting Publications, 1966.

Brooks, Tim, and Earle Marsh, *The Complete Directory to Prime-Time Network and Cable TV Shows, 1946—Present*. New York: Ballantine Books, 1995.

Brophy, Phillip. "Horrality: The Textuality of Contemporary Horror Films." *Screen* 27, no. 1 (1986): 2–13.

Bruschini, Antonio, and Antonio Tentori. *Operazione paura: I registi del gotico italiano*. Bologna: Editrice Puntozero, 1997.

Bryce, Allan, ed. *Amicus: The Studio That Dripped Blood*. Liskeard, Eng.: Stray Cat Publishing, 2000.

Bunkersmith, P. "Horror/épouvante: La decadence d'un genre." *Amis du Film et la Télévision* 294 (November 1980): 3–7.

Bussing, Sabine. *Aliens in the Home: The Child in Horror Fiction*. New York: Greenwood Press, 1987.

Butler, Ivan. *The Cinema of Roman Polanski*. New York: A. S. Barnes and Co., 1970.

———. *Horror in the Cinema*. New York: Warner Books, 1970.

Canby, Vincent. "When Movies Take Pride in Being Second Rate." *New York Times* 130 (June 7, 1981): 2:19.

Carroll, Noël. "King Kong: Ape and Essence." In *Planks of Reason: Essays on the Horror Film*, ed. Barry Keith Grant. Metuchen, N.J.: Scarecrow Press, 1984.

———. *The Philosophy of Horror; or, Paradoxes of the Heart*. New York: Routledge, 1989.

Cassady, Ralph Sr. "Impact of the Paramount Decision on Motion Picture Distribution and Price Making." *Southern California Law Review* 31 (1958): 150–80.

Cassady, Ralph Sr., and Ralph Cassady III. "Damage Measurement in Motion Picture Industry Trade and Antitrust Actions." *Southern California Law Review* 37 (1964): 389–399.

Castle, William. *Step Right Up! I'm Gonna Scare the Pants Off America!* New York: Pharos Books, 1992.

Chambers, D. "Joan Crawford and Michael Gough: The Herman Cohen Superstars." *Midnight Marquee* 29 (October 1980): 26–29.

Chatman, Seymour. *Story and Discourse: Narrative Structure in Fiction and Film*. Ithaca: Cornell University Press, 1978.

Cieutat, M. "Les fantômes de l'Amerique: Typologie d'un sous genre." *Positif* 362 (April 1991): 36–38.

Clarens, Carlos. *An Illustrated History of the Horror Film*. New York: Praeger, 1968.

Clover, Carol. *Men, Women, and Chain Saws: Gender in the Modern Horror Film*. Princeton: Princeton University Press, 1992.

Coates, Paul. *The Gorgon's Gaze: German Cinema, Expressionism, and the Image of Horror*. Cambridge: Cambridge University Press, 1991.

Cocchi, J. "The Second Feature: A History of B Movies—Horror, Science Fiction, and Fantasy." *Classic Film/Video Images* 137 (November 1986): 27–30.

Colombo, Maurizio, and Antonio Tentori. *Lo schermo insanguinato: Il cinema italiano del terrore, 1957–1989*. Rome: Marino Solfanelli, 1990.

Conant, Michael. *Antitrust in the Motion Picture Industry: Economic and Legal Analysis*. Berkeley: University of California Press, 1960.

Corman, Roger, and Jim Jerome. *How I Made a Hundred Movies in Hollywood and Never Lost a Dime.* New York: Da Capo Press, 1998.

Coulteray, George. *Le sadisme au cinéma.* Paris: Le Terrain Vague, 1964.

Cozzi, Luigi. *Mario Bava: I mille volti della paura.* Rome: Mondo Ignoto, 2001.

Crandall, Robert W. "Postwar Performance of the Motion Picture Industry." *The Antitrust Bulletin* 20 (spring 1975): 48–88.

Creed, Barbara. "Horror and the Monstrous-Feminine: An Imaginary Abjection." *Screen* 27, no. 1 (1986): 44–70.

Croydon, John. "A Reminiscence: Ghouls, Stranglers, Surgeons." *Classic Film/ Video Images* 135 (September 1986): 53–66.

Dadoun, Roger. "Fetishism in the Horror Film." *Enclitic* 1, no. 2 (1979): 39–63.

Daniels, Les. *Living in Fear: A History of Horror in the Mass Media.* New York: Scribner, 1975.

Delson, Donn. *The Dictionary of Marketing and Related Terms in the Motion Picture Industry.* Thousand Oaks, Calif.: Bradson Press, 1979.

Derry, Charles. *Dark Dreams: A Psychological History of the Modern Horror Film.* New York: A. S. Barnes and Co., 1977.

Dettman, B. "Children and Chills!" *FilmFax* 31 (February/March 1992): 34–37.

Dickstein, Morris. "The Aesthetics of Fright." *American Film* 5 (September 1980): 32–37, 56–59.

Dillard, R. H. W. "Drawing the Circle: A Devolution of Values in Three Horror Films." *Film Journal* 2, no. 2 (1973): 6–35.

———. "Even a Man Who Is Pure in Heart: Poetry and Danger in the Horror Film." In *Man and the Movies,* ed. W. R. Robinson. Baltimore: Penguin, 1969.

Dixon, Wheeler. *The Charm of Evil: The Life and Films of Terence Fisher.* Metuchen, N.J.: Scarecrow Press, 1991.

———. "The Child as Demon in Films since 1961." *Films in Review* 37 (February 1986): 78–83.

Doherty, Thomas. *Teenagers and Teenpics: The Juvenilization of American Movies in the 1950s.* Philadelphia: Temple University Press, 2002.

Ebert, Roger. "Just Another Horror Movie — Or Is It?" *Chicago Sun-Times.* January 5, 1969, p. C1.

Edgerton, Gary. *American Film Exhibition and an Analysis of the Motion Picture Industry's Market Structure, 1963–1980.* New York: Garland, 1983.

Eisner, Lotte. *The Haunted Screen: Expressionism in the German Cinema and the Influence of Max Reinhardt.* Berkeley: University of California Press, 1976.

Evans, Walter. "Monster Movies and Rites of Initiation." *Journal of Popular Film* 4 (1975): 124–42.

———. "Monster Movies: A Sexual Theory." *Journal of Popular Film* 2 (fall 1973): 353–64.

Eyles, Allen. *ABC: The First Name in Entertainment.* London: BFI Publishing, 1993.

Fischer, Lucy, and Marcia Landy. "'The Eyes of Laura Mars': A Binocular Critique." *Screen* 23, nos. 3–4 (September–October 1979): 4–19.

Flynn, Charles, and Todd McCarthy. "The Economic Imperative: Why Was the

B Movie Necessary?" In *Kings of the Bs: Working within the Hollywood System*. New York: E. P. Dutton, 1975.

Fowler, Douglas. "*Alien, The Thing,* and the Principles of Terror." *Studies in Popular Culture* 4 (1981): 16–23.

Fox, Julian. "The Golden Age of Terror." *Films and Filming* 22 (June 1976): 16–23; (July 1976): 18–24; (August 1976): 20–24; (September 1976): 20–25; (October 1976): 18–25.

Friedman, Dave. *A Youth in Babylon: Confessions of a Trash Film King.* New York: Prometheus Books, 1992.

Fuller, R. "First Love: A Personal Comment on Horror Movies." *Film Journal* 2, no. 2 (1973): 66–68.

Gaudreault, André. *Du littéraire au filmique: Système du récit.* Paris: Méridiens Klincksieck, 1988.

Gomery, Douglas. *The Hollywood Studio System.* New York: St. Martin's Press, 1986.

———. *Shared Pleasures: A History of Movie Presentation in the United States.* Madison: University of Wisconsin Press, 1992.

Gordon, Mel. *The Grand Guignol: Theatre of Fear and Terror.* New York: Amok Press, 1988.

Grant, Barry Keith, ed. *Planks of Reason: Essays on the Horror Film.* Metuchen, N.J.: Scarecrow Press, 1984.

Greenberg, Harvey R. *The Movies on Your Mind.* New York: E. P. Dutton/Saturday Review Press, 1975.

Grixti, Joseph. *The Terrors of Uncertainty: The Cultural Contexts of Horror Fiction.* London: Routledge, 1989.

Guback, Thomas H. *The International Film Industry.* Bloomington: Indiana University Press, 1969.

Gunning, Tom. "The Cinema of Attractions: Early Film, Its Spectator, and the Avant-Garde." *Wide Angle* 8, nos. 3–4 (1986): 63–70.

———. *D. W. Griffith and the Origins of American Narrative Film: The Early Years at Biograph.* Urbana: University of Illinois Press, 1991.

———. "Now You See It, Now You Don't: The Temporality of the Cinema of Attractions." *Velvet Light Trap* 32 (fall 1993): 3–12.

Gustafson, Robert. "'What's Happening to Our Pix Bix?': From Warner Bros. to Warner Communications, Inc." In *The American Film Industry,* rev. ed., ed. Tino Balio. Madison: University of Wisconsin Press, 1985.

Hardy, Phil, ed. *The Aurum Film Encyclopedia: Horror,* rev. ed. London: Aurum Press, 1993.

"Have Horror Films Gone Too Far?" *New York Times* (June 20, 1982): 2:1, 21.

Hawkins, Joan, *Cutting Edge: Art-Horror and the Horrific Avant-Garde.* Minneapolis: University of Minnesota Press, 2000.

Hayes, R. M., *3-D Movies: A History and Filmography of Stereoscopic Cinema.* Jefferson, N.C.: McFarland and Co., 1989.

Heffernan, Kevin. "The Hypnosis Horror Films of the 1950s: Genre Texts and Industrial Context." *Journal of Film and Video* 54, nos. 2–3 (summer/fall 2002).

————. "Inner-City Exhibition and the Genre Film: Distributing *Night of the Living Dead.*" *Cinema Journal* 41, no. 3 (spring 2002): 59–77.

————. "Michael Powell's *Peeping Tom*: A Film Maudit Reconsidered" (forthcoming).

Hincha, Richard. "Twentieth Century-Fox's CinemaScope: An Industrial, Organizational Analysis of Its Development, Marketing, and Adoption." Ph.D. diss., University of Wisconsin–Madison, 1989.

Hoberman, Jim, and Jonathan Rosenbaum. *Midnight Movies*. New York: Harper and Row, 1983.

Holden, S. "Critic's Notebook: Cheap Thrills and Fantasy From the Drive-In Era." *New York Times* 140 (October 26, 1990): C1.

Howarth, Troy. *The Haunted World of Mario Bava*. London: FAB Press, 2002.

Hurst, Walter E., and William Storm Hale. *Motion Picture Distribution: Business and/or Racket?!* Hollywood, Calif.: Seven Arts Press, 1975.

Huss, Roy, and T.J. Ross, eds. *Focus on the Horror Film*. Englewood Cliffs, N.J.: Prentice-Hall, 1972.

Hutchings, Peter. *Hammer and Beyond: The British Horror Film*. Manchester: Manchester University Press, 1993.

Hutchinson, Tom. *Horror and Fantasy in the Cinema*. London: Studio Vista, 1974.

International Motion Picture Almanac. New York: Quigley Publications, 1953–1968.

James, David. *Allegories of Cinema: American Film in the Sixties*. Princeton: Princeton University Press, 1989.

James, Gilbert. *A Cycle of Outrage: America's Reaction to the Juvenile Delinquent in the 1950s*. New York: Oxford University Press, 1986.

Jancovich, Mark. *Rational Fears: American Horror in the 1950s*. Manchester: Manchester University Press, 1996.

King, Stephen. *Danse Macabre*. New York: Viking, 1983.

Knutsch, Jim. "From the 'A's' to the 'B's' to the 'See 3-D's': Hollywood Hype Redefines the Art of Advertising." *FilmFax* (March/April 1987): 10–12.

Lafferty, William. "Feature Films on Prime-Time Television." In *Hollywood in the Age of Television*, ed. Tino Balio. Boston: Unwin and Hyman, 1990.

Lamson, Robert D. "*Motion Picture Exhibition: An Economic Analysis of Quality, Output, and Productivity*." Ph.D. diss., University of Washington, 1968.

Laurence, G. "TV Trailers Help Market Shock Films." *Boxoffice* 116 (July 14, 1980): 1–2.

Lavery, D. "The Horror Film and the Horror of Film." *Film Criticism* 7, no. 1 (1982): 47–55.

Lears, Jackson. *Fables of Abundance: A Cultural History of Advertising in America*. New York: Basic Books, 1995.

Lenne, Gérard. *Cela s'appelle l'horror: Le cinéma fantastique anglais, 1955–1976*. Paris: Éditions Universitaires, 1990.

————. "La proie et le monstre." *Écran* 28 (August–September 1974): 65–69.

————. "Le cauchemar est un autre forme de rêve." *Revue du Cinéma* 37 (April 1988): 71–74.

———. *Le cinéma fantastique et ses mythologies, 1895–1970.* Paris: Éditions Universitaires, 1988.

Leutrat, Jean-Louis, ed. *Mario Bava.* Liège: Éditions du Céfal, 1994.

Levin, Ira. *Rosemary's Baby.* New York: Random House, 1967.

Litman, Barry R. "The Economics of the Television Market for Theatrical Movies." *Journal of Communication* (autumn 1979): 20–33.

Lowrie, Edward. "Genre and Enunciation: The Case of Horror." *Journal of Film and Video* 36, no. 2 (spring 1984): 13–20.

Lucas, Tim. "*Black Sabbath*: The Unmaking of Mario Bava's *Three Faces of Fear.*" *Video Watchdog* (May/June 1991): 32–59.

———. "Dial 'W' For Wallace! The West German 'Krimis.'" *Video Watchdog* (November/December 1989): pp. 138–161.

———. "William Castle on Laserdisc." *Video Watchdog* (September/October 1995): 58–66.

Lucas, Tim, ed. *The Video Watchdog Book.* Cincinnati: Video Watchdog, 1992.

Martin, Leonard. *Movie and Video Guide.* New York: Signet, 2001.

Marchon, Rolland. *Advertising the American Dream: Making Way for Modernity, 1920–1940.* Berkeley: University of California Press, 1985.

Martinet, Pascal. *Mario Bava.* Paris: Edilig, 1984.

Maxford, Howard. *Hammer, House of Horror: Behind the Screams.* Woodstock, N.Y.: Overlook Press, 1996.

McCarthy, Todd, and Charles Flynn, eds. *Kings of the Bs: Working within the Hollywood System.* New York: E. P. Dutton, 1975.

McConnell, Frank D. *The Spoken Seen: Film and the Romantic Imagination.* Baltimore: Johns Hopkins University Press, 1975.

McGee, Mark Thomas. *Faster and Furiouser: The Revised and Fattened Fable of American International Pictures.* Jefferson, N.C.: McFarland and Co., 1996.

Medved, Harry, and Michael Medved. *The Golden Turkey Awards: The Worst Achievements in Hollywood History.* New York: St. Martin's Press, 1981.

Meikle, Denis. *A History of Horrors: The Rise and Fall of the House of Hammer.* Lanham, Md.: Scarecrow Press, 1996.

Morgan, Hal, and Dan Symmes. *Amazing 3-D.* Boston: Little, Brown, 1982.

National Catholic Office of Motion Pictures. *Films 1968: A Comprehensive Review of the Year in Motion Pictures.* New York: National Catholic Office of Motion Pictures, 1969.

Neale, Stephen. *Genre.* London: British Film Institute, 1980.

———. "*Halloween*: Suspense, Aggression, and the Look." *Frame-Work* 14 (spring 1981): 25–29.

Packard, Vance. *The Hidden Persuaders.* New York: David McKay and Co., 1957.

Palmerini, Luca, and Gaetano Mistretta. *Spaghetti Nightmares: Il cinema italiano della paura é del fantastico visto attraverso gli occhi dei suoi protagonisti.* Rome: M and P Edizioni, 1994.

Paul, William. *Laughing/Screaming: Modern Hollywood Horror and Comedy.* New York: Viking, 1994.

Pezzota, Alberto. *Mario Bava.* Milan: Editrice Il Castoro, 1995.

Pignone, R. "A Brief History of 3-D Horror Films." *Cinemacabre* 4 (1981): 24–29.

Pirie, David. *A Heritage of Horror: The English Gothic Cinema, 1946–1972.* New York: Avon, 1974.

Piselli, Stefano, and Riccardo Morrocchi, eds. *Horror all' italiana, 1957–1979.* Florence: Glittering Images, 1996.

Prawer, S. S. *Caligari's Children: The Film as Tale of Terror.* Oxford: Oxford University Press, 1980.

Ray, Fred Olen. *The New Poverty Row: Independent Filmmakers as Distributors.* Jefferson, N.C.: McFarland and Co., 1991.

Rebello, S. "Selling Nightmares: Movie Poster Artists of the Fifties." *Cinefantastique* 18, nos. 2/3 (1988): 40–75.

Rockett, W. H. "The Door Ajar: Structure and Convention in Horror Films That Would Terrify." *Journal of Popular Film and Television* 10, no. 3 (fall 1982): 130–36.

———. "Landscape and Manscape: Reflection and Distortion in Horror Films." *Post Script* 3 (1983): 19–34.

Ross, Phillipe. "Le gothique americain: Le noir à l'ame." *Revue du Cinéma* 471 (May 1991): 72–73.

———. "Spaghetti Horror Express." *Revue du Cinéma* 435 (February 1988): 45.

Schaefer, Eric. *Bold! Daring! Shocking! True! A History of Exploitation Films, 1919–1959.* Durham: Duke University Press, 1999.

———. "Gauging a Revolution: 16mm and the Rise of the Pornographic Feature." *Cinema Journal* 41, no. 3 (spring 2002): 3–26.

Schatz, Thomas. *The Genius of the System: Hollywood Filmmaking in the Studio Era.* New York: Pantheon Books, 1988.

———. *Hollywood Genres: Formulas, Filmmaking, and the Studio System.* New York: Random House, 1981.

Schnapper, Amy. "The Distribution of Theatrical Films to Television," 2 vols. Ph.D. diss., University of Wisconsin—Madison, 1975.

Sconce, Jeffrey. "'Trashing' the Academy: Taste, Excess, and an Emerging Politics of Cinematic Style." *Screen* 36, no. 4 (winter, 1995): 371–93.

Scruton, David L., ed. *Sociophobics: The Anthropology of Fear.* Boulder: Westview Press, 1986.

Siegel, Joel E. *Val Lewton: The Reality of Terror.* New York: Viking Press, 1973.

Skal, David. *The Monster Show: A Cultural History of Horror.* New York: Penguin, 1993.

Slusser, George. "Fantasy, Science Fiction, Mystery, Horror." In *Shadows of the Magic Lamp: Fantasy and Science Fiction in Film,* ed. George Slusser. Carbondale: Southern Illinois University Press, 1985.

Smith, Jeff. *The Sounds of Commerce: Marketing Popular Film Music.* New York: Columbia University Press, 1998.

Sobchack, Vivian Carol. *The Limits of Infinity: The American Science Fiction Film, 1950–1975.* New York: A. S. Barnes, 1980.

Spigel, Lynn. *Make Room for TV: Television and the Family Ideal in Postwar America.* Chicago: University of Chicago Press, 1992.

Stuart, Frederic. *The Effects of Television on the Motion Picture and Radio Industries.* New York: Arno Press, 1976.

Suarez, Juan Antonio. *Bike Boys, Drag Queens, and Superstars: Avant-Garde, Mass Culture, and Gay Identities in the 1960s Underground Cinema.* Bloomington: Indiana University Press, 1996.

Svehla, Gary. "Dream Reality: Horror from a Child's Point of View." *Midnight Marquee* 41 (fall 1990): 30–40.

———. "The Thirty-Second Horror: An Analysis of Motion Picture Trailers." *Gore Creatures* 25 (September 1976): 34–37.

Telotte, J. P. *Dreams of Darkness: Fantasy and the Films of Val Lewton.* Urbana: University of Illinois Press, 1985.

———. "Faith and Idolatry in the Horror Film." *Literature/Film Quarterly* 8 (1980): 143–55.

———. "Through a Pumpkin's Eye: The Reflexive Nature of Horror." *Literature/Film Quarterly* 10 (1982): 139–49.

Todorov, Tzvetan. *The Fantastic.* Trans. Richard Howard. Ithaca: Cornell University Press, 1975.

Tudor, Andrew. *Monsters and Mad Scientists: A Cultural History of the Horror Movie.* Oxford: Basil Blackwell, 1989.

Twitchell, James B. *Adcult USA: The Triumph of Advertising in American Culture.* New York: Columbia University Press, 1995.

———. *Dreadful Pleasures: An Anatomy of Modern Horror.* New York: Oxford University Press, 1985.

U.S. Congress. Senate. Select Committee on Small Business. *Motion Picture Distribution Trade Practices.* Hearings before a subcommittee of the Select Committee on Small Business, 83d Cong., 1st sess., 1953. Washington, D.C.: Government Printing Office, 1954.

———. Select Committee on Small Business. *Motion Picture Distribution Trade Practices, 1956.* Report of the Select Committee on Small Business, 84th Cong., 2nd sess., July 27, 1956. Washington, D.C.: Government Printing Office, 1957.

———. Select Committee on Small Business. *Motion Picture Distribution Trade Practices, 1956.* Hearings before a subcommittee of the Select Committee on Small Business, 83d Cong., 2nd sess., 1956. Washington, D.C.: Government Printing Office, 1957.

———. Select Committee on Small Business. *Problems of Independent Motion Picture Exhibitors Relating to Distribution Trade Practices.* Report of the Select Committee on Small Business, 83rd Cong., 1st sess., August 13, 1953. Washington, D.C.: Government Printing Office, 1954.

U.S. Department of Commerce, Business and Defense Services Administration. *U.S. Industrial Outlook 1968.* Washington, D.C.: Government Printing Office, 1967.

U.S. Federal Trade Commission. *Paramount Pictures, Inc. et al. Consent Judgements and Decree Investigation Report.* February 25, 1965. Washington, D.C.: Government Printing Office, 1966.

Vale, V., and Andrea Juno, eds. *Re/Search #10: Incredibly Strange Films.* San Francisco: Re/Search Publications, 1986.

Variety Film Reviews. New York: Garland Publishing, 1983.

Waller, Gregory A. "Seeing It Through: Closure in Four Horror Films." *Proceedings of the Purdue Conference on Film 7* (1983): 17–24.

Warshow, Robert. "St. Paul, the Horror Comics, and Dr. Wertham." *Commentary* 17 (June 1954): 596–604.

Waters, John. *Crackpot: The Obsessions of John Waters.* New York: Vintage, 1987.

———. *Shock Valve.* New York: Thunders Mouth Press, 1997.

Weaver, Tom. *Interviews with B Science Fiction and Horror Movie Makers.* Jefferson, N.C.: McFarland and Co., 1988.

———. *Science Fiction Stars and Horror Heroes: Interviews with Actors, Writers, and Directors from the 1940s through the 1960s.* Jefferson, N.C.: McFarland and Co., 1994.

Weinberg, Robert. *Horror of the Twentieth Century: An Illustrated History.* Portland, Ore.: Collectors Press, 2000.

Weldon, Michael. *The Psychotronic Encyclopedia of Film.* New York: Ballantine Books, 1983.

———. *The Psychotronic Video Guide.* New York: Vintage, 1996.

Wertham, Frederic. *Seduction of the Innocent.* Port Washington, N.Y.: Holt, Rinehart, and Winston, 1953.

Wexman, Virginia Wright. *Roman Polanski.* Boston: Twayne Publishers, 1985.

White, Dennis L. "The Poetics of Horror: More than Meets the Eye." *Cinema Journal* 10, no. 2 (spring 1971): 1–18.

Wilinsky Barbara, *Sure Seaters: The Emergence of Art-House Cinema.* Minneapolis: University of Minnesota Press, 2000.

Williams, Linda. "Film Bodies: Gender, Genre, and Excess." In *Film Genre Reader II*, ed. Barry Keith Grant. Austin: University of Texas Press, 1995.

———. *Hard Core: Power, Pleasure, and the "Frenzy of the Visible."* Berkeley: University of California Press, 1990.

———. "When the Woman Looks." In *Re-Vision: Essays in Feminist Film Criticism*, ed. Mary Ann Doane, Patricia Mellencamp, and Linda Williams. Frederick, Md.: American Film Institute, 1984.

Williams, Tony. "American Cinema in the 70s: Family Horror." *Movie* 27/28 (1981): 117–26.

———. *Hearths of Darkness: The Family in the American Horror Film.* New York: Associated University Presses, 1988.

Wood, Robin. "The American Family Comedy: From *Meet Me in St. Louis* to *The Texas Chain Saw Massacre.*" *Wide Angle* 3, no. 2 (1979): 5–11.

———. *Hollywood from Vietnam to Reagan.* New York: Columbia University Press, 1986.

———. "An Introduction to the American Horror Film." In *Movies and Methods*, vol. 2, ed. Bill Nichols. Berkeley: University of California Press, 1985.

Wood, Robin and Richard Lippe, eds. *American Nightmare: Essays on the Horror Film.* Toronto: Festival of Festivals, 1979.

INDEX

SuperScope widescreen process, 104–105

Surrender—Hell!, 79

Susina Associates. *See* William Castle

Sweet Ride, 201

Swinging Along, 207

Swope, Herbert, 68

Sword-and-sandal films, 162, 165–166

Sylbert, Anthea, 195

Sylbert, Robert, 195

Tailor's Maid, The, 174

Tales from the Crypt (1972), 47

Tannenbaum, Julius, 208

Tarantula, 41

Targets, 181

Taste of Fear, A, 184

Taylor, Don, 124

Teenage Bad Girl, 123

Teenage Bride, 78

Teenage Thunder, 72

Television Enterprises Corporation (TEC), 169, 176

Television ownership, 5. *See also* Color television

Television syndication, 15, 152, 155–179; of post-1948 feature films, 156; "vaulties," 158. *See also* Color Television; Philadelpha; UHF television

Teleworld, 169

Tempest (1959), 137

Terror in the Crypt, 167

Terror Is a Man, 173

Texas Chain Saw Massacre, The (1974), 224, 225

Texas Consolidated theater chain, 130

Texas Interstate theater chain, 78, 94, 130

Theater Guild, 214

Theater Owners of America (TOA), 19, 69, 166

Them!, 10, 93

They Came From Within, 219

Thing from Another World, The, 10, 39

Thirteen Ghosts (1960), 8, 9, 96

This Is Cinerama, 18–19

3-D films: as example of post-studio technological change, 17; critical dismissal of, 17; cost of, to exhibitors, 17–18, 21–23; and voyeurism of the female body, 28–31. *See also House of Wax; The Creature From the Black Lagoon*

Thriller (TV series), 142

Thunderbird Films, 169, 170–171, 176, 183

Time Limit, 81

Time of Indifference, 208

Times Films, 119, 170

Tingler, The, 8, 14, 68, 92, 96, 98–104, 109, 120, 128, 143, 161, 173; and Percepto Stunt, 98, 102–103, 106

Titanus Studio, 142

Titra Sound Corporation, 141

Toho Studios, 120, 121, 217

Tol'able David, 103

Tomb of Ligea, 10, 112

Tonight Show, 171, 179

Torture Garden, 47

Tourneur, Jacques, 81

Trailers. *See* Advertising

Trans-Lux, 174

Tremayne, Les, 168

Trial, The (1961), 133

Triangle Program Sales, 170

Triangle Publications, 172

Triangle TV station group, 170

Trip, The, 181

Truth, The, 132

Tudor, Andrew, 6

TV horror hosts. *See* Ghoulardi; Zacherley

Twentieth Century-Fox, 19, 93, 178; and CinemaScope, 19; and Hammer

Kevin Heffernan is Assistant Professor
of Cinema and Television at Southern
Methodist University. He is coauthor of
the book *My Son Divine*.

Library of Congress
Cataloging-in-Publication Data
Heffernan, Kevin.
Ghouls, gimmicks, and gold : horror
films and the American movie business,
1953–1968 / Kevin Heffernan.
p. cm.
Includes bibliographical references and
index.
ISBN 0-8223-3202-7 (alk. paper)
ISBN 0-8223-3215-9 (pbk. : alk. paper)
1. Horror films—United States—History
and criticism.   I. Title.
PN1995.9.H6H45   2004
791.43'6164—dc22   2003016429